AMERICA'S TEENAGERS— MYTHS AND REALITIES

Media Images, Schooling, and the Social Costs of Careless Indifference

AMERICA'S TEENAGERS—
MYTHS AND REALITIES

Media Images, Schooling, and the Social Costs of Careless Indifference

Sharon L. Nichols
Thomas L. Good
University of Arizona

LAWRENCE ERLBAUM ASSOCIATES, PUBLISHERS
2004   Mahwah, New Jersey   London

Cover Headline Credits:

1. Goodnough, A. (2001, October 24). Most 8th graders again fail New York's Statewide exams. *New York Times*, p. A20.
2. Jackson, D. Z. (1997, September 12). TV exaggerates juvenile crime, scaring public. *Arizona Daily Star*, p. A17.
3. Baumpel, J. (1997, June 21). A stress test for third graders. New York Times, op-ed, p. 21.
4. Associated Press. (1998, May 22). 'Friends' hang PA girl, 15, then beat her to death. *Arizona Daily Star*, p. A9.

Copyright © 2004 by Lawrence Erlbaum Associates, Inc.
   All rights reserved. No part of this book may be reproduced in any form, by photostat, microform, retrieval system, or any other means, without prior written permission of the publisher.

Lawrence Erlbaum Associates, Inc., Publishers
10 Industrial Avenue
Mahwah, New Jersey 07430

Cover design by Kathryn Houghtaling Lacey

CIP information can be obtained by contacting the
   Library of Congress

        p.   cm.
Includes bibliographical references and index.
ISBN 0-8058-4850-9 (cloth : alk. paper)
ISBN 0-8058-4851-7 (pbk. : alk. paper)

Books published by Lawrence Erlbaum Associates are printed on acid-free paper, and their bindings are chosen for strength and durability.

Printed in the United States of America
10 9 8 7 6 5 4 3 2 1

Contents

Preface

Since 1998, we have been collecting examples of the ways in which the media negatively exaggerates and oversimplifies the lives of today's youth. The media's presentation of youth falsely suggests that youth today are the most violent, sexual, and amoral youth culture in history. Given such negative stories, it's not surprising that many adults report in various polls that youth are lazy and dangerous. Concurrently, we have also been researching youth's behavior to document actual rates of violence, educational accomplishments, and so forth. As our library of examples has grown, so has our resolve to put forth a more appropriate image of youth: that they are better than commonly depicted and deserve to be viewed as a social priority. There are many media examples of how youth's bad behavior is exaggerated but there are also notable examples of teens' prosocial contributions that the media and many adults ignore. This imbalance needs to be addressed, and we write this book because we want more adults to recognize and value the positive contributions of youth.

One goal in writing this book is to deconstruct the negative images of American teenagers held by large numbers of adults, and to influence a more positive view of youth. We do not suggest, in general, that society harbors a strong active dislike, but rather a *careless indifference* toward youth in general. Many adults simply do not think about adolescents in a knowledgeable or careful way. Yet when they do think of youth, they do so in terms of averages. For example, as we illustrate in chapter 4, using averages to describe the sexual behavior of youth is misleading because youth vary widely in their attitudes toward and knowledge about sex. Similarly, as we describe in chapter 8, average student performance in achievement is highly mis-

leading because of the extreme variation in the quality of American education. A major problem is that highly visible media accounts of youth are excessively pejorative and use averages to tell their story. Our goal is to help
readers to become much more critical consumers of these stories.

A good example of the problem with averaged, negative depictions is illustrated by the statement that "On average, American youth vote less than
other groups." Although true on one level, this statement fails to recognize
why many youth do not vote. Is this because youth are politically indifferent
or self-absorbed? If so, does this lack of "appropriate" motivation stem from
poor parent models or from inadequate schools that fail to spark students'
sense of civil responsibility? In September 2000, a survey co-sponsored by
the Kaiser Family Foundation and MTV, found that young adults ages
18–24 hold *very strong* political convictions. Why do so few vote? Seventy percent of those polled don't vote because they believe that politicians are out
of touch with the concerns of youth and election results will not impact
them personally.[1]

In reality, many youth are highly motivated to participate in adult society. In Arizona, a group of teenagers were persistent in petitioning the state
legislature for the right to vote.[2] However, such prosocial youth subcultures
are seldom recognized or celebrated. As described in the book *Vanishing
Voter,* written by Thomas Paterson, an expert on voting, many nonvoting
Americans are among the "savvy," better-educated and more affluent citizens.[3] Should youth be blamed because they emulate their successful adult
role models?[4]

Critical Views of Youth Impede Meaningful Help

A second goal of the book is to recognize that growing numbers of youth
are left to socialize themselves and that youth need more resources, especially in the form of adult time. A general careless indifference toward
youth as a group permeates adult society and prevents the proactive policies necessary to provide them with better education, better healthcare,
higher quality work and play environments, and active recognition and
support. As a case in point, in 2002 one survey reported that 51% of youth
had not been advised of possible career paths by their parents or school
counselors.[5] Such lack of guidance—a laissez-faire approach to socialization—is one of many examples of the ways society fails to help youth.

Indeed, when youth are devalued they become a burden to society instead of a priority. The potential costs to society of these overly critical views
of youth are enormous. For example, in the late 1980s an exaggerated fear
was voiced that the next generation of adolescents would include some of

the most vicious and remorseless ever.[6] This prediction never materialized, yet the response to this "averaged" belief led to harsh policies such as the creation of tougher sentences for younger and younger youth to stop them before they "get out of control." Such beliefs also led judges to allow youth to be tried as adults, or to be sent to corrective camps where many are abused, degraded, and sometimes lose their lives.[7] Attempts to punish and incarcerate youth are heavily used despite the fact that there is little evidence to support the institution of harsh punishments as a way to decrease teen violence.[8] Of course, there are some blemished youth who hold antisocial attitudes and who behave in shockingly inappropriate ways, but these youth are the exceptions, not the norm. And, it is important to recognize that, in large measure, these youth *learned* these antisocial attitudes from a society that failed to support them.

In the book we explore how and why many citizens in the U.S. have vastly deficient knowledge about adolescents, and how and why they generally are not sensitive to the various pressures to which youth must respond. We hope that by providing a more accurate picture, we can influence how Americans think about youth and enhance their willingness to develop proactive, positive policies for them. More broadly, we describe the pressures that youth face in varied aspects of their life—health, education, and employment among others. Yet despite their pressures which stress, if not fracture, youth, society depends largely on a laissez-faire approach to youth socialization.

Throughout the book we point out various reasons why leaving youth alone is problematic. When adults don't spend time with youth, or when youth are excluded from decisions that affect them directly, it sends a powerful message that they are not respected or valued. Similarly, youth who are left alone to socialize themselves become the stepchildren of a vast media culture. In this role, and when surrounding adults are largely absent, they become more susceptible to the insidious presence of an advertising culture that overwhelms them with messages that to fit in, they should eat fast food, drink soda, buy expensive clothes, and worry excessively about appearance. Across a wide array of topics, we discuss how the media works against goals of helping youth.

Chapter Descriptions

In chapter 1, we describe what American adults generally think of youth as a group. A nationwide poll of adults' attitudes about youth sponsored by Public Agenda highlights this chapter. Adolescence is hard to define because it is a changing subculture, influenced by social class and embedded within a changing society.[9] We address and dismiss the pervasive myth that today's youth are more ill behaved, less motivated, and worse off academically than their counterparts from previous generations.[10]

In chapter 2, we analyze the critical role of media in shaping American adults' perceptions of youth. Since 1900, American technology has changed dramatically—with some of the fastest changes occurring since 1980. We analyze research that attempts to understand how the media culture affects youth, especially the role media violence plays in influencing youth violence.

In chapter 3, we explore research on youth violence. Importantly, many newspapers have reported that youth violence is decreasing; however, the wide ranging media coverage of tragic but rare incidents of violence (school shootings) are so salient that both students' and citizens' fear of school-related violence are exaggerated. Lost in the media's portrayal of youth violence is that youth violence is more likely to be expressed as self-violence (suicide) rather than as violence to others. Also missing from the discussion of youth violence is the amount of violence directed at youth by adults.

In chapter 4, we explore youth sexuality. Adolescent sexuality has a pervasive presence in modern media. Images of youthful sexuality (often distorted), are prominently displayed on television, in cinema, newspapers and magazines, and on the Internet. In part, the widespread availability of sexualized messages distributed by sophisticated technology has contributed to ambiguous values and belief systems about sexuality. Unfortunately, many teens are denied valuable information about sexuality because of adults' confused beliefs, and wide disagreements about what they think teens should know about sex. Hence, teens are forced to learn about sexual activity from peers and the media.

In chapter 5, we provide a comprehensive discussion of teenage drug, alcohol, and tobacco consumption, and analyze the role of media in advancing societally created, attractive ideologies around substance use. On Superbowl Sunday, television shows are inundated with beer commercials prominently pairing drinking alcohol and sports activities. To some adolescents, caught between childhood and adulthood, these messages provide encouragement to engage in adult-viewed behaviors such as drinking because it is perceived as "accepted" and even "expected" behavior.

In chapter 6, we discuss the health and well-being of youth. If youth are viewed as proactive investments for the future, it is logical to take steps to ensure that they have the skills and dispositions to maximize the quality of their lives. Unfortunately, current policies often contradict and sometimes undermine this philosophy. For example, in an era with record high numbers of obese adults and children, there are fewer physical education programs in schools now than in the past. We discuss how youths' decisions about health are made more difficult by the larger society.

In chapter 7, we explore the role of youth employment in American society and discuss why youth work, the types of jobs they hold, and the effects of work on youth's decisions (e.g., use of drugs and educational goals). We also explore the growing influence of media as it shapes attitudes and preferences for consumer products. Advertisements in television commercials and print ads present products so seductively that acquiring them is a powerful motivator for youth to obtain jobs. It is no coincidence that a whole new generation of belly-button showing, crop-top wearing adolescents emerged on the heels of singer Britney Spears' popularity.

In chapter 8, we present an analysis of youth and their life in schools. Education is an acutely important social and political issue. Here, we examine students' educational performance and consider the media and various other societal influences that shape students' academic performance. Among issues discussed are high stakes testing and its consequences for what American youth learn in schools. Furthermore, we note the wide ranging conditions in which youth are taught including the varying quality of teachers and learning resources that are provided.

In chapter 9, we pull together themes generated throughout the book and provide examples of policies that would underscore the value of seeing youth as an investment. We provide some general guidelines for teachers, parents, policymakers, and citizens to facilitate their ability to react to youth in meaningful and proactive ways that serve both to improve the quality of life for youth and the broader society.

ACKNOWLEDGMENTS

Several individuals helped us greatly as we wrote this book. Their contributions helped to enhance the quality of our work. We would like to thank Jason Siegel, who offered his expertise on issues of youth smoking and on the persuasion literature. We would like to thank Jeaneen Vogel, who spent much time with the first author discussing various aspects of the book and helping her to clarify many of our arguments. We value the general good advice Mary McCaslin provided and especially her thoughts about small-wins solutions that appear prominently in chapter 9. We acknowledge the good advice and constructive editing we have received from Naomi Silverman, our editor at Lawrence Erlbaum Associates, and from Evelyn Somers Rogers. Their help added greatly to the clarity of this work.

Reviewers' comments were also helpful. We thank an anonymous reviewer for challenging us to clarify many of our arguments. We especially thank David Berliner and Rhona Weinstein, who read an earlier version of the book and provided a wealth of good suggestions and critical comments.

There are several individuals at Lawrence Erlbaum Associates who helped us throughout the production phase of the book and this work couldn't have been completed without them. We want to acknowledge the assistance of Erica Kica, who greatly facilitated the book's production and always answered our questions thoroughly and quickly. We would also like to thank Nadine Simms, who answered our many questions and facilitated the editing process. Finally, we acknowledge Elisabeth Yahl for her help tracking down references and conducting extensive Internet searches for our reports on youth.

—*Sharon L. Nichols*
Thomas L. Good

ENDNOTES

1. Kaiser Family Foundation/MTV (2000, September). Youth, voting, and the 2000 election [online]. Available at: http://www.kff.org or http://www.chooseorlose.com.
2. Teen-age voters (2001, February 1). *Arizona Daily Star*, B6.
3. Patterson, T. E. (2002). *Vanishing voter: Public involvement in an age of uncertainty*. New York: Alfred A. Knopf.
4. Patterson notes that in 1960, half of the adult population had not finished high school and that most recently, 25% have graduated from college and another 25% have attended college. Yet, despite this increase in the number of educated voters, the voter turnout from 1960 to today has declined. Clearly, America's voting problem should not be blamed on youth.
5. National Women's Law Center (2002, June). Title IX and equal opportunity in vocational and technical education: A promise still owed to the nation's young women: A report of the National Women's Law Center.
6. U.S. Department of Health and Human Services (2000). *Youth violence: A report of the surgeon general*. Rockville, MD: U.S. Department of Health and Human Services, Centers for Disease Control and Prevention, National Center for Injury Prevention and Control, Substance Abuse and Mental Health Services Administration, Center for Mental Health Services, and National Institutes of Health, National Institute of Mental Health.
7. Talbot, M. (2000, September 10). The maximum security adolescent. *The New York Times Magazine* (section 6), pp. 40–47, 58, 60, 88, 96.
8. In fact, there is much evidence to show that violence begets violence and that harsher consequences for youth violence only leads to higher recidivism, not rehabilitation. See Males, M. A. (1996). *The scapegoat generation: America's war on adolescents*. Monroe, ME: Common Courage Press; U.S. Department of Health and Human Services (2000). *Youth violence: A report of the Surgeon General*. Rockville, MD: U.S. Department of Health and Human Services, Centers for Disease Control and Prevention, National Center for Injury Prevention and Control, Substance Abuse and Mental Health Services Administration, Center for Mental Health Services, and National Institutes of Health, National Institute of Mental Health. Also, see a report by the American Youth Policy Forum that compiles data

on how harsher treatment of juveniles has led to *increases* in juvenile crime, not *decreases*. Mendel, R. (2000, June). *Less hype, more help: Reducing juvenile crime, what works—and what doesn't*. Washington, DC: American Youth Policy Forum. Available online: http://www. aypf.org/mendel/index.html.

9. Hine, T. (1999). *The rise and fall of the American teenager*. New York: Avon Books Inc.

10. Berliner, D., & Biddle, B. (1995). *The manufactured crisis: Myth, fraud and the attack on America's public schools*. Reading, MA: Addison-Wesley.

Chapter 1

The Continuing Myth
of Adolescence

> *It was the best of times, it was the worst of times, it was the age of wisdom, it was the age of foolishness, it was the epoch of belief, it was the epoch of incredulity, it was the season of Light, it was the season of Darkness, it was the spring of hope, it was the winter of despair, we had everything before us, we had nothing before us, we were all going direct to Heaven, we were all going direct the other way . . .*
>
> —C. Dickens[1]

> *By any standards, America's young adolescents have a great deal of discretionary time. Much of it is unstructured, unsupervised, and unproductive for the young person. Only 60% of adolescents' waking hours are committed to such essentials as school, homework, eating, chores, or paid employment, while fully 40% are discretionary.*
>
> —Carnegie Council on Adolescent Development, 1992[2]

> *Adam suffered from nothing more serious than adolescence, a disease that would eventually pass, like a particularly virulent episode of chicken pox: ugly to look at but temporary and certainly not life-threatening.*
>
> —R. Russo, 2001[3]

Charles Dickens's vivid description of life in 18th century Paris might also be said to capture the contradictory experiences of adolescence. Adolescence is riddled with ups and downs, defined by radical biological transformations and characterized by boundless energy and enormous pressures to excel academically and to fit in socially. At a time when teens must cope simultaneously with numerous social, academic, and biological pressures, they are also experiencing a lot of firsts: first kiss, first dance, first taste of alcohol, first car wreck, first steady boyfriend or girlfriend, first breakup. As they experience these and other daily struggles, they may also be confronted with negative adult attitudes ("I told you the child was a loser") and media reports ("You attend a failing school").

Given the enormous pressures and numerous and varied expectations adolescents face, it is distressing that so much of their time is unstructured and devoid of adult guidance and supervision.[4] We must point out, though, that how teens spend their discretionary time varies greatly. Many reflect the "Hurried Youth" stereotype that David Elkind described and lamented more than 30 years ago—scheduled from dawn to dusk with structured activities.[5] At the other end of the spectrum are young people who return to empty homes in dangerous neighborhoods and have little opportunity for constructive activity. Of course, most teens fall somewhere between these two extremes.

WHY WE SHOULD VALUE YOUTH

American teenagers are not valued—or not valued highly enough—by many American citizens. Even more baffling than society's devaluation of youth is the large number of Americans who fear and distrust them.[6] Increasingly, young Americans are seen as needing harsher sanctions to make them behave in a civil manner. But to view teenagers as out of control and in need of correction is inaccurate and a dangerous underestimation of their capabilities and potential—teenagers are vital to society as its future workers, citizens, and decision makers. The quality of American life in decades to come will depend on decisions that our youth will make and initiatives they will take when they become adults.

We should view our youth as a critical resource. Birthrates are down, and older Americans represent an increasingly larger percentage of the total population. As baby boomers and echo boomers age,[7] fewer Americans will be available to maintain the various roles required by a productive society. In 1960, children represented 36% of the U.S. population. By 2025, the proportion of children in the United States is expected to be less than 24%. In 2025, there will be more Americans 65 years of age or older than Americans between the ages of 5 and 17 years.[8] Given these demographics, the health and education of American teenagers and the formation of their attitudes toward society should be of acute concern to parents and policymakers. The first step toward cultivating the resource America has in its youth is to understand why young people are generally not valued or seen as good investments.

CHAPTER OVERVIEW

In the first part of this chapter, we explore the origins of youth devaluation. We present evidence that young people have been heavily criticized by adults for a significant period of time. In addition to showing that adult conceptions of youth are pejorative, we illustrate that negative beliefs have grown *more prevalent* over the past 50 years.

We then explore why youth are more seriously devalued by society today than ever before. This brief historical analysis reminds readers of what life was like in the past and also illustrates that both the social conditions in which teenagers live and society's expectations for them have changed markedly. We ask readers to reflect on their own youth. One reason why many adults devalue youth is because it is easy to forget what being an adolescent was like.

We end the chapter with an analysis of public attitudes toward today's youth, based on evidence from two national polls sponsored by Public Agenda. Data from these polls are frequently cited as evidence of adult devaluation of youth.

HOW ARE YOUTH DEVALUED?

Youth as a Time of Storm and Stress

Pejorative perceptions of youth in the United States can be traced at least as far back as 1900, when adolescents, as an emerging subculture in America, began to be viewed as a separate and strange culture. G. Stanley Hall introduced the concept of adolescent *sturm und drang* (or storm and stress) to explain the strangeness of youth.[9] He argued that adolescence is a separate phase of development marked by antisocial behaviors and attitudes that invariably "spring up" with a rush of hormonal activity and changes resulting from physical development. Hall's descriptions of youth were internalized by society as a way to describe the typical teenager.[10]

This powerful argument has become difficult to reverse. In the 1960s Albert Bandura reported that published research data showed that the then popular view of adolescence as a time of storm and stress was unwarranted.[11] Bandura argued that, in general, teens were not excessively combative and did not experience the conflicts with parents that many assumed took place. One reason he cited for the widespread belief in the storm-and-stress phenomenon is consistent with our argument; namely that the mass media sensationalizes adolescent behavior.

In a 1999 *American Psychologist* article, Jeffrey Arnett revisited the notion of storm and stress. He documented the current pervasive belief that storm and stress is a universal adolescent experience but also noted that data strongly refute this view of adolescence. He pointed out that although some adults understand that characteristics of storm and stress may not apply to every individual adolescent, when asked about teens as a group, adults were more likely to characterize them in universal terms:

> studies that have investigated perceptions of storm and stress inquire about people's perceptions of adolescents *in general*. People's responses endorsing the storm-and-stress statements indicate simply that they see storm and stress as characteristic of adolescents taken as a group, not that it is characteristic of all adolescents without exception.[12]

Because teenagers' "bad behavior"[13] is often viewed as inevitable and unchangeable, youth tend to be treated not as an investment worth nurturing but as a *group* to be feared and punished for bad things they do or will do.

Notably, it isn't just the average citizen who holds a storm-and-stress view of youth. There is evidence to suggest that experts also view the typical adolescent experience as a stormy time of life. Daniel Offer found that when asked to describe the normal teenager, psychiatrists were likely to describe the psychology of a normal teen as significantly more disturbed (e.g., characterized by mood difficulties and relational conflicts) than normal teens would actually report themselves. Furthermore, before taking a course on adolescent psychology, undergraduate students were more accurate in describing normal teenage psychology than were the psychiatrists.[14] Perhaps these psychiatrists' perceptions are biased as a result of their extensive contact with "troubled" youth. This is a provocative finding that raises questions as to mental health diagnostic accuracy in the mental health profession. It also reflects how difficult it is for even mental health professionals to accurately characterize what normal teen life is like.

Recent research on adolescent depression also illustrates the complexity of differentiating normal from abnormal teenage mood difficulties. The number of diagnosed cases of adolescent depression has risen over the past decade, which raises the question of whether more adolescents are depressed or whether medical and psychological professionals are becoming better at diagnosing depression. Some have argued that teenage depression was underdiagnosed previously because adults attributed the depressive symptoms they witnessed in the teens with whom they were involved as the normal storm-and-stress-induced downs of adolescence.[15] Fortunately, we are learning more about the relationship among youth depression and social pressures, inadequate coping skills and support systems, and biochemical causes.[16] Still, many professionals and nonprofessionals alike have far to go in understanding the difference between normal and unhealthy adolescent behavior.

Evidence of Increasing Devaluation of Youth

Throughout history, the younger generation has always been viewed with suspicion by adults;[17] however, evidence suggests that Americans are becoming more negative toward teens. Adults' views of teenagers going back to at least the 1940s are low and have been declining ever since.[18] In 1946, a poll sponsored by the Gallup Organization found that 43% of Americans thought youth were behaving worse than when they were teens. In 1965, the Gallup Organization asked adults, "In what ways would you say teenagers are different today than when you were a teenager?"[19] The top response (41%) was that teens were "more irresponsible, too wild today, drink too much, more independent, less restricted, and freer in action."[20] By the 1970s, in another poll sponsored by the Gallup Organization, only 24% of adults said they had a "great deal of confidence in teens facing up to their own and the country's problems in a responsible way."[21]

Another study conducted in 1989, asked adults to compare teens of that time with teens of 20 years earlier. In comparing 1989 teens with those from two decades before, more adults viewed 1989 teens as selfish (81% vs. 6%), materialistic (79% vs. 15%), and reckless (73% vs. 14%), whereas fewer described them as patriotic (24% vs. 65%). In her review of polls on youth, Margaret Bostrom, a researcher for the Frameworks Institute, argued that adults' skepticism about the morals of youth is perhaps more widespread today than ever before. She noted that the percentage of adults who believe young people today do not have a strong sense of right and wrong has grown from a minority 50 years ago (34%) to an overwhelming majority today (82%).[22]

Many adults characterize today's youth negatively, using adjectives such as "irresponsible, wild, and rude."[23] They fear youth and believe them to be violent, remorseless, and amoral. More adults today view youth with suspicion, skepticism, and negativity than ever before.[24]

WHY ARE YOUTH DEVALUED?

Role Expectations Have Changed Over Time

What accounts for this increasing devaluation of youth, at a time when young people's future contributions to society are clearly so essential?[25] One hypothesis is that adults are not sensitive to how youth's roles have changed over time. Although there are many ways life for youth has changed since

1900, two of these changes seem especially significant. Youth's economic value to adults has changed over time in that modern youth generally contribute less to the economic stability and vitality of the family and more to society than the youth of the past. Second, adults' knowledge of youth has changed from a localized context (e.g., living in the same location together) to a more diffuse, unfamiliar, globalized one. There are less enduring face-to-face relations between adults and young people.

Economic Value and Family Expectations. In the 1900 teens' economic value and contributions were viewed primarily as immediate. Teens worked on the family farm or in the family business, served an apprenticeship, or worked for a neighbor. Commonly, a teen's role in helping to sustain the health of the family business was critical. Families were more stable because most parents stayed together longer—80% of women and 81% of men ages 35–44 were married, whereas only 3% of women and 0.5% of men (ages 35–44) were divorced.[26] Families tended to stay in the same community; many teens were known by their neighbors since birth. And it was common for families to spend much time together. Many families worked together, especially since they often worked together in a family business. Youth got married and obtained full-time jobs at an early age and were therefore viewed as adults very early in life. The period of adolescence was relatively brief.

By the 1950s this pattern was evolving, and teens had both immediate and future economic value. Teens still primarily married young and were expected to have children soon after marriage. But a larger percentage of youth were attending college than before, and, although the suburb was in its infancy, the shift to urbanization was occurring. Many families moved, and teens were less likely to be acquainted with their adult neighbors. Teens were teens for a longer period of time, too, though some still left school early to work and to help sustain the family. In contrast to families of the early 1900s, 1950s families spent much more leisure time together, going on vacations, recreating, and relaxing or together, even if it was only having dinner while watching *The Ed Sullivan Show*. Many 1950s families were "happy" because men and women had stable role expectations (which some women found stifling), and family compositions were ethnically homogeneous and "traditional" in nature (e.g., few, if any, homosexual or interracial parents). However, family life varied sharply depending on income, social class, and ethnicity.[27]

Today, teens offer a different sort of immediate economic value—they are primarily seen as an economic commodity, valued for how their tastes drive the consumer market. However, they are not seen as adults because today's youth delay marriage and children, and they are spending more years in higher education. Adults are less concerned with youth's long-term goals than with their immediate impact on the economy as consumers. The adolescent stage is much longer—lasting well into the second decade—and role definitions are fluid and unstable.

Today's families tend to be more heterogeneous and busier with more varied tasks. Divorce is common, and although it saves many youth from abusive households others are also harmed when messy divorces inappropriately involve them. Family activities are also more varied today than in 1900 or even 1950. Long gone are the days when many families regularly sat together for a family meal or watched television together, or when children felt confident that their parents would remain together. Families are busy, and members are consumed with their own activities. Parents work late, kids are involved in extracurricular activities, everyone has their own favorite TV shows, and teens and adults spend considerable time surfing the Web or communicating in chat rooms—alone.[28]

Adult Familiarity With Youth. In 1900, adults' knowledge of teens was based on the young people they knew personally. A teenager would be known by his or her work in the community and at church; more generalized information about teens was sparse. In 1900, most teenagers did not feel the enormous pressure to succeed in schools as teens do today because there were many good jobs available for those capable of physical labor, but they felt pressures to get a good job, fulfill family obligations, get married, and have children. Of course, these pressures varied dramatically depending on where the family lived. Teens who lived on farms had notably different lifestyles and pressures than those from inner-city neighborhoods. Many teens experienced acute stress over having to support the family financially. Indeed, in some working-class families, fathers had to retire at young ages (e.g., 40–45 years of age) due to the strain of hard laboring at the steel mills, in coal mines, or as bricklayers, thereby increasing the pressure on teens to step up to the plate.

By the 1950s, things were changing. Adults' opinions of youth were still primarily based on individuals in a local context, but the media was certainly a stronger force in providing global knowledge about teens than it had been (e.g., *American Bandstand,* shared information about teen culture), and, as noted previously, Americans were moving to the suburbs and finding themselves surrounded by new neighbors.

Today adults still possess knowledge of teens through local contacts, but they are also swamped with information about teen culture via mass media sensationalism, marketing, and entertainment. More adults work, too, and have less time to interact with youth, and youth often attend schools that are not in their immediate neighborhoods. Given a more diffuse set of adult–teen contacts, many adults are less likely to know many teens personally, as was the case in 1950.

TABLE 1.1
Comparisons of Youth's Role Expectations Over a Century

1900	Work *or* school
	Full-time employment by age 15—considered to be adult
	Married with children at young age
	Shared teen-adult work and activities
	Limited mobility
	Little media knowledge
	Isolated from the teen experience in other parts of the state, country, and world
1950	School *or* work
	Full-time employment by age 18—considered to be adult
	Married with children at young age
	Decreased teen-adult shared work and activities
	Increased mobility
	Increased media knowledge
2000	Work *and* school, plus more
	Delayed full-time employment
	Married later—children less likely
	Markedly decreased teen-adult shared activities
	Increased mobility and job choices
	Expanded media knowledge
	Instant communication with peers from all over the world

In addition, the families in which youth are raised have changed enormously from 1900 to today. More teens come home to empty houses after school, and within families there is increased ambiguity about how teens can demonstrate their success. Further, youth are socialized in a more diffuse, confusing society. Simply expressed, society's expectations for teens are notably different today than in 1900 or 1950. Youth face a different set of expectations and life conditions that leave them less connected on a personal level than in the past and that are vague as to how youth can prove themselves as successful emerging adults. These trends are summarized in Table 1.1.

Media Influence

Our second hypothesis on why adults have increasingly devalued youth is that the media have a profound impact on how we view youth. Data suggest that entertainment and news media both provide a negatively skewed perspective on youth and children. Therefore, it isn't surprising, given the rapid media growth over the past five decades, that there is an increase in the number of adults who view youth negatively. An analysis of the portrayal of children and adolescents in prime-time, weekend, and daytime television programming between 1969–1985 found that youth were underrepresented in such programs and presented pejoratively when they did appear.

Researchers have noted, "The overall image is one that conveys a sense of unimportance and devaluation of children and childhood."[29]

A 2001 report examined media newscasts for a month in 1999 in several cities. The study found that the national media seldom reported on youth. In the local news, 8% of the stories focused on youth, and most of these focused on specific events, with little attempt to explain or understand the event (more on this in chap. 2). Most youth stories (47%) focused on high school–aged students, 16% focused on middle school–aged young teens, and 20% focused on 18- to 20-year-olds. The three most frequently reported news topics were youth as crime victims, accidents involving youth (e.g., falling down drunk), and violent youth crime. Consumers of such media therefore saw youth in problematic terms. Although youth spend considerable time in jobs and community service, these topics were, in contrast, rare news items. As we show in subsequent chapters, media (both entertainment and journalistic) continue to present youth in largely pejorative terms.

Forgetting Adolescence

After generational differences and the impact of media, our third hypothesis is that adults describe the typical teen experience negatively because they forget what it was like to be one. The further adults are from high school, the fuzzier high school memories become. Many adults forget the impact of the daily struggles of adolescence in light of all the responsibilities incurred over time (college debt, mortgages, families, etc.). Memories of adolescence tend to involve the more salient episodic events (both positive and negative) of adults' histories—the moments that define them and contribute to their identities:[30] receiving academic or extracurricular honors, being class president or being on the yearbook committee, being rejected by peers, losing a girlfriend/boyfriend, not making the team, not getting into a college of choice, or dropping out of high school. For many adults, adolescence becomes a mythical time, and memories of that time become exaggerated, repressed, or forgotten[31] (unless we are reminded, as we were in Richard Russo's eloquent description of the difficulty of high school life in his 2001 Pulitzer Prize–winning book *Empire Falls*[32]). As adults, we forget the many normal and calm days we experienced as teens. Thus, whether we remember good or bad events, our memories are more influenced by a few highlights, and the many uneventful days are ignored or forgotten.[33]

Some adults look back on high school years as the apogee of their lives. In many small towns across America, adults relive their lives through this year's band, athletic team, or cheerleading squad—a theme depicted in many movies (e.g., *The Last Picture Show*) and books. Fiction writer Susan Grafton expressed the point this way:

He's a local boy, a blueblood, high society: good looks, ambitious, an ego big as your head. More charisma than character . . . not to speak ill of the dead,

but I suspect he'd peaked out. You must know people like that yourself. High
school's the glory days; after that, nothing much. It's not like he did poorly,
but he never did as well. He's a fellow cut corners, never really earned his
stripes, so to speak.[34]

Many adults leave adolescence and discover new highs. Some teenagers
have horrible experiences but self-correct and have rewarding adult lives.
In contrast, some teens never fully recover from these years (e.g., a pregnancy at an early age has repercussions that may last a lifetime).

As memories become fuzzier, it becomes easier for adults to label teenage behavior as typical or expected, thus allowing them to discount the importance of events that may seem life altering to a teen. There is considerable research on autobiographical memory to illustrate that negative
emotions fade over time and that more positive reflections of past events
tend to become more salient. Hence, many adults may now remember
more of the positive experiences they had when they were in school than
the negative ones.[35]

As a case in point, most teens experience a breakup at one point or another, but most adults view these breakups as inevitable. Just as we expect
fashion to come and go, we also expect teenage relationships to be fluid.
Parents and teachers know that teenagers recover from the loss of a first
love. But this insight has been validated by decades of additional experiences. Adults must recognize that what appears insignificant to them is vi-
tally important to teens.

Differentiated Experiences

Our last hypothesis is that adults are insensitive to the range of young people's situations. American teens' economic and social circumstances vary
enormously, which means that teens experience their teenage years in
unique, individual ways. It makes sense to talk about teens' experiences
only if we keep in mind the differences. It is our belief that oddly enough,
despite these vast differences, citizens are not keenly sensitive to the variation in youth.

CURRENT BELIEFS ABOUT YOUTH

We have established that attitudes toward youth have grown more critical
over time, and we proposed a few hypotheses as to why this is the case. We
now turn to data that reflect the current climate youth live in. The most recent survey data available (for years 1997 and 1999), sponsored by Public

Agenda (PA) suggest that citizens view the next generation largely in negative terms.

The Public Agenda Polls

Public Agenda is a nonprofit organization based in New York City that strives to impact social policy by tapping into the heart of public opinion on a wide array of political issues.[36] Founded in 1975, the organization has worked to present to the nation's leaders the spectrum of public views on topics such as welfare reform, public schooling, and, relevant to this book, adults' attitudes toward youth and what can and should be done for them. The goal of the agency is to reflect the public's primary concerns back to policymakers.

In the late 1990s, in reaction to evidence of declining valuation of youth, PA sponsored two polls—one in 1997 and a follow-up in 1999—to gauge current attitudes of adults toward the next generation. Public Agenda's 1997 survey was based on interviews with randomly selected adult members of the general public and with an oversampling[37] of African American and Hispanic parents of children under the age of 18 living at home. They collected data from approximately 2,000 adults (with Hispanic and African American citizens overrepresented) and 600 teens (ages 12–17), as well as from six focus groups organized in six different American cities.

The follow-up survey in 1999 was also based on a random sample telephone survey of 1,005 members of the public, including 384 parents of children under 18. The main findings from both surveys are presented in Figs. 1.1 and 1.2.

Finding 1: The Moral Meltdown. According to the 1997 PA report, and the follow-up in 1999, a majority of adults thought that lack of core values and personal morality are a major problem for society generally and for youth specifically.[38] In 1997, when asked to report what first comes to mind about today's teenagers, 67% of adults used negative adjectives, such as *rude, irresponsible,* and *wild.* These sentiments changed little by 1999, when 71% of citizens (and 74% of parents) viewed teens as rude, irresponsible, and wild. Strikingly, findings suggested that even more than the worsening conditions in which many youth live (e.g., poverty-stricken families and neighborhoods[39]), parents and nonparents worried most about what they saw as youth's growing character deficits. Adults described youth in terms of their unwillingness to help out (only 12% believed teens are friendly and helpful[40]), and they described them as irresponsible and narcissistic.[41]

In striking contrast to adults' negative attitudes toward youth, 66% of teens[42] stated, "faith in God is an important part of my life" and 68% reported that they attend religious services at least once a month. As for their

---

FINDING ONE: *The Moral Meltdown.* Americans believe that youth face a moral crisis, and they view teens as undisciplined, disrespectful, and unfriendly.

FINDING TWO: *It's Not Just Teens.* Public dissatisfaction extends beyond teens to include even young children, whom they believe are out of control, unfriendly, and not helpful. This applies to children from all socioeconomic backgrounds.

FINDING THREE: *Caring Parents.* Most believe that parents are the fundamental reason teens and children are in a disappointing state. Indeed, they believe parents fail to teach children right from wrong and to give them guidance.

FINDING FOUR: *Mitigating Circumstances.* Americans acknowledge that it is hard to be a parent or a child in today's society. They recognize the potentially powerful social influences of drugs and crime, and sex and violence in the media that can undermine parents' efforts. Further, they recognize that sometimes schools even fail to provide safe institutions where children and teens can flourish.

FINDING FIVE: *Never Give Up.* Americans continue to care deeply about their children and continue to believe in the well-being of youth. Most are stubbornly optimistic about the chances of reclaiming the lives of even the most troubled teens.

FINDING SIX: *Solutions that Miss the Mark.* Government programs aimed at improving the health and economic circumstances of young people miss the mark in three important ways. First, Americans define the major issue of young people in terms of morality. Second, people believe the crux of the problem is parents, not government. And third, welfare has left a skeptical legacy as to the benefits of government intervention on behalf of the family.

FINDING SEVEN: *Solutions that Show Promise.* Americans gravitate toward solutions that encourage character development. They believe schools should teach kids discipline, honesty, respectfulness towards themselves and others. They believe community centers can be helpful also.

FINDING EIGHT: *Will Individual Americans Help?* Americans are convinced that young people need adults to help them in their lives. However, they fear their efforts might embarrass the ones they are trying to help or be unappreciated. Only 1/3 of adults volunteer regularly, but most say they have time to do so.

FIG. 1.1.   A summary of findings from Public Agenda's 1997 poll of citizens' views of teenagers.

willingness to help out, in 1997, 67% of youth were very comfortable running an errand for a neighbor who needed help, and 51% reported they had done something like that in the past 6 months. Fifty-nine percent indicated they would feel very comfortable watching a younger child for a neighbor as a favor without getting paid, and 55% said they were very comfortable doing volunteer work once a week at a place like a hospital or a

FINDING ONE: *Negative Reactions.* Most Americans are deeply disappointed with kids these days with 70% ascribing words such as "rude" "irresponsible," and "wild." Few believe that today's youngsters will grow up to make America a better place.

FINDING TWO: *A Focus on Values and Respect.* The American public believes that youth lack character and values and are severely short on basic civility.

FINDING THREE: *Putting Blame on Parents.* Most believe that parents are the fundamental reason teens and children are in a disappointing state. They believe parents fail to teach children right from wrong and to give them guidance.

FINDING FOUR: *Difficult Circumstances.* Americans acknowledge that it is hard to be a parent or a child in today's society. A majority of citizens believe that it is much harder to parent children today than in the past.

FINDING FIVE: *Little Willingness to Write Off Kids.* Americans believe that helping kids get a good start in life is one of the most important issues facing the country. Many citizens believe that given the right guidance, even the most troubled teenager can get "back on track."

FINDING SIX: *The Role of Government.* Americans endorse a variety of solutions for helping youth; however, a majority of citizens focus mostly on those that build character and involve children in structured activities. The public looks to schools, employers, and community-based organizations, not the government. Minority parents are more likely to view governmental programs as important and sorely needed to help their children.

FINDING SEVEN: *Positive Attitudes Among Teens.* Teenagers today report warm relationships with their parents and other adults, a strong faith in God, and reliable friends. Few confront gangs on a regular basis. However, many teens report having a lot of extra time on their hands.

Reproduced from *Kids these days '99: What Americans really think about the next generation* by permission of Public Agenda. © Copyright 1999. We gratefully acknowledge that the material in this book is adapted from *Kids these days '99: What Americans really think about the next generation* by permission of Public Agenda. For information about these national surveys and other Public Agenda research, please call Public Agenda at 212-686-6610, fax 212-889-3461, email info@publicagenda.org or visit www.publicagenda.org.

FIG. 1.2. Updated findings from Public Agenda's 1999 poll on adults and youth.

church. Though adults tend to view teens as narcissistic or self-absorbed, a large number of teens report wanting more contact with surrounding adults. Many teenagers do voluntary community service[43] and believe helping others is important. And polls also show that youth have a positive outlook on life. In May 2000, *Newsweek* reported that teens believed they were more "spiritual, optimistic, and ambitious" than their parents' generation.[44]

Why do so many adults describe adolescents as morally impaired? Why do they perceive youth, on average, as selfish and lacking in character when teens themselves generally believe that they have a strong moral and spiritual code? Why do adults see youth as primarily narcissistic, when many young people say that they want closer ties with their family members and friends? Perhaps adults do not listen to youth or take their perspectives very seriously. Possibly, adults and youth define *character* differently. Just as many adults disagree on notions of morality, teenagers also vary widely in how they define and practice morality. Some readily admit that lying and cheating are common among their peers and view these as deplorable behaviors. However, for others, these are small infractions compared with violence, substance use, and pregnancy.[45]

The reasons for the discrepancies between adults' perceptions of teens and teens' own self-perceptions are not easy to identify—especially in light of the way youth are socialized. Clearly, it is hypocritical to blame youth for immorality when they learn their immorality from surrounding adults. Also, there is no absolute consensus in our culture as to what constitutes morality. The following example illustrates the difficulty of defining morality. In a fall 2002 episode of *Boston Public,* a male student makes money by renting out to other teens an empty high school room in which they can have sex. He also rents out blankets, condoms, and so forth. The student donates all of the money he collects to a youth AIDS charity group. After he is caught, the vice principal sarcastically asks how he plans to list this activity on his résumé. The student's straightforward answer is that he would say, "I worked through high school to give money to charity!"

Finding 2: It's Not Just Teens.   Tragically, younger children (between ages 5 and 12 years) are also targets of scathing judgments and unrealistically high expectations. In 1997, 53% of PA poll respondents described young children as spoiled, out of control, or unwilling to help others, and 48% asserted that children do not appreciate what they have. By 1999, the percentage of respondents who criticized young children remained high at 53%. By contrast, only 12% of 1997 respondents found it very common for children to treat people with respect, and only 17% considered it usual for children to be friendly and helpful toward their neighbors. And, in 1999, 22% of respondents ascribed positive attributes to children, and 15% did so with teens. According to PA, it seems that adults believe even very young children are "unwieldy," "unhelpful," "spoiled," and "unappreciative."

In both 1997 and 1999, a majority of adults (58%) believed children either "won't make any difference in the world" or will "make it even worse." Perhaps one result of this sense that youth won't cut it is the current push to urge younger children to do more. Increasingly, even very young children are asked by surrounding adults (parents, educators, and policymakers) to engage in high-stakes testing, to play less, and to work harder, and they are bashed if they "fail." One reporter put it this way:

> Increasingly rare are the days when children had the time and ability to organize their own games of marbles, stickball or cops and robbers. In their place is more time doing homework, more time running around with parents doing errands and more time participating in organized sports like soccer.[46]

These shifting expectations of children and adolescents are seen most vividly in the educational realm. For example, today students as young as 5 or 6 years of age can, in some schools, expect upwards of 20 minutes of daily homework.[47] Recess times are being shortened and in some schools eliminated.[48] Kindergarten is becoming less about exploration and socialization, and more about academic pressure. Some grade schoolers are so busy they have little time to relax or reflect and play.[49] And President Bush has threatened to alter the highly successful Head Start program because it does not address systematic development of reading skills.

Why do adults believe that even very young children are willfully obstinate, spoiled, or selfish? Citizens and parents acknowledge how difficult it is to be a parent today—partly because there are so many undesirable influences in their children's lives (e.g., drugs, gangs). However, we suspect part of the problem rests in how society fails to help parents. For example, there are many laws designed to protect children. In today's age of accountability, skepticism, and even nanny cams, parents are put in the precarious position of being judged for actions toward their children. Thus, parents who are publicly unsuccessful at redirecting bad behavior are often judged as having no control over an unwieldy, "spoiled" child or a child who is violent or destructive toward others. This overly generalized perspective must be challenged.

Finding 3: Uncaring Parents. Poll respondents tended to blame parents for the plight of many teenagers. Only 22% of poll respondents in 1997 said it was "very common to find parents who are good role models for their kids." Half complained that parents failed to provide discipline, and more than half (55%) believed that parents break up marriages too easily instead of trying to make than work for the sake of the children. Even parents who were polled questioned the skills of parents. About 65% of parents who were polled said, "It's common for parents to have children before they are ready for the responsibility." And only 19% said it was very common for parents to be good role models and to teach their children right from wrong. Overall, a majority of respondents were quick to blame parents for the problems of teens and children.

By 1999, these views had changed little. Citizens who were polled continued to hold parents responsible for the problems of today's youth. The number of citizens who blamed parents for the problems today's kids face increased from 1997 to 1999 (from 44% to 49%). And fewer respondents in 1999 blamed the social and economic pressures on families for problems (41% vs. 37%).

Saying parents are to blame for what is wrong with today's teenagers is no more accurate than blaming teens themselves. Families live in remarkably varied circumstances. Although some parents do a poor job of caring for their children, many do the best they can with the support systems and social opportunities available to them. To blame parents is counterproductive. For many families who receive very little support and guidance from community or government services, recent welfare reform (i.e., the federal government's Welfare-to-Work Initiative) is making it even tougher to parent effectively. Both teens and parents are being asked to do more and do it well without being given adequate support and guidance.

Finding 4: Mitigating Circumstances.   According to both polls, respondents felt that being a parent or a teenager is difficult to some extent because of circumstances such as drugs and gangs. Eighty-one percent believe environmental factors such as these make it harder to be a parent and to do their job than it was in the past. Similarly, 83% said it is harder to be a kid growing up in America now. In 1999, citizens continued to view social circumstances as barriers to effective parenting; 78% reported that it was much harder to be a parent today, again due in part to the range of dangers and temptations in their environment.

Citizens who were polled acknowledged that some social circumstances hinder effective parenting and child rearing, but this recognition still has not led to services or programs to help parents and youth in such circumstances. For example, researchers found that many working mothers who live in poverty (compared with those who do not) are not afforded the flexible schedules or paid sick leave necessary for even minimal involvement in their child's schooling[50] (see Table 1.2). Employers make it extremely hard for struggling parents—especially single mothers—to be physically present to support their children.

Society's attitude has become harsher toward welfare recipients over the past decade, a fact that further endangers young people living in poverty. Near the end of his term, President Clinton, with strong political support from both parties, signed legislation requiring most mothers on welfare to return to the workplace. The negative effects of these policies are now emerging. A 2002 report suggests that when welfare mothers go back to work, adolescents are hurt even more than younger children and tend to do worse in school than adolescents with mothers who stay on welfare.[51] Unfortunately, as a consequence of welfare reform in the 1990s, more adolescents in poor homes are left to socialize themselves.

Finding 5: Never Give Up.   Citizens who were polled in 1997 reported that they continue to care deeply about youth, despite their negative descriptions of them. Most respondents were "stubbornly optimistic about the chances of reclaiming the lives of even the most troubled teens." In 1997, 85% of respondents believed that "given enough attention and the right guidance, almost all teens can get back on track." Additionally, 72% be-

TABLE 1.2
Working Conditions Faced by Mothers Whose Child
Scores in the Lowest Quartile on the PIAT-Reading
Comprehension and PIAT-Math

	Reading		Math	
	Family Living in Poverty?		Family Living in Poverty?	
	No (%)	Yes (%)	No (%)	Yes (%)
No paid sick leave	40.4	66.5	36.5	70.3
No paid vacation leave	23.4	38.3	24.1	25.6
No paid sick/vacation leave	21.1	36.5	20.7	39.3
No flexibility	51.0	63.2	46.2	59.4
No paid sick leave, vacation leave, or flexibility	12.5	25.1	10.8	29.3

Note.   From "Low-Income Parents: How Do Working Conditions Affect Their Opportunity to Help School-Age Children at Risk?" by S. J. Heymann and A. Earle, 2000, *American Educational Research Journal, 37*(4), 833–848.

lieved that "given enough love and kindness, just about any kid can be reached." Only 11% thought that many of these teens (i.e., the teens who were already in trouble) were beyond the point where they could be helped. By 1999, even more citizens believed that even the most troubled teens could be reached (89% said that given enough attention and the right kind of guidance, almost all teenagers can get back on track).

Adults believe that in spite of all the bad things youth do they are likely to turn out okay. Perhaps part of this optimism—youth will turn out okay—is a social desirability artifact of the survey[52] or perhaps a form of deep cynicism. In a January, 2002, *New York Times* column, Frank Rich cynically wrote that youth who are out of work, undereducated, and have no health plan should join the army and "see Iraq."[53] This view—that if parents can't socialize their children, the army or prison system is a viable alternative—is curious. Even if the belief is valid, it is not clear how this turnaround will be achieved. Who will help socialize youth and help them make better decisions about sexuality, work, drugs, and careers? Increasingly, society is asking its adolescents to self-socialize and then blaming them when they get into trouble. Effective guidance and social support is largely absent for many youth, even though a significant number are asking for more adult contact.[54]

Finding 6: Solutions That Miss the Mark.   Many poll respondents in both 1997 and 1999 reported believing that government programs aimed at helping youth miss the mark and that increased funds for programs isn't the solution. Only 34% of respondents in both surveys said that more government funding for child and health care programs would be a very effective way to help young people. Similarly, only 27% of 1997 respondents (and 25% of 1999 respondents) believed that a shortage of government programs was a problem.

A primary source of reluctance about the government's ability to help is owing to the legacy of the welfare system. Only 10% said that increasing government funding for welfare programs would be a very effective way to help young people. Just 5% said the reason for the failure of these programs was lack of money; 38% said programs are poorly designed, and 51% said those who need the programs fail to take advantage of them. Citizens who were polled also blamed parents and guardians for not using programs intended to help them—a view seemingly independent of whether the relevant program is effective or helpful.

In 1997, PA also asked an oversampling of minority parents to comment on these various issues. Relevant to this specific finding is that minority parents were more likely to view government programs as effective and to believe that a shortage of these programs was a serious problem. For example, 34% of the general public polled said that more government funding for child care and health care programs would be *very effective*. In contrast, 56% of African American parents, 45% of Hispanic parents, and 36% of White parents had the same response. Similarly, when asked about after-school programs and activities for kids in places like community centers, 60% of all parents polled said it would be *very effective* for helping youth, whereas 75% of African American, 67% of Hispanic, and 57% of White parents believed it would be very effective.

Many of the adults who were polled believe that current government programs, especially the welfare system, miss the mark and that increased funding isn't an appropriate answer. These Americans asserted that part of the problem is poorly designed programs. Ironically, however, many of the same respondents asserted that parents who don't take advantage of available programs are at fault. It is odd that citizens expect participants to seek out and accept help and guidance from flawed programs.

Even more egregious in this accusation is that those who need the greatest amount of help often lack the know-how to ask for help. What is called for is a greater sensitivity to developing programs that are effective and accessible to those in greatest need.

We agree with those citizens who believe that increased funding for government programs without appropriate structure misses the mark. Money is needed for high-quality programs. Foster care is a prime example of a need that requires spending money to help youth, but the system now in place typifies the horrors that result when funding is allocated or supervised inappropriately. Although the foster care system was designed to protect children,[55] its implementation has been woefully inadequate.[56] Conservative estimates suggest that the incidence of torture, neglect, and abuse among the 550,000 children in foster care is somewhere around 7,500.[57] In November of 2000, *Time Magazine* did a cover story on the atrocities that have largely gone unnoticed. The article highlights the plight of a 5-year-old African American boy (approximately 50% of children in foster care are Black) who, after being taken away from his drug-addicted mother, was placed in what seemed like the ideal environment—with the maternal grandparent of one of his siblings. However, this little boy's life ended abruptly when he was found battered and so bruised that the medical examiner gave up counting the number of bruises on his body. This atrocious incident is but one of the many occurrences within the foster care system. In Georgia alone more than 513 kids have died while in the foster care system.[58] In January of 2003, the State of New Jersey admitted that it lost track of many children believed to have been abused.[59] Despite increasing news coverage of deficiencies in foster homes since at least year 2000, the problems are still largely unaddressed.

Foster care is only one example of a government program that exists to help many disadvantaged children but which could be improved significantly. Obviously, some foster care homes provide rich, loving support for children. And some children are abused in stable, affluent, two-parent homes. Still, too many teens live in poverty, and being young and poor is vastly different from being young and affluent. Poverty does not cause bad behavior, but it makes it more likely,[60] especially when youth are abandoned.[61]

Finding 7: Adults Provide a "Solution."   The PA polls provide strong evidence that adults believe the problems with today's teenagers are primarily their low moral character and general disdain for others. Although many respondents believe that parents are most to blame for these problems, a large number think that schools, too, are failing to build the character of youth. A majority of those polled wanted schools to educate all students in values and standards of behavior, such as being responsible, on time, and disciplined (83%), knowing the value of hard work (78%), and being honest and tolerant of others (74%).[62] In 1999, these views were repeated, with the larger proportion of citizens (33% of White adults, 31% of minority adults) ranking "not learning values like honesty, respect, and responsibility" as the most serious problem facing kids out of 10 possible choices. The next most-serious problem, according to those polled, was drug and alcohol abuse (23% of White adults, 29% of minority adults).

In November of 1999, presidential hopeful George W. Bush fueled the character debate when he described teenagers who engage in "evil" acts of violence or criminal activity as lacking in character. He attributed this to a failure of education and called for character education to be provided more systematically in today's schools:

Yes, we want our children to be smart and successful. But even more, we want
them to be good and kind and decent. Yes, our children must learn how to
make a living. But even more, they must learn how to live, and what to love.
"Intelligence is not enough," said Martin Luther King, Jr. "Intelligence plus
character—that is the true goal of education."[63]

Unfortunately, as beneficial as this plan sounds, empirical data are lacking that show a connection between character education and a reduction in
violent acts. After all, many violent crimes have been committed by presumably moral individuals with deep religious beliefs. Currently, the number of
cases in which priests have been found to abuse children or nuns is alarming, and the role of the church in denying or hiding these abuses is even
more alarming.[64]

Bush is calling for a systematic character curriculum in the schools. However, this has obvious problems in that character is such a value-laden con-
struct that it is unclear how such a curriculum would be defined, implemented, or assessed. Will character education be deemed successful if more
students volunteer to help out? Or will success be defined by fewer disciplinary problems in school? How would such a curriculum coincide with
school-specific philosophies, such as codes of conduct and disciplinary consequences for disobeying them?[65] For example, in one school a student was
punished for not telling administrators who had been involved in a cheating scam that was uncovered. How is a student to understand character
when he or she is strongly punished for being a good friend?

There are numerous examples within and across schools of contradictions in how character is defined and communicated. Some schools employ
a zero-tolerance disciplinary stance, whereas others take the position of
three strikes, you're out. The former communicates that some behaviors
are simply unforgivable, whereas the latter suggests that second chances are
possible. How should students attending these two schools who make undesirable decisions negotiate what adults think of them? How can we hold
youth accountable when they are asked to understand and negotiate numerous and contradicting messages of character?

At the classroom level, management techniques that conflict with goals
of instruction are ineffective for building warm, collegial, and productive
learning environments.[66] It is hypocritical to tell students they must unques-
tionably comply with arbitrary classroom rules if a classroom is one that pur-
ports to foster independent thinking skills. The same rationale applies to
societally imposed punishment. It seems ludicrous to suggest that we can
teach youth morality when there are often blatant inconsistencies and contradictions in the actions taken against youth. This is especially the case
when school offenses and societal crimes are treated so differently. A good

example of this hypocrisy is provided in the movie *Election*. The student running for president is disqualified when election fraud is discovered, but in society (e.g., in the 2000 presidential election), by the rule of the Supreme Court, it was ruled acceptable not to count all the ballots that voters cast in Florida. Youth notice these things.

Finding 8: Will Individual Americans Help? In 1997, the citizens who were polled strongly believed that young people need adults in their life; however, only one third of adults volunteered with young people, even though many more said they have the time. In the 1999 poll, many teens reported having a lot of time on their hands. Unfortunately, it appears that few adults are willing to become involved with them. Some adults reported that they withheld their help for fear of embarrassing a teen or being unappreciated. In another 2002 report, sponsored by The Search Institute, it was found that nonparents believed strongly that they are not and should not be responsible for other people's children.[67]

Who will help make things better for youth? Despite the empathy for young people's struggles reflected in the PA poll, most Americans are unwilling to help. Similarly, it is clear that many adults today resent the presence of youth in their surroundings. For instance, when adult couples who chose not to have children were interviewed for a feature story in the *New York Times Magazine*,[68] many said they viewed the presence of youth in their neighborhoods or workplaces as distracting, unappealing, and irritating. This view is apparently shared by enough adults that many retirement communities, and even newer developments, have emerged that don't allow children. Similarly, it was reported that childless workers are increasingly irritated when asked to do a job that is unfinished when co-workers must leave work for children's medical emergencies or other family- or child-related reasons. They argue that employers should not have the right to take advantage of them just because they do not have kids. We, too, feel that some adults abuse their co-workers with their child-care hardships. Still, it is a notable shift in cultural attitudes that youth are now viewed as excuses at the workplace and as a nuisance to neighbors.

These eight PA findings[69] suggest that adults are critical of youth and their parents, even though at the same time other data suggest that youth describe themselves favorably. The findings also underscore how many adults do not think realistically about how American youth can emerge as flourishing adults from problematic conditions. Many adults are negative about teenagers, but few are invested in enhancing their socialization. If these attitudes persist, the time that teenagers spend unsupervised could increase as adults continue to pull away from them.

So What Are the Costs of Ignoring Youth?

In the rest of the book, we deal with this question. The failure to see youth as a varied group has real consequences. Some youth are subjected to low expectations, denied resources, and ignored unless they commit a crime. Other youth are overscheduled, subjected to multiple, often contradictory, and inappropriately high expectations. One recent study[70] illustrated that more than 5.5 million youth between the ages of 16–24 years are out of work, out of school, and, as Bob Herbert[71] put it, "out of hope." He argues, "This army of undereducated, jobless young people, disconnected in most instances from society's mainstream, is restless and unhappy, and poses a severe long-term threat to the nation's well-being on many fronts."[72]

Yet elsewhere we learn that many youth who attend college receive little career guidance both before or after they enter college. These youths are left largely to socialize themselves, as are the number of youth, both rich and poor, who return after school to homes that are empty of adults and helpful guidance. It is not a mystery as to why the bulk of juvenile crime—committed by both rich and poor kids—takes place in the after-school hours. Such crime, whether driven by desperation, boredom, or opportunity, could be markedly reduced if adults were more responsive to youth. Similarly, as we argue later in the book, youth's violence, inappropriate sexuality, and health could be addressed in ways that benefit both youth and society.

CONCLUSION

American citizens hold negative attitudes about youth, including young children. Furthermore, citizens express little interest in working with youth or in supporting government programs designed specifically for youth. In terms of core values, youth are seen as less moral than they were in post–World War II America. We considered several reasons for the decline of youth's value in the eyes of their elders. In part, youth may be less valued because their "real" contributions (marriage, full-time job, living away from home) begin at a considerably later age than even 50 years ago. Also, we believe that it is easy for adults to forget the pressures that youth face, and it is arguable that youths' role in a modern society is more ambiguous and more multifaceted than it was in earlier times.

We argued that the presence of an active media that is critical of youth also negatively impact adult beliefs about youth. In particular, the media provides citizens with negative and stereotyped images of youth. Finally, we argued that adults are more susceptible to media influences because their relations with teens are fewer and less personal than they were even 50 years ago.

As noted in the second epigraph at the start of the chapter, much of youth's time (upwards of 40%) is discretionary. It is critical that adults recognize that for many youth this percentage is more illusion than fact. Scheduled activities leave many youth stressed and exhausted. Some youth are free to choose among free time or organized activities of their choice, yet other youth have considerable time available but no opportunities to participate in organized activities. The highly publicized generalization of youth's time illustrates the problem with averaged depictions of youth in the media. As we show in later chapters, the media stereotypes of youth are highly distorted and paint youth's sexuality, substance abuse, and violence in blatantly excessive ways. It is our thesis that only if citizens become more consciously aware of youth's diversity, can they demand appropriate policies that can help youth to become productive citizens.

General Considerations

Following the atrocities of September 11, 2001, policymakers worked to ensure that the public did not generalize the fault of those horrendous deeds to all Arab and Islamic peoples. Society needs to work equally hard to ensure that negative actions of some youth are not generalized to all. Some youth are aggressive, rude, or irresponsible but many are not. Further, many youths who behave badly learned the behavior from their community. However, society is inclined to blame individuals, not the environment.

It seems tragic that society is willing to disparage the character of youth at a time when there are evident flaws in the morality of the broader society. We have federal agencies, such as the CIA and FBI, squandering valuable time and resources trying to blame one another for the tragedy of September 11. We witness the decay of morality in the Catholic Church and in big businesses (Enron, Firestone, Ford, Arthur Anderson, and many more). Rather than blaming youth for cheating in schools, we should better understand their pressures and teach them how to learn from their mistakes and those made by adults. Of course, some schools and parents address these complex issues in meaningful ways with their students and children. However, they must also become part of the national dialogue. Only then will adults be more sensitized to the complexities of adolescence today and in the future.

That the experiences of an age cohort are viewed as unique by a member of that group is understandable. After all, teens growing up in post–World War II America, or the post-Vietnam era recall highly salient events that capture the struggles of their teenhood in common ways. Similarly, today's teens have to cope with threats of terrorism and will carry with them the horrific images of September 11, 2001.

We noted that citizens recognize the difficulties of being a teen or a parent but are still highly critical of teens and are unwilling to help them with personal time or to support government programs for them. Recognition of the issue is an important first step for helping. Perhaps there are ways that citizens' recognition of youth problems can be turned into active support. We will return to this consideration in chapter 9.

Needed Research

More research is needed on adults' conceptions of youth. Although the evidence suggests that adults hold negative attitudes about youth, the number of studies in the area is small. We need more information about why adults perceive teenagers negatively. Do they form opinions on the basis of personal experience, print media, television, or Internet sources? Perhaps more important, we need to know the intensity with which these beliefs are held. Research needs to focus more closely on citizens' attitudes toward children and what leads adults to make pejorative judgments of preteens. More information is needed, too, to explore how citizens believe that immoral and rude teens will turn out to be effective citizens.

It would be instructive to ask today's citizens to reflect on growing up and its varied meanings in the decades since the 1940s to more fully depict the stressors that teens felt in growing up. For example, some see the teens of the 1950s as living in a simple world of stable families and simple decisions. However, youth of the 1950s were expected to marry early and to stay married to the same person. Imagine the pressure on 1950s youth to marry young, stay married, and have babies. Youth of the new millennium do not face these pressures because they can choose to delay marriage, change partners, or decide not to marry and not to have children with minimal stigma. But the teens of the 1980s faced drugs, HIV, and gun violence unknown to the youth of the 1950s, and teens of the millennium cope with the threats of local terrorism that never existed before.

Perhaps the culture would benefit from more perspectives on what it means to be a teenager in different eras. How are suburban or rural youth in the 1950s different or the same as urban youth in the 1980s or today? It has become increasingly popular in the last two decades to pay attention to differences in life experiences and the perceptions of such experiences as a function of gender, race, ethnicity, culture, and so forth. It is perhaps useful to pay more attention to how life conditions have varied for teenagers (and other subcultures) over time.

Most important, it would be useful for youth's views to be more systematically researched. How do youth perceive the fact that society criticizes them—their character, intelligence, and civility? Although advertisers assiduously attempt to understand youth's needs, policymakers, including educators, have not sought conceptions of how youth see and experience their world.

ENDNOTES

1. Dickens, C. (1938). *A tale of two cities.* New York: Heritage Free Press.
2. Carnegie Council on Adolescent Development. (1992, December). *A matter of time: Risk and opportunity in the nonschool hours* (Report of the Task Force on Youth Development and Community Programs). New York: Carnegie Corporation of New York.
3. Russo, R. (2001). *Empire falls.* New York: Knopf.
4. Carnegie Council on Adolescent Development. (1992, December). *A matter of time: Risk and opportunity in the nonschool hours* (Report of the Task Force on Youth Development and Community Programs). New York: Carnegie Corporation of New York.
5. Elkind, D. (1981). *The hurried child: Growing up too fast, too soon.* Reading, MA: Addison-Wesley.
6. Farkas, S., & Johnson, J. (with Duffett, A., & Bers, A.) (1997). *Kids these days: What Americans really think about the next generation.* New York: Public Agenda.
7. Howe, N., & Strauss, W. (2000). *Millennials rising: The next great generation.* New York: Vintage Books.
8. Estimates are taken from population projections calculated by the U.S. Census Bureau. For specific estimates, see http://www.census.gov/population/projections/nation/summary/np-t3-f.pdf (retrieved November 13, 2002).
9. Hall, G. S. (1904). *Adolescence: Its psychology and its relations to physiology, anthropology, sociology, sex, crime, religion, and education.* New York: D. Appleton & Company.
10. Several psychologists have argued this point. See Bandura, A. (1964). The stormy decade: Fact or fiction? *Psychology in the Schools, 1,* 224–231; Offer, D., & Schonert-Reichl, K. A. (1992). Debunking the myths of adolescence: Findings from recent research. *American Academy of Child and Adolescent Psychiatry, 31*(6), 1003–1014. Researchers on adults' perceptions of adolescence as a stormy period of life have documented that storm-and-stress theories of adolescence are prevalent. For example, see Holmbeck, G. N., & Hill, J. P. (1988). Storm and stress beliefs about adolescence: Prevalence, self-reported antecedents, and effects of an undergraduate course. *Journal of Youth and Adolescence, 17*(4), 285–306.
11. Bandura, A. (1980). The stormy decade: Fact or fiction? In R. E. Muus (Ed.), *Adolescent behavior and society: A book of readings* (3rd ed., pp. 22–31). (Original work published 1964)
12. Arnett, J. J. (1999). Adolescent storm and stress, reconsidered. *American Psychologist, 54*(5), 317–326.
13. Research has shown that adults stereotype adolescents as more "internalizing, conforming, risk-taking, rebellious, and involved in problem behaviors" than younger children. See Buchanan, C. M., & Holmbeck, G. N. (1998). Measuring beliefs about adolescent personality and behavior. *Journal of Youth and Adolescence, 27*(5), 607–627.
14. Offer, D., Ostrov, E., & Howard, K. I. (1981). The mental health professional's concept of the normal adolescent. *Archives of General Psychiatry, 38,* 149–152.
15. Koplewicz, H. S. (2002). *More than moody: Recognizing and treating adolescent depression.* New York: Putnam.

16. Koplewicz, H. S. (2002). *More than moody: Recognizing and treating adolescent depression.* New York: Putnam.

17. Bostrom, M. (2001). *The 21st century teen: Public perception and teen reality: A summary of public opinion data.* Washington, DC: The Frameworks Institute.

18. Bostrom, M. (2001). *The 21st century teen: Public perception and teen reality: A summary of public opinion data.* Washington, DC: The Frameworks Institute.

19. For a list of poll citations, see Bostrom, M. (2001). *The 21st century teen: Public perception and teen reality: A summary of public opinion data.* Washington, DC: The Frameworks Institute. Also, for more information on Gallup polls, go to www.gallup.com

20. Bostrom, M. (2001). *The 21st century teen: Public perception and teen reality: A summary of public opinion data.* Washington, DC: The Frameworks Institute.

21. Bostrom, M. (2001). *The 21st century teen: Public perception and teen reality: A summary of public opinion data.* Washington, DC: The Frameworks Institute.

22. See Bostrom, M. (2001). *The 21st century teen: Public perception and teen reality: A summary of public opinion data.* Washington, DC: The Frameworks Institute. Results are based on a CBS news poll of 878 adults nationwide, April 13–14, 1999.

23. Farkas, S., & Johnson, J. (with Duffett, A., & Bers, A.) (1997). *Kids these days: What Americans really think about the next generation.* New York: Public Agenda.

24. Polls have found that adults tend to criticize youth rather than describe them in positive terms. For example, the organization Connect for Kids (http:www.connectforkids.org) conducted research to examine adult attitudes about teens. With support from the William T. Grant Foundation, they found that adults are excessively critical of teens. See Bales, S. N. (2000). *Youth today: Adult perceptions may be misperceptions.* Retrieved from http://www.connectforkids.org/content1555/content_show.htm?attrib_id=334&doc_id=30516

    In another research project, the W. T. Grant Foundation awarded a multiyear grant to the UCLA Center on Communications and Community and the Frameworks Institute to apply the perspective of strategic frame analysis to youth issues. The research was conducted in 1999 and 2000 to discern what Americans think about youth, why they think what they do, and how advocates might best engage Americans in a discussion about positive youth development. The resulting research included an analysis of existing survey research, an analysis of the conceptual frames that people use to reason about teenagers, a content analysis of the representation of teenagers in TV entertainment programming, a catalog of framing options, and a summary of the six focus groups. See the following publication from the Frameworks Institute: Bales, S. N. (2000). *Reframing youth issues for public consideration and support.* Retrieved from http://www.frameworksinstitute.org/products/reframing.pdf

    See also a report sponsored by the Center for Media and Public Affairs, which discusses the ways the media perpetuate a negative, averaged view of youth. This project supplemented the work by the Frameworks Institute. See Amundson, D. R., Lichter, L. S., & Lichter, S. R. (2001). *What's the matter with kids today: Television coverage of adolescents in America?* Washington, DC: The Frameworks Institute (http://www.frameworksinstitute.org/products/cmpa.pdf)

25. In 2025, more Americans will be 65 or older than between the ages of 5 and 17 years. Estimates are taken from population projections calculated by the U.S. Census Bureau. For specific estimates, see http://www.census.gov/population/projections/nation/summary/np-t3-f.pdf (retrieved November 13, 2002). See also Zollo, P. (1999). *Wise up to teens: Insights into marketing and advertising to teenagers* (2nd ed.). Ithaca, NY: New Strategist Publications.

26. U.S. Department of Commerce (1975, September). *Historical statistics of the United States, Colonial times to 1970* (bicentennial ed., Part I, pp. 20–21). Washington, DC: U.S. Bureau of the Census.

27. Books like *Warriors Don't Cry* make it clear, for example, that Black youths who integrated American schools were treated with blatant hostility and abuse.

28. Roberts, D., Foehr, U. G., Rideout, V. J., & Brodie, M. (1999, November). *Kids and media @ the new millennium: A comprehensive analysis of children's media use.* Menlo, CA: The Kaiser Family Foundation.

29. Signorielli, N. (1987). Children and adolescents on television: A consistent pattern of de-valuation. *Journal of Early Adolescence, 7*(3), 225–268.

30. Erikson, E. (1968). *Identity: Youth and crisis.* New York: Norton.

31. Interestingly, in a longitudinal study led by Daniel Offer, it was found that adult memories of adolescence were flawed and inaccurate. Although most participants in the study were White men, it was found that when adult men were asked to recall their high school experiences for investigators, many of their responses were completely different from their responses when asked as an adolescent. Therefore, although more research needs to be done, some data suggest that our recollections of adolescence become faded and fuzzy over the years. Offer, D., Kaiz, M., Howard, K., & Bennett, E. (2000). The altering of reported experiences. *Journal of the American Academy of Childhood and Adolescent Psychiatry, 39*(6), 735–742.

32. Russo, R. (2001). *Empire falls.* New York: Knopf.

33. The authors thank an anonymous reviewer for helping to clarify this point.

34. Grafton, S. (1999). *"O" is for outlaw* (p. 303). New York: Henry Holt.

35. For a review on the autobiographical memory research, see Walker, W. R., Skowronski, J. J., & Thompson, C. P. (2003). Life is pleasant—and memory helps to keep it that way! *Review of General Psychology, 7*(2), 203–210. It is important to note that participants who suffered from dysphoria (mild depression) had pleasant and unpleasant memories that faded at the same rate over time. However, for other participants, it was clear that unpleasant emotions faded more quickly than pleasant emotions.

36. For more information, see www.publicagenda.org

37. Oversampling a portion of the population ensures better representation of that segment.

38. For example, when asked to choose between decline in moral values and the economic pressures on the family, 51% attribute the general state of society to a decline in moral values, whereas only 37% believe the general state of society can be blamed on familial economic factors.

39. Males, M. A. (1996). *The scapegoat generation: America's war on adolescents.* Monroe, ME: Common Courage Press.

40. Farkas, S., & Johnson, J. (with Duffett, A., & Bers, A.) (1997). *Kids these days: What Americans really think about the next generation.* New York: Public Agenda.

41. Putnam, R. (2000). *Bowling alone: The collapse and revival of American community.* New York: Simon & Schuster.

42. Telephone interviews were conducted with 600 young people ages 12–17. Youth were selected through a random sample of households using a random-digit-dialing technique, whereby every household in the region covered had an equal chance of being contacted (including those with unlisted numbers).

43. Youniss, J., & Yates, M. (1997). *Community service and social responsibility in youth.* Chicago: University of Chicago Press; Wichner, D. (2000, June 6). All booked up. *Arizona Daily Star,* p. B3.

44. Chessum, J. (2000, May 8). A world of their own. *Newsweek,* 53–74.

45. Steinberg, L. (1996). *Beyond the classroom: Why school reform has failed and what parents need to do about it.* New York: Simon & Schuster; Good, T., Nichols, S., & Sabers, D. (1998). Under-

estimating youth's commitment to schools and society: Toward a more differentiated view. *Social Psychology of Education, 3,* 1–39.

46. Holmes, S. (1998, November 11). Children study longer and play less, a report says. *New York Times,* p. A18; see also Ohanian, S. (2002). *What happened to recess and why are our children struggling in kindergarten.* New York: McGraw-Hill.

47. Winerip, M. (1999, January 3). Homework bound. *New York Times Magazine: Education Life,* 28–31. Also, for more information on the history of homework, the reader is directed to Gill, B., & Schlossman, S. (1996). A sin against childhood: Progressive education and the crusade to abolish homework, 1897–1941. *American Journal of Education, 105,* 27–66.

48. Ohanian, S. (2002). *What happened to recess and why are our children struggling in kindergarten?* New York: McGraw-Hill.

49. Blatchford, P. (1998). *Social life in schools: Pupils' experience of breaktime and recess from 7–16 years.* Bristol, PA: Falmer Press.

50. Heymann, S. J., & Earle, A. (2000). Low-income parents: How do working conditions affect their opportunity to help school-age children at risk? *American Educational Research Journal, 37*(4), 833–848.

51. Rothstein, R. (2002, June 5). When mothers on welfare go to work. *New York Times,* p. B8. See also the report by Gennetian, L. A., Duncan, G. J., Knox, V. W., Vargas, W. G., Clark-Kauffman, E., & London, A. S. (2002, May). *How welfare and work policies for parents affect adolescents: A synthesis of research.* New York: Manpower Demonstration Research Corporation.

52. Social desirability is when research participants misrepresent themselves to look as if they hold socially desirable qualities. For example, when adults report they are optimistic about youth's potential, it could simply be because they want researchers to see them as caring individuals as opposed to being viewed as someone who doesn't care about youth. Admitting to a critical view of youth is seen as a socially undesirable quality by some.

53. Rich, F. (2003, January 18). Joe millionaire for president. *New York Times,* p. A35.

54. Horatio Alger Association. (2001). *The state of our nation's youth, 2001–2002.* Alexandria, VA: Horatio Alger Association of Distinguished Americans. Retrieved from http://www. horatioalger.com/. See also Loven, J. (2001, August). Teens want strong family ties, survey finds. *Arizona Daily Star,* p. A4.

55. George, V. (1970). *Foster care: Theory and practice.* New York: Routledge and Kegan Paul.

56. The number of children referred to foster care has increased over the past three decades—since the 1970s, the foster care population has grown to more than 500,000 children. Geiser, R. L. (1973). *The illusion of caring: Children in foster care.* Boston: Beacon Press. Over the past 5 years, the number of children committed to foster care nearly doubled from about 250,000 in 1995 to between 550,000 and 560,000 in 2000. Brick-Panter, C., & Smith, M. T. (Eds.). (2000). *Abandoned children.* Cambridge, UK: Cambridge University Press.

57. Roche, T. (2000, November 13). The crisis of foster care. *Time, 156*(20), 74–82.

58. Roche, T. (2000, November 13). The crisis of foster care. *Time, 156*(20), 74–82.

59. Kocieniewski, D. (2003, January 11). State admits losing track of children. *New York Times,* p. A14.

60. In an authoritative review of data on youth and poverty, violence, and drug use, Michael Males provides statistics showing the relationship between poverty and at-risk youth outcomes. Males, M. A. (1996). *The scapegoat generation: America's war on adolescents.* Monroe, ME: Common Courage Press.

61. Brick-Panter, C., & Smith, M. T. (Eds.). (2000). *Abandoned children.* Cambridge: Cambridge University Press.

62. Farkas, S., & Johnson, J. (1997). *Kids these days: What Americans really think about the next generation.* New York: Public Agenda.

63. Excerpts from Bush's campaign speech on education. (1999, November 3). *New York Times,* p. A23.

64. Dillon, S. (2002, December 8). Files on priests called "slovenly." Leader of panel studying sex abuse faces other obstacles, too. *New York Times,* p. A8; Belluck, P. (2002, December 9). With criticism mounting, cardinal heads to Rome. *New York Times,* p. A15.

65. Jackson, P., Boostrom, R., & Hansen, D. (1993). *The moral life of schools.* San Francisco, CA: Jossey-Bass.

66. McCaslin, M., & Good, T. (1992). Compliant cognition: The misalliance of management and instructional goals in current school reform. *Educational Researcher, 21*(3), 4–17.

67. For example, see Belkin, L. (2000, July 23). Your kids are their problem. *New York Times Magazine,* 30–40; see also The Search Institute. (2002). *Grading grown-ups 2002: How do American kids and adults relate?* Retrieved from http://www.search-institute.org/norms/gg2002.pdf

68. Belkin, L. (2000, July 23). Your kids are their problem. *New York Times Magazine,* 30–40.

69. We acknowledge that these polls are based on a small but random sample of adults. Further, these results do not comprehensively reflect how all adults feel about all teens. Still, the wide press release of this report and the reporting practices of youth are all indicators of the primarily negative way adults view youth.

70. Sum, A., Khatiwada, I., & Trub'skyy, M. (with Fogg, N., Palma, S.) (2002, November). *Left behind in the labor market: Labor market problems of the nation's out-of-school, young adult populations.* Chicago: Center for Labor Market Studies, Northeastern University. (Available online at http://www.nupr.neu.edu/2-03/left_behind.PDF)

71. Herbert, B. (2003, February 6). Young, jobless, hopeless. *New York Times,* p. A35.

72. Herbert, B. (2003, February 6). Young, jobless, hopeless. *New York Times,* p. A35.

Youth and Media

Every generation
Blames the one before
And all of their frustrations
Come beating on your door
      —Lyrics from the "The Living Years," by Mike and the Mechanics

Expressions of concern about children and media—or more accurately, about
content from "outside" that media make available to children—can be traced
back at least to Plato's defense of censorship in The Republic, *and have contin-*
ued with the introduction of each new medium.
      —Kaiser Family Foundation Report, *Kids and Media* (1999)[1]

The stories the press tell are shaped not by a "liberal agenda" or a "right-wing
conspiracy" but by the desire to case the news in a dramatic, easily packaged
form.
      —*The Press Effect,* 2003[2]

In the 2001 report published by the Frameworks Institute, *What's the Matter*
With Kids Today,[3] the authors' analysis of how youth are portrayed on TV
leads them to the observation that youth are commonly depicted in the
news as dangerous or endangered and involved in some personal crisis or
social conflict. But before we despair of the state of today's youth, we might
wish to ask whether news stories about youth are fair and accurate.

    The media provide a selective lens on what makes "good" news, whether
it is tragic, sensational, ironic, or threatening. From the *New York Times*
motto "All the news that's fit to print" to the legendary Walter Cronkite's

salutation "That's the way it is" to today's online and televised media that report 24 hours a day, 7 days a week, the media suggest what is important and what to value. However, numerous scholars and media critics have noted that those who control the media bring biases (both intentional and unintentional) to their selection and presentation of the news.[4] And it is clear the media, although charged with presenting the "facts," sometimes allow egregious falsehoods to go unchallenged.

In their 2003 book *The Press Effect,* Kathleen Hall Jamieson and Paul Waldman describe how the press frames its stories and how those frames can help or hinder the communication of "facts." They assert, "The stories that journalists tell and the lenses that color this interpretation of events can sometimes dull their fact-finding investigative instincts."[5] In part, the stories that we create of ourselves, and indeed "the stories we live by,"[6] are shaped by the media. Nancy Signorielli[7] writes, "Our children are born into a home which for the first time in human history, a centralized commercial institution rather than parents, church, or school tells most of the stories most of the time."[8] The awareness that the media can and do shape the truth to its own ends, and that its influence helps form our individual identities, leads to two questions: What are the stories the media tell to youth and what are the stories they tell about youth?

In this chapter, we debunk common misconceptions about media effects by providing a systematic description of the relationship between youth and the media that they consume. We explore the role of media in three main ways.

First, we discuss youth's use of media. A brief historical survey of media's cultural presence illustrates, comparatively, how vast and varied youth's current media options are and note that adults believe youth engage in excessive media indulgence. We posit this is because they compare the relationship between today's youth and media with their own relationship to media in their youth. This discussion leads to a description of the current state of youth and their media choices. There is no single accurate profile of the young television viewer. One young person may watch several hours of sitcoms a day; another may watch only a few hours a week of educational programming such as the Discovery Channel or the History Channel. For the former, television may be purely entertainment, but for the latter it may offer valuable new information and even spark vigorous critical thinking on a wide array of subjects.

Second, we discuss the media as storytellers of events (specifically violence), both real and fabricated. Adults have always worried about how media messages affect youth, as noted in the second epigraph of this chapter. In 1900, citizens worried about the content of literature and theater, and books with even implicit sex or violence were condemned (sometimes burned). Throughout the first half of the 20th century, parents were concerned that new technological forms of entertainment, such as radio, movies, and television, would influence youth negatively.[9] In the 1920s, one author asked, "Had a whole generation indelibly learned its manners and morals, unattended at Saturday matinees?"[10] In the 1950s, Elvis's suggestive hip movements caused so much concern that they were edited from his TV performances. Today, media violence and sex are virtually everywhere, and the subject of their ostensibly deleterious effects on youth is both controversial and to many parents and educators a source of escalating concern.[11]

Despite century-old concerns about the effects of media content, today's media portray sex and violence in ways that would have shocked earlier generations. Journalistic reporting of violence includes real-time images of gun battles and death. Entertainment violence has become so real (and common) that audiences are desensitized to fierce explosions, brutal physical fights, threatening hostage situations, and gory deaths. Sex and sexuality pervade media culture. The swimsuit edition of *Sports Illustrated* would have alarmed those of the 1950s, who were more accustomed to women in long skirts and one-piece bathing suits.

In light of these century-long pervasive concerns, in this section we describe what is currently known about the effects of media on behavior. To illustrate the complexity of the relationship between media and behavior, we discuss the most current debates on the role of violence in entertainment and journalism.

Last, we discuss the media as storytellers about youth. The media's slanted representation of youth give the false impression that today's youth are part of the most violent, "sexed," and amoral youth culture in history.[12] However, as we show in chapters 3 and 4, youth violence and sexual behavior have decreased notably—especially in the last few years (e.g., youth violence rates have reached a 33-year low).

MEDIA OVER TIME

Media are vastly different today than in the previous century. Especially since the 1960s, media advances have changed the way we get information, communicate, and are entertained. Summoning a doctor in 1900 might have required a 2- or 3-mile walk to the doctor's office, and the only way for rural residents to communicate with the outside world was by making long treks to their post offices (one Missouri farmer estimated that in 15 years he had traveled more than 15,000 miles to and from his post office[13]). Youth primarily obtained their information through books and personal contact with teachers, peers, parents, or other adults. By the 1940s and early 1950s, youth could listen to the radio and read the newspaper; however, radio did not broadcast around the clock, and newspaper coverage was not instantaneous. Now, youth have numerous media choices, and most choices are available 24 hours a day. The telephone, television, and personal computer have changed how we live. A 1999 Kaiser Family Foundation report put it this way:

> Readers [of this report] who are nearing retirement age likely recall a childhood media environment consisting of magazines and newspapers, radio (drama, game shows, music, 5-minute news broadcasts), possibly a phonograph, and an occasional Saturday matinee at a neighborhood movie theater—with two or three television channels perhaps joining the mix during adolescence. In contrast, most of today's high school students cannot recall a time when the universe of television channels was fewer than three dozen (even without cable or satellite, many homes can receive more than 20 broadcast channels), and their younger siblings have never known a world without interactive video games, personal computers, and the World Wide Web.[14]

Television

Television revolutionized the daily life of an entire society. The first transmission of a televised picture occurred in 1925, but TVs weren't available to most Americans until much later. In 1948, approximately 100,000 televisions were available, and by 1959 7 out of 10 U.S. homes had television sets (approximately 50 million). Today, 98–99% of homes in the United States have at least one TV, and these televisions bear little resemblance to televisions of the mid-20th century. Whereas early televisions had three to five channels and were connected to a ground cable, today's televisions can be hooked up to satellite systems that provide hundreds of channel options controlled from the comfort of a lounge chair. The nuisance of having to actually get up to change channels is obsolete.

Advances in television technology have shaped our cultural experiences. In the 1950s, most youth and adults watched the same TV shows—there was a common media culture. In some families, favorite TV shows became a sacred ritual—no family member would miss *The Ed Sullivan Show* or *I Love Lucy.*

Early television programming portrayed mostly White middle-class values. Ethnic Americans were largely absent from television programming, and, when they made brief cameo appearances, they generally played roles that reinforced stereotypical conceptions of minorities. Gender roles were also stereotypical. Wives were "happy" homemakers, donning aprons and doing housework while husbands went off to work every morning and returned each evening to obedient children and wives who were still wearing their aprons. Children were portrayed as cooperative, cheerful, and helpful, and teens were often presented as largely compliant and frivolous.

In marked contrast to a largely shared media culture of the 1950s, to-day's youth vary more widely in television choices—mostly because there are so many choices available. According to Nielson ratings of 2001, female teens' top five choices in 2001 were *Temptation Island,* a reality-based show highlighting the complexities of relationships and breaking up, *Seventh Heaven, Survivor, Malcolm in the Middle,* and the *Wide World of Disney.* Among young males, the preferred choices included *The Simpsons,* a satirical cartoon aimed at an adult audience, *Malcolm in the Middle, Temptation Island,* and *WWF Smackdown!*[15] Youth's entertainment preferences vary greatly.

Unlike 1950s programming, today's television markets target a range of ethnic groups. On cable there are several Spanish-speaking channels and channels committed to the African American audience. There are several situation comedies that feature Black families (e.g., *One on One, My Wife and Kids,* and *The Bernie Mac Show*). Further, an analysis of television programming suggested that 51 television shows introduced in the 2002–2003 season had multiethnic casts.[16] Still, although there are growing numbers of ethnic shows, mainstream TV programming has a long way to go to provide a balanced representation of all ethnic groups and both genders.[17]

Ultimately, the variation in youth's television preferences spans the scope of choices available. Some youth enjoy television that is geared toward their age group (*Buffy the Vampire Slayer, Dawson's Creek*); others prefer adult-oriented shows, such as *Friends, Frasier,* or *CSI,* and others enjoy educational channels, such as the Discovery Channel or the Learning Channel. A real challenge for today's TV programmers is the lack of predictability in the youth market. Because there are so many choices in television programming and movies, television-watching behavior is much more fragmented today than even 20 years ago. Writers of the Kaiser Foundation report on kids and the media note the following:

> . . . there may be nothing so elusive as "the average kid." Every bit as noteworthy as the substantial amounts of time that some youngsters devote to communication media is the remarkable variation among kids in how much of what they are exposed to, and under what conditions.[18]

The movie *Pleasantville* illustrates how television culture has changed. In the movie, there is a radical transformation from the simplicity of life in the 1950s, where characters were one-dimensional and compliant and where life was predictable, to the more colorful, diverse, and creative life of the late 1990s. The 1950s section of the movie is filmed in black and white and plays on the conventions of programming in that era. For example, one of the main male characters comes home every day, hangs up his coat and hat, and states, "Honey, I'm home." Every day, the wife is there to respond to his entrance with snacks and a smile (reminiscent of *Leave It to Beaver, I Love Lucy,* and *The Honeymooners*).

As the movie progresses, the characters begin to question and challenge their existence—something is wrong with such a simple life. They ultimately break from their 1950s lifestyles to forge new identities that lead to a world they see as more interesting and colorful (and, indeed, aspects of the movie are subsequently displayed in color to represent this change). Those who are incapable of experiencing this change see those who break free as forming a world that is too chaotic and dangerous. Predictability and monolithic story lines defined media of the past, whereas today's media are defined by more vivid and varied story lines.

Computers

The modern computer has profoundly affected our lives. The personal computer allows its user to do simple writing, accounting, and other office-related activities faster and more expertly than before. Individuals and business owners have gained increased flexibility with software that lets them organize and manage their own data systems. The Internet's appearance in the 1990s forever changed how information is disseminated, and, at the same time, it provided a market for creative entrepreneurs to establish new businesses. The 1990s was an era of seemingly limitless possibilities that were realized by hundreds of motivated young people who ended up millionaires.

Having grown up with them, youth tend to know more about computers than many technophobic adults; as a result, teens are often in high demand for their precocious computer expertise. This trend was cleverly parodied on the popular television show *Saturday Night Live,* in a skit that featured a young acne-ridden teenager who grows increasingly frustrated with adults' computer incompetence. The skit depicted a typical office where adults sit in cubicles at their desks, each with a personal computer. Whenever a computer problem arose, they called in their resident 16-year-old expert to help them. It soon became painfully obvious the young expert found these adult workers excruciatingly incompetent.

When a computer-related question was asked—such as "How do you merge addresses into Word to create labels?"—the expert's response was often laced with sarcasm and impatience, which further confused the adult. In his last bit of patience, the expert ultimately executed the request himself. Finally, the teenager walked away, convinced the adults are idiots, and they, in turn, went back to work filled with wonderment because their computer magically performed such complex tasks. The skit is not so far-fetched. Today, it is common for teens to provide technology apprentice-ships for their parents and other adults. And there is evidence that adults' technophobia may hinder their ability to communicate with youth about appropriate use of the Internet for meeting and chatting with friends (e.g., chat rooms, instant messaging). Growing numbers of unsuspecting youth are preyed on through online outlets—in part because parents don't know how to protect them.[19]

The Internet has forever changed the way youth gather and dissemi-nate information and communicate. Instead of late-night phone conversa-tions, youth use instant messaging services to talk long into the night with a number of peers at once. High school research projects no longer re-quire a trip to the library because volumes of information can be readily found online. Indeed, as Bob Dylan noted in his lyrics, "times are a changin'."

Movies

In contrast to the 20th century films, today's movies feature a crisp, high-quality sound system that virtually surrounds viewers, as well as makeup and costume technology so advanced it is difficult to discern image from reality. Special-effects technology has come so far it is difficult to believe Keanu Reeves can't jump from skyscraper to skyscraper (*The Matrix, The Matrix Re-loaded*), Drew Barrymore can't beat up eight men at once with her hands tied behind her back (*Charlie's Angels*), or that ants don't talk to one an-other (*A Bug's Life*). Computer technology allows filmmakers to render such violence with such verisimilitude that it appears entirely real. Deaths depicted on the screen are not real, even when based on historical facts. Still, part of the reason real-life violence is blamed on media violence is be-cause movie magic makes even the impossible seem so real and possible.

> Most graybeards can remember when chocolate syrup dabbed on a shirt sleeve served as blood in Gene Autry westerns; today's teens take for granted films and video games in which blood, gore, and severed limbs, complete with spasmodic nerve endings, are the norm.[20]

The movie rating system, developed by the FTC in the late 1960s,[21] is used by many parents and average citizens to assess the level of explicit vio-lence and sexuality in films. To those who worry about the potential effects of violence-themed stories on youth's attitudes and behavior, this system is meant to act as a filter. However, there is evidence that adults have different definitions of movie labels and that the rating system has the opposite effect of enticing youth.[22] Ultimately, parents want a system in place but not one that simply restricts access of violent films to minors. Rather, parents call for a system that describes the movie's content and therefore allows parents to determine the appropriateness of the film for their child.[23]

YOUTH'S USE OF MEDIA

Today's youth are immersed in media (see Fig. 2.1). Almost every household in the United States has a television set (99% of homes nationwide), as well as access to a radio (97%), CD player (90%), and cable/satellite TV (74%). And many households have more than one of those types of media sources. Sixty percent have three or more televisions, 63% have three or more radios, and 21% have two computers (6% have three or more computers).

Despite the obvious availability of television, youth do not watch as much TV as most people believe. According to one study, youth spend 7.2% of their waking time watching TV and 29% of their time engaged in productive activities, including doing class work, studying, and working.[24] Other researchers have concluded that adolescents watch the least amount of television of any age group.[25] However, in comparison to other types of media, television is their most popular media choice. In general, 8- to 18-year-olds watch approximately 3 hours of television a day. In the case of youths ages 14 to 18 years, their second-longest exposure to media is to CDs and tapes (1 hour, 29 min per day), followed by radio (1 hour, 5 min per day), print media (37 min per day), computer (30 min per day), and, finally, movies (11 min per day).

Youth generally watch TV by themselves; only 2% of youth's television-viewing time is spent with their parents. Many parents work late or are too busy to spend time with their children, thus television provides an easy (and free) entertainment option when children cannot be supervised. However, we must note that some youth actively choose to watch television alone as a way to unwind from a stressful day, catch up on popular culture, or explore issues that either don't interest adults or are uncomfortable for teens to share with them. In other words, solitary TV viewing is not in and of itself predictive of youth's attitudes toward adults. Still, when youth use TV as a substitute for interaction with parents, or without any mediation from parents regarding troubling events, then it is problematic.

Other media are also experienced primarily in solitude. A majority of youth plays video games alone (55%), plays computer games alone (64%), and uses chat rooms or surfs the Web alone (61%). Similarly, many teens use media in the privacy of their bedrooms (25% watch TV there, 41% play video games, 47% read, and 36% listen to music). In contrast, movies are social experiences. Data collected from 7th- through 12th-grade teens suggest that 56% watched videos with siblings or peers and 60% watched mov-

FINDING ONE: *The Media Environment.* Children are immersed in media. Over half have televisions, tape players, or CD players in their bedrooms; 70% report having their own radios; and a third have video game systems. Higher income kids are more likely to have computers in their rooms while lower income kids are more likely to have television in their rooms.

FINDING TWO: *Media Exposure/Media Use.* Youth use media a great deal. Most kids are actively using at least one or two different media on a daily basis. Media use peaks around age of 12 or 13 with an average exposure of just over 8 hours daily. Media use begins to decline as students enter high school age. High school students ultimately read less, watch less TV and play fewer video games. Computers have made an impact on youth's use of media—on any given day 42% of 2-18-year-olds report using a computer at home or at school and 30% report playing a video game.

FINDING THREE: *Sub-Group Differences in Media Use.* On average, black kids are exposed to 2 more hours of media content—especially television—per day than white or Hispanic kids. Kids in higher income groups report less daily media exposure than kids in lower income groups. On average high income youth report a few more minutes of daily print and computer use than their lower income peers. In general, as family resources decrease media exposure increases.

FINDING FOUR: *Heavy Versus Light Media Use.* When kids are heavy users of one form of media, it is not necessarily the case that they are less frequent users of another form. That is, heavy use of one medium is strongly associated with the heavy use of another. There are simply a faction of youth are extremely into media. For example, kids who spend more than an hour a day on the computer use other media over 4 hours per day more than those who use the computer less or not at all.

FINDING FIVE: *Computers.* About 40% of youth report using computers on any given day and the average youth spends about a half an hour a day with the computers. However, the "digital-divide" does exist. Youth who live or go to school in low-income areas have less access to computers at home or at school and therefore are less likely to use a computer in a typical day. Similarly, black and Hispanic youth use computers less than their white counterparts. Interestingly, the amount of time youth spend on computers does not differ by ethnicity, suggesting that although a smaller proportion of minority youth use computers, those who do tend to sit down and use them do so for longer periods of time.

FINDING SIX: *Absence of Adults.* Given that a large number of youth have television and other media outlets in their own bedrooms, it is not surprising that a large amount of time engaged with media occurs when youth are alone. Secondarily, youth spend their time with peers or siblings watching television or playing video games. Parents are largely absent from their child's media experiences.

FINDING SEVEN: *Psychological and Social Adjustment.* Less contented kids (kids who are not as happy in school or do not feel they have many friends) spend more time with almost all media than kids who fall into the most contented/well-adjusted group. Further, substantially more kids who score high on the contentedness index come from families where there are controls on watching television and where the television is less likely to be on during meals. Further investigation needs to be done to examine characteristics of youth who are "less contented" and their relative media habits and experiences. That is, we do not know if less contented kids use more media, or if those who use more media tend to be less contented.

FIG. 2.1. A summary of findings from the Kaiser Foundation report on kids and the media. From *Kids and Media @ the New Millennium: A Comprehensive Analysis of Children's Media Use* (pp. 78–82), by V. J. Rideout, U. G. Foehr, D. F. Roberts, and M. Brodie, 1999. Menlo, CA: Kaiser Family Foundation. Copyright Kaiser Family Foundation. Adapted with permission.

ies with others.[26] Thus, media is used for different purposes and in different ways. It is clear that although most media are generally experienced in isolation, all can be experienced in groups, and certain kinds—movies for example—are far more likely to serve a social purpose.

Variation

Personal income and ethnicity are directly related to TV viewing habits, computer ownership, and Internet access.[27] African American teens live in homes that are more television oriented than homes of White or Hispanic teens. They are more likely to have the television on most of the time, to have three or more television sets, and to subscribe to satellite/cable systems. Similarly, a greater percentage of African American teens have television sets in their bedrooms. Watching an average of 4.41 hours a day, African American teens engage in significantly more hours of daily television viewing than do White (2.47 hours per day) or Hispanic youths (3 hours, 50 min per day).[28]

In residential areas where the yearly median income is below $25,000, only 49% of homes have a computer. Where the median income is between $25,000 and $40,000, 66% have computers, and where incomes are more than $40,000, 81% have computers. Similarly, 23% of families with yearly incomes less than $25,000 have Internet access, compared with 58% of homes with yearly incomes above $40,000. There are also marked differences in the availability of computers and the Internet by ethnicity. Seventy-eight percent of White homes have computers, in comparison to 55% of African American and 48% of Hispanic homes; 54% of White homes have Internet access, compared with 29% of African American and 24% of Hispanic homes.[29] Although public schooling has the potential to equalize access to technology, tragically it does not. Low-income neighborhood schools have fewer computers than do schools in richer neighborhoods with richer resources.[30] See chapter 8 for further discussion on this issue. Inevitably, the amount of time youth spend accessing the Internet is heavily dependent on opportunity and resources.

Media as a Socializer

Correlational data suggest that teens who enjoy healthy social relationships watch less TV than their peers who do not. Researchers report a significant relationship between youth's contentedness in relationships with others and the amount of TV they watch. Those who agree with statements such as "I have a lot of friends," "I get along with my parents," "I have been happy at school this year," and those who report a greater happiness overall, spend less time watching television than their counterparts who are less satisfied with their relationships.[31] It is difficult to determine, however, whether contentment reduces TV viewing in youth or whether watching less TV leads to increase contentment. Watching TV may be an adaptive choice if unhappy teens seek out television for comfort. While TV viewing is clearly not an answer, and we should be concerned if youth are turning to TV for help rather than to adult advisors, the other possibility is more disturbing: that youth become less contented because they watch a lot of TV.

Watching TV may be helpful for teens, and researchers argue that adolescents' media use (especially within the privacy of their own bedroom) is vital to their identity development.[32] With an increased capacity for abstract thought, adolescents are more capable than their preadolescent peers of imagining complex social roles and opportunities.[33] A fairly normal response to heightened self-awareness, self-doubt, or both, is for youth to seek out solitary activities, such as listening to music or watching TV for solace and validation.[34] The classic withdrawn teenager is the subject of a popular comic strip, where one teen comes across a copy of his picture taped to a milk carton. In response to his parents' message that their child seems to be missing, he notes, "I **like** spending time in my room. Okay???"[35]

MEDIA EFFECTS: A FOCUS ON VIOLENCE

Teens today are exposed to a plethora of violence. Research shows that about 60% of TV programs contain violence. By the time the average American child graduates from elementary school, it is estimated that he or she will have viewed more than 8,000 murders and more than 100,000 other assorted acts of violence (e.g., assaults, rapes) on television—numbers that go up if the child has access to cable television or videocassette players.[36] Not surprisingly, many adults worry about how the insidious presence of violence on television, in video games, and in movies may affect youth. This concern is legitimate but also ironic, given that daily news broadcasts report the true horrors of local and global violence in gory detail.

Insidious Presence of Violence in the News

The question of how and when to report on real-life violence is especially skewed in American journalism, where the common practice is to lead with the bloodiest story available. And, the images of war across the past several years have been especially bloody displays of violence. During the war in Iraq we were witnesses to the day-by-day movement of the war's progression. These images were replete with bomb explosions and the deadly aftermath of attacks on Iraqi communities—complete with bodies of dead soldiers. Even after the war was over we were not spared from the war's violence as the dead bodies of Uday and Qusay Hussein were gruesomely displayed across American media. During the Balkan war of the winter of 2001, images of death and destruction were common throughout the press. For example, one photo on the front page of the January 24, 2001 edition of the *New York Times* showed people lying face down on a wet sidewalk; above them stood a Serb militiaman kicking the head of one of the victims.[37] In the background, two soldiers are walking by without a glance, displaying a casual acceptance of the violent scene. In another front page photo, a man is staring directly at the camera, his hands on his head as if in a surrendering position. He is pleading for his life with Serbian soldiers. This man's fear and despair are displayed for the world to witness.

Or take the coverage of one Israeli-Palestinian conflict. Television footage captured the violent death of an Israeli soldier at the hands of an angry Palestinian mob. At the center of this group, a young Palestinian college student proudly displayed the blood of the dead soldier on his hands, waving them high above his head. In another horrifying incident from the same conflict, news cameras filmed the death of a 10-year-old boy struggling to hide behind his father, both of whom were caught in the cross fire of an Israeli-Palestinian gunfight.

Now that terror has hit our own soil, with the destruction of the World Trade Center, few young people have been sheltered from the images of violence against innocent Americans. News coverage of the September 11 attacks included replay after replay of airplanes hitting the towers, followed by their ultimate collapse. The enormity of the attack and its aftermath kept most Americans glued to their televisions and radios. Initially, news media, unsure of how to cover the event, simply replayed the footage of the tragedy. However, after about a week of reporting, journalists and television news producers began to edit more carefully the September 11 story. Indeed, in an almost unprecedented display of concern over the effects of repeated exposure to violence, most stations ordered reporters and newscasters not to show the footage again unless it was absolutely critical to a story. In a time of uncertainty, fear, and tragedy, the media ultimately responded by holding back—but only after a week of rehashing the horror that had been experienced.

That the journalistic dictum "if it bleeds, it leads" has never been more true, brings us to an important question: "Is real footage required to understand tragic violence or death?" The death of famous race car driver Dale Earnhardt ignited a debate in Florida, where a local newspaper fought with his wife over the rights to autopsy photos. The newspaper claimed the right to these photos, so citizens could make their own judgments about his death. His wife, and many others, argued that publishing the pictures went beyond the media's role and feared that if the paper did win rights to the photos, the images would end up on the front page of their newspaper—

and on the Internet. In this case, at least, it seems untenable to argue that the public needs to see pictures of a dead Dale Earnhardt strapped in his car to make judgments about the cause of a death that only experts are capable of determining.

In the 90 days prior to the execution of Oklahoma City bomber Timothy McVeigh, there was ongoing debate about whether to televise his death. Politicians and citizens argued they had a right to see the man who killed so many innocent people put to death to satiate feelings of revenge and anger. Finally, a judge decided media coverage was unnecessary, and only a few of the victims' relatives watched his execution live, while the remaining victims' relatives and survivors watched it on closed-circuit TV. While it might be argued that for families of murder victims, watching the killer die provides a sense of closure, it is clearly more arguable whether there is any benefit to letting an entire nation see a real-life execution. The question is especially problematic given the widespread concern with violent teens and what they watch. If fictional violence is viewed as an incentive to real violence, how much more dangerous is it to prominently display a methodically violent real and legal act? Public executions provide strong symbolic support for the legal use of violence in a democracy.[38]

Responsible Portrayals of Violence

Inarguably, violent human behavior is deplorable, yet a responsible news media must report violence realistically at times to inform its audience of the truth. Photos depicting dead American soldiers in Vietnam, for instance, came at a time when policymakers were still underestimating American involvement in the Vietnam War and helped change public sentiment about the war. More recently, the coverage of America's 2003 bombing of Iraq and the day-by-day advance of our army gave Americans a vivid account of the war's progress.

In addition to its evidentiary role in the news, depictions of violence, like depictions of other human attributes, both noble and ignoble, deserve a forum in art, music, and media. Exposure to good literature can help youth understand the role of violence in society, including its necessity under some circumstances. Even news reports of violence can provide information to counter the confusion and alarm that commonly erupt in wartime. For example, a study of media effects on Israeli adolescents during the Persian Gulf War concluded that media information increased teens' ability to cope with the reality of the war.[39] Adolescents sometimes seek out media depicting volatile emotional issues as well because the depictions help them cope with and negotiate life's ups and downs.[40]

Violence in Entertainment

Perhaps a larger concern to adults than the evidentiary role of media to report on real-life violence is the extensive presence of violence in youth's entertainment media culture (music, movies, video games, television, especially cartoon shows for children). Indeed, the entertainment industry is laced with so much violence that the message sent to youth is that violence is normal. Of course, this message worries concerned parents and politicians, who are quick to blame Hollywood executives for youth violence. Still, it is important to delineate legitimate use of violence from irresponsible exploitation.

Arguably, there are examples of responsible depictions of violence in entertainment media. For example, the 2001 Academy Award–winning film *Traffic* (which won Best Director, Best Supporting Actor, Best Adapted Screenplay, and Best Film Editing awards) elegantly captured the historical role of violence in society, as did many before it (e.g., *Braveheart, High Noon, Apocalypse Now*) and subsequent to it (e.g., *Gangs of New York*). Indeed, American history is replete with violence, and it is hard to imagine how it could be accurately chronicled without violence. These stories are an important part of the culture meriting truthful expression and wide audiences.

Responsible depictions of violence can also be extremely valuable for youth. In two episodes of the TV show *Boston Public,* the potential repercussions of gang membership were powerfully demonstrated. One segment involved a young high school student whose gang membership eventually led him to commit a violent act. In school, the young man was pleasant, a capable student, and a prominent member of the choir. Despite his positive character in school, his actions led him to be killed by a hostile gang. The message was clear: Bad decisions may be irreversible. In a subsequent episode, a teacher took students to the morgue to see the body. As one might expect, some parents in this episode found the trip highly objectionable. The teacher's motivation was to prove to students gang membership is not cool. It is worth noting that both episodes made their point without showing a murder or a headless body in the morgue.

Movies, too, can depict violence responsibly. The previously mentioned movie *Traffic,* for example, has been described by some as educational:

> "I saw *Traffic* with my 16-year-old daughter," Senator John McCain told me [a movie critic and reporter], "and it had a very powerful effect. It's caused me to rethink our policies and priorities." That's a pretty amazing thing for a movie to do. Which is why I'm not neutral about which film wins Best Picture this year. Shouldn't we reward a movie that is not only great enough to move us, but great enough to move our world?[41]

In contrast to the *Boston Public* episodes or movies such as *Traffic,* there are some especially egregious examples on TV and in the movies of indulgent, even gratuitous violence. On TV, examples include the World Wrestling Federation; murder mysteries that graphically show dead bodies; and law and courtroom shows, such as *NYPD Blue, Law and Order,* and *Crime Scene Investigation (CSI)* that involve the viewer in an in-depth investigation into murder, deception, and lies; and real-life police dramas, such as *Scariest Police Chases* and *Cops.* There are numerous examples of films depicting gratuitous violence (e.g., *The Substitute, Rambo, Natural Born Killers*). A particularly shocking example is the 1995 movie *Kids,* which tells the story of a 17-year-old on a self-destructive path of drugs and violence. The movie provides an especially exploitative view of youth by suggesting such behavior is normative when it is not. In these TV shows or movies, which capitalize on violence, dead bodies are almost requisite, as are violent rampages—complete with blood, guts, and gore.

Does Violent Media Make Kids Violent?

There is no question that media is laced with violence. And, as discussed previously, violence can be used gratuitously or, in some cases, appropriately to realistically tell a story. Therefore, the critical question is does viewing violence—in any form—cause violence? This question remains unanswered, despite a rich literature to show a strong relationship between viewing violence and aggression. In 2001, Bushman and Anderson reviewed this literature and noted the strong negative effects of media violence.[42] They lament that this evidence has not been productively used:

> Indeed, since the mid-1980s, the average news story has actually softened a bit on the media violence problem, even though the cumulative evidence is now more overwhelming in showing that short- and long-term exposure to media violence causes significant increases in aggression.[43]

Further, they note that six professional societies, including the American Medical Association and the American Psychiatric Association, acknowledge the hazards of watching media violence. Bushman and Anderson quote from this joint statement: "At this time, well over 1,000 studies . . . point overwhelmingly to a causal connection between media violence and aggressive behavior in some children."[44]

Although strong associations have been found between viewing violence-themed media and violent behavior, there is no conclusive evidence to show how a violent media culture may lead to violent behavior.[45] Indeed, since it is impossible to conduct randomized experiments in naturalistic settings to look at the effects of different types of violence on behavior, it is impossible to decipher what it is in the media that is related to violent behavior and what types of individuals are prone to that influence. As we note in chapter 3, predicting violence is difficult. Still, there are tragic examples where youth explicitly emulate what they see on TV. For example, after the movie *Deer Hunter* was released, there was a rash of youth who committed suicide by playing the game Russian roulette.[46] The macho portrayal of Russian roulette may have induced some teens to mimic this behavior for attention or for status recognition among peers.[47] The problem is that there are plenty of examples where youth don't imitate actions on TV. Therefore, we can't conclude definitively that violent movies, television programming, or video games cause youth to be violent.

It is not only movies that are suspect; anecdotal evidence suggests news coverage of violence may influence subsequent behavior. On March 6, 2001, for instance, a 15-year-old boy took a gun to his California high school and shot and killed two classmates and injured 13 others. In the week following the saturated coverage of this event, there was a shooting incident in Pennsylvania (March 8, 2001) and a host of threats were reported from around the country (see Fig. 2.2). Again, there is no proof that the coverage of this shooting caused the subsequent incidents of violence, but it is logical to conclude that in some cases, there may be a contagion effect that is energized by the media.

In his original studies on aggression, Albert Bandura found that when children watched other children being violent (e.g., hitting a large plastic doll), it increased the likelihood that the children viewing this behavior would imitate it. The power of modeling effects is well known; however, as

---

- A 14-year-old Wisconsin boy allegedly authored a hit list of 70 fellow students in a computer chat room.
- A 17-year-old student was arrested for bringing a loaded handgun to his Albany high school.
- Several Bucks County, Pennsylvania, students were suspended after allegedly making violent threats.
- Two middle school children were accused of threatening to bring guns from home to shoot their classmates.
- A 13-year-old middle school boy from Cincinnati was charged with inducing panic after officials found a list of 22 names of potential targets.
- A Miami high school student was suspended and recommended for expulsion after making threats against a teacher and classmates.
- A student in Upper Merion, Pennsylvania, was arrested after confessing to taping a threatening note to a bathroom door inside the middle school.

FIG. 2.2.   A list of reported incidents following the coverage of the Santee shooting in California. Adapted from an article by the Associated Press (2001, March 8). Wave of school threats shocks U.S. Retrieved March 8, 2001, http://www.wire.ap.org/

Bandura persuasively argues, the act of viewing someone else's aggression doesn't singularly predict aggression.[48] Bandura argued that genetic dispositions, personality traits, and perception of events influence one another in complex ways to energize behavior.[49] Thus, violence is not attributable to only one or two variables, such as watching too much violence on TV. Many variables lead to its expression, such as individual circumstance, perception, and experience.

One example of the complexity of predicting youth violent behavior rests in a 2003 study that explored the effects of playing violent video games on the brain's selective attention skills. In contrast to the widespread belief that immersion in violent video games is bad for youth, this study showed that individuals who played violent video games had better attention skills than those who did not play or those who only played nonviolent video games (e.g., Mario Brothers).[50] Of course, the study said nothing about other behaviors (violence) and skills (impulse control) or the extent to which better attention skills are desired; however, it is another piece of the puzzle in understanding the effects of media violence on youth. Historically, violent video games have been blamed for youth violence (e.g., it was widely known that Eric Harris and Dylan Klebold were fans of violent video games). And the modeling literature by Bandura heavily influenced this belief. However, this brain study should raise another critical awareness—that the relationship between playing violent video games or watching violent TV or movies and violent behavior is complex and uncertain, having yet unknown positive and negative effects on youth. Like anything else, video games have trade-offs. Youth who play video games typically do so alone. Hence, excessive use of video games may leave youth with too little time to engage in shared, social activities with other youth and adults.

The key issue is that media violence cannot be linked to violence in specific individuals—its predictive power is exceedingly low. We do not wish to suggest that parents should allow their children unlimited access to images of violence—especially gratuitous violence—or that media should not strive to reduce their use of needless violence. But we do want to stress that teens live in a violent society and that exposure to some images of media violence may help them to anticipate it, deal effectively with it, or even minimize it. One thing we can say with assurance: Although exposure to violence is at its apogee, actual teen violence is decreasing (see chapter 3).

STORIES TOLD ABOUT YOUTH

Perhaps more important than the impact of media stories on youth is the impact on the adult culture of the stories that the media tell about youth. A comprehensive 2003 study details how youth are presented negatively.

Heintz-Knowles studied the content of one show of each prime-time series between September 20th and November 21st, 1999, and found that youth were primarily presented as self-absorbed and unconnected to community or family.[51] Primarily, entertainment shows emphasized romantic issues or friendships. Problems depicted were almost always solved without adult help. Despite young peoples' apparent responsibility for their own difficulties, adults' language in these shows indicated that they saw youth as children.

As for news coverage, one recent study by the Berkeley Center for Media and Public Affairs found that in newscasts, youth appeared in only 1 of 12 local programs and only 1 of 25 newscasts at the national level. When they did appear in the news, youth were presented in negative situations. Roughly 50% of local stories featured youth accidents, violent youth crime, or youth as crime victims.[52]

These two studies, and many others, consistently show that the real problems youth experience are avoided (poverty, homelessness, suicide, etc.), while youth's violence, sexuality, and other undesirable behaviors are exaggerated and often inaccurately reported.[53] Although the entertainment and news media present somewhat different views of youth, their combined effects are to depict youth as self-absorbed and frivolous or disconnected and dangerous. As Susan Bales argued, these stereotypes are so powerful that when adults receive positive information about youth they reject the facts or shape them to fit their stereotyped views.[54] When actively forced to reflect on positive news about youth, adults' retort is often "Not good enough."

We show that the stories the media tell about youth's violence (chap. 3), sexuality (chap. 4), drug and alcohol use (chap. 5), health (chap. 6), employment (chap. 7), and education (chap. 8) are excessively pejorative.

CONCLUSION

Parents have always worried, with reason, about the potential damaging effects of harsh societal messages on youth. In the 1920s through the 1950s, even implicit references to violence were censored. Youth (and adults) today have more exposure to far more types of media than did previous generations. Citizens believe that teens watch TV too much and too passively. Yet adolescents watch less TV than do adults. Although parents may worry that the media's focus on violence encourages youth to be more violent (as well as more sexual), many youth choose not to watch violent programs; the media choices of today's teens are notably varied.

Clearly, technological advances have made possible the immediate exchange of information, including violent images, as dramatically exhibited in the 2003 Iraq invasion. Media depiction of violence can be both educative and detrimental, and the unnecessary exposure of violence in the media is hotly debated. In a democratic society, the truth should not be suppressed on the sole grounds that it is violent. However, we believe that the media's excessive marketing of violence too often places entertaining (i.e., shocking) "news" over educative reporting.

General Considerations

Adults tend to infer that most youth overuse media, and that by doing so they stunt their social intellectual growth. However, in light of our research that shows how youth use media in a wide variety of ways, for many different purposes, we believe that parents, teachers, and policymakers need to think more about the educative role of media. How can that role be enhanced while helping youth increase their ability for self-monitoring and mediating the potential effects of gratuitous violence?

It is unfortunate that teens' advanced technological skills aren't more readily recognized. Many teens and children, even those as young as 4 and 5 years of age, have developed advanced hand-eye coordination, multitasking capabilities, and knowledge of computers that transcend those of adults. We probably won't be able to tabulate the advantages and disadvantages of these early developed skills, or say what the costs are for disadvantaged youth who have few opportunities to develop them for at least another generation. Still, the sooner we begin to acknowledge the technological know-how of teens and children, the more likely we are to be able to use it to their advantage—especially in the academic realm.

When youth are more skilled than adults on computers, it challenges the age-old notion that adults know more. Why shouldn't a 17-year-old computer geek wonder why college is so important? After all, his or her skills surpass those of many college-educated adults. And if learning itself is so important, why do many adults refuse to learn how to use technology and advanced communication systems?

The media technology explosion has affected teens' dispositional development in still unknown ways. The first generation of youth born into an era of CD writers, DVD players, Digital Video Recorder technology (e.g., TiVo), advanced interactive gaming systems, and satellite television is only now in elementary school, and it is still unclear exactly what effect these fast-paced, informationally rich technological capabilities will have on skill and social development. In retrospect, some may conclude that youth who supervise their own play without adult help learn many valuable social and organizational skills. Yet despite a paucity of empirical information, many adults believe that youth do not ever benefit from their media but that they are captives of media that have deleterious effects.[55] Although it is possible that there may be some important negative effects of media use (e.g., the inability to delay gratification) there is emerging evidence that shows there may be a positive effect of video game playing.[56] However, anything done to excess is likely to lead to reduced opportunities in other areas, such as the chance to develop cooperative social skills.

In one, among a long line of examples of how society communicates contradictory messages to its youth, is that although Hollywood ratings have deemed many movies as inappropriate for young audiences, Hollywood markets *directly* to teenagers and children. In a pivotal investigation of how violent movies are marketed to teens conducted by the Federal Trade Commission (FTC), it was found that *80%* of the movies were targeted to children under 17.

> Marketing plans for 28 of those 44, or 64% [of films selected for study] contained express statements that the film's target audience included children under 17. For example, one plan for a violent R-rated film stated, "Our goal was to find the elusive teen target audience and make sure everyone between the ages of 12–18 was exposed to the film."[57]

Because disadvantaged and some ethnic minority youth watch disproportionately more television than White and typically more advantaged counterparts, it is critical that we find ways to provide healthy alternatives to media for those who have fewer resources. When youth spend more time with TV and other media, they are likely to spend less time exercising and engaged in social interaction with peers. As we show in chapter 6, more Americans, including children and teens, are obese and suffering acute health problems. In terms of community service, it might be helpful to encourage the local media to run focused brief programs describing how twenty minutes of exercise can be completed while watching TV, listening to the radio, or reading the newspaper.

The rich variety of media—especially media entertainment—places yet another demand on youth. To keep current, young people must track more TV shows, films, and music to converse with their peers. The desire to challenge adults' knowledge (or lack of it) isn't the only impediment to young people's education. There is also the question of the disposition that is developed by youth who watch few shows in depth but abstract many of them in a culture that already abstracts most of the news of the day. Are these pressures contributing to make youth explore more but in markedly less depth?

Needed Research

Although media often help youth to conceptualize complex situations more fully and to develop strategies for coping in prosocial ways, ironically, social scientists (like the media) are more likely to explore the media's negative effects on youth. More research identifying media's positive influences on youth would be a valuable contribution. Such research might encourage the media to explore its role in socializing youth and model ways in which positive effects could be increased.

Many youth are exposed to media when they are alone. Thus, they are often left to mediate and understand the contents of media without much guidance or support. Because more teens reside in homes with two working parents, or with one (working) parent, teens are left unsupervised more often than ever before. Currently, there are no data that comprehensively assess how teens understand the media they view. Many teens are left to their own devices in Internet chat rooms, and when they talk about their understanding of media products, it is most likely with peers, not adults. Because entertainment media, especially film and TV, often address adult-oriented themes, such as premarital sexual relationships, power struggles over children, homicides, and abuse, it seems important to understand more fully how youth are internalizing these messages and story lines and whether their impact is different or greater when teens experience the media while alone.

Youth are also left alone to converse in Internet chat rooms with their peers and, in rare but highly publicized incidents, predator adults. The content and forms of discussion are essentially unregulated. Research could usefully explore what youth seek from the Internet, what they perceive, what they receive, and how this varies by gender, income level, and ethnicity.

We believe it is important to conduct more rigorous research into how youth cope with media violence. Investigating the ways in which youth internalize violence is vital if we are to understand how much media culture affects youth's decisions. Earlier it was noted that Senator McCain's views were altered by watching the movie *Traffic*. As is too often the case, the perceptions of youth (in this case, his daughter, who attended the movie with him) went unnoticed. Similarly, it is important to understand what role, if any, media play in adolescent coping strategies. Preliminary data suggest that some media can offer an adaptive socialization outlet for some youth. However, it is not clear what kinds of support media provide and for what kinds of youth they are most beneficial. Research that explores how students internalize movie images and how they differentiate and reflect on this and other content would be useful information.

As technology continues to advance our capabilities to display violence, data on how youth use, understand, and internalize violence in the media and what they witness in their immediate environment are critical for understanding how they cope with and mediate the messages they receive. Perhaps more important, it is critical that adults' roles in youth's mediation of media content be better understood and advocated.

ENDNOTES

1. Roberts, D., Foehr, U. G., Rideout, V. J., & Brodie, M. (1999, November). *Kids and media @ the new millennium: A comprehensive analysis of children's media use* (p. 3). Menlo Park, CA: Kaiser Family Foundation.

2. Jamieson, K. H., & Waldman, P. (2003). *The press effect: Politicians, journalists, and the stories that shape the political world* (back cover). Oxford, UK: Oxford University Press.

3. Amundson, D. R., Lichter, L. S., & Lichter, S. R. (2001). *What's the matter with kids today: Television coverage of adolescents in America.* Washington, DC: Center for Media and Public Affairs, The Frameworks Institute. Retrieved May 1, 2003, from http://www.frameworksinstitute.org/products/cmpa.pdf

4. As one example, scholars write about the biases in how student achievement and their education are presented. See Maeroff, G. (Ed.). (1998). *Imaging education: The media and schools in America.* New York: Teachers College Press. See also Jamieson, K. H., & Waldman, P. (2003). *The press effect: Politicians, journalists, and the stories that shape the political world.* Oxford, UK: Oxford University Press.

5. Jamieson, K. H., & Waldman, P. (2003). *The press effect: Politicians, journalists, and the stories that shape the political world* (p. 1). Oxford, UK: Oxford University Press.

6. The book by Dan P. McAdams provides an interesting analysis of how we form "the stories we live by." McAdams, D. P. (1993). *The stories we live by: Personal myths and the making of the self.* New York: Guilford Press.

7. Nancy Signorielli is a prominent researcher of media effects on adolescent attitudes and beliefs. She has investigated how the media shapes adolescents' perceptions about work and sex roles. See Signorielli, N. (1993). Television and adolescents' perceptions about work. *Youth and Society, 24,* 314–341; and Signorielli, N. (1989). Television and conceptions about sex roles: Maintaining conventionality and the status quo. *Sex Roles, 21,* 341–360.

8. Signorielli, N. (1987). Children and adolescents on television: A consistent pattern of devaluation. *Journal of Early Adolescence, 7*(3), 255–268 (quote on p. 255).

9. Sklar, R. (Ed.). *The plastic age (1917–1930).* New York: G. Braziller.

10. Sklar, R. (Ed.). *The plastic age (1917–1930)* (p. 43). New York: G. Braziller.

11. Roberts, D., Foehr, U. G., Rideout, V. J., & Brodie, M. (1999, November). *Kids and media @ the new millennium: A comprehensive analysis of children's media use.* Menlo Park, CA: Kaiser Family Foundation.

12. Farkas, S., & Johnson, J. (1997). *Kids these days: What Americans really think about the next generation.* New York: Public Agenda; Public Agenda. (1999). *Kids these days '99: What Americans really think about the next generation* (A Report from Public Agenda). Retrieved November 13, 2002, from http://www.publicagenda.org/aboutpa/pdf/Kids99.pdf/
    Princeton Survey Research Associates (sponsored by *Newsweek* and NBC News). Based on a national telephone survey of 656 adults, conducted in April of 1997 in response to the question, "Which of the following is a bigger threat to the United States, foreign nations working against us or young Americans without education, job prospects, or connections to mainstream American life?," 18% said foreign nations, 74% said young Americans, and 8% said, "Don't know."

13. More information on the history of the post office can be found at http://www.usps.com/history/his2.htm/

14. Roberts, D. F., Foehr, U. G., Rideout, V. J., & Brodie, M. (1999, November). *Kids and media @ the new millennium: A comprehensive national analysis of children's media use* (p. 1). Menlo Park, CA: Kaiser Family Foundation.

15. Taken from Salamon, J. (2001, March 13). Independence fueled by puberty and cable. *New York Times,* p. B1, B8. Neilson ratings were based on TV shows rated through March 4, 2001.

16. Based on a study conducted by Initiative Media, part of the partnership division of the Interpublic Group of Companies. Study results are discussed in the *New York Times.* See Elliott, S. (2003, April 21). Prime-time differences. *New York Times,* C12.

17. For an analysis of how male and female roles have been portrayed over the last three decades, see Signorielli, N., & Bacue, A. (1999). Recognition and respect: A content analysis of prime-time television characters across three decades. *Sex Roles, 40,* 527–544.

18. Roberts, D. F., Foehr, U. G., Rideout, V. J., & Brodie, M. (1999, November). *Kids and media @ the new millennium: A comprehensive national analysis of children's media use* (p. 77). Menlo Park, CA: Kaiser Family Foundation.

19. U.S. Department of Justice (2001, December). *Internet crimes against children.* Washington, DC: Office of Justice Programs, Office for Victims of Crime. Retrieved May 1, 2003, http://www.ojp.usdoj.gov/ovc/publications/bulletins/internet_2_2001/NCJ184931.pdf

20. Roberts, D. F., Foehr, U. G., Rideout, V. J., & Brodie, M. (1999, November). *Kids and media @ the new millennium: A comprehensive national analysis of children's media use* (p. 1). Menlo Park, CA: Kaiser Family Foundation.

21. For a history of the rating system, see Federal Trade Commission. (2000). *Marketing violence to children: A review of self-regulation and industry practices in the motion picture, music recording, and electronic game industries.* Washington, DC: Author.

22. Bushman, B. J., & Cantor, J. (2003). Media ratings for violence and sex: Implications for policymakers and parents. *American Psychologist, 58*(2), 130–141.

23. Kaiser Family Foundation. (2001). *Parents and the V-chip: How parents feel about TV, the TV ratings system, and the V-chip.* Menlo Park, CA: Author. See also Woodard, E. H. (2000). *Media in the home 2000: The fifth annual survey of parents and children.* Philadelphia: Annenberg Public Policy Center. However, the FTC has yet to act on parents' cries for a different system. For a review of the research regarding the public's knowledge and use of movie, TV, video game, and computer rating system, see Bushman, B. J., & Cantor, J. (2003). Media ratings for violence and sex: Implications for policymakers and parents. *American Psychologist, 58*(2), 130–141.

24. Csikszentmihalyi, M., & Larson, R. (1984). *Being adolescent: Conflict and growth in the teenage years.* New York: Basic Books.

25. Signorielli, N. (1993). Television and adolescents' perceptions about work. *Youth and Society, 24*(3), 314–341.

26. Roberts, D. F., Foehr, U. G., Rideout, V. J., & Brodie, M. (1999, November). *Kids and media @ the new millennium: A comprehensive national analysis of children's media use* (p. 11). Menlo Park, CA: Kaiser Family Foundation.

27. Gladieux, L., & Swail, W. (1999, April). *The virtual university and educational opportunity: Issues of equity and access for the next generation.* Washington, DC: College Board.

28. Roberts, D. F., Foehr, U. G., Rideout, V. J., & Brodie, M. (1999, November). *Kids and media @ the new millennium: A comprehensive national analysis of children's media use.* Menlo Park, CA: Kaiser Family Foundation.

29. Roberts, D. F., Foehr, U. G., Rideout, V. J., & Brodie, M. (1999, November). *Kids and media @ the new millennium: A comprehensive national analysis of children's media use* (p. 1). Menlo Park, CA: Kaiser Family Foundation.

30. Snyder, T. D., & Hoffman, C. (2001). *Digest of education statistics, 2000* (p. 475). Washington, DC: U.S. Department of Education, National Center for Education Statistics (NCES 2001—034).

31. Roberts, D. F., Foehr, U. G., Rideout, V. J., & Brodie, M. (1999, November). *Kids and media @ the new millennium: A comprehensive national analysis of children's media use.* Menlo Park, CA: Kaiser Family Foundation.

32. Larson, R. (1995). Secrets in the bedroom: Adolescents' private use of media. *Journal of Youth and Adolescence, 24*(5), 535–550.

33. Erikson, E. (1968). *Identity, youth and crisis.* New York: W. W. Norton.

34. Broughton, J. M. (1981). The divided self in adolescence. *Human Development, 24,* 13–32.

35. Scott, J., & Borgman, J. (2002, March 13). Zits (comic). *Arizona Daily Star,* p. E4.

36. Bushman, B. J., & Anderson, C. A. (2001). Media violence and the American public: Scientific facts versus media misinformation. *American Psychologist, 56,* 477–489.

37. The story and images were captured by a journalist (who smuggled them out of the country before death threats against him could be carried out).

38. See the front page of *New York Times,* April 30, 2003; see also *New York Times* front page on May 1, 2003, depicting enraged and hurt Iraqis, and one dead Iraqi, during a confrontation with American soldiers in Iraq.

39. Zeidner, M. (1993). Coping with disaster: The case of Israeli adolescents under threat of missile attack. *Journal of Youth and Adolescence, 22,* 89–108.

40. Larson, R. (1995). Secrets in the bedroom: Adolescents' private use of media. *Journal of Youth and Adolescence, 24*(5), 535–550, Steele, J., & Brown, J. D. (1995). Adolescent room culture: Studying media in the context of everyday life. *Journal of Youth and Adolescence, 24*(5), 551–576.

41. Huffington, A. (quotation in ad for the movie *Traffic*). (2001, March 4). *New York Times,* p. A14.

42. Bushman, B. J., & Anderson, C. A. (2001). Media violence and the American public: Scientific facts versus media misinformation. *American Psychologist, 56,* 477–489.

43. Bushman, B. J., & Anderson, C. A. (2001). Media violence and the American public: Scientific facts versus media misinformation. *American Psychologist, 56,* 486.

44. As quoted in Bushman, B. J., & Anderson, C. A. (2001). Media violence and the American public: Scientific facts versus media misinformation. *American Psychologist, 56,* 480 (Original work published in 2000). Retrieved December 4, 2000, from http:///www.senate.gov/~brownback/violence1.pdf

45. For some of the most recent debates on media effects and violence, see Bushman, B. J., & Anderson, C. A. (2001). Media violence and the American public: Scientific facts versus media misinformation. *American Psychologist, 56,* 477–489.

46. Collins, J. M. (1982, July/August). Can movies kill? Twenty-eight people died from playing Russian roulette—apparently after watching *The Deer Hunter. American Film, 4,* 32–41. (Available at http://www.geocities.com/ResearchTriangle/Forum/6370/dhanalysis.html); see also Gado, M. (2002). *Bad to the bone.* Retrieved from http://www.crimelibrary.com/criminal_mind/psychology/crime_motivation/12.htm http://www.geocities.com/ResearchTriangle/Forum/6370/dhanalysis.html

47. Bandura has argued elsewhere the role of social rewards in shaping violence behavior. See Bandura, A. (1973). *Aggression: A social learning analysis.* Englewood Cliffs, NJ: Prentice-Hall.

48. For an overview of Bandura's theory of aggression, see Bandura, A. (1973). *Aggression: A social learning analysis.* Englewood Cliffs, NJ: Prentice-Hall.

49. For example, see Bandura, A., Ross, D., & Ross, S. A. (1963). Imitation of film-mediated aggressive models. *Journal of Abnormal and Social Psychology, 66,* 3–11; Bandura, A., & Walters, R. H. (1959). *Adolescent aggression.* New York: Ronald Press Co.; see also Bandura, A. (Ed.). (1971). *Psychological modeling: Conflicting theories.* New York: Aldine.

50. Green, C. S., & Bavelier, D. (2003). Action video game modifies visual selective attention. *Nature, 423*, 534–537.

51. Heintz-Knowles, K. E. (2000, April 9). *Images of youth: A content analysis of adolescents in prime-time entertainment programming.* Washington, DC: Frameworks Institute. (Available at http://www.frameworksinstitute.org/)

52. Dorfman, L., & McManus, J. (2002). Youth violence stories focus on events, not causes. *Newspaper Research Journal, 23*(4), 6–20; Dorfman, L., Woodruff, K., Chavez, V., & Wallack, L. (1997). Youth and violence on local television news in California. *American Journal of Public Health, 87*(8), 1311–1316.

53. Males, M. A. (2000). *Kids and guns: How politicians, experts, and the press fabricate fear of youth* (p. 10). Philadelphia: Common Courage Press. (Available at http://www. commoncouragepress.com/). See also Males, M. (1996). *The scapegoat generation: America's war on adolescents.* Philadelphia: Common Courage Press.

54. Bales, S. (1999). Communicating early childhood education: Using strategic frame analysis to shape the dialogue. *Zero to Three, 19*(6), 18–26.

55. And some research supports this view. See, for example, Kilmartin, C., Kliewer, W., Myers, B., & Polce-Lynch, M. (April 2001). Adolescent self-esteem and gender: Exploring relations to sexual harassment, body image, media influence, and emotional expression. *Journal of Youth and Adolescence, 30*(2), 225–244.

56. Green, C. S., & Bavelier, D. (2003). Action video game modifies visual selective attention. *Nature, 423*, 534–537.

57. Federal Trade Commission (2000, September). Marketing violent entertainment to children: A review of self-regulation and industry practices in the motion picture, music recording and electronic gaming industries (p. iii). Washington, DC: Author.

Chapter 3

Youth Violence

They finally found an answer to overcrowded prisons. Smaller prisoners.
—American Civil Liberties Union, 1996[1]

TV exaggerates juvenile crime, scaring public.
—D. Z. Jackson, 1997[2]

In international comparisons, the United States has the highest firearm-related homicide rates with Northern Ireland as the next closest competitor.
—Office of Juvenile Justice and Prevention Program, 1999[3]

Fear of our children is a fear well grounded in fact, as juvenile crime, particularly violent crime, has ripped through our cities and suburbs like a new and deadly virus . . . children are killing children, violently, inhumanly, forcing one another to duck bullets, spraying whole crowds in order to take out a single intended victim, transforming urban American teenagers into the psychological equivalent of war orphans.
—E. Humes, 1996[4]

Americans are misinformed about youth violence, and, as the second quote suggests, the media play a large role in fueling citizens' fears of youth. Perhaps as a result of this fear, more young people convicted of crimes go to jail with adults or serve adult sentences than ever before.[5] Part of the problem is access to firearms, but a larger part is the way our society views its youth and withholds proactive guidance and socialization.

In the late 1980s, policymakers predicted that society should prepare for the onslaught of the teenage "superpredator," who in growing numbers would commit serious violent crimes (e.g., assault, rape, and murder) without remorse.[6] These predictions were based on two salient factors. First, the 1990s was about to experience one of the largest adolescent populations ever seen. Also, gun violence was increasing in the late 1980s, leading experts to predict that violent crimes would increase substantially with a growing youth population. A second prominent factor in the belief that society should hunker down and prepare for an onslaught of adolescent offenders was the media's imbalanced and distorted reporting of youth crime. Violent crime declined substantially throughout the 1990s, but media coverage of it increased substantially.[7] Because of this misleading media attention, it was widely held that teens would become increasingly unmanageable. Ironically, an epidemic of white-collar crime during this same period went largely unrecognized (until recently). Labaton, a *New York Times* columnist writing in 2002, notes that while there has been a decline in property and violent crimes in the last decade, there has been a large increase in white-collar crimes (e.g., accounting and corporate crimes, health care fraud, intellectual property piracy).[8] Still, youth violence is by far more visible than adult crime in the media.[9] Apparently, the media choose to attack less powerful youth more often than the crimes of powerful adults.

The 1980s prediction of superpredator teens damaged the reputations of teens in the 1990s and beyond. More alert now to the possibility of youth violence, we have, as a culture, developed exaggerated notions of adolescent offenders. Policymakers and law officials created harsher and swifter consequences for youth crimes, including zero tolerance, three-strikes-you're-out policies and death sentences for minors.[10] Policymakers, citizens, and journalists anticipate that dangerous youth exist anywhere, "even in suburbia."[11] Tragically, these expectations led to a barrage of ill-conceived policies meant to punish youth, not help them.

Reports on teen crimes fail to note that juvenile violent crime has been decreasing over the past decade, not increasing, and the harsher punishments that were put into place to offset a predicted surge in crime that never materialized have had mostly negative consequences. More youth are sent to adult prisons, where many are abused and mistreated. When juveniles are detained as adults, they are much more likely to become repeat offenders, and they are also more likely to become victims themselves; children in adult institutions are 500% more likely to be sexually assaulted, 200% more likely to be beaten by staff, and 50% more likely to be attacked with a weapon than juveniles incarcerated in juvenile facilities.[12] These are tragic and preventable outcomes.

In this chapter, we want to debunk the myth of wild adolescents and explore how media exaggerate youth violence. Research clearly documents the dramatic disparity between youth crime rates and media reporting—violent crimes by youth are *falling;* reporting of them is *exploding.* Not only do the numerous stories about youth crime create the illusion that it is out of control, but the content of the stories, especially the headlines, distorts and exaggerates youth violence to the point that it suggests youth should be feared.

Public terror over the wave of school shootings is an example of how fear of youth is generated by sensational reporting. The chance of being shot in school is extremely tiny. The surgeon general and the U.S. Department of Education estimate that on any given school day, the likelihood of being shot at school is about one in a million.[13] However, the public's perception that if it can happen it will ignores these odds. The shootings at Columbine received so much national attention that school officials and parents worried, thinking "When will it happen here?"—as if it were inevitable. School administrators and policymakers also jumped on the bandwagon and have furiously recommended laws to create safe schools. Even President Bush called for safer schools in his 2002 policy agenda No Child Left Behind[14] (see Fig. 3.1). Bush's policy financially rewards states that adopt a zero tolerance stance against "persistently disruptive" students. This problematic stance has resulted in students being expelled, suspended, and arrested at alarming rates.[15]

YOUTH VIOLENCE IN THE MEDIA

Distorted media coverage on teen violence has created mistaken beliefs about youth violence. Test your knowledge by reading the statements in Box 3.1. Which of the 10 assertions are accurate?

As reported in Satcher's "Facts of Youth Violence" (a) youth offenders are not necessarily more antisocial, remorseless, or vicious than their nonoffending peers; (b) incidents of youth violence, especially weapons-related violence, are decreasing, but are far from solved; (c) there are prevalent racial disparities in victimization and perpetration of violence; and (d) youth violence is difficult to predict (see Box 3.2). The prediction that the 1990s would see an increase of violent youth has proved unsubstantiated—fewer youth are committing crimes, and youth are not more vicious now than in the past.

The Problem With Media

Michael Males, a leading advocate for balanced and fair reporting on youth, explains why youth receive pejorative attention for their violence. First, a youth who commits an especially egregious act is newsworthy because the act is unexpected:

I. Improving the academic achievement of the disadvantaged
   a. Institutes academic accountability and high standards
   b. Institutes annual academic assessments
   c. Provides for consequences to schools that fail to educate disadvantaged students
II. Preparing, training, and recruiting high quality teachers and principals
   a. Grants states and districts more flexibility for effective professional development and high standards and accountability
   b. Allows for alternative routes for teacher certification
   c. Allows for new local activities, including teacher recruitment and retention initiatives, signing bonuses, and merit pay
   d. Calls for class size reductions
   e. Promotes innovative teacher reform
III. Providing language instruction for limited English proficiency and immigrant students
   a. Sets performance objectives for improving English fluency
   b. Imposes sanctions for poor performance
IV. Creating 21st century schools—safe and drug free schools and communities
   a. Consolidates and simplifies funding for the safe and drug free schools program and the 21st century learning centers program
   b. Establishes accountability for school safety and achievement
   c. Grants teachers control over their classrooms: *States must adopt a zero-tolerance policy for violent or persistently disruptive students*
   d. Facilitates crime prevention and prosecution
   e. Allows community-based organizations to receive grants for after-school programs
V. Promoting informed parental choice and innovative programs
   a. Promotes charter schools
   b. Expands school choice
   c. Broadens education savings accounts
   d. Consolidates categorical grant programs to send more dollars to classrooms
   e. Increases funds for character education
VI. Encouraging flexibility and accountability
   a. Creates charter option for states and districts on the cutting edge of accountability and reform
   b. Increases accountability for improved student achievement
   c. Expects states to improve academic achievement
   d. Creates sanctions for low-performing states
   e. Rewards high-performing states and schools
   f. Provides bonuses to schools that reduce the achievement gap among its students
VII. Indian, Native Hawaiian, and Alaska Native education
   a. Established to meet the unique educational and culturally related academic needs of American Indians and Alaska Natives and the education of Indian children and adults
   b. Calls for the training of Indian persons as educators and counselors, and in other professions serving Indian people
   c. Calls for research, evaluation, data collection, and technical assistance

FIG. 3.1.   An overview of President Bush's 2001 No Child Left Behind Act.

For the paradox of the press is that if a type of crime is common, it becomes un-newsworthy. The unexpected is news. Thus, a heinous crime by an 11-year-old such as the Jonesboro, Arkansas, school shooting is big news because it is unexpected; "children," by popular stereotype, are supposed to be "innocent." A similar shooting by an adult is more expected and therefore less newsworthy.[16]

Highlighting shocking events is wrong because it shapes and sustains dangerous stereotypes:

We are shocked when a young child commits murder because younger kids only rarely kill. Now, how does the press handle the rare murder by an 11-year-old versus the three-a-week murder by a 40 year old? It turns the picture upside down: the occasional 11-year-old killer is depicted as a symbol of today's supposedly more violent grade-school generation, while the 40-year-old gunman is treated as an isolated case in no way reflective of "mature" middle-agers. Result: the media have transformed the stereotype of 11-year-olds from "innocent" to "murderous" by making one murderer this prototype.[17]

Males also reasons that youth are especially good targets because they have no power. "Politicians, institutions, and the press do not wage fear campaigns against population groups with the power to fight back." Consider the story presented in Box 3.3, written by Males. The vignette highlights true accounts of violence perpetrated by elder Americans; however,

---

BOX 3.1. Test your understanding of youth violence.

1. The epidemic of violent behavior that marked the early 1990s is over, and young people—as well as the rest of society—are much safer today.
2. Most future offenders can be identified in early childhood.
3. Child abuse and neglect inevitably lead to violent behavior later in life.
4. African American and Hispanic youths are more likely to become involved in violence than other racial or ethnic groups.
5. A new, violent breed of young "superpredators" threatens the United States.
6. Getting tough with juvenile offenders by trying them in adult criminal courts reduces the likelihood that they will commit more crimes.
7. Nothing works with respect to treating or preventing violent behavior.
8. In the 1990s, school violence affected mostly White students or students who attended suburban or rural schools.
9. Weapons-related injuries in schools have increased dramatically in the last 5 years.
10. Most violent youths will end up being arrested for a violent crime.

Note. From *Youth Violence: A Report of the Surgeon General,* by D. Satcher, 2001, Rockville, MD: Department of Health and Human Services.

BOX 3.2.   The facts of youth violence.

1. Fact: Although statistical indicators of violence such as arrests and gun possession are down, we are far from having solved the problem of youth violence.

2. Fact: Exhibiting uncontrolled behavior or being diagnosed with a conduct disorder will not predict future violent behavior. Further, a majority of adolescent violent offenders were not highly aggressive or out of control in early childhood.

3. Fact: Physical abuse and neglect are weak predictors of violence.

4. Fact: Although there are ethnic and racial differences in homicide arrest rates, data from self-reports indicate that race and ethnicity have little bearing on the overall proportion of nonfatal violent behavior. There are also differences in timing and continuity of violence over the life course, which account in part for the overrepresentation of these groups in U.S. jails and prisons.

5. Fact: There is no evidence to indicate increased seriousness or callousness of youth offenders.

6. Fact: Youths transferred to adult prison systems have a much higher likelihood of committing subsequent felonies than those committed to juvenile centers. Additionally, they are more at risk for being victims of sexual and physical abuses.

7. Fact: There are some intervention/prevention models that have some effectiveness in combating youth violence.

8. Fact: Inner-city, poverty-stricken neighborhoods disproportionately house African American and Hispanic males who stand the greatest risk of becoming victims or perpetrators of violent acts at schools.

9. Fact: Weapons-related injuries in schools have not changed over the last 20 years.

10. Fact: Most youths involved in violent behavior will never be arrested for a violent crime.

Note.   From *Youth Violence: A Report of the Surgeon General,* by D. Satcher, 2001, Rockville, MD: Department of Health and Human Services.

the story adopts language and strategies we are accustomed to seeing in reports on teen violence. The result shows how manipulative "true" stories of youth violence may be.

Deconstructing Delinquents

In the aftermath of violent crimes by young people, we want to know why. The media dissects the incident, offenders' backgrounds—their family life, their friends, their aggressive past—the victims they shot, the schools they

---

BOX 3.3. Excerpt from "Senior Violence" Alarms Experts.

A 71-year-old sprays a quiet church with gunfire, four dead or wounded. Another septuagenarian guns down two in a bloody office slaughter. On successive days, graying residents open fire with automatic weapons on dozens of people in senior citizens' centers in Arizona and Michigan, killing or maiming eight. In a picturesque beach community on Monterey Bay, an enraged 61-year-old shoots two neighbors to death over a trivial falling out. An elderly Santa Ana man beats a 14-year-old to death in a rage, tossing his corpse in a ditch.

Once seen as sweet, doting grandparents incapable of violence, America's and California's senior citizens are committing mass murders and displaying surges in violent crimes unknown to previous generations. In a particularly shocking trend, more people were murdered in mass, public shootings by senior citizens in the last 12 months than in all of America's schools put together.

A generation ago, old folks didn't act like this.

Californians age 50 and older once had violence levels considerably lower than grade school kids'. But in the last two decades, senior citizens' violent crime rates doubled. Today, elderly Californians are 40% more likely to commit serious violence than their grade school grandchildren. Social disadvantage is not the reason. Five-sixths of the state's aged murderers are white and middle class.

The kindly, rocking-chair codgers of yesteryear are a vanishing breed. Seniors' felony rates jumped 80% from 1975–1999. Today's elderly Californians suffer skyrocketing addiction and death from hard street drugs once unheard of in the grandparent set. In 1998, twice as many Californians over age 60 than under age 20 died from abusing heroin, cocaine, crack, or methamphetamine.

As a result, the number of Californians 50 and older sentenced to prison leaped 1,200%, from 233 in 1977 to 2,919 in 1999. Taxpayers will shell out $60 million to imprison 1999's superannuated felons, a group once thought long past their criminal years . . .

Note. From *Kids and Guns: How Politicians, Experts, and the Press Fabricate Fear of Youth,* by M. A. Males, 2000, Philadelphia: Common Courage Press. Copyright 2000 by Common Courage Press. Reprinted with permission from author.

attended, and the communities in which they lived. Is this practice meaningful? Or does it simply satisfy society's voracious appetite for horror and gore—giving further momentum to erroneous stereotypes? It likely does both. We want information, so we can make informed judgments about the potential of violence in our own lives; however, the act of deconstructing a young criminal's life and background is irresponsible and pointless if it leads to erroneous stereotypes and elevated levels of fear about youth.

In the wake of the Columbine incident, thousands of schools were on edge, and students who in some way resembled Eric Harris and Dylan Klebold were viewed suspiciously. Suddenly, students who wore anything remotely like a trench coat became suspects because of the notoriety of the trench coat mafia. In a special A&E television newscast, reporters asked New Jersey high school students to carry video cameras to document what high school was like for them following Columbine. Jocks and nerds in the TV program said they feared being future targets. Students whose dress wasn't mainstream reported that suddenly teachers and other students were afraid of them. Columbine coverage raised issues of bullying and peer-group conflicts (jocks vs. nerds) to such exaggerated levels that many students felt unsafe or distrusted in school.

Michael Moore's 2003 Academy Award–winning documentary *Bowling for Columbine* offered a very different view of incidents leading up to the shooting, exploring possible explanations for these two boys' horrific actions. In contrast to what the press offered, which essentially blamed parents, violent video games, and violent lyrics in music, the movie explored the broader societal context in which these two youths lived. For example, Moore highlights the dramatic contradiction of living in a "peaceful" community, such as Littleton, which is significantly contrasted by the presence of Lockheed Martin, the world's largest mass weaponry manufacturer, whose weapons were used in military action that was vividly shown on TV. That we raise children in a violent society but are shocked when they are violent is notable.

Deconstructing the Media

Journalistic reporting can be seen as falling into two broad categories: episodic (stories that focus only on the main event, without reporting contextual information), and thematic (stories that provide a more balanced representation by incorporating important contextual information surrounding the event).[18] Most journalistic reporting is episodic,[19] and therefore significant public concerns are seldom covered in depth.[20] One social studies high school teacher put it this way:

> Most commercial TV news is a hodgepodge of fast-paced reports of unconnected and sometimes insignificant events that do not help viewers to be informed about important public issues. News items are immersed in advertising and the eyes, ears, and minds of viewers must shift from world events to soft drinks and laxatives, from congressional decisions to running shoes and headache pills, all in rapid colorful presentations . . . "television news operates on 'borrowed time' in a commercial entertainment-oriented media system."[21]

Episodic reporting sensationalizes information to seize readers' attention, while neglecting significant details that might provide a context for understanding events.

Decontextualizing Youth

Episodic reporting on youth's "bad" behavior is rampant.[22] A study of roughly 8,000 television newscasts from 26 different California stations found that 68% of the stories focused on youth violence and that 84% of those focused only on the most salient aspects of violence.[23] Television reporting tends to overly represent the negative aspects of youth's lives—not just in their headlines but also in their general reporting. Similarly, many newspaper stories employ headlines that grab the reader's attention via an episodic slant. Consider these episodic and decontextualized headlines:[24]

- "Shooting was planned and calmly carried out, police say" (*New York Times,* 2001 March 7)
- "Girl in shooting was seen as dejected" (*New York Times,* 2001 March 9)
- "Santee Is Latest Blow to Myth of Suburbia's Safer Schools" (*New York Times,* 2001 March 9)
- "A life of guns, drugs, and now, killing, all at 6" (*New York Times,* 2000 March 2)
- "Multiple killings in school violence rises" (*New York Times,* 2001 December 5)

Obviously, the *New York Times* is not the only paper to exaggerate youth violence in the headlines. There are numerous examples of these sorts of headlines from around the country.

- "Boy faces jail term for shooting at neighbor: Teen violence cases are growing concern." (*The Washington Post,* 2003, July 13).
- "Teens apathetic about school shootings, violence." (*The Jupiter Courier,* 2001, May 2).
- "Police say Lutcher teen gunned down his parents; Bloody violence shocks tiny community." (*Times Picayune,* 2001, April 6).
- "What leads to violence? Latest school shooting has professionals wondering which young person might lash out next." (*Morning Star,* 2001, March 10).

It is typical that newspaper headlines sensationalize the story; however, it is particularly damaging for youth because it misleads readers about youth in general. In the first headline, the statement claiming that a youth "calmly planned" and "carried out" a violent crime leads the reader to believe that a youth knowingly and methodically shot others. Even before this youth is tried in court, the newspaper is shaping how citizens think about his intent. The second headline highlights the dejection of the girl offender in the story, suggesting that typically negative emotions in youth lead to violence. Using the phrase the "myth of suburbia's safer schools" in the third headline simply perpetuates the common beliefs that violence doesn't happen in middle-class suburbia and that schools in general are unsafe. Schools are as safe as ever before, and violence can erupt in any type of neighborhood for varied reasons. The fourth headline is misleading because it feeds the belief that even very young children are naturally vicious. And the fifth headline exaggerates the incidence of violence, an exaggeration that is even acknowledged in the first sentence of the article: "The number of violent deaths at American schools is dropping, but the rare outbursts are increasingly likely to claim more than one life." This same type of analysis can be applied to the remaining headlines.

Males commented on a particularly outrageous story that appeared in the *LA Times,* claiming that "gangs" had invaded South Orange County Haven—a community of mostly White, upper middle-class families. Males noted that crime statistics in Los Angeles County indicated that the murder rate among Black, Hispanic, and Asian youths in Los Angeles County fell by 85%, reaching three-decade lows by 1999, and that one Black youth per month was arrested for murder in 1999, down from one every 80 hours in 1990. Perhaps because minority youths weren't providing enough excitement, the press constructed a newer version of youth violence—the suburban threat of middle-class youths. Again, the press exaggerated the threat of youth, alluding to the proliferation of violence in suburbia when there had been but three killings in the county in 10 years (not dozens, as the press implied). The implication here, and in numerous news stories across the country, was that dangerous youths were striking in all neighborhoods.

Sensationalizing Youth Violence

Youth violence is overreported.[25] Researchers in Hawaii compared trends of crime with crime reporting. During 1987–1996, there was a 9% increase in juvenile arrests (nationally, there was a 35% increase in juvenile arrests during this same time period). A closer investigation of these arrests in Hawaii revealed that 91% of them were for noncriminal status offenses, such as running away and curfew violation—not serious violent crime. When all noncriminal status offense arrests are subtracted from the overall arrest rates for more serious offenses, Hawaii ends up with an 11% decrease in juvenile arrests for violent crimes. Although statistics verify a decrease in violent crime by juveniles in Hawaii, the media coverage of juvenile crime there rose dramatically. During 1991–1996, for instance, the number of articles about juvenile delinquency increased 690%, and the number of articles about gangs specifically increased 720%. And these percentages increased respectively to 2,800% and 4,000% when a 10-year time period was studied.[26]

A similar story is told by Males who found that news reports of youth violence in California had reached exaggerated levels. In 1997, Males collected all stories written in the *Times'* Orange County edition on violence, broken down by age of perpetrator (adult vs. youth). He found that youth were 3.2 times more likely to be featured in violent crime stories than adults, even though the crime rate of the 30- to 40-year-old population was growing rapidly (criminals in this age group better deserved the epithet "superpredator"). Perhaps more disparaging to the reputation of youth is that half of the stories on violent crime featured youth, which was 6 to 10 times more frequently than actual youth violence rates.[27]

Creating Pessimism About Youth

Does exaggerated reporting about youth affect consumer perceptions of them? Although it is impossible to prove a causal link between media coverage and consumer attitudes, it is possible to at least hypothesize regarding its effects. In 1998, 62% of individuals believed that youth crime was increasing, at a time when it had dropped to a 25-year low.[28] Similarly, school violence is extremely rare, yet because of sensational media coverage of shootings like the one at Columbine, parents and youth are more fearful than ever before that violence may erupt in their hometown schools. And citizens believe that the disciplinary problems facing schools are more numerous and more extreme,[29] even though there are no data to show that this is the case.

Why are adults poised to embrace such bad news? Andrew Sullivan, a prominent social-policy writer, has argued that our media is so laced with pessimism, in the forms of violence, sarcasm, and political debate, that as a society we are skeptical about any good news:

> It's not hard to see why optimism gets such a bad rap. It doesn't fit into our ideological framework. The right won't believe that without reviving religion, censoring Hollywood, stigmatizing homosexuals and restricting divorce, people can actually behave more morally or responsibly. The left won't believe that without hefty government programs and a paleoliberal in the White House, the lives of most Americans can get better. The good news of the last decade has proved both sides wrong.[30]

Sullivan's argument points to a definitive trait of our culture: as a society—influenced by the media's insatiable appetite for the bad news of the world, an appetite reinforced by our collective interest in it—we are much more likely to embrace pessimism than optimism. Perhaps the pervasiveness of our problem-oriented culture is one impetus behind the American Psychological Association's call for a positive psychology.[31] This call is to encourage professionals to abandon a deficit-oriented perspective (how do we fix problems?) and to embrace a proactive, positive one (how can we promote and maximize healthy living?). It is clear evidence of a problem when a large organization of psychological professionals has to explicitly advocate for a positive outlook from their members.

It is important to note that this widespread witch hunt for bad news is especially prevalent in reporting that involves youth. Youth crime, on the decrease, gets the limelight, whereas white-collar crime, which has increased substantially, is quickly forgotten—or at least not exaggerated to the point of stereotyping all CEOs of major companies in the press. Indeed, the image of miscreant youth is so established in adult minds that adults seem to write off favorable images of youth formed by direct personal contact and instead embrace—and believe—negative media messages.

YOUTH OFFENDERS AND THEIR CRIMES

Citizens must become more critical consumers of youth violence reports. We suggest three strategies for becoming better informed, but to do so requires not only accurate information but also a conscious effort to discover the truth behind the misrepresentations. First, accurately quantifying youth violence is difficult even for experts; therefore, citizens must become better educated about the different conclusions that can be drawn depending on which crime indicators are used. Second, the media focus on crimes youth commit against others, while often failing to report the thousands of stories of crimes committed against youth by adults. More inclusive information about all kinds of crimes involving youth can help put youth violence into proper perspective. Third, contextual factors, such as types of opportunities or neighborhood conditions in which youth live, must be more widely understood.

QUANTIFYING YOUTH VIOLENCE

Two types of data are commonly used to describe youth violence: the Federal Bureau of Investigation's (FBI) annual Uniform Crime Reports (UCR), based on voluntary arrest-rates reports from approximately 98% jurisdictions nationwide[32] and self-report measures that typically ask individuals to comment on violence they have directly experienced, observed, or committed. Both data sources have strengths and weaknesses.[33] Arrest rates are useful in clarifying the relative levels of violence; however, they under-report youth violence because a majority of violent offenses are never reported to the police, and fewer than half of those end up in arrests. Arrest rates also don't take into account instances where the same person is being arrested repeatedly; therefore the incidences of violence within a subgroup are difficult to determine. Lastly, arrest rates say nothing about actual conviction rates—judgments where offenders are found guilty. In contrast, self-report measures can provide a better account of incidences of violent crime. However, critics of self-report methods argue that the data are biased because respondents tend to answer in ways that make them appear favorable and because most self-report research employs small samples. However, sound methodological techniques, such as guaranteeing respondents' anonymity and representative sampling strategies, can diminish these impediments to accuracy. Despite these weaknesses, self-report measures provide useful supplemental information about violence that is not expressed in official reports.[34]

Self-Reporting: A Closer Look

There are two main types of self-report data. The first asks respondents to report on the nature, type, and frequency of violence that occurs directly to them (i.e., victimization data). One commonly used data source is the National Crime Victimization Survey (NCVS) that has been sponsored by the Department of Justice since 1973.[35] The federal government established the NCVS to obtain a more representative index of violence that complements the UCR. The NCVS consists of interviews with approximately 120,000 randomly selected persons (over the age of 12 years) from 60,000 U.S. households nationwide.

A second type of self-report asks respondents to confess their level of violence against others. Respondents are asked to report, for example, whether they have hurt anyone during a specified time frame. Two large-scale self-report measures commonly used to track youth violence rates and prevalence are the Youth Risk Behavior Surveillance System (YRBSS)[36] and Monitoring the Future (MTF).[37]

Both types of self-reporting data are susceptible to measurement error and are potentially misleading. When reporting on violence that is observed or directly experienced (as in victimization surveys) there are potential differences in how respondents define violence. The NCVS asks respondents to define the crime and to describe characteristics of the offenders and the situation as a way to minimize these effects. However, even with these specifications, it is likely that individuals vary in their perceptions of violence. Similarly, asking a respondent to confess their sins opens things up for the respondent to lie or exaggerate to look better or worse.[38]

What the Data Report: Youth Arrest Rates

Evidence from official arrest records shows that crime in the general population has declined sharply in the past 10 years—reaching a 33-year low in 1999.[39] A significantly larger than average decrease in juvenile arrests accounted for a substantial proportion of the decline in violence rates. During 1993–1997, juvenile violent crime decreased by 33%, and adult violent crime decreased by 25%.[40] Between 1995 and 1999 arrest rates for juveniles dropped significantly for serious crimes such as murder (56%), robbery (39%), burglary (23%), and auto theft (35%). Juveniles and older youth combined (ages 24 years and younger) made up 38% of the increase in violent crime arrests in the years 1985–1995, whereas they accounted for 51% of the decrease in years 1995–1999.[41]

However, although arrest rates for more serious crimes were falling, rates for less serious offenses were climbing.[42] For example, in 2000 the arrest rates of 10- to 17-year-olds for homicide, rape, and robbery were below their peak 1983 rates. In contrast, arrest rates for aggravated assault were 70% higher than the 1983 rates.[43] And the rates of arrest for other crimes are increasing—36% for drinking and driving, 31% for violating liquor laws, and 9% for curfew violations.

Self-Report Data

Self-report data, on the other hand, support a view that many youth are aggressive. In a comprehensive summary of scientific evidence on youth violence, the Surgeon General's Office concluded that, although arrest rates (UCR) show violence has declined, self-report evidence suggests that many acts of violence go unreported. In any given year in the late 1990s, at least 10 times as many youths reported that they had engaged in unreported violent behavior that could have seriously injured or killed another person than what is reflected in arrest data.[44] Similarly, victimization reports (NCVS) indicated that 3–5 times more crimes occur than arrest data confirm.[45] Thus, although arrest rates for serious violent crimes have decreased dramatically since 1993–1994, self-report data document that the incidence of juvenile crime (including serious assaults and robberies) has remained at least at a steady level since 1993–1994.[46]

Not surprisingly, discrepancies between official and self-report data are common.[47] The challenge lies in determining how best to interpret the data. Criminologists who study self-report and official data on violence continue to debate the relative accuracy of either method as a barometer of violence.[48]

Incarceration Rates of Youth in Adult Prisons

Another type of data source, perhaps less accessible to the public, are incarceration rates of youth in adult prisons. Data on incarceration rates from 1985 to 1997 reveal very little change in the number of persons under the age of 18 years who went to adult correctional facilitates. For example, since the mid-1980s, less than 1% of inmates in state prisons have been under the age of 18 years. Although overall there hasn't been a change, the likelihood that a juvenile will be sentenced to adult prison has grown significantly over time. In 1985, 18 per 1,000 violent teens arrested went to adult prisons, whereas by 1997 this proportion had nearly doubled, to 33 out of 1,000 violent teens arrested going to adult prison.[49] Shockingly, it isn't just violent offenses by youth that send them to adult prison. Between 1985 and 1997 the number of youths sent to adult prison for robbery offenses nearly tripled, and for aggravated assault they quadrupled.[50]

The Role of Guns[51]

The availability of guns separates the *Black Board Jungle*[52] youth culture from the *Dangerous Minds*[53] culture. Data overwhelmingly suggest that juvenile homicide rates are closely correlated with firearm use.[54] The surge in homicide rates from 1980 to 1993 is significantly related to increased gun use during crimes. Similarly, the decline in homicides since 1993 is widely attributed to a decrease in firearm use. Hospitalization records confirm this—a large number of youth were killed by firearms between 1987 and 1993, followed by a decrease in gun-related deaths from 1993 to 1999. Emergency room records also show a 50% drop in firearm-related injuries between 1993 and 1998 for youth ages 10 to 19 years.[55]

Evidence shows that a prominent risk factor for teens using firearms is related to the availability of guns in the home. In fact, when there is a gun in the home (about half the homes in the United States have a gun), household members (of any age) are 8 times more likely to kill or to be killed by a family member or intimate acquaintance and 5 times more likely to commit suicide than someone in a home without a gun.[56] One simple solution seems promising: Eliminate access to guns and homicide and suicide rates will drop.

WHEN YOUTH ARE VICTIMS

Media emphasize the violence youth commit against others. Yet the preponderance of violence committed against youth by adults is staggering.[57] According to FBI data, juveniles make up 12% of all crime victims (known to police) including 71% of all sex crime victims and 38% of all kidnapping victims.[58] Simple assault is the most commonly reported crime against juveniles (41%), followed by larceny (22%), sexual offenses (12%), and aggravated assault (11%). Girls are the primary victims of sexual assault and kidnapping, whereas boys are more frequently associated with all other crimes. Children under 12 make up approximately one fourth of all juvenile victims (possibly a conservative estimate as young children look up to adults and may be more easily coerced into silence). Another factor influencing this estimate is that children and teens who say they've been victimized may not be listened to. In some cases, like abuse by priests, young children's reports, before the recent notoriety of such incidents, were not believed— even by their parents. Adult offenders are responsible for 55% of all juvenile victims, most disproportionately for kidnapping, sex offenses, and victimization of children under 6 years old and older than 15 years old.

Tragically, family perpetrators commit 20% of all offenses against children and represent a majority of offenders against children under the age of 4 years and a majority of kidnappers and sex offenders. Except for robbery, a large proportion of violent crimes against juveniles is perpetrated by family members or acquaintances. For example, 38% of juvenile kidnappings are by family members, and 25% are by acquaintances. Similarly, 86% of all sexual offenses against juveniles are committed by a family member (28%) or acquaintance (58%).

Victims in Schools

Juvenile victimization is also prevalent in schools, where in some instances violence against youth is sanctioned. Amazingly, although most school districts have banned paddling of students as a method of punishment, there are still those who believe that hitting children is an effective disciplinary tool for keeping them "in line."[59] Fundamentalist Christian schools, in particular, may have such a philosophy.[60]

Among other types of school-related abuses, sexual abuse is one of the more prevalent. New York City schools experienced an increase in the number of sexual attacks suffered by students, both those perpetrated by staff and those committed by other students. The 2000–2001 rates of attacks in New York City schools was nearly 4 times the national rate, more than twice the 2000–2001 rate for schools in urban areas, and more than double the rate of attacks reported in Los Angeles (the country's second largest school district). The rise in sexual attacks (including groping, grabbing, sexual abuse, rape, and sodomy) increased by 13% over the 1999–2000 reports.[61]

Amazingly, there is evidence that adults protect one another when they prey on youth. Throughout the summer of 2003, the extent of the cover ups within the Catholic Church over sexual abuse was slowly revealed. And abhorrently, we learned in August of 2003 that these cover ups were sanctioned for over three decades when the Associated Press reported on a 1962 Vatican document that ordered priests to keep sexual abuse allegations under secrecy or face excommunication from the church.[62] In St. Louis, Missouri, an elementary school counselor, formerly a priest, who was accused of sexually abusing youth in the 1970s, was simply moved to another school when allegations resurfaced that he continued to sexually abuse students at his school.[63] Unfortunately, school officials took their time in responding to complaints that the counselor unnecessarily accompanied young boys to the bathroom and watched them use the urinals. When one teacher brought his actions to the principal's attention, she was met with criticism and her complaint was put down to a collegial spat.

Although schools are getting better at confronting allegations of sexual abuse by teachers, there are still too many schools where students are unprotected targets. Only 35 states require criminal background checks for school employees, and only 4 states require fingerprinting. In large school districts, screening more than 6,000 applicants per year for past criminal behavior is nearly impossible. Thus, although most schools are safe environments, these rare, egregious acts of adults preying on youth and other adults failing to protect youth need to be better addressed.

Suicide Culture

Suicide rates among youth have been increasing (they have doubled among the Black male population, though a disproportionately greater number of suicides are committed by White males). Between 1980 and 1996, suicides increased by 9% overall and soared by 113% for youth younger than age 15 years. In international comparisons, the United States has the highest firearm-related homicide rate for children (nearly twice that of Finland, the country with the next highest rate) and the second highest youth suicide rate (behind Northern Ireland).[64]

It is ironic that rates of youth homicide and suicide are very close, yet youth suicide gets very little media attention. In 1996, approximately 2,119 teens committed suicide.[65] By comparison, in 1997, approximately 2,300 youths were involved in the commission of homicides. These rates are only approximations (and in both cases are likely conservative estimates[66]). Still, it is ironic that the violence youth commit against others is a primary media target when suicide is an equally tragic, and increasing, phenomenon. For example, the three major television networks (ABC, NBC, and CBS) aired 296 stories on the Columbine incident;[67] yet youth suicide or youth death by accidental drowning in bathtubs (both of which account for more youth fatalities than school shootings) are rarely mentioned in TV news.

The image of the externally violent teen is very different from the de-spondent, desperate, and depressed one. One fuels a sense of retaliation (let's punish them); the other engenders a sense of support, help, and con-cern. Importantly, depression and the tendency to kill oneself is sometimes correlated with the desire to take others out as they go, as in the case of Col-umbine. It would be a much more proactive and helpful message if the me-dia put outward and inward violence in better perspective.

Why Is Youth Suicide on the Rise?

Higher suicide rates today are associated with other tragically increasing so-cial phenomena, including higher divorce rates, more parental abuse, in-creased availability of handguns, inadequate access to mental and physical health services, and higher expectations of educational success.[68] It is espe-cially clear that youth are under growing educational stress. One 2003 study conducted by Sherry A. Benton and her colleagues at Kansas State Univer-sity reports that more college students are expressing feelings of heavy stress, anxiety, and depression.[69] A national survey conducted in 2002 found that 80% of counseling-center directors reported an increase in the number of students displaying serious psychological disorders over the past few years.[70] Thus, it is clear that high stress levels and need of support are growing youth issues.

Although high suicide rates are troubling, what is more so is that for ev-ery teenager who commits suicide, 100 more will try. Even more teens re-veal that at some point they have contemplated suicide. Literally millions of youth engage in some form of suicidal ideation sometime in their adoles-cence. Suicidal tendencies, and the depression that often accompanies them, are mental health concerns that need to be more effectively con-fronted. Although adults are learning more about how to help youth when confronted by depression or other mental health afflictions, American culture has far to go in diagnosing mental health problems accurately. Part of the challenge is that adults' cultural views of youth are so distorted in the first place (mood swings are written off as "nothing" or "typical teenage stuff"). This blasé attitude can have serious repercussions to youth who need serious attention but who feel marginalized.

CONTEXT IS CRITICAL

Examining the backgrounds of youth offenders suggests that violence is as-sociated with either a pattern of aggressive behavior that emerges during childhood (early onset) or a sudden emergence of aggression during ado-lescence, following a relatively calm and nonviolent childhood (late onset) (see Table 3.1). Although ultimately youth violence can be described by

TABLE 3.1

Early and Late Risk Factors for Violence at Ages 15–18 Years
and Proposed Protective Factors, by Domain

	Risk Factor		
Domain	Early Onset (ages 6–11)	Late Onset (ages 12–14)	Protective Factor
Individual	General offenses	General offenses	Intolerant attitude toward deviance
	Substance use	Psychological conditions	High IQ
	Being male	Restlessness	Being female
	Aggression**	Difficulty concentrating	Positive social orientation
	Psychological condition	Risk taking	Perceived sanctions for transgressions
	Hyperactivity	Substance use	
	Problem (antisocial) behavior	Aggression**	
	Exposure to television violence	Being male	
	Medical, physical	Physical violence	
	Low IQ	Crimes against persons	
	Antisocial attitudes, beliefs, dishonesty**	Problem (antisocial) behavior	
		Low IQ	

(Continued)

TABLE 3.1
(Continued)

| | Risk Factor | | |
Domain	Early Onset (ages 6–11)	Late Onset (ages 12–14)	Protective Factor
Family	Low socioeconomic status/poverty Antisocial parents Poor parent-child relations Harsh, lax, or inconsistent discipline Broken home Separation from parents Other conditions Abusive parents Neglect	Poor parent-child relations Harsh, lax discipline Poor monitoring, supervision Low parental involvement Antisocial parents Broken home Low socioeconomic status/poverty Abusive parents Other conditions Family conflict**	Warm, supportive relationships with parents, other adults Parents' positive evaluation of peers Parental monitoring
School	Poor attitude, performance	Poor attitude, performance Academic failure	Commitment to school Recognition for involvement in conventional activities
Peer Group	Weak social ties Antisocial peers	Weak social ties Antisocial, delinquent peers Gang membership	Friends who engage in conventional behavior
Community		Neighborhood crime, drugs, disorganization	

**males only

Note. From *Youth Violence: A Report of the Surgeon General*, 2000, Rockville, MD: U.S. Department of Health and Human Services.

one of these two trajectories, in general, it is a result of knowledge gained through hindsight. Predicting violence early is difficult. Many aggressive children do not become violent, and most calm children do not suddenly become violent juveniles. In short, researchers cannot say definitively who will become violent.

However, a body of research compiled over the past 50 years suggests that youth violence is associated with several environmental factors, such as poverty, availability of firearms, childhood abuse or harassment, bullying, and neglect.[71] Youth crime is partly a product of opportunities (or lack thereof) and socialization; therefore, it is no surprise that its perpetrators show distinguishable demographic characteristics. For instance, girls are less violent than boys—either due to socialization or genetics.

Ethnic Disparities in Crime and Punishment

Data suggest that a disproportionate number of poor, ethnic minority youth are arrested and jailed for crimes.[72] Incarceration statistics show that minority youth are overrepresented in the prison system,[73] and minority youth are 2 to 3 times more likely to receive a harsher sentence for *equivalent* crimes than their White counterparts.[74] In Los Angeles, 12% of the slightly more than 24,000 juveniles arrested for felonies in 1996 were White, 56% were Hispanic, 25% were Black, and 6% were Asian. More profound, however, are the proportions that were actually tried as adults. Of the 561 cases transferred to adult court, only 5% were White, 6% were Asian, 30% were Black and 59% were Hispanic.[75] Similarly, in Arizona (where the number of criminals younger than 18 years of age serving time in Arizona adult prisons doubled between 1985 and 1997), more than half of the Arizona youths sent to adult court and prison in 1997 were Hispanic.[76]

It is difficult to say with certainty if this overrepresentation is due to bias in the justice system or to minority youths committing more violent crimes. Do ethnic minority youths commit more crimes? Are they more violent? There is no easy answer to these questions, and data are mixed—some studies report evidence of racial bias in arrest and conviction practices; others have found no evidence of bias.[77]

Still, there is growing concern that minority youths are being unfairly treated. According to one report by an alliance of youth advocacy groups including the Youth Law Center, American Bar Association Juvenile Justice Center, Justice Policy Institute, Juvenile Law Center, Minorities in Law Enforcement, National Council on Crime and Delinquency, and Pretrial Services Resource Center, African American teens are more likely than White teens to be formally charged in juvenile court, even when referred for the same type of offense. Similarly, minority youths are more likely to be waived to adult criminal court than are White youths—a statistic true for all offense categories.[78]

A disproportionate number of minorities live in environmental conditions that heighten the risk factors for committing criminal offenses—minorities are more likely to be poor, to live in crime-ridden neighborhoods, and to come from broken homes. The nature of the legal system, as evidenced in the profiling and conviction literature, suggests that too many law officials, prosecutors, judges, and juries hold pejorative stereotypes of minority youths that in some cases probably result in self-fulfilling prophecies. We have far to go in understanding the role of bias and the role of opportunity in ethnic minority youth populations. But, a critical first step is to stop blaming and embrace a better awareness of the scope of issues.

Girls and Their Crimes

Girls and boys are arrested at different rates because they commit different kinds of crimes.[79] A larger proportion of boys are arrested for violence and weapons violations; girls are more typically arrested for status offenses[80] (running away, prostitution, theft, and curfew violations). Boys continue to be arrested and convicted more frequently than girls, but the ratio of male to female arrests has shrunk noticeably over time. In 1983, for every crime committed by a girl, boys committed 7.4 crimes. By 1999, the ratio had shrunk to 1 female crime for every 3.5 male crimes.[81] And the rate of increase in violent offenses was greater for girls than for boys from 1981 to 1993, with the male rate in 1997 rising 24% above the 1987, rate and the female rate rising 85%.[82]

Another aspect of female violence that has gained media notice is the vicious verbal wars that some girls wage against others. A study by Rosalind Wiseman, for instance, shows that girls are becoming purveyors and targets of vicious gossip, backstabbing, and just plain meanness.[83] It is difficult to know how widespread this problem is; however, Wiseman suspects it is becoming more prevalent as girls grow more assertive and vocal in their attitudes.

Why are more females aggressive and violent today? One reason is that gender-typed social expectations have changed over time. The macho male expectation has been challenged by psychologists for its deleterious effects on young boys' development,[84] yet it still contributes widely to societal tolerance of male violence and aggression. However, the women's movement in the 1960s and 1970s spawned a new generation of independent-minded, "strong" women. During the past 40 years it has slowly become more acceptable, if not more common, for women to assert themselves in the workplace and at school.

Still, violence represents only a small proportion of all female offenses. Two main offenses endemic to young girls are running away and prostitution. It is estimated that 60% of all runaways are girls (a figure that has increased by 29% since 1983). Girls who run away are mostly White, middle class, and age 13 or 14. A majority of them run away from home to escape abusive environments—statistics show that 25% of runaways were born to mothers under the age of 17 years, 70% were drug users, 60% had parents who abuse drugs or alcohol, and 50% were victims of sexual or physical abuse.[85] Prostitution often goes hand in hand with running away because it is a means by which a young, unskilled girl can survive on her own. Most juvenile prostitutes are White, ages 16 or 17, come from upper and middle-class backgrounds, and typically have experienced some form of sexual or physical abuse.[86]

Although some runaways leave home because of conflicts with parents or guardians, many do so for self-protection. Female runaways seek to escape abusive and violent homes where they are mistreated and neglected; they may opt for taking risks on the street rather than suffer continued abuse at home. Tragically, too many see drugs, prostitution, and shoplifting as better ways to survive.

SCHOOL VIOLENCE

Inflammatory stories, written about a few tragic instances of school violence and based on misrepresentation of the facts, have led to the public perception that school violence is rapidly increasing. This skewed belief is held by citizens, parents, and policymakers at the highest levels and is so pervasive that when President Bush introduced his public education program, he said, "We must face up to the plague of school violence, with an average of three million crimes committed against students and teachers inside the public schools every year. That's unacceptable in our country. We need real reform."

The president's exaggerated claim contributed to the widespread illusion of a surge in school violence. Richard Rothstein argued that Bush's reference to "three million crimes" "comes from rounding up the results of a Census Bureau survey in which teenagers said they were victims of 2.7 million school crimes in 1998. But fewer than one tenth of these were categorized by the survey as serious."[87] Rothstein notes, "when only 1 percent of teenagers report a serious school crime, there is no 'plague of school violence.'"[88]

History of School Violence

Have students become more violent, and does that violence threaten the safety of our schools? There are no data to show that schools are more dangerous places today than in the past. However, perceptions that they are

run rampant. Many policymakers and influential citizens, William Bennett
for instance, have compared the supposedly primary problems of today's
schools (violence, rape, burglary) to those of yesterday's (cheating, gum
chewing, cutting class).[89] In fact, there is no evidence that the biggest problems of today's schools are worse than yesterday's, and many of today's
teachers report the same problems of the 1940s—cutting class, chewing
gum, lying. However, because the media make violence more visible today,
the public is misled to believe that violence dominates the concerns of
school personnel.[90]

School Violence Today

School violence is difficult to define because it exists in varied forms. Does
violence only include conflicts involving a weapon? If so, what kinds of
weapons? Can it involve verbal threats, harassment, peer rejection, assault,
or theft? Is direct violence the same as indirect violence (e.g., spreading ru-
mors and lying vs. face-to-face verbal abuse)? As we try to define violence for
the purpose of quantifying violent incidents, we need to take into account
its consequences: There is research to suggest that indirect violence—in
the form of bullying and social rejection—can have very serious effects.[91]

The incidence of serious violent crimes (including rape, sexual assault,
robbery, aggravated assault, theft, and simple assault) and of thefts occurring on or near school property has declined since 1992 for all age ranges,
both genders, and geographic location (rural and suburban). The percentage of students who report being threatened or injured with a weapon on
school property has remained relatively stable since 1993, with boys being
more likely to be threatened than girls and younger students being more
likely than older ones to experience threats.[92] High school students are
much less likely to carry weapons of any kind to school today than in 1991
(see Table 3.2).

TABLE 3.2
Percentage of High School Students Who
Carried Weapons: 1991–1999

	Carried Weapon (%)	Carried Weapon at School (%)	Carried Gun (%)
1991	26	NA	NA
1993	22	12	8
1995	20	10	7.5
1997	18	8	6
1999	17	7	5

Note. Data is based on responses for 1 or more of the 30 days preceding the survey. From
Youth Violence: A Report of the Surgeon General (p. 23), 2000, Rockville, MD: Department of Health
and Human Services.

And, public perceptions to the contrary, murder and suicide are extremely rare on school grounds. Of all homicides of children ages 5–19 years during the 1997–1998 year, 1% of them occurred on or near school grounds, and of all suicides in the same year 0.3% of them took place on or near school grounds.[93]

Perceptions of School Violence

The annual *Phi Delta Kappan*/Gallup polls from 1985 through 1994 show a dramatic increase in the percentage of citizens who are concerned about school violence and safety. In 1985, only 1% of those polled thought fighting was a problem in public schools—a percentage that remained stable until it rose to 9% in 1992, 13% in 1993, and 18% in 1994.[94] By 1999, the top two major concerns held by citizens regarding public schools were lack of discipline/control (18%) and fighting/gang violence (11%). One third of parents and nonparents combined were concerned that youth were violent and that schools were not able to control their students.[95] In the 2000 poll, opinions shifted slightly. The top two concerns citizens had for their schools were inadequate financial support (18%) and lack of discipline and student control (15%). A newer picture is slowly emerging.[96] Perhaps citizens are growing more aware of the challenges schools have when they don't have resources to combat the complexity of modern problems.

Students also report growing concern about school danger. Despite stable or declining rates of school violence, students felt less safe in schools in 1999 than previously. In 1989, 6% of youth ages 12–19 years reported fears that they would be harmed at school; by 1995 the percentage of students who feared physical danger at school had increased to 9%. Yet these fears seem unrelated to an actual threat because the percentage of students who came to school carrying a weapon declined from 12% in 1993 to 9% in 1997.[97]

Promising Solutions

Over the past decade, policymakers, educators, and youth advocates have demonstrated a growing awareness of and desire to thwart youth violence.[98] Because researchers who evaluate violence-prevention programs use a variety of methods and measurements for establishing connections between program components and youth outcomes, it is impossible to establish definitive conclusions about individual program effectiveness. Still, results of a wide array of studies can, in combination, provide some initial clues about what program elements are essential to facilitating youth's prosocial development.[99]

In their review of the literature, Eccles and Templeton describe two types of successful programs, each with strengths and weaknesses for reducing youth violence.[100] On the one hand, school-based programs, such as Social Competence Program for Young Adolescents and Seattle Social Development Program, are often incorporated into the school's curriculum—all students are exposed to them whether they like it or not. On the other hand, participation in community-based programs, such as Outward Bound and Big Brothers Big Sisters, is often voluntary, and therefore youth who enroll in them are typically more motivated.

There is evidence that both types of programs can be successful,[101] even though they differ dramatically in design and implementation. Still, as Eccles and Templeton note, there are essential core elements that span all types of programs and are critical to their success. Programs that are youth centered, knowledge centered, and assessment centered are more effective than those that are not. Similarly, as other researchers have noted, programs that intentionally pair adult mentors with youth are especially critical for ethnic minority, low-income, high-risk teens.[102]

CONCLUSION

We attempted to show that reporting on youth crime is exaggerated. Youth crime rates are decreasing, yet the public believes that youth violence is escalating, and policymakers continue to implement harsher legislation—legislation that is self-defeating (e.g., sending younger children to jail, treating juveniles as adults). The subject of teenage violence is complex, involving questions about what constitutes violence, about accuracy of official and self-report data, and about how to predict future violence in young people. However, within this complexity, some factors are salient. Juvenile arrests rates are down, and although self-reports of juvenile crime are up, it is clear that the feral juvenile society of superpredators that the media predicted in the late 1980s has not emerged. Given that violent youth crimes are down, it is ludicrous to suggest that today's teens are more violent than those in the past. Americans must learn the facts about youth violence (see Boxes 3.1 and 3.2) and press policymakers to launch reforms that more proactively help youth.

Teens from all ethnic backgrounds have received less than optimal opportunities to develop their productive potential. White boys commit suicide (Black boys are gradually catching up). White girls are more likely to run away from home and to become prostitutes than girls of other ethnic groups. And it is well documented that Hispanic and Black students, especially boys, are more likely to be arrested and punished than White students. The various acts of violence against youth of all ethnic and socioeconomic groups suggests an indifference or hostility to youth generally. These are serious dangers that we have not begun to deal with adequately.

American society and its media largely ignore the issue of youth suicide—an area where new approaches and programs are acutely needed. And society continues to ignore adult violence against youth. Why does our culture exaggerate youth violence against others while being virtually oblivious to the fact that more youth are killing themselves or being harmed by adults? If the media presented youth as victim more often than youth as criminal, perhaps more adults would be compelled to argue for better programs for youth rather than for better police protection from them.

General Considerations

Do crimes committed by youth always merit front-page news coverage? Do youth's good deeds only deserve coverage in the entertainment section of the paper? In 2000, NBC's *Today* show ran a series of "odd and unique" stories. One of these related the success of a high school chess team considered to be the most successful chess team in the country, having won numerous national championships. The news coverage stressed the strangeness of a national champion chess team's return home and of the welcoming rally—complete with cheerleaders. This type of upbeat story about youth accomplishment is almost always relegated to the oddities section of the news.

The school building itself has become an increasing target of concern for American adults and teens, with policy leaders—including the president of the United States—calling for safer schools. Although no one would argue against safety at school, demands to tackle the problem of unsafe schools can only be seen as misguided when statistics show that schools are relatively safe. Needless spending on violence prevention (hall guards, random drug checks, expelling students from school, shooting-spree drills) occurs at the expense of other potentially more effective forms of guidance (e.g., supervised after-school programs, skills-training courses). In addition, it has been clearly demonstrated that students' behavior is better in schools where they perceive fair and open communication.[103] To stress punishment (and not guidance) is self-defeating because it reduces the likelihood that peers will report dangers.

Even more disturbing is the trend of treating juveniles as adult offenders. Students who are incarcerated and treated as adults are exposed to models and abuse that harden them. The number of inmates in jails nationally has quadrupled over the past two decades, reaching 2 million by 2000, and the current cost to Americans is about $40 billion a year. Although some believe the number of prisoners accounts for an 8-year decline in criminal activity, there are too may other variables associated with this trend to convincingly argue this point.[104] Criminal justice experts generally dismiss the role of increased jail sentences in reducing crime—less poverty and higher employment rates are more significant factors in crime reduction.

The recent prison building boom is a vivid metaphor for the lack of foresight to invest in youth. Or is it just a lack of foresight? Our troubling suspicion is that unwillingness to invest in youth often stems from indifference to youth and tragically, in some cases, from active hostility toward youth. Do Americans feel somehow safer because more criminals are being locked up? It seems illogical—and reactive—to think that taking young criminals off the streets and putting them into jails at higher rates makes society safer. After all, most young offenders eventually return to society, often as young adults who are more capable and more likely to commit crimes.[105]

The long overdue alternative is to help youth. Youths who consistently or blatantly engage in violence must be incarcerated. But to keep this tragedy from happening—and it is a tragedy when youth adopt criminal rather than productive lifestyles—we should invest in proactively preventing their negative behavior. Why not invest more in at-risk prevention programs? Why not improve after-school programs that engage youth in enjoyable and educational social activities? How we answer these questions in the coming decade will have profound consequences for the quality of life for all Americans—especially youth. The small minority of teens who engage in antisocial behavior need to be punished and, if possible, helped to change. It is time to stop blaming youth because of their potential for violence and to help them to develop their talents. Unfortunately, federal, state, and local governments refuse to prioritize the needs of teens.

Needed Research

In light of the gap between the widespread myth that youth violence is proliferating and the actual truth that it is decreasing, it would seem important to research strategies for conveying actual crime rates to the public and for assessing the extent to which more accurate information would educate citizens. Research into the factors that influence certain types of youth crime is also in order: Although overall juvenile crime rates are down, some types of crimes for certain groups of teens are increasing. Female juvenile crime, for instance, is growing, and this topic merits careful scrutiny and more research.

Context is a critical mediator of violent events and must be evaluated in empirical investigations of violence prevention in schools. For example, in one high school, a large percentage of school fights occurred in the cafeteria. One preventive measure could have been to staff the lunch period with more teacher monitors. Closer investigation revealed that the frequency of fights increased substantially on pizza day—the day when pizza was ordered out for approximately half of the lunch crowd. The problem was that there was not enough pizza for all the students who wanted it; therefore, fights started when students cut in line and argued over who would get the limited slices of pizza. Instead of putting more teachers in the cafeteria, the school simply ordered more pizza—less fighting ensued.[106] Incidents of violence do not occur in isolation from their contexts, and blanket statements that youth are vicious—and that they need to be tamed—are misleading if they do not take into account contexts of violence. Research is needed that investigates how individual and contextual variables interact if youth violence is to be more effectively reduced.

Following the publicity surrounding Columbine and other school-related tragedies, the problems of bullying, peer harassment, and rejection have been in the limelight[107] (despite the fact that there have probably been school bullies as long as there have been schools). Early investigations of school bullying were conducted by Dan Olweus in Sweden in the late 1960s.[108] Olweus found the social hierarchy of bullies and their victims to be relatively stable—once a bully always a bully—and that, in general, approximately 10% of students become bullies. There has been much research that documents bullying behavior, but effective research into reducing or eliminating that behavior is scarce, as is research that identifies the traits of the typical victim—an equally important issue.

The 2001 surgeon general's report on youth violence called for stronger empirical analyses of antiviolence prevention and intervention programs (more on this in chap. 9). To determine what works and what does not, it is vital that better program evaluation studies be conducted. More experimental research must be performed to assess which elements of which programs effect changes in youth's violent attitudes, behaviors, and tendencies. Similarly, more qualitative studies must be conducted to assess students' perceptions of their relationships with teachers and peers within school settings.

ENDNOTES

1. American Civil Liberties Union. (1996). *ACLU fact sheet on the juvenile justice system.* New York: Author. (Available at http://www.aclu.org/library/fctsht.htm./)

2. Jackson, D. Z. (1997, September 12). TV exaggerates juvenile crime, scaring public. *Arizona Daily Star*, A17.

3. Snyder, H. N., & Sickmund, M. (1999). *Juvenile offenders and victims: 1999 national report.* Washington, DC: Office of Juvenile Justice and Delinquency Prevention.

4. Quote taken from Humes, E. (1996). *No matter how loud I shout: A year in the life of juvenile court.* New York: Simon & Schuster; quoted in Males, M. A. (2000). *Kids and guns: How politicians, experts, and the press fabricate fear of youth* (p. 15). Philadelphia: Common Courage Press. (Available online at http://www.commoncouragepress.com/)

5. Strom, K. J. (2000). Profile of state prisoners under age 18, 1985–1997. *Bureau of Justice Statistics, Special Report* (NCJ 176989). Washington, DC: U.S. Department of Justice.

6. The prediction that a teenage superpredator was on the horizon was first brought to our attention in the surgeon general's report on youth violence in 2001. U.S. Department of Health and Human Services. (2000). *Youth violence: A report of the surgeon general.* Rockville, MD: Author. More recently, arguments of the youth superpredator have been viewed as a myth. Snyder, H. N., & Sickmund, M. (1999). *Juvenile offenders and victims: 1999 national report.* Washington, DC: Office of Juvenile Justice and Delinquency Prevention.

7. Males, M. A. (2000). *Kids and guns: How politicians, experts, and the press fabricate fear of youth* (p. 10). Philadelphia: Common Courage Press. (Available online at http://www.commoncouragepress.com/); see also, Males, M. (1996). *The scapegoat generation: America's war on adolescents.* Philadelphia: Common Courage Press.

8. Labaton, S. (2002, June 3). Downturn and shift in population feed boom in white collar crime. *New York Times,* pp. A1, A22.

9. Males, M. A. (2000). *Kids and guns: How politicians, experts, and the press fabricate fear of youth* (p. 10). Philadelphia: Common Courage Press. (Available online at http://www.commoncouragepress.com/); see also Dorfman, L., Woodruff, K., Chavez, V., & Wallack, L. (1997). Youth and violence on local television news in California. *American Journal of Public Health, 87*(8), 1311–1316.

10. Streib, V. (1987). *Death penalty for juveniles.* Bloomington: Indiana University Press. Information on the statistics of juvenile death sentences and executions can also be found online: Streib, V. (2000). *The juvenile death penalty today: Death sentences and executions for juvenile crimes, January 1, 1973–June 30, 2000.* Ada, Ohio: Ohio Northern University. (Available at http://www.law.onu.edu/faculty/streib/juvdeath.pdf); see also, Gray, M. (2003). *The death game: Capital punishment and the luck of the draw.* Philadelphia: Common Courage Press.

11. One author frequently cited throughout this chapter, Michael Males, argues specifically about the skewed nature of media reporting on the "dangers" of youth who live in middle-class neighborhoods. See Males, M. A. (2000). *Kids and guns: How politicians, experts, and the press fabricate fear of youth.* Philadelphia: Common Courage Press. (Available online at http://www.commoncouragepress.com/)

12. American Civil Liberties Union. (1996). *ACLU fact sheet on the juvenile justice system.* New York. (Available at http://www.aclu.org/library/fctsht.htm./) Austin, J., Johnson, K. D., & Gregoriou, M. (2001). *Juveniles in adult prisons and jails: A national assessment.* Washington, DC: U.S. Department of Justice; see also Smith, J. S. (2002, July). Adult prisons: No place for kids. *USA Today,* pp. 34–35; see also Brown, G. F. (2002). Adolescents incarcerated with adults: A growing problem. *Brown University & Child Adolescent Behavior Letter, 18*(11), 8.

13. Reddy, M., Borum, R., Berglund, J., Bossekuil, B., Fein, R., & Modzeleski, W. (2001). Evaluating risk for targeted violence in schools: Comparing risk assessment, threat assessment, and other approaches. *Psychology in the Schools 38*(2), 157–172.

14. Bush, G. W. (2001, January 29). *No child left behind* [online]. (Available at http://www.ed.gov/inits/nclb/)

15. Astor, R. A., Meyer, H. A., & Behre, W. J. (1999). Unowned places and times: Maps and interviews about violence in high schools. *American Educational Research Journal, 36*(1), 3–42.

16. Males, M. A. (2000). *Kids and guns: How politicians, experts, and the press fabricate fear of youth* (p. 10). Philadelphia: Common Courage Press. (Available online at http://www.commoncouragepress.com/)

17. Males, M. A. (2000). *Kids and guns: How politicians, experts, and the press fabricate fear of youth* (pp. 10–11). Philadelphia: Common Courage Press. (Available online at http://www. commoncouragepress.com/)

18. Iyengar, S. (1991). *Is anyone responsible?* Chicago: University of Chicago Press.

19. Dorfman, L., Woodruff, K., Chavez, V., & Wallack, L. (1997). Youth and violence on local television news in California. *American Journal of Public Health, 87*(8), 1311–1316; Iyengar, S. (1991). *Is anyone responsible?* Chicago: University of Chicago Press.

20. Hepburn, M. A. (1998). The power of the electronic media in the socialization of young Americans: Implications for social studies education. *The Social Studies, 89*(2), 73.

21. Hepburn, M. A. (1998). The power of the electronic media in the socialization of young Americans: Implications for social studies education. *The Social Studies, 89*(2), 73. Insert quote comes from Neumann, W. R. (1987, Winter). Knowledge and opinion in the American electorate. *Kettering Review,* 56–64.

22. Dorfman, L., Woodruff, K., Chavez, V., & Wallack, L. (1997). Youth and violence on local television news in California. *American Journal of Public Health, 87*(8), 1311–1316.

23. Dorfman, L., Woodruff, K., Chavez, V., & Wallack, L. (1997). Youth and violence on local television news in California. *American Journal of Public Health, 87*(8), 1311–1316.

24. Sterngold, J. (2001, March 7). Shooting was planned and calmly carried out, police say. *New York Times,* p. A14; Barboza, D. (2000, March 2). A life of guns, drugs, and now, killing, all at 6. *New York Times,* pp. A1, A25; Egan, T. (2001, March 9). Santee is latest blow to myth of suburbia's safer schools. *New York Times,* pp. A1, A16; Hanley, R. (2001, March 9). Girl in shooting was seen as dejected. *New York Times,* p. A16; Associated Press. (2001, December 5). Multiple killings in school violence rises. *New York Times,* p. A21.

25. Violence on TV: A lot of it is on the network news. (1997, August 12). *Washington Post,* p. D1; see also Males, M. A. (2000). *Kids and guns: How politicians, experts, and the press fabricate fear of youth* (p. 10). Philadelphia: Common Courage Press. (Available online at http://www.commoncouragepress.com/)

26. Perrone, P., & Chesney-Lind, M. (1997). Representations of gangs and delinquency: Wild in the streets? *Social Justice, 24*(4), 96–116 (quote on p. 100).

27. Males, M. A. (2000). *Kids and guns: How politicians, experts, and the press fabricate fear of youth* (p. 10). Philadelphia: Common Courage Press. (Available online at http://www. commoncouragepress.com/)

28. Juvenile crime at lowest since '88. (2000, December 15). *Arizona Daily Star,* pp. A1, A21.

29. Elam, S. M., Rose, L. C., & Gallup, A. M. (1994). The 26th annual Phi Delta Kappa/Gallup poll of the public's attitudes toward the public schools. *Phi Delta Kappan, 75*(1), 41–56; Rose, L. C., & Gallup, A. M. (2000). The 32nd annual Phi Delta Kappa/Gallup poll of the public's attitudes toward the public schools. *Phi Delta Kappan, 82*(1), 41–57.

30. Sullivan, A. (1999, November 7). The assault on good news. *New York Times Magazine,* pp. 38–39.

31. Seligman, M. E., & Csikszentmihalyi, M. (Eds.). (2000). Special issue on happiness, excellence, and optimal human functioning [Special issue]. *American Psychologist, 55*(1).

32. UCR measures violent crime, including murder, forcible rape, robbery, aggravated assault, and property crimes, including burglary, larceny-theft, and motor vehicle theft. Obtained from Kempf, K. L. (Ed.). (1990). *Measurement issues in criminology* (pp. 28–29). New York: Springer-Verlag.

33. U.S. Department of Health and Human Services. (2000). *Youth violence: A report of the surgeon general.* Rockville, MD: Author.

34. Klein, M. (1989). (Ed.). *Cross-national research in self-reported crime and delinquency. Series D: Behavioural and social sciences—volume 50.* Dordrecht, The Netherlands: Kluwer; Coleman,

C., & Moynihan, J. (1996). *Understanding crime data: Haunted by the dark figure.* Philadelphia: Open University Press; Kempf, K. (1990). (Ed.). *Measurement issues in criminology.* New York: Springer-Verlag; U.S. Department of Health and Human Services. (2000). *Youth violence: A report of the surgeon general.* Rockville, MD: Author.

35. The NCVS was previously known as the National Criminal Survey.

36. For more information on the YRBSS, see http://www.cdc.gov/nccdphp/dash/yrbs/index.htm (retrieved June 28, 2002).

37. Monitoring the Future is a national survey on adolescent drug use stemming back to 1975, conducted by researchers at the Institute for Social Research, University of Michigan, and sponsored by U.S. Department of Health and Human Services and the National Institute on Drug Abuse (NIDA). For copies of annual reports see http://monitoringthefuture.org/

38. Coleman, C., & Moynihan, J. (1996). *Understanding crime data: Haunted by the dark figure.* Philadelphia: Open University Press.

39. Juvenile crime at lowest since '88 (2000, December 15). *Arizona Daily Star,* pp. A1, A21.

40. Snyder, H. N., & Sickmund, M. (1999). *Juvenile offenders and victims: 1999 national report.* Washington, DC: Office of Juvenile Justice and Delinquency Prevention; Butts, J. (2000). *Youth crime drop.* Washington, DC: Urban Institute, Justice Policy Center. (Available online at http:www.urban.org)

41. Butts, J. A. (2000). *Youth crime drop.* Washington, DC: Urban Institute, Justice Policy Center.

42. However, part of the explanation could be a tougher crackdown on youth, yielding larger numbers of arrests.

43. Butts, J. A. (2000). *Youth crime drop.* Washington, DC: Urban Institute, Justice Policy Center.

44. U.S. Department of Health and Human Services. (2000). *Youth violence: A report of the surgeon general.* Rockville, MD: Author.

45. Kempf, K. (1990). (Ed.). *Measurement issues in criminology.* New York: Springer-Verlag.

46. U.S. Department of Health and Human Services. (2000). *Youth violence: A report of the surgeon general.* Rockville, MD: Author.

47. Kempf, K. (1990). (Ed.). *Measurement issues in criminology.* New York: Springer-Verlag.

48. Klein, M. (1989). (Ed.). *Cross-national research in self-reported crime and delinquency. Series D: Behavioral and social sciences—volume 50.* Dordrecht, The Netherlands: Kluwer.

49. Strom, K. J. (2000). *Profile of state prisoners under age 18, 1985–1997* (Special Report NCJ 176989). Washington, DC: Bureau of Justice Statistics.

50. Strom, K. J. (2000). *Profile of state prisoners under age 18, 1985–1997* (Special Report NCJ 176989). Washington, DC: Bureau of Justice Statistics.

51. Information on firearm use and trends is taken from U.S. Department of Health and Human Services. (2000). *Youth violence: A report of the surgeon general.* Rockville, MD: Author.

52. *The Blackboard Jungle* is a 1955 movie about a well-intentioned teacher who attempts to influence inner-city school students. Retrieved November 19, 2001, from http://us.imdb.com/Title?0047885; information can also be obtained from Yahoo! Movies at http://movies.yahoo.com/movies/ (retrieved November 19, 2001).

53. *Dangerous Minds* is a more modern depiction of inner-city classrooms and can also be reviewed on Yahoo! Movies at http://movies.yahoo.com/movies/

54. Snyder, H. N., & Sickmund, M. (1999). *Juvenile offenders and victims: 1999 national report.* Washington, DC: Office of Juvenile Justice and Delinquency Prevention.

55. U.S. Department of Health and Human Services. (2000). *Youth violence: A report of the surgeon general.* Rockville, MD: Author.

56. Reiss, A. J., Jr., & Roth, J. A. (Eds.). *Understanding and preventing violence.* Washington, DC: National Academy Press. As referred to in Seppa, N. (1996, April). APA releases study on family violence. *Monitor of the American Psychological Association, 12;* see also *Violence and the family: Report of the APA Presidential Task Force on Violence and the Family.* (Available online at http://www.apa.org/pi/pii/viol&fam.html; full report is available from the American Psychological Association.)

57. See Wilson, J. W. (2000, June). Characteristics of crimes against juveniles. *Juvenile Justice Bulletin.* Washington, DC: U.S. Department of Justice, Office of Juvenile Justice and Delinquency Prevention.

58. Snyder, H. N., & Sickmund, M. (1999). *Juvenile offenders and victims: 1999 national report.* Washington, DC: U.S. Department of Justice, Office of Juvenile Justice and Delinquency Prevention.

59. High court rules against spanking. (2001, November 16). *Arizona Daily Star,* p. A12; Wilgoren, J. (2001, May 3). Lawsuits touch off debate over paddling in schools. *New York Times,* pp. A1, A22.

60. See, for example, Berliner, D. (1997). Educational psychology meets the Christian right: Differing views of children, schooling, teaching, and learning. *Teachers College Record, 98*(3), 381–416.

61. Wyatt, E. (2001, June 5). Support, and caution, for a school crime-report law. *New York Times,* p. B4; Wyatt, E. (2001, June 3). Data show sexual attacks in city schools are up sharply. *New York Times,* pp. A1, A39.

62. Associated Press (2003, August 8). Vatican defends 1962 sex abuse document. *New York Times.*

63. Hardy, L. (2002). Trust betrayed. *American School Board Journal, 189*(6), 14–18.

64. Snyder, H. N., & Sickmund, M. (1999). *Juvenile offenders and victims: 1999 national report.* Washington, DC: U.S. Department of Justice, Office of Juvenile Justice and Delinquency Prevention.

65. Snyder, H. N., & Sickmund, M. (1999). *Juvenile offenders and victims: 1999 national report.* Washington, DC: U.S. Department of Justice, Office of Juvenile Justice and Delinquency Prevention.

66. Four main reasons for underreporting are (1) parents often hide suicide notes that are needed to classify a death as a suicide in some states, (2) those who determine causes of death are often local sheriffs or some other community-appointed designate ill-educated to make appropriate death determinations, (3) local sheriffs or police members fail to recognize suicidal intents of car accidents when there are no skid marks or any other evidence that it was an accident, or (4) many youths escape gang life by provoking cops to shoot them, otherwise known as suicide by cop. (There are reports that many gang affiliated youths wish to escape gang life but feel the only way out that is noble is to die by the hand of a cop.) See, for example, Portner, J. (2000). Complex set of ills spurs rising teen suicide rate. *Education Week, 19*(31), 23.

67. Stossel, J. (1999, October 22). Give me a break: Media coverage of school shootings is up though violence in schools is down. *20/20* [Television series]. New York: ABC News.

68. Portner, J. (2000). Complex set of ills spurs rising teen suicide rate. *Education Week, 19*(31), 23.

69. Benton, S. A., Robertson, J. M., Tseng, W., Newton, F. B., & Benton, S. L. (2003). Changes in counseling center and client problems across 13 years. *Professional Psychology: Research and Practice, 34*(1), 66–72.

70. As reported in Goode, E. (2003, February 3). More in college seek help for psychological problems. *New York Times,* p. A11.

71. U.S. Department of Health and Human Services. (2000). *Youth violence: A report of the surgeon general.* Rockville, MD: Author.

72. Words, M., Bynum, T. C., & Corley, C. J. (1994). Locking up youth: The impact of race on detention decisions. *Journal of Research in Crime and Delinquency, 31*(2), 149–165; Conley, D. J. (1994). Adding color to a black and white picture: Using qualitative data to explain disproportionality in the juvenile justice system. *Journal of Research in Crime and Delinquency, 3*(2), 135–148; Strom, K. J. (2000). *Profile of state prisoners under age 18, 1985–1997* (Bureau of Justice Statistics, Special Report NCJ 176989). Washington, DC: U.S. Department of Justice; see also the report *Building Blocks for Youth: And Justice for Some.* (Available online at http://www.buildingblocksforyouth.org/justiceforsome/jfs.pdf)

73. Strom, K. J. (2000). *Profile of state prisoners under age 18, 1985–1997* (Bureau of Justice Statistics, Special Report NCJ 176989). Washington, DC: U.S. Department of Justice; see also the report *Building Blocks for Youth: And Justice for Some.* (Available online at http://www.buildingblocksforyouth.org/justiceforsome/jfs.pdf)

74. Justice Policy Institute. (2000). *The color of justice: An analysis of juvenile adult court transfers in California.* Washington, DC: Author. (Available online at http://www.cjcj.org/colorofjustice/)

75. Lewin, T. (2000, February 3). Discrepancy by race found in the trying of youths. *New York Times,* p. A21; also see Justice Policy Institute. (2000). *The color of justice: An analysis of juvenile adult court transfers in California.* Washington, DC: Author. (Available online at http://www.cjcj.org/colorofjustice/)

76. African American juveniles are also overrepresented in the adult prison system (12% of youths in Pima County, Arizona, sent to adult court were Black, when only 5% of the population are Black). See Innes, S. (2000, April 10). Fearing for the future. *Arizona Daily Star,* pp. B1, B5; see also an article in the *Arizona Daily Star* that argued that minority youths have fewer opportunities for rehabilitation than their White counterparts: Machelor, P. (2002). Fewer ways out for minority teens. *Arizona Daily Star,* pp. A1, A11.

77. For a review of this debate, see Pope, C. E., & Snyder, H. N. (2003). *Race as a factor in juvenile arrests.* Washington, DC: U.S. Department of Justice, Office of Juvenile Justice and Delinquency Prevention. (Available online at http://www.ojjdp.ncjrs.org/)

78. See Justice Policy Institute. (2000). *The color of justice: An analysis of juvenile adult court transfers in California.* Washington, DC: Author. (Available online at http://www.cjcj.org/colorofjustice/)

79. Warner, B. S., Weist, M. D., & Krulak, A. (1999). Risk factors for school violence. *Urban Education, 34*(1), 52–68.

80. A status offense is one that involves a minor or someone under the age of 18 years.

81. Flowers, R. B. (1995). *Female crime, criminals and cellmates: An exploration of female criminality and delinquency.* Jefferson, NC: McFarland & Company.

82. Bilchik, S. (2000). Challenging the myths: 1999 National Report Series. *Juvenile Justice Bulletin.* Washington, DC: U.S. Department of Justice, Office of Juvenile Justice and Delinquency Prevention.

83. Wiseman, R. (2002). *Queen bees and wannabes: A parent's guide to helping your daughter survive cliques, gossip, boyfriends, and other realities of adolescence.* New York: Crown; Simmons, R. (2002). *Odd girl out: The hidden culture of aggression in girls.* New York: Harcourt; see also Talbot, M. (2002, February 24). Girls just want to be mean. *New York Times Magazine,* 24–29.

84. Pollack, W. S., & Schuster, T. (2001). *Real boys' voices.* New York: Penguin.

85. Flowers, R. B. (1995). *Female crime, criminals and cellmates: An exploration of female criminality and delinquency.* Jefferson, NC: McFarland & Company.

86. Flowers, R. B. (1995). *Female crime, criminals and cellmates: An exploration of female criminality and delinquency.* Jefferson, NC: McFarland & Company.

87. Rothstein, R. (2001, February 7). Lessons: Of schools and crimes, and gross exaggeration. *New York Times,* p. B9.

88. Rothstein, R. (2001, February 7). Lessons: Of schools and crimes, and gross exaggeration. *New York Times,* p. B9.

89. O'Neill, B. (1994, March 6). The history of a hoax. *New York Times Magazine,* 46–49.

90. Kaufman, P., Chen, X., Choy, S. P., Ruddy, S. A., Miler, A. K., Fleury, J. K., Chandler, K. A., Rand, M. R., Klaus, P., & Planty, M. G. (2000). *Indicators of school crime and safety, 2000* (NCES 2001-017/NCJ-184176). Washington, DC: U.S. Department of Education, U.S. Department of Justice.

91. For example, see Keltikangas-Jarvinen, L. (2002). Aggressive problem-solving strategies, aggressive behavior, and social acceptance in early and late adolescence. *Journal of Youth and Adolescence, 31*(4), 279–289. Importantly, effects of indirect aggression are more commonly investigated as they pertain to females. See Bjorkqvist, K. (1994), Sex differences in physical, verbal, and indirect aggression: A review of recent research. *Sex Roles, 30*(3/4), 177–189. See also Simmons, R. (2002). *Odd girl out: The hidden culture of aggression in girls.* New York: Harcourt; Wiseman, R. (2002). *Queen bees and wannabes: Helping your daughter survive cliques, gossip, boyfriends and other realities of adolescence.* New York: Crown.

92. National Center for Education Statistics. (1999, June). *The condition of education 1999* (NCES 1999–02). Washington, DC: U.S. Department of Education, Office of Educational Research and Improvement.

93. See Kachur, S. P. et al. (1996). School-associated violent deaths in the United States, 1992–1994. *Journal of the American Medical Association, 275*(22), 1729–1733.

94. Elam, S. M., Rose, L. C., & Gallup, A. M. (1994). The 26th annual Phi Delta Kappa/Gallup poll of the public's attitudes toward the public schools. *Phi Delta Kappan, 75*(1), 41–56.

95. Rose, L. C., & Gallup, A. M. (2000). The 32nd annual Phi Delta Kappa/Gallup poll of the public's attitudes toward the public schools. *Phi Delta Kappan, 82*(1), 41–57.

96. Citizens are concerned that schools aren't receiving the support they need. Indirectly, this suggests that adults believe an adequate distribution of funds is necessary for schools to be effective. Indeed, this is echoed in other public opinion polls that suggest citizens are willing to pay more to help schools but only if they know their monies are being used in meaningful ways. However, many still believe that students are wild and need to be controlled.

97. Kaufman, P., Chen, X., Choy, S. P., Ruddy, S. A., Miler, A. K., Fleury, J. K., Chandler, K. A., Rand, M. R., Klaus, P., & Planty, M. G.(2000). *Indicators of school crime and safety, 2000* (NCES 2001-017/NCJ-184176). Washington, DC: U.S. Department of Education, U.S. Department of Justice.

98. As argued by Eccles, J. S., & Templeton. J. (2002). Extracurricular and other after-school activities for youth. In W. G. Secada (Ed.), *Review of research in education* (Vol. 26, pp. 113–180). Washington, DC: American Educational Research Association.

99. See Eccles, J. S., & Templeton. J. (2002). Extracurricular and other after-school activities for youth. In W. G. Secada (Ed.). *Review of research in education* (Vol. 26, pp. 113–180). Washington, DC: American Educational Research Association; see also Catalano, R. F., Berglund, M. L., Ryan, J. A. M., Lonczak, H. S., & Hawkins, J. D. (1999). *Positive youth development in the United States: Research findings on evaluations of the positive youth development programs.* New York: Carnegie Corporation; Connell, J. P., Gambone, M. A., & Smith, T. J. (2000). Youth development in community settings: Challenges to our field and our approach. In P. P. Ventures (Ed.), *Youth development: Issues, Challenges and directions* (pp. 281–300). Philadelphia: Public/Private Ventures.

100. Program reviews can be found in Catalano, R. F., Berglund, M. L., Ryan, J. A. M., Lonczak, H. S., & Hawkins, J. D. (1999). *Positive youth development in the United States: Research findings on evaluations of the positive youth development programs.* New York: Carnegie Corporation; Roth, J., Brooks-Gunn, J., Murray, L., & Foster, W. (1998). Promoting healthy adolescents: Synthesis of youth development program evaluations. *Journal of Research on Adolescence, 8,* 423–459; Greenberg, M. T., Domitrovich, C., & Bumbarger, B. (2001). The prevention of mental disorders in school-aged children: Current state of the field. *Prevention and Treatment, 4,* 1–71; Kirby, D. (2001). *Emerging answers: Research findings on programs to reduce teen pregnancy.* Washington, DC: National Campaign to Prevent Teen Pregnancy.

101. Eccles and Templeton (2002) provide a synthesis of effective school-based and after-school programs for promoting healthy adolescent development. Eccles, J. S., & Templeton. J. (2002). Extracurricular and other after-school activities for youth. In W. G. Secada (Ed.), *Review of research in education* (Vol. 26, pp. 113–180). Washington, DC: American Educational Research Association.

102. McLaughlin, M. W. (1993). Embedded identities: Enabling balance in urban contexts. In S. B. Heath, & M. W. McLaughlin (Eds.), *Identity and inner-city youth: Beyond ethnicity and gender* (pp. 36–68). New York: Teachers College Press.

103. Battistich, V., Solomon, D., Kim, D., Watson, M., & Schaps, E. (1995). Schools as communities, poverty levels of student populations, and students' attitudes, motives, and performance: A multilevel analysis. *American Educational Research Journal, 32*(3), 627–658; Battistich, V., Solomon, D., Watson, M., & Schaps, E. (1997). Caring school communities. *Educational Psychologist, 32*(2), 137–151; Bushman, B. J., & Anderson, C. A. (2001). Media violence and the American public: Scientific facts versus media misinformation. *American Psychologist, 56*(6/7), 477–489.

104. See Blumstein, A., & Wallman, J. (Eds.). (2000). *The crime drop in America.* Cambridge, UK: Cambridge University Press; see also Butterfield, F. (2000, September 28). Effect of prison building on crime is weighed. *New York Times,* p. A16.

105. Butterfield, F. (2000, November 29). Often, parole is one stop on the way back to prison. *New York Times,* pp. A1, A32.

106. Gavin, T. A. (2000). Bringing SARA to school: A commonsense problem-solving model is your first defense against school violence. *American School Board Journal, 187*(3), 36–39.

107. Following Columbine, the press more frequently documented instances of harassment and bullying in schools. For example, see Angier, N. (2001, May 20). Bully for you: Why push comes to shove. *New York Times* (Section 4), pp. 1, 4.

108. Olweus, D. (1978). *Aggression in the schools: Bullies and whipping boys.* New York: Wiley.

Chapter 4

The Sex Lives of Teenagers

Young adolescents don't seem to know a lot about sex.
— National Campaign to Prevent Teen Pregnancy, 2003[1]

Worldwide, 15- to 24-year-olds account for half of all new infections. Almost 12 million young people now have H.I.V., and an additional 6,000 young adults become infected every day.
— L. K. Altman, July 3, 2002[2]

Every child needs to have equity of opportunity for sex education.
— D. Satcher[3]

One hallmark of adolescence is puberty—a biological and social transformation that emerges seemingly overnight. An overwhelming onslaught of awkward physical developments assault young people during puberty, including noticeable hair growth and vocal changes for boys and breast development for girls. At no other time in the human life span other than in early infancy do such sudden and radical bodily changes occur. In addition to these inevitable biological changes, adolescents must simultaneously grapple with social changes, notably increased emphasis on peer groups and potential romantic partners.

The adolescent's sexual curiosity is developmentally appropriate,[4] yet many adults see youth's blooming sexuality as threatening—feral behavior to be controlled.[5] Fear tactics and other strategies are employed to stop youth from having sex or even thinking about it. Religious groups hold that premarital sex is a sin. Policymakers claim that sexually active teens are morally deficient. Policymakers, pressured by influential conservative and

91

religious organizations, politicize the sex education curricula in schools with the aim of prohibiting educative material on sexually transmitted disease (STD) prevention and birth control. School administrators, answering to nonrepresentative parent groups and school boards, dance around what can and cannot be discussed in sex education classrooms (e.g., can availability of birth control pills be acknowledged in abstinence-only approaches?). The public, whose primary information about all youth sex comes from media accounts of pregnancy or abortion rates, erroneously believes that youth are hormonally driven sexual beings with little self-control or responsibility.[6] Strangely, those who judge the average youth as oversexed and irresponsible often strive to deprive them of the knowledge about sexuality that might encourage responsible decision-making behavior.

As with widely held views about violent youth, these mostly negative beliefs about youth's sexual behavior are damaging because they spur the development of ineffective policies and programs. Labeling youth as oversexed or amoral also reflects a general lack of awareness of how widely young people vary in decision-making capabilities, sexually related knowledge, and relationship skills.[7] Many teens have sex before they get married; some do so responsibly, others recklessly. Many teens choose to have sex only when they are in a committed relationship; others do so haphazardly. Still others delay sex until they are married—a trend that varies with age.[8]

The disparity between what our culture communicates about sexuality and what parents and mentors tell teens is appropriate is striking. Our vast media culture is replete with explicit and implicit messages about youth sex and its role. Entertainment and advertising saturate the market with sexual content and images of youthful physical beauty. According to these messages, sex is exciting, healthy, and a powerful determiner of individual worth. In striking contrast, many parents, teachers, and other mentors are determined to convince youth that premarital sex is a bad choice. Ultimately, it is futile and counterproductive to withhold knowledge about sex from teens because information about sex is easily accessible from peers and our extensive media culture.[9]

In this chapter we debunk the notion that increasing media coverage of sex that has grown more frequent—and more explicit—over time has influenced a more oversexed youth culture. Adults have always been concerned about the suggestion of sex in literature, theater, and other forms of entertainment, and at no other time has there been such wide, varied, and immediate access to sexually related information. Yet despite this growing gratuity of sexual content, youth's responsible sexual behavior seems to be increasing. In fact, there is some evidence that sex in the media helps youth make decisions and sort out complex sexual situations.[10]

We then provide a more positive, and accurate, depiction of a contemporary youth culture in which teens today make a range of good (and bad) decisions about their sexuality. We discuss teens' knowledge about sex and explore how it relates to their behavior. Data suggest that today's teens are having less sex today than the teens of 10 years ago and that pregnancy rates are rapidly declining. Still, many teens have inadequate or erroneous information about sex and its consequences.[11] While politicians continue to invest in ineffective abstinence programs,[12] recent polls suggest that many teens lack critical information about the consequences of their sexual behavior (e.g., some—especially very young youth—do not understand the STD risks of oral sex[13]).

Lastly, we turn to schools as a valuable venue for equalizing normative information about sexual health for all teens. Perhaps surprisingly, teens' preferred source for information about sex is their parents.[14] However, increasing numbers of parents are turning to schools for help in educating their children about sexual behavior.[15] Tragically, many policymakers are reluctant to support expanded sex education in public schools, especially if it includes a discussion of safe-sex practices—even though that knowledge can save lives and prevent serious illnesses. This reluctance is especially ironic since many policymakers who oppose expanding sex education in the school curriculum also advocate for expanded roles of charter public schools and voucher programs because they increase schools' sensitivity to parents' needs! Despite parents' expressed need for more comprehensive sex education in the curriculum,[16] these same politicians violently oppose such additions to the curriculum. These efforts to restrict the information teens receive about sexuality have dangerous consequences. It seems plausible to argue that other cultures have fewer issues with teenage pregnancies and related issues in part because their school curricula openly teach students about the consequences of unsafe sexual behavior.[17]

MEDIA, SEX, AND THE ADOLESCENT

The media's capacity for shaping our collective consciousness of sex and promoting normative values, beliefs, and tolerance regarding sexual behavior is enormous. Early in the last century, before television and movies, parents' biggest worries about their suddenly sexualized teen had to do with either preventing exposure to dirty magazines, illicit books, and other "sexy" literature or monitoring peer influence. Though sex was exploited in 1900 (i.e., through advertisements in magazines), sexual conduct and images were extremely conservative compared with today's standards. Women in advertisements were mostly covered, and women's fashion was defined by long skirts; high, buttoned shirts; and one-piece, extra-long bathing suits. By the 1950s, and with the emergence of TV, sex was sold more explicitly (i.e., women in ads were more scantily clad). Still, in comparison to today's media, the 1950s generation was one of sexual modesty. In *I Love Lucy* and other television shows, parents slept in separate beds. The romantic and passionate moments on TV or in movies were long kisses good-bye or the implied sexual tension in scenes where first-time lovers held hands or gazed into one another's eyes.

Today, the portrayal of sex in the media is insidious. More than one half of television programming has sexual content,[18] and some have estimated that as many as 65,000 instances of sex are portrayed during the afternoon and early evening hours. Television viewers—especially teenage viewers— are literally bombarded with sexually explicit material.[19]

Media Can Be Useful

The media can help youth by suggesting useful coping strategies to young viewers facing complicated or troubling social and personal situations. Through realistic story lines and character development, popular television shows sometimes provide possible answers to complex socialization questions, such as, "How do I break up with someone?" and "How does someone else handle rejection?" In a 2002 survey of teens sponsored by the Kaiser Family Foundation, 43% of teens ages 15 to 17 say they learned how to talk with a partner about safer sex, and 60% said they learned about how to say no to a sexual situation that makes them uncomfortable, from TV programs.[20] In this role, the media validate youth's decisions, especially the decisions of those who do not have immediate or safe access to answers about sensitive issues.

Unfortunately, the impact of sexually explicit media content can also be damaging. When television characters make poor decisions, or, for example, when outcomes of their poor decisions are not portrayed, young viewers may be misled to believe that such choices are desirable or without repercussions. There are numerous examples of this potential media hazard. During the 2002–2003 season of *Friends*, Rachel, a 30-something, becomes a single mom. The challenges of raising an infant alone were rarely portrayed—or were portrayed unrealistically.

A second role of the media is to define societal norms. American media do this both by reflecting the current sexual climate of our youth and by pushing the boundaries of what is acceptable. One *Dawson's Creek* episode created a national stir when the main teen characters were going to have sex for the very first time. Although some advocates believed it was valuable to realistically portray young people contemplating their first sexual experience, others argued that a popular show with this story line would influence many teens to emulate it.

Common Themes Throughout Media

The sheer volume in the entertainment media of material centered on youth sexuality reveals a society preoccupied by the difficulties of adolescent sexuality. For example, parents are often uncomfortable with their teenagers' emerging interest in sex, and the media reflect (and sometimes distort) parental attitudes in numerous ways. In the popular television show *My So-Called Life* (produced in the mid-1990s by MTV), the mother of a budding teenage daughter exclaims with confusion and utter surprise, "She's like a stranger." Indeed, much of the show's appeal was owing to the reality with which mother–daughter conflicts are portrayed. As the daughter rapidly develops, her physical transformation is paralleled by her psychological and emotional one. She needs her mother less and turns to her rebellious friend more. The mother's loss of control over her suddenly rebellious and independent-minded daughter is a familiar American phenomenon.

In the 2000 movie *Almost Famous,* this psychological reaction of maternal horror is revisited in the story of an overprotective mother of a 15-year-old boy who is immersed in the life of a traveling rock-and-roll band. In this movie, the mother's incredible fear is that her young boy will be seduced by the sexy rock-and-roll lifestyle that is defined by sex and drugs. Fathers, too, react to the seemingly abrupt sexual changes in their daughters. For example, in the movie *Dirty Dancing,* the father character strongly opposes his daughter's first sexual love interest. Or consider the father character from *My So-Called Life,* who is so threatened by his daughter's sexual development that he asks his wife to tell her not to walk around in a towel.

Because of their real-life relevance, parent–teen conflicts over dating are also common themes in the media. Shakespeare's story *Romeo and Juliet* is perhaps the most notable example. Indeed, the movie version of the story was released eight times in the 20th century (in 1936, 1954, 1960, 1968, 1983, 1996 [twice], and 1998). The two most modern versions of the story include the 1996 *Romeo and Juliet,* starring Leonardo DiCaprio and Claire Danes, and the 1998 film *Shakespeare in Love,* which won nine Academy Awards, including Best Picture, Best Original Screenplay, and Best Actress (Gwyneth Paltrow). Many versions of the story have been recast in a multitude of ways.[21]

There are literally millions of media references to the ways in which American culture struggles with youth's developing sexuality. And, despite adults' worries about their impact, many youth are left alone to mediate these scenarios. This creates a complex dilemma for adults. When adults ignore youth's healthy sexual curiosity and blindly hope they will abstain, they guarantee that some youth will make poor decisions based partly on their own interpretations of what the media portray as acceptable behavior.

Adults must share media experiences with youth to help them integrate media information in ways that promote good decisions.

TEENAGE SEX: THE FACTS

American society judges the sexual morality and decisions of its youth by the teenage pregnancy, abortion, and STD rates reported in the media. Unfortunately, these statistics tell relatively little about the complicated nature of youth's sexual lives, and although they are useful indicators for gauging youth's sexual activity, they fail to provide accurate accounts of the conditions under which sexual behavior occurs. Rate data say nothing about the underlying nature of youth's sexual relationships; pregnancy rates fail to describe the context of a young female's pregnancy, and abortion rates say nothing on the role of parents or other adults who may have failed to guide youth. Adults often see pregnancy rates as proof of irresponsible behavior. Although some teenage pregnancies are the result of sex between two teenagers, the majority (52%) are the result of sexual relations between young females and older males (i.e., over 18 years).[22] When we realize that many pregnancies happen because young females are vulnerable to the persuasion and threats of older men, we see a strikingly different picture from the common notion that young teens are irresponsibly following hormonal desires with each other.

Journalistic media have fueled adults' pejorative and shallow views of youth sex. As only one example, every spring break newspapers print articles like the one that appeared in the spring of 2002, "Booze, skin rule as spring break overtakes Cancun." This story stressed the lax morals of teens (thereby increasing readers' disdain for youth), while failing to note the immoral behavior of the hotel bar owners who provided free drinks to women but not to men. It was billed as an establishment where customers ". . . need some sexy ladies dancing on the bar . . ."[23]

You can test your knowledge about teenage sex by answering the questions presented in Box 4.1 and comparing your responses with the answers in Box 4.2. If your answers were wrong, is it because you are not exposed to media or because the media misrepresent these data? Or is it a combination of these factors?

Measuring Sex

One common belief adults hold is that more youth today are having sex than ever before. But are more teens having sex? Newspapers want readers to think so—and not only that more of them are having sex but also that they do so irresponsibly. In media accounts, youth's sexual behavior is often narrowly described and presented in misleading ways. Take the

---

BOX 4.1   Statements associated with teenage sex.

True or False:

1. Teenagers don't care about what parents think or say.
2. The high incidence of teen births is not a new development in America.
3. The recent decline in the teen birth rate (e.g., the past decade) is due to an increase in abortions.
4. Sex education and access to contraception tend to increase sexual activity.
5. Most Americans believe that sexually active teens should have access to birth control measures.
6. Teen pregnancy is only a problem of minority populations.

Note. From *When Teens Have Sex: Issues and Trends*, by Annie E. Casey Foundation, 1998, Washington, DC: Author. Copyright 1998 by Annie E. Casey Foundation. Reprinted with permission.

egregious example of the headline "Teenage prostitution ring broken in Detroit."[24] The headline implies that teens played a major role in forming a prostitution ring, when the truth couldn't be further from this. The gruesome fact was that one adult was kidnapping, raping, and forcing young females into prostitution.

The numerous, conflicting, and sometimes vague definitions of sex make it difficult to accurately gauge how many youth have sex. For exam-

---

BOX 4.2   The facts about teen sex.

1. False: Young people rank parents as the *preferred* source of information about sex and health.
2. False: The rate of teen births in the United States has been high for a long time including back to the 1950s. What has changed is the number of unmarried teens.
3. False: Abortion rates and pregnancy rates have *both* declined.
4. False: In programs that provide access to contraception and safe sex education, there has been no increase in sexual activity.
5. True: A majority number of Americans agree that if teens are sexually active, they should have access to contraception.
6. False: Pregnancies are a problem across all ethnic groups.

Note. From *When Teens Have Sex: Issues and Trends*, by Annie E. Casey Foundation, 1998, Washington, DC: Author. Copyright 1998 by Annie E. Casey Foundation. Reprinted with permission.

ple, many youth, as well as adults, believe that oral sex is not really sex. According to one Gallup poll conducted in the late 1990s, 20% of adults believed that oral sex does not constitute sexual relations. In another survey, 59% of college students from a midwestern university did not believe that oral sex constitutes sex, and, according to another poll, the proportion of 1998 undergraduates who believed oral sex was not sex increased if they were asked specifically about oral sex that did not result in orgasm.[25] That even adults don't consistently define oral sex as sex (especially visible adults—former President Clinton claimed that oral sex was not sex during the Monica Lewinsky incident) adds to an already confusing culture in which youth live and make choices. If adults can't consistently define the boundaries of sexual behavior, how can we expect youth to do it?

Another obstacle to obtaining accurate statistics about young people's sexual activity is that questions regarding intimate sexual behavior are usually not asked. Parents (and policymakers who create human subjects laws) worry that these questions will give youth "ideas."[26] Surveys designed to gauge youth's sexual behavior often reflect a community's politics. More conservative communities could demand surveys that ask less direct questions than liberal communities, whose concerns are not so much suggestibility as discovering ways to keep youth safe.

Comparing sexual practices of youth today with those of youth from even a decade ago may be difficult because some questions asked now either weren't asked then or were asked differently. For example, in one longitudinal research project among adolescent males, questions about vaginal intercourse were asked differently during two time periods. In 1988, males were asked to answer the following items: "I put my penis in a girl's vagina but I did not come or ejaculate," and "I put my penis in a girls' vagina and I came or ejaculated." In 1995, respondents were asked to quantify: How often did you "put your penis in a female's vagina (vaginal intercourse)."[27] This question did not address whether respondents had ejaculated. Thus, different probes yield different responses and therefore are impossible to reliably compare.

Changing social conditions also make it next to impossible to identify changes in youth's behavior over time. In the 1920s and 1930s, the teen pregnancy rate was high—but teens were getting pregnant as married teens, legitimizing their behavior. Today, record numbers of teens are getting pregnant out of wedlock. In 1960, 15% of teen births were to unmarried teens, but in 1996 the figure was 76%.[28] Thus, to say that more teens are getting pregnant today is not necessarily accurate. What has changed is the age at which young people typically marry and the socially-defined expectation that teenage males who impregnate their partners out of wedlock will marry them.

Youth Sexual Behavior

Despite a wide range of methodological problems in measuring youth sexual activity, a rough picture of youth's sexual practices can be obtained from practitioners' reports, from research with smaller samples of youth, and from large-scale surveys that are beginning to ask tougher, more specific questions of larger numbers of youth.[29] According to one study, the percentage of youth who report having sex has decreased over the past decade. The decrease in sexual activity is more pronounced for boys (61% had had sex in 1990, whereas 49% had had sex in 1997) than girls (the percentage having had sex in 1990 was the same in 1997: 48%). While there is a general (and significant) decrease in young people's reported sexual activity, there is notable differentiation among different ethnic groups. Black teens are the most active. Among this group, 72% had had sex in 1990, a figure that actually increased marginally to 73% in 1997. The number of Hispanic youths who report having sex[30] has remained stable, with 53% having had sex in 1990 and 52% in 1997, whereas Whites' rates of sexual activity decreased from 52% in 1990 to 44% in 1997.

Rates of sexual activity also vary with age. For example, the decline in sexual activity for younger students was less pronounced than for older students. Specifically, 40% of ninth graders in 1990 reported having had sex, whereas 38% of them had had sex in 1997. In marked contrast, 72% of 12th graders had had sex in 1990, whereas 61% had had sex in 1997.[31] In a more recent study, the proportion of teen girls ages 15–19 years who had sexual intercourse decreased between 1988 and 1995, but the proportion of unmarried teen girls who had sexual intercourse at age 14 and younger increased during the same time period.[32]

A 2003 report by the Kaiser Family Foundation on adolescents' attitudes, knowledge, and experiences with sex documents variation in youth's sexual behavior. For example, among polled youths ages 15–17 years, more boys (65%) reported being with someone in an intimate way (including, but not limited to, intercourse) than girls (47%). And Black and Latino youth had sex at earlier ages than Whites, and girls (51%) were more likely to report one lifetime partner than males (35%).[33]

The variation among youth subgroups (by age, ethnicity, and gender) and their level of sexual activity is notable and provides important information about how to address youth sex. Fewer males are having sex than females, significantly fewer White youths are having sex, whereas a large proportion of minority youths continue to have sex. And more younger youths have sex, whereas older teens' activity levels are dropping.

Although these percentages quantify teen sexual activity, it isn't clear what kinds of sex teens are having. For example, one disturbing trend more commonly being reported is the growing numbers of youths—especially younger ones—who engage in oral sex.[34] One study estimated that 50% of young boys received oral sex.[35] In 2003, the Kaiser Family Foundation reported that 38% of 15- to 17-year-olds had oral sex, and 46% reported that oral sex is not as big a deal as intercourse. Further, 33% of girls (and 18% of boys) reported they had oral sex to avoid intercourse. Oral sex is rapidly becoming a popular way for girls to engage in sex without the worry of pregnancy and, according to some respondents, without the complexities associated with intimacy—many young girls seem to believe that oral sex is not an intimate act.

In an episode of *Boston Public* (a 1-hour television show in its first season on the Fox network during 2000–2001), a teacher catches a young girl giving oral sex to a male peer. As the story unfolds, we learn that she provided this "service" in return for his endorsing her candidacy for student body president (an endorsement that would guarantee her election). During a meeting with the principal, the female student argues the appropriateness of the act: "It wasn't like it was intimate or anything. We didn't even kiss!" According to some practitioners, this accurately represents how many youths view oral sex. One Manhattan psychologist noted the following:

> I see girls, seventh and eighth graders, even sixth graders, who tell me they're virgins, and they're going to wait to have intercourse until they meet the man they'll marry. But then they've had oral sex 50 or 60 times. It's like a good-night kiss to them, how they say good bye after a date.[36]

Too many teens simply don't know the risks of oral sex. In 2003, the Kaiser Family Foundation found that 19% of 15- to 17-year-olds reported that they didn't know you could get an STD through oral sex and a larger 39% (47% male and 30% female) considered oral sex to be safe sex. It is disturbing that youth are uninformed about the risks of oral sex.

RATE DATA

In this section, we explore teen pregnancy, abortion, and STD rates—the three aspects of teen sexual health most commonly reported. It is encouraging that all of these rates seem to be falling; however, we have a long way to go before youth are adequately protected from the negative consequences of early sexual activity. And, again, rates are only part of the story. Quality of relationships, the pleasure of sex, and parental attitude and guidance are rarely explored aspects of the sexual lives of youth.

Pregnancies

According to a report compiled by the Surgeon General's Office in 2001, nearly one half of all pregnancies in the United States were unintended, with the highest rates of them occurring among adolescents, lower income women, and Black women. Teen pregnancies are an acute national problem because when young girls have children, the risk of poor developmental outcomes, such as poverty or lost career and educational opportunities, increases substantially for both mother and child.[37] Tragically, when babies are born to young, unwed mothers who are high school dropouts, they are 10 times more likely to be living in poverty than a child born to a mother with none of these characteristics. The child's financial security is further compromised because few fathers of children born to teenagers provide financial help. Census data indicate that only 10% of mothers ages 15 to 17 years received child support payments in 1997.[38] Additionally, children born to single mothers are twice as likely to drop out of high school, twice as likely to have a child before the age of 20 years, and 1.5 times as likely to be out of work and school in their late teens or early 20s.[39] Teenage pregnancies are costly to mother, child, and society.

The good news is that there has been a steady decrease in the teen pregnancy rate in the last 10 years. In 1998, the rate of teen pregnancies in the United States was lower than it had been for two decades, and these rates declined for teens from all races and socioeconomic backgrounds. Unfortunately, despite these dramatic decreases,[40] the United States still has the highest teenage pregnancy rate among all industrialized nations (the next-closest nation is the United Kingdom, with half the teen birthrate of the United States[41]).

Abortions

Some citizens believe that the decrease in teen pregnancy rates nationwide is because of higher abortion rates. This is not true, however; teenage abortion rates have also declined over the past 10 years. Specifically the rates of abortions among youths ages 15–19 years decreased from 41 per 1,000 in 1990 to 30 per 1,000 in 1995.[42] And in a study conducted by the Alan Guttmacher Institute, there was a 39% decrease in abortions between 1994 and 2000 among young girls ages 15–17 years.[43] It is worth noting that women in their 20s constitute the age group with the highest number of abortions. Still, proportionately, more adolescent pregnancies end in abortion (29%) than do pregnancies for women over 20 (21%).[44]

In the last few years, there have been a few notable and tragic cases where teens have left newborn babies behind to die. In these stories, teens are described as cold and uncaring, with selfish motives. In New Jersey, for example, one teen had a baby in the bathroom during her senior prom, only to return to the dance floor for another dance after leaving her baby behind in the toilet. In another example, a teenage couple left their newborn wrapped in newspaper in a trash bin. Although these are tragic events, it is surprising that so many are shocked at youth's coldness when babies are thrown away. Our society has made it exceptionally difficult for teens to make reasonable, rational choices about sex and pregnancy. Forty-four states require parental notification or permission for youth to get an abortion.[45] The implication in this policy, of course, is that parents should take ultimate responsibility for guiding their children's decisions about moral and sexual issues. Yet many parents of pregnant teens have no idea their teens are even having sex or have never even discussed sex with them. This dynamic makes it hard for most teens to approach a parent about an unwanted pregnancy. Legislation that requires parental consent makes a difficult choice more difficult and influences desperate actions, such as leaving babies in trash cans.

Sexually Transmitted Diseases

Five of the 10 most commonly reported infectious diseases in the United States are STDs, and in 1995 STDs accounted for 87% of cases reported among the top 10 of all infectious diseases. Still, public awareness about STDs is limited, and understanding of STDs and their causes varies widely across subpopulations. For example, chlamydia, the most commonly reported STD, occurs more frequently among women ages 15–19 years old and is more common among Black and Hispanic women than among White women.[46] Approximately two thirds of persons who acquire STDs are younger than 25 years of age, with minority girls representing the highest at-risk group. Since the early 1990s, when rates of STDs among youth peaked, there has been a dramatic decrease in the rate of chlamydia (from 13% to 6% in the 17-and-under age group) and gonorrhea (decreasing from 6,000 per 100,000 to 4,000 per 100,000 from 1981 to 1997).

The 2003 Kaiser Family Foundation's survey of teens revealed that some youths are unaware of the risks of STDs. For example, 1 in 10 youths ages 15–17 years doesn't think an STD can be acquired from oral sex, and 1 in 6 think STDs spread only when the diseases are physically present. Many youths are unaware that STDs can cause some types of cancer (60%) and that they increase the risk for contracting HIV/AIDS (35%). Further, a minority of youths hold the misperception that they would be able to tell if someone they were dating had an STD (20%). And 12% believe that unless you have sex with a lot of people, STDs are not something to worry about. When it comes to testing for STDs, one fourth of youths don't know to ask to be tested because they mistakenly believe it is a routine part of health exams. Youth must be better informed on how to protect themselves from STDs.

HIV/AIDS

Although some STDs are curable, AIDS is incurable and life threatening. Statistics suggest that AIDS is growing rapidly among certain subgroups—specifically the Black, female community.[47] Blacks are just 13% of the American population, but more than half of new HIV infections occur among Blacks. AIDS is the leading cause of death for African Americans between the ages of 25 and 44 years, and 1 in every 50 Black American men is infected with HIV. Furthermore Blacks are 10 times more likely to be diagnosed with AIDS and 10 times more likely to die from it than their White counterparts, both male and female. African American women represent one of the fastest-growing risk groups. One in every 160 Black women is infected with HIV, whereas 1 in 250 White men and 1 in 3,000 White women are infected.[48] Of all new infections among women, 64% of them are in Blacks.

The good news is that the number of AIDS cases among youth has been decreasing steadily ever since peak rates of infection in 1993, with only small increases in the past 2 years. Still, the rate of new AIDS cases among youth disproportionately affects minority youth. Although 15% of the adolescent population is Black, 64% of AIDS cases among all 13- to 19-year-olds were among Blacks, and 20% were among Hispanics. Additionally, younger girls are at higher risk for contracting HIV and AIDS than older girls. In 2000, the Centers for Disease Control and Prevention (CDC) reported that the majority of HIV infections existed among young girls ages 13–19 years (61%).[49]

Adults are not doing enough to educate youth on the risks of HIV/AIDS, and obviously this is especially the case for minority youths who disproportionately contract the disease (through sexual contact or through blood transfusions from the birth mother). Research suggests that part of the problem could be because AIDS continues to be presented as a primarily homosexual disease in sex education curricula in schools.[50]

Stigma of HIV/AIDS for Youth

With advances in the treatment of HIV, many more babies born with HIV live to be teens. Before the mid-1990s, children with HIV lived to an average age of 9 years. Since 1996, the average age has risen to 15 years and is still going up. Further, according to the CDC, many teens have contracted it through blood transfusions. Thus, it is critical that teens not only be taught about how to avoid the disease through appropriate decision making but also be taught that HIV/AIDS is a faultless disease and that learning how to live with it is as important as learning how to avoid it. This is especially critical for developing youth.

Teens infected with HIV have to live with the stigma of a disease many do not know how to talk about. For teens born with HIV, the challenges are even harder when they have to watch their mothers die of AIDS. The typical teen stressors associated with dating and sexual exploration are compounded in teens with HIV, who must struggle with whether and how to disclose their disease to potential partners. Uninfected teens may fear rejection because of acne or large ears—HIV-positive teens fear rejection and taunting because of their disease. According to one 17-year-old, "I kept it to myself because it's none of anybody's business. I don't care what people think really, but I hear what they say about people. I hear them talking about girls who got pregnant, saying they like to sleep with so many men. I got this thing from my mother, but still, can you imagine what they'd say about me?"[51]

Alternative Lifestyles: Teenage Homosexuality

The risks associated with sexual encounters (pregnancy, STDs, and AIDS) are more complicated for youths who have alternative sexual lifestyles. Some estimates suggest that approximately 10% of teens identify themselves as gay, lesbian, bisexual, transgender, or questioning their sexuality (GLBTQ). The culture in which GLBTQ youths live has changed considerably since the Stonewall uprising in New York City in 1969—with the most pronounced changes occurring in the past decade.[52] There are more visible gay characters on TV and in films (such as *Will and Grace* and *The Birdcage*) and more legislation that acknowledges the civil rights of homosexual lifestyles (with the 2003 Supreme Court decision to eradicate anti-sodomy laws perhaps one of the most significant to date). Youth, too, have become more accepting of their homosexual peers. Whereas in 1991, 17% of teens said they had no problem with homosexuality, 54% of teens in 1999 reportedly had no problem with homosexuality; only 39% said it made them uncomfortable, and 15% said they had actually fooled around with someone of the same sex.[53]

Despite greater acceptance of their sexual preferences, GLBTQ teens continue to face difficulties because of their sexuality. GLBTQ youths are subject to harsher stigmatization than heterosexual teens (see Fig. 4.1), making an already confusing part of their identity development (How do I approach a love interest? How will I know if it is safe to approach someone?) even more difficult.[54] It is no coincidence that GLBTQ teens are 3 to 4 times more likely to commit suicide than their heterosexual peers.[55] Their chances for acceptance, although better today than 30 years ago, continue to be hampered by discrimination on the basis of sexual orientation or gen-

1. Gay/lesbian adolescents are subject to the "assumption of heterosexuality," of feeling "guilty until proven innocent" in the social arena to invert our legal principle.

2. Because they are not heterosexual, these teenagers are, therefore, assumed to be "inverts," according to our cultural presumption of the inversion.

3. They are, then, stigmatized as persons, which oppression has real-life consequences for their development and adaptation.

4. Finally, as homosexuals, they are subject to the assumption of homogeneity: the idea that gays and lesbians the *world over* are the same in "coming out" experience, identity, and cultural organization.

Note. From "Gay and Lesbian Youth, Emergent Identities, and Cultural Scenes at Home and Abroad," by G. Herdt, 1998, in P. M. Nardi and B. E. Schneider (Eds.), *Social Perspectives in Lesbian and Gay Studies: A Reader* (p. 280), New York: Routledge. Copyright 1998 by Routledge. Reprinted with permission.

FIG. 4.1.   Four ways homosexual teens are stigmatized.

der identity, a type of discrimination tolerated by too many citizens and institutions. To give just one example, the military is notorious for forcing homosexuals out of service.[56]

Society continues to communicate intolerance for sexual differences through legislation and reaction to discrimination-based hate crimes. Consider the U.S. Supreme Court's ruling that the Boy Scouts are justified in their discriminatory practices against a gay Boy Scout leader. In light of the organization's good reputation and rich history of positively impacting the lives of many young boys, it is incredible that the Boy Scouts of America condones outright discrimination against any group. Sadly, this stance by the Boy Scouts sends a message of intolerance to any and all youths who might identify themselves as gay, lesbian, or bisexual—a message with potentially harmful effects.[57] The 1998 slaying of young, gay college student, Mathew Shepard, is a notable example of how hatred and intolerance of alternative sexuality can escalate to deadly levels.[58] And unfortunately these acts of hate are not isolated, rare cases. In Tucson, Arizona (presumed to be a moderately tolerant community), more than 50% of 1999 reported hate crimes were against gay and lesbian community members.[59]

Still, things are getting better for the "invisible minority."[60] Hate crimes legislation is being passed in states and communities around the nation, and many communities, in response to the Boy Scouts ruling, are coming together to promote an organized ban against the Boy Scouts. For example, in Tucson, Arizona, city board officials unanimously voted to stop giving funds to the United Way—a primary supporter of the Boy Scouts. And some schools and other institutions refused to let the Boy Scouts meet in their facilities. Finally, many older Eagle Scouts handed in their coveted badges in protest against the Boy Scouts's policy of barring homosexual leaders from the organization.

Evidence suggests that education can affect school climate and increase tolerance for sexual diversity. In one large-scale survey in Massachusetts, researchers found that students' attitudes toward GLBTQ youths were more tolerant after the students participated in a program promoting sexual diversity and acceptance. Education can also reduce some of the dangers faced more frequently by GLBTQ youths. The GLBTQ population is at higher risk for substance use, high-risk sexual behaviors, suicidal thoughts or attempts, and personal safety issues than their heterosexual peers. Yet in Massachusetts, GLBTQ youths who attended schools that promoted gay-sensitive HIV training had fewer sexual partners, less recent sex, and less substance use before their last sexual experience than did GLBTQ youth who attended schools without sensitivity training.[61] More programs should be created to address the numerous risk factors associated with a sexually diverse youth culture and high quality research must be conducted to illuminate program strengths and weaknesses.

SEX EDUCATION

Where should American youth get information about sex? If you ask teens, most of them say they want to learn about sex from their parents. If you ask parents, most of them say they want their children to learn about sex from the schools. However, if you ask policymakers and religious rights organizations, they say that youth should not get any information about sex (except from their parents). President Bush has called for increased allocation of funds to schools that promote an abstinence-only approach to sex. This policy glaringly contradicts the desires of both teens and their parents by favoring a program built on the assumption (an assumption based on no empirical data) that abstinence is the best choice for all youth.[62] Further, it denies youth needed information about what to do if they become pregnant or are raped. Tragically, in some places where safe havens have been created (i.e., hospitals that accept babies within the first 48 hours of life without questioning or prosecuting mothers), teens are still not informed of these opportunities and abort babies who could otherwise have been saved.

What Most Citizens Want, What Many Politicians Do Not

Historically, parents have not wanted schools to teach human sexuality because they believed that sex education classes would promote the sexual behavior of students. These beliefs have changed remarkably—perhaps because of the mounting evidence showing no relationship between sex information and sexual behavior. For example, in Massachusetts, a study looking at the sexual activity of teens attending two different schools revealed that students at schools that provide condoms are no more likely—

and in fact are slightly less likely—to have had sex in the past 3 months than teens at schools without condom availability.[63]

Current data indicate that parents not only want schools to teach their children about sex, but also they want sex education to be more frequent and more comprehensive.[64] Most parents even want schools to teach the core elements of sex education (HIV/AIDS, 98%; other STDs, such as herpes, 98%; the basics of pregnancy and birth, 90%; and abstinence, 97%). A large majority also want schools to teach topics that historically few schools have discussed—homosexuality and sexual orientation (76%) or what to do if you or a friend is sexually assaulted (97%). In addition, parents want schools to teach their children how to talk with them about sex and their relationships. Parents are strongly urging schools to help them (and their children) communicate more effectively with one another about sexuality.

A 2003 survey of youth and parents confirmed that adolescents and their parents want (and need) more information about sex. When asked what are the biggest concerns facing 15- to 17-year-olds today, an overwhelming majority of both parents (88%) and teens (88%) reported that sexual health issues (such as STDs, HIV, and pregnancy) were the biggest problems, above sexual violence or other physical violence; drug use; discrimination because of race, ethnicity, or sexual orientation; excessive drinking or smoking; or depression or other mental illness.

The Surgeon General's Report

The surgeon general's 2001 report on the sexual health of Americans represents a vital yet highly politicized comment on the importance of addressing the sexual health of all Americans (see Fig. 4.2). Specifically, the report described the effectiveness of programs on youth sexual health. In an exploratory comparison of abstinence-only versus comprehensive sexual health education programs, the report found abstinence-only approaches to be ineffective and so diverse in content emphasis that it is difficult to even establish what the core program components are.

The publication of the report sparked renewed national debate over the role of sex education in schools. Not surprisingly, after its release, members of the Bush administration distanced themselves from the report because of its suggestions for addressing the sexual health of American youth. Church-based conservative groups vilified the report as "ideology disguised as science from the beginning to end."[65] Despite the political heat around the surgeon general's recommendations, many youth advocacy groups were empowered by its recommendations for frank discussions with youth about sexual health. These recommendations were also backed by national polls that documented parents' desire for schools to be more involved in their children's sexual education.[66]

- STDs infect approximately 12 million persons each year.
- 774,467 AIDS cases, nearly two thirds of which were sexually transmitted, have been reported since 1981.
- An estimated 800,000 to 900,000 persons are living with HIV.
- An estimated one third of those living with HIV are aware of their status and are in treatment, one third are aware but not in treatment, and one third have not been tested and are not aware.
- An estimated 40,000 new HIV infections occur each year.
- The AIDS epidemic is shifting toward women. Whereas women account for 28 percent of HIV cases reported since 1981, they accounted for 32 percent of those reported between July 1999 and June 2000. Similarly, women account for 17% of AIDS cases reported since 1981, but 24% of those reported between July 1999 and June 2000.
- An estimated 1,366,000 induced abortions occurred in 1996.
- Nearly one half of pregnancies are unintended. Unintended pregnancy is not only medically costly, it is also socially costly in terms of out-of-wedlock births, reduced educational attainment and employment opportunity, increased welfare dependency, and later child abuse and neglect.
- An estimated 22% of women and 2% of men have been victims of rape.
- An estimated 104,000 children are victims of sexual abuse each year, and the proportion of women in current relationships who are subject to sexual violence is estimated at 8%.
- In their extreme form, antihomosexual attitudes lead to antigay violence. Averaged over two dozen studies, 80% of gay men and lesbians had experienced verbal or physical harassment on the basis of their orientation, 45% had been threatened with violence, and 17% had experienced a physical attack.

Note. From *The Surgeon General's Call to Action to Promote Sexual Health and Responsible Behavior*, by U.S. Department of Health and Human Services, 2001, Washington, DC: Author.

FIG. 4.2. Sexual health in the United States as reported by the surgeon general.

Findings of the Surgeon General's Report: Sex Education Exists in Many Forms

Currently, about 89% of schools nationwide teach some form of sex education; however, curricula vary widely. Most schools commit to one of two main philosophies, labeled comprehensive or abstinence-only. Most teachers (61%) and principals (58%) report that their school's main message about sex is comprehensive—young people should wait to have sex, but if they don't, they should use birth control and practice safe sex. In contrast, a minority of teachers (33%) and principals (34%) report that their schools promote an abstinence-only approach—young people should only have sex when they are married.

A large majority of teachers and students report that their schools cover core elements of sex education independent of the model implemented (e.g., abstinence-only and comprehensive). Core elements that students and teachers generally agree are covered include HIV/AIDS, STDs other than HIV/AIDS (such as herpes), the basics of reproduction, and abstinence. Topics covered in addition to the core elements of sex education include birth control, abortion, sexual orientation, and negotiation skills (e.g., how to talk to a partner about birth control, how to talk to someone about a rape or sexual assault). Unfortunately, these other topics are covered much less frequently, and more unevenly, across schools nationwide.

What Is Abstinence? Sex education programs vary in how they are implemented, in part because there is disagreement as to how to define *sex* and *abstinence*. Although many abstinence-only approaches do not include lessons about safe sex practices, some do. Fifty-one percent of abstinence-only programs provide information about how to use and where to get birth control (other than a condom), and 10% specifically discuss condom use. Some abstinence-only approaches include discussions about STDs and HIV/AIDS but without informing students on methods to stay protected from these risks. It is arguably confusing for youth to hear such conflicting messages. On the one hand, youth are told not to even think about having sex. On the other hand, they are informed of STDs and life-threatening HIV but then are not told how to stay protected. Ultimately, if sex education programs are spotty in their coverage, youth may be left to figure it out among themselves.

What Is Sex? Comprehensive approaches aren't necessarily any clearer. Thirty-seven percent of students who attended schools that boasted a comprehensive approach reported that information about how to use and where to get birth control was not included, and 28% said that condom use was not discussed. Discussions about sex are notably varied. For example, schools may report that they teach students about condoms, but it isn't clear how condoms are discussed. Some schools may simply inform students to "wear a condom" for protection against STDs and pregnancy. In contrast, other schools may provide students with detailed information on how to choose a condom, how to put it on in the dark, and how to address condom use with a partner.

Implementation of Sex Education

Students, parents, principals, and teachers generally agree that all aspects of sex education, including birth control and safer sex, should be delayed until high school grades. However, some believe that some information is appropriate for seventh and eighth graders or even fifth and sixth graders. More parents want sex education to be taught to boys and girls separately

(54%) than want it taught together (40%). And more think it should be taught for at least half a semester or a quarter (27%) than think it should be confined to one class period or several class periods or special sessions (26%) or for an entire semester or quarter (21%).

What is lacking in this data is authoritative information about the content and form of sex education curricula. Data suggest that education focusing on the future can be a powerful way to communicate to youth—especially teens with few opportunities—about options other than early pregnancy. An evaluation of an after-school program instituted in high-poverty neighborhoods suggests that quality sex education supplemented by job tutoring, SAT preparation, and other life-building skills training can positively impact the sexual attitudes and behaviors of youth.[67] Providing youth with skills and a more positive outlook on life reduced the pregnancy rate by one third (when compared with a control group who did not receive the program intervention). Notably, the pregnancy rates for girls were cut in half, whereas it actually increased for boys (i.e., boys continued to father babies at high rates). When girls receive job training they are introduced to options other than becoming a mother at a young age.

Students Lack Critical Information

Regardless of whether they have actually had sex, students are knowledgeable about some areas of sexuality yet extremely uninformed about others. Although many students know that a teenage girl can get pregnant the first time she has sex (88%), fewer understand that youth under 18 can get birth control without parental permission (48%), or that a doctor's prescription is needed to buy birth control pills (72%), or that emergency contraceptive pills can be taken after unprotected sex (40%). Students also want more information about what to do if you or a friend has been raped (56%), or how to get tested for HIV/AIDS or other STDs (53%), or how to talk to parents about sex and relationship issues (48%).

Promising Solutions

In a review of research on effective programs targeting teen sex and pregnancy, Douglas Kirby[68] differentiated effective programs that targeted teenage sex and sexuality according to their primary focus.[69] These included a focus on either sexual behavioral antecedents, nonsexual behavioral antecedents, or a focus on both. Programs that focused on sexual behavioral antecedents included school-based programs that incorporated discussion about concrete behaviors (such as how to say no or how to ask a partner to use a condom). These programs also promoted skill building, included a strong social support component, and were sensitive to peer relationships by promoting positive social norms. Studies of programs with this focus suggest that they increase individual efficacy and can lead to reduced teen pregnancy rates.

Programs that focused on nonsexual behavioral antecedents can also be effective and include after-school, service-learning activities. Studies on these types of programs result in increased achievement and lower rates of pregnancy. One especially promising program that includes both sexual and nonsexual behavioral antecedent components is the Children's Aid Society Carrera Program. Research on this program shows delayed initiation of sex among girls, increased contraception use, and decreased pregnancy and birth rates for up to 3 years.[70] Thus, we have the tools and knowledge for affecting teen sexual health. But the critical issue is to convince policymakers to invest in data-driven programs rather than supporting ineffective abstinence-focused ones.

CONCLUSION

Sexuality dominates our culture, figuring prominently in cultural products, including books, movies, television, and advertising. The prevalent message that sexuality is desirable for youth as well as adults conflicts with cultural mores that say youth should delay sexual activity until maturity. But like many forbidden fruits, sex is attractive, and youth will inevitably open the gate to sexual activity though the age for opening this gate varies widely within society. Parents and many other adults—especially policymakers— seem to want to deny sexual information to teens, even though such data might help youth to prevent health problems or even death. Withholding information and medical treatment (e.g., abortions) may have terrible consequences for them, their children, and the broader society. It seems especially unfortunate to deny today's teens information, when they appear to be handling sexuality better than teens in the recent past.

More than 1 in 10 girls who first have sex prior to age 15 years describe it as nonvoluntary or relatively unwanted.[71] Therefore, it is necessary to better inform not only young women but also young men and their parents about the predatory behavior of older men. Principles of public health education suggest that it is wise to teach youth the issues involved in sexual practices and diseases and how to handle these situations when they arise. Although some youths get this information from TV, it seems ludicrous not to let children and teens know they can seek help from adults when they find themselves in abusive relationships with adults. Failure to help children protect themselves, physically and emotionally, from potentially harmful sexual situations of any kind has tragic consequences for youth and the broader society.

The facts are relatively straightforward: Teens want information about sex and prefer to obtain it from their parents. Parents feel awkward in discussing these issues and increasingly want schools to supplement, if not replace, their role in discussions of sexuality. According to Dr. Bruce Bagley, chairman of the board of the American Academy of Family Physicians, "The only way we're going to change approaches to sexual behavior and sexual activity is through school. In school, not only at the doctor's office."[72] Oddly, despite the overwhelming support from parents and physicians for sex education in the schools, many policymakers are determined to prevent such programs or to restrict the range of content included in them.

How can schools best provide sex education and introduce it early in the curricula? There is considerable debate on these questions. Since younger teens (and even children) have sex, should more explicit sex education come as early as the elementary grades? We think so. What should sex education look like in these grades? As in other areas of life, students are often exposed to increased sexual standards. Although it is unlikely that anyone would want to stop friends from hugging in public places (e.g., a PTA meeting), students in some schools are actually expected not to hug in school.[73] And in some schools, an elementary-aged boy can get expelled for kissing a female classmate on the cheek because it is considered to be sexual harassment. What are the standards for appropriate behavior, how consistently are they monitored, and what are appropriate sanctions? These are important questions schools must address. We believe that the earlier issues of intimacy are discussed, the better.

General Considerations

Although youth of past generations were exposed to their fair share of sexualized media, the scope, intensity, and explicitness of sex in the world has never been as great as they are today. Today's youth live in a world riddled with images of sexuality—images explicitly paired with consumerism. And sexual content in the media is not only becoming increasingly more explicit, but it is also being aimed at younger people.

Teens are clearly not going to stop seeking information about sex. So the question for policymakers and parents is, where do they want teens to learn about sexuality? From parents, schools, or well-conceived educational materials? Or from peers, the Internet, or pornography? Ignoring the need for sex education programs in schools and elsewhere has clear costs: death, STDs, and unwanted pregnancy. Ironically, the same political agenda that wants to limit sex education programs also champions parents' rights for charter schools and voucher programs to make schools more responsive to parental values.

Perhaps the most salient dilemma is that the presence of sex in society has never been greater, yet the delay between puberty and adulthood has never been longer. Teens in 1903 commonly were married by age 16 years; now the average age for young adults to marry is about 26 years. Adults who advocate abstinence are asking today's teens, who biologically experience puberty at younger ages than ever, to wait a decade longer to have sex than did teens in the past.

We should be more alarmed about reckless sex among youth than about sex that is between two loving individuals. The insensitive, too-casual nature of sexual relations among some youth demonstrates a lack of intimacy that may be a predictor of future loveless, unfulfilling relationships. Our current divorce rate reflects in part the unstable nature of many adult sexual relationships.[74] In one sense, what teens need most is more knowledge about the pleasurable aspects of mutually shared sexuality, a message presently provided to only a few teens (mostly boys). For a variety of reasons, some cultural and some political, society actively works to prevent youth from getting useful information about sexuality.

Media have always provided one avenue for youth to gain sexual knowledge. Despite criticisms of the blatant sexuality in the current media, it can be argued that one cultural duty of the media is to educate the public about certain forms of sexuality that may cause death (e.g., AIDS) and about abuse of younger children, which is at horrifying levels.

Most parents want schools to provide comprehensive sex education courses, and the surgeon general issued recommendations for sex education programs that address parents' and students' interests. Still, some parents—and many policymakers—oppose school-based sex education programs, contending that they encourage sexual behavior. Importantly, data supporting this contention is weak[75] and typically correlational in nature.

Needed Research

Development and evaluation of programs that teach adolescent boys how to prevent pregnancies is needed. Existing programs need to be modified—some appear effective for girls, but they are largely ineffectual for boys. Fathers in general feel differently about the chastity of their daughters than they did about the chastity of their wives before marriage. What causes these developmental shifts in perspectives, and can young boys be helped to develop more prosocial attitudes about shared responsibility for sexual behavior?

Given the enormous impact of advertising in American culture, it would make sense to use advertisements to get sexual health messages out quickly and succinctly. One advertising campaign in Arizona that targets youth's condom use through the slogan "Use Condom Sense" is seen as a contributing factor in the decisions of the 64% of sexually active teens who say they always use condoms during sex. As part of the campaign, youths are used as models. In one advertisement, a young, 15-year-old girl sits inside a bus holding a condom and relating the importance of condom use.[76] (This ad should remind us that sometimes peer advice has more credibility than advice given by an adult.[77]) More studies are needed to better understand when and how to use peers as effective sources of information about safe sex.

Clearly, the United States can learn teen-pregnancy prevention methods from other industrialized societies. As noted earlier, the United States leads the world in teenage pregnancies. What factors in other countries—education, social norms, and so on—serve to sharply reduce teenage pregnancies? Comparative research on this point could yield rich dividends.

If better programs are to be developed to teach students positive and negative aspects of sexuality, more research is needed into the questions and misconceptions that students, especially younger ones, have about sex. Special attention should be given to language, concepts, and activities that are appropriate for young students. Especially important is further consideration of when and how to teach issues of sexuality in single-gender and mixed-gender settings. Table 4.1 outlines the surgeon general's vision for the future of educating Americans about sexual health. This tripartite vision includes awareness, intervention, and research as its core components. The report stridently calls for more resources to be directed toward communities, schools, and educators to ensure the availability of programs for all individuals. Additionally, the report calls for increased empirical attention to evaluating sexual health interventions. We believe this is a good first step in acknowledging how crucial it is to address teen sex and sexuality in this rapidly changing society.

ENDNOTES

1. Albert, B., Brown, S., & Flanigan, C. (Eds.). (2003). *14 and younger: The sexual behavior of young adolescents* [Summary]. Washington, DC: National Campaign to Prevent Teen Pregnancy.

2. Altman, L. K. (2002, July 3). U.N. forecasts big increase in AIDS death toll. *New York Times*, p. 3.

3. Quoted in Schemo, D. J. (2001, June 29). Surgeon general's report calls for sex education beyond abstinence courses. *New York Times*, p. A14.

4. A primary stage of identity development, according to Erik Erikson, a notable developmental theorist, is to achieve a balance between a sense of isolation and intimacy. See Erikson, E. (1968). *Identity: Youth and crisis*. New York: Norton. Although Erikson believes the struggle for intimacy to be a primary aspect of identity development for older teens, others have suggested that the search for intimacy in teens is a precursor to the identity struggle. See Gilligan, C. (1982). *In a different voice: Psychological theory and women's development*. Cambridge, MA: Harvard University Press.

TABLE 4.1
Risk and Protective Factors for Sexual Health

Risk	Protective
Family—Adolescents living with a single parent or in homes with older siblings (especially when older siblings have sex or older sisters get pregnant) are more likely to have sex. For girls, sexual abuse as a child is linked to increased risk of pregnancy. Excessive parental control is associated with intercourse.	**Family**—Adolescents whose parents have higher education and income, and who have warm relationships with their parents, are more likely to postpone sexual intercourse and to use contraception if they do engage in sexual intercourse.
Schools—Dropping out is associated with a higher likelihood to initiate sexual activity earlier, failure to use contraception, pregnancy, and birth.	**Schools**—Higher school attendance, and for some the completion of elementary school, is associated with decreased adolescent birth rates. Greater involvement with school athletics is associated with lower birth rates and less sexual risk taking (later age of initiation of sex, lower frequency of sex, pregnancy, and childbearing).
Community—Defined by geography, ethnicity, socioeconomic status, and cultural beliefs, community is associated with sexual risk taking based on several factors. Communities that are more organized, and which offer more opportunities, are generally associated with fewer pregnancies, abortions, and STDs.	**Community**—Organized communities and those with opportunity and structure are associated with fewer risk-taking sexual behaviors, STDs, abortions, and unwanted pregnancies. Similarly, the rigidness of community members (how willing they are to talk about sex) is associated with lowered levels of sexual risk taking.
Religion—No known association with sexual risk taking behavior.	**Religion**—No known association with sexual risk taking behavior.

Note. From *The Surgeon General's Call to Action to Promote Sexual Health and Responsible Behavior,* by U.S. Department of Health and Human Services, 2001, Washington, DC: Author.

5. As evidenced by increased legislation to abstinence-only model programs. See a review of legislation published in Devaney, B., Johnson, A., Maynard, R., & Trenholm, C. (2002). *The evaluation of abstinence education programs funded under Title V Section 510: Interim Report.* Princeton, NJ: Mathematica Policy Research.

6. Consider the movie *Kids,* which portrays 24 hours in the lives of a group of teens who do nothing but think about and have sex, do drugs, and engage in violence. This is an especially gratuitous portrayal of the sex drive of teens.

7. One researcher discusses the problem with how our culture defines *teen pregnancy* that doesn't allow for a broader understanding of the role that pregnancy and motherhood play in the school careers and future roles of low-income women of color. Mainstream portrayal of pregnancy is monolithic and insensitive to the diversity of the teen population. See Schultz, K. (2001). Constructing failure, narrating success: Rethinking the "problem" of teen pregnancy. *Teachers College Record, 103*(4), 582–607.

8. A recent report by the Centers for Disease Control and Prevention states that there has been a decrease in the percentage of youth who report having had sexual intercourse, from 54.1% in 1991 to 45.6% in 2001. Brener, N., et al. (2002). Trends in sexual risk be-

haviors among high school students—United States, 1991–2001. *Morbidity & Mortality Weekly Report, 51*(38), 856–859. Data released by the National Campaign to Prevent Teen Pregnancy show that rates of initial sex experiences of younger youth (ages 12–14 years) is increasing. Albert, B., Brown, S., & Flanigan, C. (Eds.). (2003). *14 and younger: The sexual behavior of young adolescents* [Summary]. Washington, DC: National Campaign to Prevent Teen Pregnancy.

9. A 2002 poll sponsored by the Kaiser Family Foundation shows that many teens learn something about sex and sexually related decisions from TV. See Kaiser Family Foundation. (2002). *Teens, sex, and TV.* (Available online at http://www.kff.org/)

10. See Kaiser Family Foundation. (2002). *Teens, sex, and TV.* (Available online at http://www.kff.org/)

11. See Hoff, T., Greene, L., & Davis, J. (2003). *National survey of adolescents and young adults: Sexual health knowledge, attitudes and experiences.* Menlo Park, CA: Kaiser Family Foundation. (Available online at http://www.kff.org/)

12. Recent policy initiatives sought to invest millions in abstinence-only training opportunities. For example, in 1996, Congress authorized $50 million annually for 5 years to promote abstinence education; for every $4, states must match with $3, resulting in $87.5 million available annually to abstinence programs. A review of the research on these programs suggests that abstinence-only approaches have little effect on youth's sexual behavior. Devaney, B., Johnson, A., Maynard, R., & Trenholm, C. (2002). *The evaluation of abstinence education programs funded under Title V Section 510: Interim Report.* Princeton, NJ: Mathematica Policy Research.

13. Hoff, T., & Greene, L. (2000). *Sex education in America: A view from inside the nation's classrooms.* Menlo Park, CA: Kaiser Family Foundation. (Available online at http://www.kff.org/); see also Hoff, T., Greene, L., & Davis, J. (2003). *National survey of adolescents and young adults: Sexual health knowledge, attitudes and experiences.* Menlo Park, CA: Kaiser Family Foundation. (Available online at http://www.kff.org/)

14. Hoff, T., & Greene, L. (2000). *Sex education in America: A view from inside the nation's classrooms.* Menlo Park, CA: Kaiser Family Foundation. (Available online at http://www.kff.org/)

15. Hoff, T., & Greene, L. (2000). *Sex education in America: A view from inside the nation's classrooms.* Menlo Park, CA: Kaiser Family Foundation. (Available online at http://www.kff.org/)

16. Of course, it could be that these parents' voices are not widely heard.

17. Darroch, J. E., Frost, J. J., Singh, S., & the Study Team (2001). *Teenage sexual and reproductive behavior in developed countries: Can progress be made?* (Occasional Report No. 3). New York: Alan Guttmacher Institute. Retrieved January 25, 2002, from http://www.agi-usa.org/pubs/eurosynth_rpt.pdf

18. From *The surgeon general's call to action to promote sexual health and responsible behavior.* (2001). Washington, DC: U.S. Department of Health and Human Services. Retrieved January 16, 2002, from http://www.surgeongeneral.gov/library/sexualhealth/

19. According to one study, there are approximately 65,000 instances of sexual material per year on TV during the afternoon hours of 12:30–4:00. See Alali, O. A. (1991). *Mass media sex and adolescent values: An annotated bibliography and directory of organizations.* Jefferson, NC: McFarland & Company. This study was done before the advent of the Internet and satellite television and therefore before access to a wide range of television programming dramatically increased. Thus, it is probable that these estimates are conservative by today's standards.

20. See Kaiser Family Foundation (2002). *Teens, sex, and TV.* (Available online at http://www.kff.org/)

21. The movie *West Side Story* depicts the nuances of teenage love and sexual angst. And there are numerous other examples, including in the 1999 Academy Award–winning film *Titanic*, which shows the struggles of class differences; the movie *The Man Who Came to Dinner* and the television show *The Jeffersons*, each depicting the complexities of interracial relationships; the show *Six Feet Under*, which illustrates the complexities of homosexual relationships; and the Tony Award–winning Broadway show *Aida*, which tells the story of a prince falling in love with a princess of another culture.

22. Landry, D. J., & Forrest, J. D. (1995). How old are U.S. fathers? *Family Planning Perspectives, 27*(4), 159–161.

23. Associated Press. (2002, March 11). Booze, skin rule as spring break overtakes Cancun. *Arizona Daily Star*, p. A8.

24. Teenage prostitution ring broken in Detroit. (2003, January 16). *New York Times*.

25. Gallup Short Subjects. (1998, September). *The Gallup poll monthly* (No. 396, Survey GP 9809035 QW. 15), p. 47.

26. Remez, L. (2000). Oral sex among adolescents: Is it sex or is it abstinence? *Family Planning Perspectives, 32*(6), 298–304. Also, on May 20, 2003, on National Public Radio's *Talk of the Nation* program, Sarah Brown, coeditor of the National Campaign to Prevent Teen Pregnancy's report titled, *14 and Younger: The Sexual Behavior of Young Adolescents*, discussed the challenges of collecting data from younger youth on sensitive topics such as homosexuality and oral sex.

27. Gates, G. J., & Sonenstein, F. L. (2000). Heterosexual genital sexual activity among adolescent males: 1988 and 1995. *Family Planning Perspectives, 32*(6), 295–297, 304.

28. Annie E. Casey Foundation. (1998). *When teens have sex: Issues and trends. Kids Count Special Report*. Washington, DC: Author. (Available online at http://www.aecf.org/)

29. Gates, G. J., & Sonenstein, F. L. (2000). Heterosexual genital sexual activity among adolescent males: 1988 and 1995. *Family Planning Perspectives, 32*(6), 295–297, 304; see also Annie E. Casey Foundation. (1998). *When teens have sex: Issues and trends. Kids Count Special Report*. Washington, DC: Author. (Available online at http://www.aecf.org/)

30. Annie E. Casey Foundation. (1998). *When teens have sex: Issues and trends. Kids Count Special Report*. Washington, DC: Author. (Available online at http//www.aecf.org/)

31. This, of course, provides a strong argument for beginning school-based sex education programs at earlier ages.

32. Terry, E., & Manlove, J. (2000). *Trends in sexual activity and contraceptive use among teens*. Washington, DC: National Campaign to Prevent Teen Pregnancy.

33. See Hoff, T., Greene, L., & Davis, J. (2003). *National survey of adolescents and young adults: Sexual health knowledge, attitudes and experiences*. Menlo Park, CA: Kaiser Family Foundation. (Available online at http://www.kff.org/)

34. Remez, L. (2000). Oral sex among adolescents: Is it sex or is it abstinence? *Family Planning Perspectives, 32*(6), 298–304; Lewin, T. (2000, December 19). Survey shows sex practices of boys. *New York Times*, p. A22; Ponton, L. (2000). *The sex lives of teenagers: Revealing the secret world of adolescent boys and girls*. New York: Dutton; Jarrell, A. (2000, April 2). The face of teenage sex grows younger. *New York Times*, p. B1.

35. Lewin, T. (2000, December 19). Survey shows sex practices of boys. *New York Times*, p. A22; Gates, Gary J., & Sonenstein, F. L. (2000). Heterosexual genital sexual activity among adolescent males: 1988 and 1995. *Family Planning Perspectives, 32*(6), 295–297, 304.

36. Jarrell, A. (2000, April 2). The face of teenage sex grows younger. *New York Times*, p. B1.

37. From *The surgeon general's call to action to promote sexual health and responsible behavior*. (2001, July). Washington, DC: U.S. Department of Health and Human Services. Retrieved January 16, 2002, from http://www.surgeongeneral.gov/library/sexualhealth/

38. For example, see http://landview.census.gov/hhes/www/childsupport/chldsu97.html for statistics on child support payments to custodial mothers, based on ages of mothers.

39. For example, Brown, S., & Eisenberg, L. (Eds.). (1995). *The best intentions: Unintended pregnancy and the well-being of children and families.* Washington, DC: National Academy Press; National Campaign to Prevent Teen Pregnancy. (1997). *Whatever happened to childhood? The problem of teen pregnancy in the United States.* Washington, DC: Author; Sawhill, I. V. (1998). *Teen pregnancy prevention: Welfare reform's missing component.* Washington, DC: Brookings (*Brookings Policy Brief, 38*), 1–8; Carnegie Task Force on Meeting the Needs of Children. (1994). *Starting points: Meeting the needs of our youngest children.* New York: Author; Maynard, R. (Ed). (1997). *Kids having kids: A Robin Hood Foundation special report on the costs of adolescent childbearing.* New York: Robin Hood Foundation. See also George, R. M., & Lee, B. J. (1997). Abuse and neglect of the children. In R. A. Maynard (Ed.), *Kids having kids: Economic costs and social consequences of teen pregnancy.* Washington, DC: Urban Institute Press.

40. Teenage birth rates declined significantly from 1991–2000. See Ventura, S. J., Mathews, T. J., & Hamilton, B. E. (2002). Teenage births in the United States: State trends, 1991–2000, an update. *National Vital Statistics Reports, 50*(9). (Available online at http://www.cdc.gov/nchs/data/nvsr/nvsr50/nvsr50_09.pdf); the CDC also reports a decline in teen pregnancy rates. See Centers for Disease Control and Prevention (2000). National and state-specific pregnancy rates among adolescents—United States, 1995–1997. *Morbidity and Mortality Weekly Report, 49*(27). (Available online at http://www.cdc.gov/mmwr/PDF/wk/mm4927.pdf); Pitt, D. (2000, July 14). National teen-pregnancy rate continues downward trend. *Arizona Daily Star,* p. A14.

41. Annie E. Casey Foundation. (1998). *When teens have sex: Issues and trends. Kids Count Special Report.* Washington, DC: Author. (Available online at http//www.aecf.org/)

42. Annie E. Casey Foundation. (1998). *When teens have sex: Issues and trends. Kids Count Special Report.* Washington, DC: Author. (Available online at http//www.aecf.org/)

43. Johnes, R. K., Darroch, J. E., & Henshaw, S. T. (2002). Patterns in the socioeconomic characteristics of women obtaining abortions in 2000–2001. *Perspectives on Sexual and Reproductive Health, 34*(5), 226–235.

44. From *The surgeon general's call to action to promote sexual health and responsible behavior.* (2001). Washington, DC: U.S. Department of Health and Human Services. Retrieved January 16, 2002, from http://www.surgeongeneral.gov/library/sexualhealth/

45. For more information on which states have parental consent laws, see: http://www.plannedparenthood.org/library/ABORTION/StateLaws.html

46. From *The surgeon general's call to action to promote sexual health and responsible behavior.* (2001). Washington, DC: U.S. Department of Health and Human Services. Retrieved January 16, 2002, from http://www.surgeongeneral.gov/library/sexualhealth/

47. Herbert, B. (2001, January 11). The quiet scourge. *New York Times,* p. A31.

48. Herbert, B. (2001, January 11). The quiet scourge. *New York Times,* p. A31.

49. Based on a 2002 fact sheet released by the CDC. See http://www.cdc.gov/hiv/pubs/facts/youth.pdf

50. Fine, M. (1993). Sexuality, schooling, and adolescent females: The missing discourse of desire. In L. Weis & M. Find (Eds.), *Beyond silenced voices: Class, race and gender in U.S. schools* (pp. 75–100). Albany, NY: State University of New York Press.

51. Villarosa, L. (2001, November 20). A new generation: Teenagers living with H.I.V. *New York Times,* p. F7.

52. For example, there are increasing numbers of high schools that have adopted Gay-Straight Alliance (GSA) clubs where any member of the school can join to participate in the dialogue of tolerance. Over the past decade, approximately seven GSAs have opened

up in southwest Arizona. Anecdotal evidence from students who helped to organize these clubs throughout one southwestern city have reported that the existence of such a club has made it easier to come out and feel supported as a gay, lesbian, bisexual, or transgendered teen. Thus, there have been marked changes in some high schools throughout the nation. Unfortunately, there are many schools in which extreme forms of intolerance and hatred exist.

53. Hoff, T., & Greene, L. (2000). *Sex education in America: A view from inside the nation's classrooms.* Menlo Park, CA: Kaiser Family Foundation. (Available online at http://www.kff. org/)

54. Nichols, S. (1999). Gay, lesbian, and bisexual youth: Understanding diversity and promoting tolerance in schools. *Elementary School Journal, 99*(5), 505–519.

55. Remafedi, G., Farrow, J., & Deisher, R. (1991). Risk factors for attempted suicide in gay and bisexual youth. *Pediatrics, 87*(6), 868–875; Rotheram-borus, M., Hunter, J., & Rosario, M. (1994). Suicidal behavior and gay-related stress among gay and bisexual male adolescents. *Journal of Adolescent Research, 9*(4), 498–508.

56. Associated Press. (2002, March 15). Military gay dismissals highest since '87. *Arizona Daily Star*, p. A15.

57. See brief of *Amicus Curiae,* published by the American Psychological Association in support of James Dale, the respondent in the case of the Boy Scouts of America and *Monmouth Council v. James Dale.* (Available online at http://www.apa.org/)

58. This story is now out in book form: Loffreda, B. (2000). *Losing Matt Shepard: Life and politics in the aftermath of anti-gay murder.* New York: Columbia University Press.

59. Alaimo, C. A. (2000, October 20). If progressive Tucson can have hate crimes, then any town can. *Arizona Daily Star*, p. B4.

60. *Invisible minority* is a term that is frequently used throughout the literature to describe the population of individuals with sexual orientations that are gay, lesbian, or bisexual. These individuals represent a minority of the population and are considered invisible because of the tendency to hide their lifestyles.

61. Blake, S., Ledsky, R., Lehman, T., Goodenow, C., Sawyer, R., & Hack, T. (2001, June). Preventing sexual risk behaviors among gay, lesbian, and bisexual adolescents: The benefit of gay-sensitive HIV instruction in schools. *American Journal of Public Health, 91*, 940–946.

62. There have been many studies to evaluate the effectiveness of abstinence-only programs. To date, research has not yielded evidence that abstinence-only programs result in abstinent behavior. For example, see Kirby, D. (2000). What does the research say about sexuality education? *Educational Leadership, 58*(2), 72–76; see also, Devaney, B., Johnson, A., Maynard, R., & Trenholm, C. (2002). *The evaluation of abstinence education programs funded under Title V, Section 510: Interim Report.* Washington, DC: U.S. Department of Health and Human Services.

63. Blake, S., et al. (2003, June). Condom availability programs in Massachusetts high schools: Relationships with condom use and sexual behavior. *American Journal of Public Health, 93*(6), 955–962.

64. Hoff, T., & Greene, L. (2000). *Sex education in America: A view from inside the nation's classrooms.* Menlo Park, CA: Kaiser Family Foundation. (Available online at http://www. kff.org/)

65. Quoted in Schemo, D. J. (2001, June 29). Surgeon general's report calls for sex education beyond abstinence courses. *New York Times*, p. A14.

66. See Schemo, D. J. (2001, June 29). Surgeon general's report calls for sex education beyond abstinence courses. *New York Times*, p. A14; Schemo, D. J. (2001, April 21). Promised sex-ed report languishes. *New York Times*, p. A9; Hoff, T., & Greene, L. (2000). *Sex education in America: A view from inside the nation's classrooms.* Menlo Park, CA: Kaiser Family Foundation. (Available online at http://www.kff.org/)

67. Philliber, S., Kaye, J. W., Herrling, S., & West, E. (2002). Preventing pregnancy and improving health care access among teenagers: An evaluation of the Children's Aid Society—Carrera Program. *Perspectives on Sexual and Productive Health, 34*(5), 244–251; see also Shrier, L., et al. (2001, January). Randomized controlled trial of a safer sex intervention for high-risk adolescent girls. *Archives of Pediatric and Adolescent Medicine, 155,* 73–79.

68. Douglas Kirby is a senior research scientist at ETR Associates, a nonprofit organization that provides educational resources, training, and research in health promotion.

69. Kirby, D. (2001). *Emerging answers: Research findings on programs to reduce teen pregnancy.* Washington, DC: National Campaign to Prevent Teen Pregnancy.

70. Philliber, S., Kaye, J. W., Herrling, S., & West, E. (2000). *Preventing teen pregnancy: An evaluation of the Children's Aid Society Carrera Program.* Accord, NY: Philliber Research Associates, as described in Eccles, J. S., & Templeton, J. (2002). Extracurricular and other after-school activities for youth. In W. G. Secada (Ed.), *Review of research in education* (Vol. 26, pp. 113–180). Washington, DC: American Educational Research Association.

71. Albert, B., Brown, S., & Flanigan, C. (Eds.). (2003). *14 and younger: The sexual behavior of young adolescents* [Summary]. Washington, DC: National Campaign to Prevent Teen Pregnancy.

72. Quoted in Schemo, D. J. (2001, June 29). Surgeon general's report calls for sex education beyond abstinence courses. *New York Times,* p. A14.

73. Best, G. A. (2000, September 29). How harmless is a hug? *Arizona Daily Star,* p. A2.

74. Although we recognize that many variables contribute to the divorce rates, we argue that part of the concern should rest with attitudes youth form around sexual relationships as they exist within society.

75. Kirby, D., & Cole, K. (1997). School-based programs to reduce sexual risk taking behavior. *Child and Youth Services Review, 19,* 415–493.

76. Skinner, M. S. (2000, July 2). Getting the message. *Arizona Daily Star.*

77. Indeed, Albert Bandura has contributed the most knowledge to this area regarding appropriate modeling. For example, see Bandura, A. (1971). *Psychological modeling.* Chicago: Atherton.

Tobacco, Alcohol, Drugs, and Teens

To the dismay of cancer surgeons everywhere, the traits Hollywood chose to attribute to smokers were independence, beauty and determination.

—I. Gately, 2001[1]

The overdiagnosis of learning and behavioral disorders in ever-younger children has gone so far that even psychologists now joke that Huck Finn and Tom Sawyer, were they alive today, would be on Ritalin and in special education for hyperactivity.

—K. Zernike, 2001[2]

Based on its magazine advertising schedule in 1999, Marlboro, the favorite brand of teens, reached 89 percent of teens 5 times or more.

—American Legacy Foundation[3]

Youth take risks that most would not take as adults:[4] riding roller coasters, driving cars as fast as they can go, or riding bikes and skateboards through dangerous obstacles. Smoking, drinking alcohol, and taking drugs are especially popular forms of risk for teens, in part because they are forbidden activities reserved only for adults and in part because of their effects. Because smoking and drinking are only for adults is sufficient reason to encourage many teens to sample them: If it's taboo, it must be good.[5]

Adolescent risk taking is widely recognized as a behavior by which teens assert their independence from the constraints of their childhood years. Young children eagerly obey their parents' commands not to smoke or drink simply because they want to please them.[6] In contrast, adolescents strive to communicate that they are their own persons and deserve adults'

121

respect as adults, not children. Risk-taking behavior that is frowned on by adults is one way teens communicate their independence. Although many teens strive to make their mark irresponsibly, however, there are many others who internalize the healthy values and behaviors of surrounding adults (i.e., they don't need to rebel). Why do some take risks whereas others don't? More important, why are we inundated with stories of risk-taking actions when so many more youth avoid them?

One goal of this chapter is to provide a more balanced view of youth's relationship with tobacco, alcohol, and drugs (TAD)—forms of risk taking with notable long- and short-term health consequences. Although some teens use TAD excessively and irresponsibly, *many* don't. Tragically, deficit depictions are more prominently displayed in the media than the numerous positive stories of youth's behavior and choices. For example, a report that 33% of teens smoke, marginalizes the fact that 67% don't. Data show that at least one third of today's 12th graders have never smoked, 59% haven't ever used an illicit drug (including marijuana), 50% haven't ever had an alcoholic drink, and 68% hadn't been drunk in the previous 12 months. And, as shown in Table 5.1, 92% of 12th graders haven't recently smoked, while 37% have *never* smoked.

Of course, when average deficit depictions of youth's TAD behavior are made, they fail to tell the full story of TAD use. As a case in point, if 33% of youth smoke, how much do they smoke? Once a day? Twice a day? Every day? And how long have they been smoking? One week? One month? One year? Finally, what circumstances surround their smoking? Do their peers smoke? Their parents? Do they smoke infrequently for pleasure and peer acceptance or because they are addicted?

Unfortunately, media reports on youth's TAD behavior—like reports on teen sexuality and violence—are often negative and devoid of contextual information. The point we emphasize is that only more differentiated knowledge about why, how, where, and when youth use (and do not use) TAD will allow us to develop strategies to decrease those numbers.

We start the chapter by exploring the notable contradictions surrounding TAD. This is important because youth are blamed for using TAD—a position that glaringly overlooks the roles of competing social messages about their use. Adults tell youth that smoking can lead to life-threatening illnesses, yet many youth know someone who has smoked his or her whole life and has lived a long time, or they know adults who, seemingly oblivious to the damage caused by tobacco, invest in tobacco stocks. Adults tell youth, "Don't do drugs," yet physicians in this society routinely prescribe medication for many ailments. Such contradictions make it extremely difficult to tell youth *effectively*, "Don't do that."

The data we present on adolescent TAD use show that many youths experiment with alcohol, tobacco, and drugs, but only a small percentage be-

TABLE 5.1
Many Youth Do Not Smoke, 2000

| Question | *Percentage Who Used* | | |
	8th Grade	*10th Grade*	*12th Grade*
Have you ever smoked cigarettes?			
Never	*59.5*	*44.9*	*37.5*
Once or twice	21.5	23.2	23.1
Occasionally but not regularly	8.8	13.7	14.8
Regularly in the past	5.3	7.6	7.8
Regularly now	5.0	10.6	16.8
N	16,700	14,300	12,800
How frequently have you smoked cigarettes during the past 30 days?			
Not at all[a]	*95.8*	*94.0*	*92.4*
Once or twice	2.1	3.1	3.1
Once or twice per week	0.8	0.7	0.5
3–5 times per week	0.4	0.4	0.8
About once a day	0.2	0.3	0.3
More than once a day	0.7	1.6	2.9
N	8,400	7,200	2,100

[a]Includes "never" category from question above.

Note. From *Monitoring the Future: National Results on Adolescent Drug Use: Overview of Key Findings*, by L. D. Johnston, P. M. O'Malley, and J. G. Bachman, 2001, Ann Arbor: University of Michigan Institute for Social Research, U.S. Department of Health and Human Services.

come chronic users. Data also suggest that since the 1970s, the number of youths who use tobacco, alcohol, or drugs has declined steadily. (Of course, some youths do turn to excessive TAD use for coping because they have learned that strategy from their environment.) The learning of drug habits can be mediated, and we close the chapter by discussing some promising efforts designed to reduce TAD use.

SOCIETAL EXPECTATIONS: CONFLICTING STANDARDS FOR BEHAVIOR

Tobacco

Societal standards for TAD use are astonishingly ambiguous and contradictory. A blurry line divides good and bad drugs, and even good drugs in excess can become dangerous. For example, the first American study linking cigarette use to lung cancer was published in the May 1950 issue of the *Journal of the American Medical Association* (JAMA).[7] Yet before the 1950s, and especially since then, the media have insidiously presented smoking as sexy.

Despite incontrovertible evidence that smoking kills, tobacco companies continue to promote tobacco as attractive.

Alcohol

Alcohol, too, is portrayed as glamorous. Society is saturated with alcohol advertisements strategically designed to establish alcohol as a socially accepted and needed recreational drug. Who can forget Budweiser's famous Clydesdales, or the talking frogs and iguanas, or the Bud Bowl? One can't watch highly visible sporting events such as the World Series or the Superbowl without being assaulted by beer ads.[8] Associating alcohol with competitive and recreational events is an effective marketing strategy that reinforces the widespread notion that drinking is synonymous with fun.

Drugs

Drugs pose different social problems because, unlike tobacco and alcohol, some are illegal though many are not, and the reasons why certain drugs are illegal do not seem to make sense. Ironically, many legal drugs are dangerously addictive, whereas some illegal ones are benign. Proponents of using nonaddictive marijuana for medicinal purposes[9] argue the insanity of using strong (legal) painkillers, which are potent and addictive, when so many terminally ill patients report substantial benefits from marijuana, notably appetite recovery and pain reduction. Oddly, the government decided that morphine is an acceptable prescription drug for some patients, but marijuana (the use of which is supported by 80% of Americans[10]) is not. Are there rational reasons for this distinction?

Less ambiguity is associated with hard-core illegal drugs, such as cocaine, crystal meth, or hallucinogens, because their deleterious effects are widely known and well documented and, most important, accepted to be true by youth. Still, American attitudes about drug use vary, ranging from complete intolerance of all illicit street drugs to a willingness to accept occasional social drug use and light experimentation. During the 2000 presidential campaign, Mr. Bush admitted to trying cocaine. How are youth to accept that drugs are bad when George Bush can use drugs in moderate amounts and still be president? And how many famous people have, at some point in their careers, fallen prey to drug addiction only to kick the habit (or at least rebound temporarily) and to again be idolized (e.g., Robert Downey, Jr.). Youth are often shown role models who are admired for beating their addiction. Unfortunately, the many users who never recover from drug addiction are less visible to youth, and thus some youth fail to realize that second chances that come to the stars do not always occur for others.

Despite drug education programs, many teens who begin to use drugs are either ignorant or disbelieving of their potential damaging effects. Young people who get high from sniffing common household items are of-tentimes unaware of the risks of neurological damage that even one-time use can cause.[11] To others for whom the dangers of their drug of choice may be well known, the risks may seem small or worth it. Some youths use speed or snort cocaine to sustain energy levels required to meet multiple so-cial demands. Others snort cocaine because the high is a powerful substi-tute for food and, therefore, helps them lose weight. Consider a popular commercial in which a very thin, attractive woman violently destroys her kitchen with a skillet while saying, "This is what drugs do to you, your family, and your life." Ironically, there is a powerful, subliminal message here: Drugs cause damage, but the reward is thinness and beauty; kitchens—and therefore food—are irrelevant (more on this in chap. 6).

Overprescribing Medication

On the one hand, Americans condemn youth for illegal or nonprescription drug use. On the other, America is an overmedicating society. Prescription medication is a billion-dollar business, and there are drugs available for most common ailments. But the abundance and availability of prescription medicine per se are not what is troubling. Children are repeatedly told that drugs are not the solution to life's problems. Yet when children become a problem, a common reaction is to give them medicine.[12] Ritalin is over-prescribed for children who are misdiagnosed with behavioral disorders.[13] The overuse of drugs has led researchers to argue that even Winnie the Pooh would be diagnosed with attention deficit hyperactivity disorder (ADHD) and possibly obsessive compulsive disorder (OCD) were he a real character. Piglet would be diagnosed with generalized anxiety disorder, Eeyore with chronic dysthymia (mild depression), and Tigger would raise alarm with his tendency for risk taking.[14]

Different Standards for Different Populations

In some families, older and younger members are treated inconsistently. When elderly family members abuse prescription drugs, the response is a patronizing wink, in part because such usage makes it easier to deal with the elderly adult. In contrast, in that same family, the teenager who steals three beers from the cooler endures heavy punishment. In athletics there are also inconsistencies. Several athletes were banned from the 2000 Olympics in Sydney or stripped of their medals for a positive drug test. Andreea Raducan, the gold medal winner for the female all-around gymnastics competition, was stripped of her medal by the International Olympic Committee (IOC) because she tested positive for traces of pseudoepinephrine—a drug found in common cold remedies.[15] Raducan claimed she was just following her doctor's advice to alleviate cold symptoms (her doctor was banned from the games until 2004 for prescribing the common medicine).

Had Raducan been a Major League Baseball (MLB) player, she could have taken her medication with impunity. MLB allowed steroids and even celebrated the accomplishments of athletes who were on them. In a 2002 *Sports Illustrated* feature story, several MLB players commented on the insidious use of steroids throughout the sport. Some estimated that as many as 85% of players use the illegal substance earmarked primarily for HIV and other critically ill patients.[16] Mark McGwire, well known for his 1998 record-breaking home run year, admitted to using steroids. In sharp contrast, the IOC bans common substances with little or no performance-enhancing benefits and punishes athletes who use them.

The use of powerful painkillers among National Football League (NFL) players is widespread. In the week preceding Superbowl XXXVI (February of 2002), there was a controversial debate about the health of both teams' quarterbacks. Would St. Louis Rams' quarterback Kurt Warner take painkillers to allow him to play in the big game?[17] One has to wonder why it is okay for seasoned athletes to take dangerous and potentially addictive drugs simply to play their sport when teens are prosecuted and many times jailed for using marijuana? While at the same time, and ironically, young athletes are encouraged to use dangerous substances to bulk up for competition.[18]

The legal use of tobacco and alcohol are reserved for adults. That a 17-year-old can suddenly smoke when he or she turns 18 is an arbitrary decision (the legal smoking age is 18 in all states except Alabama, Alaska, and Utah, where it is 19). If the point of establishing age markers is to send a message that anyone under age 18 years is not able to make independent decisions about smoking, then what is so special about 18 that they suddenly can? Age markers have little bearing on a youth's ability to get cigarettes or alcohol anyway; youth widely report how easy it is to buy cigarettes or obtain alcohol from parents or older friends.[19] Still, legal age markers serve an important purpose for attempting to protect youth from harmful substances, and perhaps in some cases they do dissuade youth from harmful behavior. But we also worry that legal age markers serve another purpose—as a way to punish youth who break the law. We believe that youth shouldn't smoke, but we also believe that arbitrary age laws (you can go to war at 18 years of age but not smoke) thwart the notion that many teens are thinking, rational individuals who are brought up within a glaringly contradictory—do as I say, not as I do—society.

TEENS AND TOBACCO

The tobacco industry spends $8 billion annually to advertise its dangerous products. For that industry, as with so many others, the profit motive supersedes ethical and moral concerns. Mass marketing to sustain profits ignores the fact that the products in question are harmful—even lethal.

The time line in Fig. 5.1 depicts some milestones in the history of the tobacco industry. Prior to the 1950s, tobacco companies enjoyed relatively free and profitable operations, and cigarette consumption rose steadily. It wasn't until the mid-1960s that medical research into tobacco's side effects began to impact the use of tobacco in American culture. As information on the ill effects of tobacco became more widely disseminated, support for tobacco companies slowly subsided. After years of passing knowledge of the dangers of tobacco use, lawmakers finally took action by adding warning labels to cigarette packages, banning cigarette use in various venues (e.g., bars, restaurants, and airplanes), and heavily restricting cigarette advertising in some formats while banning it all together in others (e.g., television commercials).

By the 1980s, as more smokers were dying of lung disease, civil lawsuits filed by long-term smokers suffering from lung cancer appeared, claiming that tobacco companies knowingly promoted a dangerous, addictive substance. In the 1990s, more laws were posed restricting the sale of advertising space to tobacco companies, and in 1998 a landmark $206 billion settlement (the Master Settlement Agreement—MSA[20]) was reached between the tobacco industry and 46 states. By the terms of the settlement, tobacco companies agreed to curb youth advertising, and states would allocate settlement monies to develop antitobacco campaigns.[21]

Out of the MSA also came the American Legacy Foundation (ALF), a Florida-based group charged with creating a nationwide antitobacco media campaign and with following up on the compliance of tobacco companies with the MSA. Billions of dollars were allocated for antitobacco programs; however, states varied widely in their implementation and evaluation of such programs (some states even redirected tobacco settlement monies toward other priorities, including highway repairs[22]). Tobacco companies have not curtailed their advertising to youth, as stipulated in the MSA. In a 2001 article in the *New England Journal of Medicine,* researchers found that advertising of cigarettes to youth had not subsided. They reported that in 2000, magazine advertisements for youth brands of cigarettes (defined as cigarette brands smoked by more than 5% of youth in 8th, 10th, and 12th grades) reached more than 80% of young people in the United States, an average of 17 times each.[23]

Recently, the R. J. Reynolds Tobacco Company was fined $20 million for violating the MSA by marketing to youth. They were charged with "studi-

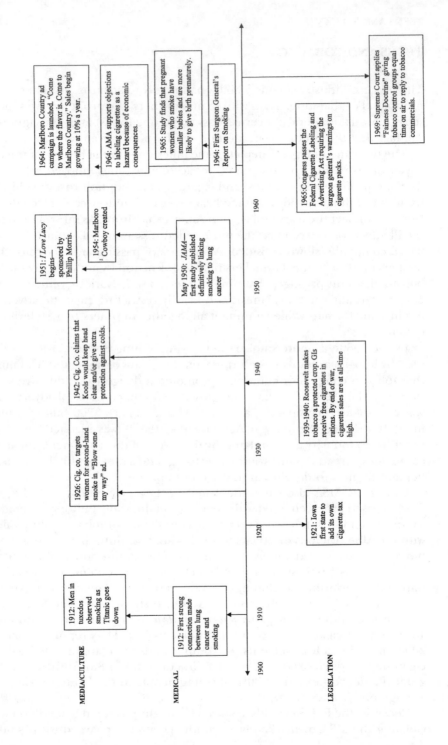

MEDIA/CULTURE

1912: Men in tuxedos observed smoking as Titanic goes down

1926: Cig. co. targets women for second-hand smoke in "Blow some my way" ad.

1942: Cig. Co. claims that Kools would keep head clear and/or give extra protection against colds.

1951: *I Love Lucy* begins—sponsored by Phillip Morris.

1954: Marlboro Cowboy created

1964: Marlboro Country ad campaign is launched. "Come to where the flavor is. Come to Marlboro Country." Sales begin growing at 10% a year.

1964: AMA supports objections to labeling cigarettes as a hazard because of economic consequences.

1965: Study finds that pregnant women who smoke have smaller babies and are more likely to give birth prematurely.

MEDICAL

1912: First strong connection made between lung cancer and smoking

May 1950: *JAMA*—first study published definitively linking smoking to lung cancer

1964: First Surgeon General's Report on Smoking

LEGISLATION

1900   1910   1920   1930   1940   1950   1960

1921: Iowa first state to add its own cigarette tax

1939-1940: Roosevelt makes tobacco a protected crop. GIs receive free cigarettes in rations. By end of war, cigarette sales are at all-time high.

1965:Congress passes the Federal Cigarette Labeling and Advertising Act requiring the surgeon general's warnings on cigarette packs.

1969: Supreme Court applies "Fairness Doctrine" giving tobacco control groups equal time on air to reply to tobacco commercials.

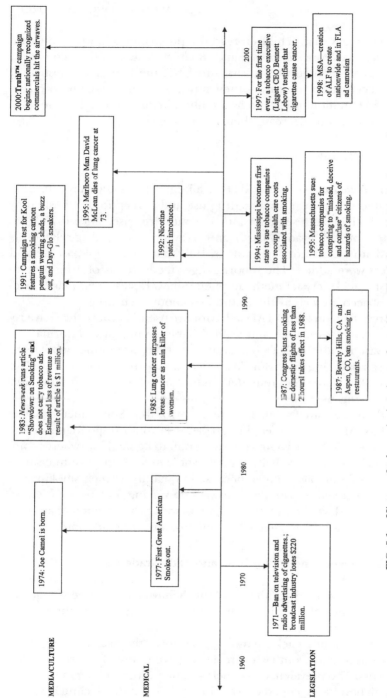

FIG. 5.1. History of tobacco in American culture. *Note.* This information was written and donated to the History Net by Gene Borio © 1997, the Tobacco BBS 212-982-4645, Web page: http://www.tobacco.org. Can be found online: http://www.historian.org/frameshn.htm

ously" tracking how many children read the publications in which they advertised, such as *Sports Illustrated* and *Rolling Stone*. Another company, Lorillard, was threatened with a suit, and UST, the nation's largest snuff maker, was accused of increasing their advertising in teen-focused magazines from $3.6 million in 1997 to $9.4 million in 2001, even after the MSA ordered companies to decrease their marketing.[24]

Teen Smoking Trends

The report *Monitoring the Future* (MTF),[25] a large scale, nationally representative longitudinal study of youth's drug use and perceptions published by University of Michigan researchers, tracks youth drug use. Since 1975, a national sample of 12th graders has been surveyed on their drug-related behaviors and attitudes, and, beginning in 1991, national samples of 8th and 10th graders were added. The report gauges teens' levels of drug use, including LSD (acid), crystal meth, amphetamines, Ecstasy, marijuana, alcohol, and tobacco, as well as their attitudes about each drug.

MTF survey data on teens' TAD behavior are useful because they have remained consistent over time and yield reliable comparative information. Given the vast amount of MTF data available, there are numerous ways to describe teen smoking behavior. We select a few trends documented in MTF to provide a more differentiated picture of youth smoking (and later alcohol and drug use).

Although the data are useful, they are not error free. Survey methods, like those used for MTF, are limited, in part because youth respondents define smoking differently. Some youth consider a puff to be smoking, whereas others think you have to smoke half a cigarette at least for it to constitute smoking. Survey results are also limited because in quantifying their smoking, respondents were asked to base their answers on varying time periods (e.g., a week, the past 30 days, their lifetime). And, as with quantification of any past behavior, the respondents' memories may not always be accurate.

Smoking Prevalence Among 8th, 10th, and 12th Graders

MTF researchers divided youth's smoking behavior into three categories based on frequency of smoking: Have you smoked at all over the past 30 days? Have you smoked at least once daily over the past 30 days? Have you smoked at least a half a pack a day, every day, over the past 30 days? These categories differentiate youth who are just experimenting from regular and heavy smokers. The prevalence of experimenting with smoking in the 12th-grade population has declined overall since 1975, but the decline has been erratic. In 1976, 39% of all 12th graders reported that they had had at least one cigarette in the previous 30 days (see Tables 5.2 and 5.3). This percent-

TABLE 5.2

Trends in 30-Day Prevalence of Cigarette Use by Subgroups for 12th Graders[a]

	1976	1977	1978	1979	1980	1981	1982	1983	1984	1985	1986	1987	1988	1989
Total (%)	38.8	38.4	36.7	34.4	30.5	29.4	30.0	30.3	29.3	30.1	29.6	29.4	28.7	28.6
White[b]	—	38.3	37.6	36.0	33.0	30.5	30.7	31.3	31.2	31.3	31.9	32.1	32.2	32.2
Black	—	36.7	32.7	30.2	26.8	23.7	21.8	21.2	19.3	18.1	16.9	14.2	13.3	12.6
Hispanic	—	35.7	32.8	26.8	22.6	23.2	24.7	24.7	25.3	25.5	23.7	22.7	21.9	20.6
College plans														
None or < 4 years	46.3	46.2	44.6	43.0	39.6	38.1	38.7	38.0	37.9	40.5	38.5	39.7	37.5	38.0
Complete 4 years	29.8	29.4	27.4	26.0	22.3	22.3	22.1	23.3	22.7	22.8	24.0	24.3	24.4	24.1

	1990	1991	1992	1993	1994	1995	1996	1997	1998	1999	2000	2001	2002	2001–2002 Change
Total (%)	29.4	28.3	27.8	29.9	31.2	33.5	34.0	36.5	35.1	34.6	31.4	29.5	26.7	-2.8*
White	32.3	32.2	31.8	33.2	35.2	36.6	38.1	40.7	41.7	40.1	37.9	35.3	32.5	-2.9*
Black	12.2	10.6	8.7	9.5	10.9	12.9	14.2	14.3	14.9	14.9	14.3	13.3	12.1	-1.2
Hispanic	21.7	24.0	25.0	24.2	23.6	25.1	25.4	25.9	26.6	27.3	27.7	23.8	21.3	-2.6
College plans														
None or < 4 years	37.5	38.1	38.6	37.3	40.9	43.5	45.0	45.7	46.7	44.9	43.6	40.8	37.5	-3.3
Complete 4 years	25.4	24.2	23.8	27.3	28.0	29.9	30.8	33.1	31.3	31.4	27.3	25.9	23.6	-2.3*

[a]Level of significance of different between the two most recent classes: *p = .05, **p = .01, ***p = .001. — indicates data not available.
[b]To derive percentages for each racial subgroup, data for the specified year and the previous year have been combined to increase subgroup sample sizes and thus provide more stable estimates.

Note. From *Monitoring the Future: National Survey Results on Drug Use, 1975–2002. Volume I: Secondary School Students* by L. D. Johnston, P. M. O'Malley, & J. G. Bachman, 2003, Lansing, MI: University of Michigan (NID Publication No. 03-5375). Bethesda, MD: National Institute on Drug Abuse.

TABLE 5.3
Trends in 30-Day Prevalence of Cigarette Use by Subgroups for 8th and 10th Graders[a]

8th Graders

	1991	1992	1993	1994	1995	1996	1997	1998	1999	2000	2001	2002	2001–2002 Change
Total (%)	14.3	15.5	16.7	18.6	19.1	21.0	19.4	19.1	17.5	14.6	12.2	10.7	−1.5*
White[b]	—	16.2	17.8	18.9	20.7	22.7	22.8	21.5	20.1	17.7	14.7	12.0	−2.7**
Black	—	5.3	6.6	8.7	8.9	9.6	10.9	10.6	10.7	9.6	8.2	7.7	−.05
Hispanic	16.7	16.7	18.3	21.3	21.6	19.6	19.1	20.1	20.5	16.6	13.0	12.7	−.20
College plans													
None or < 4 years	29.2	31.9	34.1	36.6	36.5	39.2	40.0	40.1	40.3	34.7	30.0	29.3	−.70
Complete 4 years	11.8	13.1	14.3	16.1	16.8	18.2	16.9	16.5	14.5	12.2	10.0	8.9	−1.2

10th Graders

	1991	1992	1993	1994	1995	1996	1997	1998	1999	2000	2001	2002	2001–2002 Change
Total (%)	20.8	21.5	24.7	25.4	27.9	30.4	29.8	27.6	25.7	23.9	21.3	17.7	−3.6**
White	—	24.1	26.0	27.8	29.7	32.9	34.4	33.2	30.8	28.2	25.7	22.4	−3.3**
Black	—	6.6	7.5	9.8	11.5	12.2	12.8	13.7	12.5	11.1	11.1	9.8	−1.3
Hispanic	18.3	18.3	20.5	19.4	21.4	23.7	23.0	21.3	21.1	19.6	16.8	14.3	−2.5
College plans													
None or < 4 years	36.5	35.0	41.9	42.2	46.3	46.2	47.2	45.2	44.0	38.6	38.1	33.3	−4.8*
Complete 4 years	17.3	18.6	21.0	21.7	24.7	27.8	26.8	24.5	22.7	21.5	18.5	15.1	−3.4***

[a]To derive percentages for each racial subgroup, data for the specified year and the previous year have been combined to increase subgroup sample sizes and thus provide more stable estimates.

[b]Level of significance of different between the two most recent classes: *p = .05, **p = .01, ***p = .001. — indicates data not available.

Note. From *Monitoring the Future: National Survey Results on Drug Use, 1975–2002. Volume I: Secondary School Students* by L. D. Johnston, P. M. O'Malley, & J. G. Bachman, 2003, Lansing, MI: University of Michigan (NID Publication No. 03-5375). Bethesda, MD: National Institute on Drug Abuse.

age declined slowly but steadily until 1992, when it fell to a low of 28%, peaked again at 37% in 1997, and subsequently fell to 31% in 2000. On average, approximately 33% of students in each 12th-grade class over the past 25 years has smoked "at least once in the past 30 days."

As we update this information prior to going to press, the most recent data from MTF show that experimentation with smoking is at its lowest point since the inception of the survey in 1976 with 12th graders at 26.7%, and at its lowest with 8th- and 10th-graders since the inception of reporting for these grade levels in 1991 at 10.7% and 17.7% respectively.[26]

MTF researchers described the prevalence of daily smoking among 12th graders since 1975 as a way to distinguish the percentage of those who are experimental smokers from those who are heavier users. In 1975, 27% of 12th graders said they smoked cigarettes (in an undetermined amount) on a daily basis. This rate decreased to a low of 17% in 1992, rose again to a peak of 25% in 1997, and then declined again to 21% in 2000. In differentiating lighter from heavier chronic smokers, MTF reports that 18% of 12th graders smoked at least half a pack a day on a daily basis in 1975, a percentage that dropped to 10% in 1992, rose again to 14% in 1997, and then dropped again to 11% in 2000. Thus, while approximately one third of 12th graders over time have ever smoked within the previous 30 days, approximately one quarter smoked on a daily basis and 11% smoked at least a half a pack daily. And recent data indicate that teen smoking further lessened for 2000–2002.[27]

Differentiation in Declines

Youth smoking has declined over the past 2.5 decades; however, these declines vary markedly depending on youth's ethnicity and educational goals. CDC data indicate that since 1976 the rate of smoking among Black youths dropped by 83%, whereas the rate among White youth only dropped 20%. This trend was also documented by the Monitoring the Future data (see Table 5.2). Among 12th graders, 38% of White students smoked once in the past 30 days in 1977, and, after rising to a high of 42% in 1998, the percentage declined to 38% in 2000. In contrast, 37% of Black 12th graders smoked in 1977, whereas 14% did in 2000.[28] As shown in Table 5.2, 46% of 12th graders who smoked reported that they would not go to college, whereas 30% of college-bound students smoked. In 2000, 44% of non-college-bound students smoked, whereas 27% of college-bound students did.

I Know, I Know, Smoking Is Bad for Me

Youth know that smoking is dangerous, and, as they age, more youth are likely to report that smoking one or more packs of cigarettes a day is a great health risk (see Table 5.4). In 2002, 57.5% of 8th graders, 64.3% of 10th

TABLE 5.4

Trends in Perceived Harmfulness and Disapproval of Alcohol, Tobacco, and Drugs by 8th, 10th, and 12th Graders

	1991	1992	1993	1994	1995	1996	1997	1998	1999	2000	2001	2002	2001–2002 Change
8th graders	51.6	50.8	52.7	50.8	49.8	50.4	52.6	54.3	54.8	58.8	57.1	57.5	+.4
	82.8	*82.3*	*80.6*	*78.4*	*78.6*	*77.3*	*80.3*	*80.0*	*81.4*	*81.9*	*83.5*	*84.6*	*+.1*
10th graders	60.3	59.3	60.7	59.0	57.0	57.9	59.9	61.9	62.7	65.9	64.7	64.3	–.4
	79.4	*77.8*	*76.5*	*73.9*	*73.2*	*71.6*	*72.8*	*75.3*	*76.1*	*76.7*	*78.2*	*80.6*	*+2.4**
12th graders	69.4	69.2	69.5	67.6	65.6	68.2	68.7	70.8	70.8	73.1	73.3	74.2	+1.0
	71.4	*73.5*	*70.6*	*69.8*	*68.2*	*67.2*	*67.1*	*68.8*	*69.5*	*70.1*	*71.6*	*73.6*	*+2.0*

Percentages include students who smoke one or more packs of cigarettes per day.

Percentage saying "great risk"; *percentage disapprove or strongly disapprove of drug use.*

Note. From *Monitoring the future national survey results on drug use, 1975–2002. Volume I: Secondary school students* by L. D. Johnston, P. M. O'Malley, & J. G. Bachman, 2003, Lansing, MI: University of Michigan (NID Publication No. 03-5375). Bethesda, MD: National Institute of Drug Abuse.

graders, and 74.2% of 12th graders reported that smoking was a great health risk. Although increased awareness of the perils of smoking can influence smoking behavior, there is no empirical evidence that knowledge alone deters a teen (or an adult) from smoking. Many smoke because the physical high or the social cachet of smoking outweigh potential risks.[29]

Table 5.4 also shows the percentage of students who disapprove of heavy daily smoking. In 2002, 73.6% of 12th graders disapproved of smoking, a percentage that is much higher for 8th graders. In following the underlined cohort from Table 5.4, it can be seen that fewer students disapprove of smoking in the later grades, whereas more believe it is a great risk—although all percentages are relatively high. Still, this is an interesting trend that merits further investigation. Why do younger youths disapprove of smoking more than older ones? One possibility is that as they grow older, youth become more aligned with the general portrayal of smokers in the media. Also, once they reach legal smoking age, they may view it as an acceptable adult choice.

Recent data from the 2002 survey show that students in all three grade levels (8th, 10th, and 12th) are becoming less accepting of being around smokers. The proportion of them who agree with the statement, "I strongly dislike being near people who are smoking" increased from 46% in 1996 to 54% among 8th graders in 2002, with an increase from 42% to 49% among 10th graders spanning 1997 to 2002 and from 38% to 47% among 12th graders during the same time frame. All changes are statistically significant.[30] More recently, in a 2003 study conducted by the National Center on Addiction and Substance Abuse at Columbia University, it was found that the number of teens who do not have friends that smoke is on the rise. Specifically, they report that 70% of teens polled had no friends who smoked (up from 56% in 2002). Similarly, 56% of respondents had no friends who regularly drank (up from 52% in 2002) and 68% had no friends who used marijuana (up from 62% in 2002).[31]

ANTITOBACCO CAMPAIGNS EMERGE

As smoking hazards have become more widely known, debates have arisen over how to protect consumers while also appreciating the economic contributions of tobacco companies. One early strategy (1965) for communicating the risks of smoking was to add warning labels to cigarette packages. The push for warning labels was initially resisted by many critics, including the American Medical Association (AMA), which argued that warning labels would adversely affect the economy.[32] However, as evidence mounted that smoking was a health hazard, the AMA and other critics could no longer ignore the dangers of tobacco consumption. Legislators cracked down on tobacco companies, especially on how they represented their products in advertisements. By 1971, cigarettes could no longer be advertised on radio and television, and by the 1980s smoking was banned from airplanes and some restaurants.

Appealing to Youth

Youth are continuing targets of tobacco companies because they are the next generation of smokers and because their rebellious nature makes them easier to hook. Uncovered confidential documents written by marketing executives for R.J. Reynolds Tobacco Company in 1977 argue the following:[33]

> There is a strong drive in most people, particularly the young, to try new things and experiences. This drive no doubt leads many pre-smokers to experiment with smoking, simply because it is there and they want to know more about it. A new brand offering something novel and different is likely to attract experimenters, young and old, and if it offers an advantage it is likely to retain these users.

Tobacco ads have often been designed to exploit typical adolescents. One strategy was based on a belief that many youths want to be risk takers. Marketing executives for R.J. Reynolds Tobacco Company concluded as follows:

> If the desire to be daring is part of the motivation to start smoking, the alleged risk of smoking may actually make smoking attractive. Finally, if the "older" establishment is preaching against smoking, the anti-establishment sentiment discussed above would cause the young to want to be defiant and smoking. Thus, a new brand aimed at the young group should not in any way be promoted as a "health" brand, and perhaps should carry some implied risk. In this sense the warning label on the package may be a plus.

Appallingly, tobacco executives continue to seek and find ways to attract new youth customers. In the 1980s and early 1990s, youth were bombarded directly and indirectly by numerous prosmoking campaigns: Joe Camel dressed like a teenager communicated subliminally to youth that smoking is cool and the enduring Virginia Slims slogan "You've come a long way baby" appealed to young women via an implied association with the feminist movement.

A 2002 article in the *Journal of the American Medical Association* (*JAMA*) argued that for antitobacco messages to be equally effective, they must adopt the same strategies tobacco companies have historically used to capture new, young smokers.[34] After an exhaustive review of online documents released by tobacco executives from tobacco advertising campaigns of the last 40 years, the *JAMA* authors concluded that tobacco companies have been so successful in hooking smokers because of their diligence in examining and monitoring not only the demographics of their target market but also the wide-ranging social attitudes toward their products. The authors suggested that to design approaches to keep youth from smoking campaigners must first understand the unique pressures on, motivations of, and social influences on different target populations. Although this process seems to have begun—we have a long way to go.

Antitobacco Campaign Strategies

Recently, many antitobacco media campaigns have been created at state and federal levels. However, states vary widely in the amount of funding they allocate for the creation, implementation, and evaluation of such campaigns. Some states spend billions (e.g., Florida), whereas others redirect their funds toward other priorities. One result of the MSA was to dedicate funds for creating a national mass media campaign (truth™)—the largest and most widespread attempt to target youth smokers and potential smokers. These commercials, originally created in Florida and now seen nationally, have been credited for some declines in youth smoking.[35] And perhaps, could be attributed for the increasing negative attitudes youth hold toward smoking.

In Florida from 1998–2000, smoking rates fell 40% among middle schoolers and 18% among high schoolers.[36] Although smoking rates among youth declined nationally over the same time period, some researchers noted that the decline in Florida was steeper—attributing the decline to a comprehensive approach to tobacco control that entails aggressive media campaigns and changes in laws and enforcement practices. In Florida, for example, a new state law was enacted that gave policemen the power to take teens' driver's licenses away if they were caught smoking. At the time this study was conducted, more than 4,000 underage smokers' licenses had been suspended. Thus, it is difficult to determine how much changes in laws and law enforcement contributed to this decrease and how much was a result of antismoking media campaigns. But evidence seems to suggest that an approach using both strategies can be effective.[37]

Two studies describe the effectiveness of media-based antitobacco approaches. In one study, researchers manipulated antitobacco messages to contain either explicit or implicit information provided by either teens or adults.[38] Explicit messages were parental in nature and contained a direct order not to smoke (e.g., smoking is bad for you. Don't do it). Implicit messages provided viewers information and allowed them to make their own decisions (e.g., this is what can happen if you smoke). Implicit messages conveyed by adults were found to be the most effective way to influence attitudes against smoking, whereas explicit messages failed to affect youth's attitudes. One hypothesis is that implicit messages are more powerful because they allow adolescents opportunities to make their own decisions. Indeed many adolescents dislike being told what to do. These data suggest that informative approaches are more effective than authoritarian commands.

In another study, researchers conducted focus groups with youth and adults in states where large-scale antitobacco media campaigns were running (California, Massachusetts, and Michigan). They identified eight main categories of antitobacco advertising strategies and reported viewers' predominant impressions of their effectiveness. The categories they identified were industry manipulation, secondhand smoke, addiction, cessation, youth access, short-term effects, long-term health effects, and romantic rejection.[39] Table 5.5 provides a brief overview of each approach and its rationale, including an assessment of each message as either primarily explicit or implicit (added based on other researchers' work). Industry manipulation ads and secondhand smoking ads (both containing implicit-type messages) were reported as highly effective strategies for preventing and stopping youth and adult smoking. This is perhaps not surprising and only confirms previously discussed controlled experimental findings that implicit-type messages are more powerful.

Industry Manipulation.   Industry manipulation ads depict youth as a pawn of the tobacco industry and are a hallmark approach of the nationally recognized truth™ campaign. One ad portrays an abandoned city parking lot filled with 1,200 body bags, representing the number of people who die daily because of tobacco. Another ad portrays a tobacco executive thanking a young man on a ventilator for his business while wondering where the next victim will come from—until he spots a young child in the hallway. Similarly, ads show tobacco executives winning Oscar-type awards for killing more people than Hitler. This approach is viewed as highly effective by both adults and youth.

Secondhand Smoking.   Media campaigns that stress secondhand smoking are also seen to be highly effective, perhaps because they are implicit. The approach, depicting the victimization of vulnerable bystanders, such as children or even fetuses, is a powerful way to guilt someone into quitting without having to address a smoker personally. These type of messages do not foist a do-not-smoke approach on the viewer. Rather, they provide provoca-

TABLE 5.5
Summary of the Relative Effectiveness of Tobacco Control Advertising Strategies for Youth and Adults

		Effectiveness		
Component	Main Message	Youth	Adults	Impact
Industry manipulation	Showing that tobacco company executives are manipulating the public, especially youths, into being their next victim. (Implicit)	Highly effective	Highly effective	Youth dislike being manipulated; therefore, they want to rebel against "evil" tobacco company executives.
Secondhand smoke	Viewer is an outsider who witnesses the effects of smoking on innocent third parties. (Implicit)	Highly effective	Highly effective	Youth are outside observers inadvertently witnessing the ill effects of smoking behavior on innocent third parties; appeals to a sense of what is right but allows them to decide for themselves.
Addiction	Portrays the addictive effects of nicotine use. (Implicit)	Effective	Effective	Sometimes paired with manipulation. Shows potential smokers that tobacco executives are using nicotine to hook new smokers.
Cessation information	Tries to get current smokers to quit. (Explicit)	Impact unknown	Effective	Appeals mostly to adults by providing resources to them about how to quit, and validates the difficulties associated with quitting.
Youth access	Shows how easy it is for youth to obtain cigarettes. (N/A)	Not effective	Moderately effective	Tested only with teens, but adults who saw it were angered by the easy access for teens; attempts to persuade adults to be more vigilant in keeping cigarettes from being too accessible to youth.

(Continued)

139

TABLE 5.5
(Continued)

Component	Main Message	Effectiveness		Impact
		Youth	Adults	
Short-term effects	To offset tobacco company's portrayal of smoking as glamorous by showing the immediate health and cosmetic effects of smoking. (Explicit)	Moderately effective	Not effective	Ineffective with youth because it trivializes the seriousness of smoking, and many teens do not believe they smoke enough for these effects to happen to them.
Long-term health effects	Details the potential long-term health consequences of smoking, such as lung cancer and emphysema. (Explicit)	Not effective	Moderately effective	Youth already know the risks and do not believe these hard-core effects will happen to them.
Romantic rejection	These try to convince smokers and potential smokers that if they smoke they will be found unappealing by potential romantic partners. (Explicit)	Not effective	Not effective	Adults found this message offensive and noted that their own experiences ran counter to the ad. Youth reported a similar reaction.

Note. From "Evaluation of Antismoking Advertising Campaigns," by L. K. Goldman and S. A. Glantz, 1998, *Journal of the American Medical Association, 279,* 772–777. Copyright 1998 by American Medical Association. Adapted with permission.

tive information to viewers about the potential harm of their actions and allow viewers to make their own decisions.

Long- and Short-Term Effects.   Media campaigns that portray the extreme long- and short-term effects of smoking are largely ineffective. In one commercial, we hear from different adults who suffer from tobacco-related cancers—including a gentleman with only half a jaw and a woman with a hole in her throat. Another commercial follows the life of a young smoker through a dark and dreary factory-like environment. He moves on a belt with other young smokers, all in wheelchairs and in line for throat or lung surgery, or both. The inference is that many of the young factory cogs die.

Extreme, scare approaches (emphasizing that death is a possible outcome of smoking) often fail to work because of the many real-life examples that seem to contradict their messages. Many youth have grandparents or great-grandparents who have smoked their whole lives and who live relatively full and productive lives. And there are celebrities who lived incredibly long lives despite long-term and highly public smoking patterns, such as George Burns and Bob Hope (both who lived to be 100). Attempts to frighten youth with death threats fail because youth view such media campaigns as hyperbolic, not credible, and not related to their own lives. Youth who smoke infrequently are unlikely to envision themselves ending up with holes in their throats.

In Canada, legislation mandated tobacco companies to use 50% of the space on cigarette packaging to graphically depict the hazards of smoking.[40] Packages include images of irreversible periodontal disease, diseased lungs and brains, and heart damage. Other ads include shocking messages, such as images of pregnant women smoking, a limp cigarette with the message "tobacco can make you impotent," or babies and children pictured next to messages such as "don't poison us" or "tobacco smoke hurts babies." Many worried that this tactic only served to make smoking more alluring to teens, while creating a new market for collectibles. Accordingly, some companies have even profited from making cigarette sleeves that cover these images with less threatening ones such as images of puppies.

Romantic Rejection.   Another media approach makes smoking unappealing by implying that it will lead to romantic rejection. In one commercial, a young couple is seated in a movie theater and the male is chewing tobacco and spitting in a cup. In the middle of the movie, the young female takes his "drink" and starts to drink it. The intent is to elicit a visceral reaction from viewers: Chewing tobacco is gross. In an Arizona campaign, smoking was described as a "tumor causing, teeth staining, smelly puking habit." Romantic rejection messages are believed to be ineffective because youth typically do not find a smoker to be unappealing unless they also have other unappealing personality qualities. Also, this approach completely fails with viewers who smoke and would not find a smoking partner unappealing.

Responsible Youth.   In another approach, one that was not included in the original focus group research, campaigns appeal to youth's sense of responsibility, choice, and self-control. For example, in Arizona one commercial depicts teens telling their parents that they heard them when they told them that smoking is bad. This strategy assumes that teens do listen and are capable of making reasonable choices that affect their health—an image of teens that is rarely portrayed in our culture. The message here is that it is okay to do what your parents suggest; it is okay to resist peer pressure, a message made more credible because it comes directly from teens.[41] It also makes a valuable statement to the adults that teens are responsible. Unfortunately, the effect of this strategy on smoking behavior is not yet known.

Although adults are getting smarter about ways to prevent and intervene on teen smoking, there is still a long way to go. Adults want to control youth, but it is clear an authoritarian voice won't work. Adults must become more sensitive to and respectful of teens and their range of experiences, knowledge, and lifestyles.

TEENS AND ALCOHOL

American culture embraces alcohol. Drinking is associated with recreational and social events and is promoted as both a way to unwind from a hard day and to celebrate a good day. In contrast to the strong evidence that smoking is dangerous, evidence regarding the effects of alcohol use is seemingly more ambiguous. Heavy, sustained drinking can lead to brain and liver damage and promote domestic violence. Drinking heavily and then getting behind the wheel of a car can have tragic consequences. But many argue that alcohol in moderation is harmless, and some even argue that certain types of alcohol are good for health.

Youth cannot legally buy or drink alcohol until the age of 21 years, presumably because individuals under 21 are not able to drink "wisely." The establishment of 21 years as the legal age is curious, especially when compared with the legal age of 18 years for smoking. Smoking is known to have no beneficial, only deleterious, effects, whereas some types of alcohol are viewed as beneficial. Thus, it seems odd that American society sanctions a deadlier substance for younger individuals. Teens see these arbitrary restrictions as attempts to control their behavior and to make decisions for them.

The flip side of this argument, however, is that heavy alcohol use impairs normal abilities to drive and sometimes leads to violent and out-of-control behavior, whereas heavy cigarette use does not. Thus, setting the legal drinking age at 21 years restricts youth, at least in theory, from decisions to drink heavily and then drive until they are older and more capable of making wiser choices. The problem with this logic is that age restrictions alone do not deter youth from drinking or obtaining alcohol. In 2002, 67.9% of 8th, 84.8% of 10th, and 94.7% of 12th graders reported that it was fairly easy or very easy to get alcohol. Encouragingly, these rates are lower than the previous two years.

Granted, age restrictions of some type are needed for the protection of young minors. However, that teens can smoke at 18 years of age but not drink until 21 probably resides in the fact that youth are only killing themselves by smoking but that they endanger adults when they drink.

Some Teens Drink; Many Do Not

Media reports on youth drinking are susceptible to gross exaggeration and error. In 2002, researchers at Columbia University reported that underage drinkers accounted for 25% of the total alcohol consumption nationwide.[42] Given that youth represent only 20% of the population, this statistic garnered wide media attention as a feature story for CNN, the Associated Press, NBC, and the *New York Times* Web site. The press was especially quick to report on the massive numbers of youth who were drinking. However, immediately following a flurry of criticism, the Columbia researchers reported that they had mistakenly calculated this percentage, and it was actually around 11%.[43] However, the media's correction of this was notably less visible. Clearly, the media are prepared to accept bad information about teens even when it is greatly exaggerated.

The popular belief is that alcohol and drug abuse primarily afflict those residing in poor, urban settings. Although substance abuse is prevalent in these populations, the trend has begun to change as more adolescents in rural communities and in midsize cities are consuming alcohol than are those from larger metropolitan areas. Specifically, eighth graders in rural areas were 29% more likely to have used alcohol in the past month and 70% more likely to have been drunk in the past month than eighth graders in large metropolitan areas.[44]

Defining **Drink.** Measuring teens' alcohol consumption is complicated because alcohol consumption can be defined in multiple ways. A drink, to some, is a full beer, whereas for others it is only a few sips. Or it could mean 3 oz of vodka. Thus, respondents' estimates of their drinking are subject to individual biases. When asked to remember how much they drink, respondents may not reply accurately, either out of forgetfulness, exaggeration, or the desire for social acceptance.

During the 1990s, an average of 25% of 8th, 40% of 10th, and 52% of 12th graders per year had ever tried alcohol, but these percentages changed according to how the question was asked. In 1993, MTF included in their survey an additional question that defined *drink* more clearly as "more than a few sips." For eighth graders, 26% reported they had ever had a drink, but that percentage decreased to 24% when *drink* was qualified. Similarly, 42% of 10th graders said they had ever had a drink, but 38% did when it meant more than a few sips. Finally, 51% of 12th graders stated they had had a drink, but 49% did when it meant more than a few sips. Although these differences are slight, they highlight the importance of understanding a youth's frame of reference for defining his or her behavior.

Binge Drinking and Being Drunk.   More students binge drink as they get older (see Tables 5.6 and 5.7); however, usage varies according to ethnicity and educational aspirations. Hispanic students are more likely to binge drink than White students in earlier grades, but this pattern reverses over time. The percentage of teens who drink heavily is larger for those who plan on attending less than 4 years of college (or none at all) than for those who plan on attending a 4-year university.

Strikingly, data suggest that younger youths are more likely to binge drink or drink heavily but not acknowledge that they are drunk. In 2000, 14% of 8th, 26% of 10th, and 30% of 12th graders reported they had binged on alcohol (had five drinks or more on at least one occasion) within the previous 2 weeks of the survey. In contrast, 8% of 8th graders, 24% of 10th graders, and 32% of 12th graders reported that they had been drunk during the same time period. That the number of eighth graders who acknowledge being drunk is less than half of the number of those who admit to binging is alarming but must be taken cautiously because younger teens could be defining *drink* differently. Still, the difference among eighth graders who binge drink but deny that they get drunk (or are unaware of being drunk) is alarming. Younger teens must be better educated on the effects of their choices—especially when youth are left to socialize themselves.

Targeting Drinking and Driving

Preventive education aimed to reduce (or stop) underage drinking are considerably less visible. In stark contrast to antitobacco campaigns, there are few ads that target youth specifically with an antialcohol message. In contrast, there are strategic efforts to draw in young drinkers (e.g., the popularity and widespread advertisement of fruity liquor and lemonade beer). Perhaps the unspoken assumption that young people will, as they mature, eventually experiment with alcohol, along with the widespread and socially

TABLE 5.6

Trends in 2-Week Prevalence of Five or More Drinks in a Row by Subgroups for 12th Graders[a]

	1976	1977	1978	1979	1980	1981	1982	1983	1984	1985	1986	1987	1988	1989
Total (%)	37.1	39.4	40.3	41.2	41.2	41.4	40.5	40.8	38.7	36.7	36.8	37.5	34.7	33.0
White[b]	—	40.5	42.4	43.5	44.3	44.9	44.9	44.5	43.6	41.5	40.3	40.9	40.0	37.9
Black	—	19.0	19.3	18.9	17.7	17.1	17.1	18.3	17.2	15.7	16.4	15.8	15.2	15.7
Hispanic	—	36.4	37.2	33.6	33.1	34.8	32.9	32.5	33.0	31.7	30.8	33.0	33.7	28.8
College plans														
None or < 4 years	41.8	44.7	44.3	44.5	46.3	46.7	45.7	44.9	43.5	41.6	41.3	42.7	38.5	38.2
Complete 4 years	31.5	33.9	35.9	37.7	36.7	37.4	36.5	37.2	34.6	33.0	34.1	35.0	32.8	30.5

	1990	1991	1992	1993	1994	1995	1996	1997	1998	1999	2000	2001	2002	2001–2002 Change
Total (%)	32.2	29.8	27.9	27.5	28.2	29.8	30.2	31.3	31.5	30.8	30.0	29.7	28.6	-1.1
White	36.6	34.6	32.1	31.3	31.5	32.3	33.4	35.1	36.4	35.7	34.6	34.5	33.7	-.7
Black	14.4	11.7	11.3	12.6	14.4	14.9	15.3	13.4	12.3	12.3	11.5	11.8	11.5	-.2
Hispanic	25.6	27.9	31.1	27.2	24.3	26.6	27.1	27.6	28.1	29.3	31.0	28.4	26.4	-.2
College plans														
None or < 4 years	35.8	34.4	32.8	32.7	34.0	35.2	33.9	36.2	36.3	35.4	35.7	35.9	34.0	-1.9
Complete 4 years	30.3	27.9	26.0	25.8	26.3	27.8	28.8	29.5	30.0	29.5	27.6	27.8	27.2	-.5

[a]Level of significance of difference between the two most recent classes: *p = .05, **p = .01, ***p = .001. — indicates data not available.
[b]To derive percentages for each racial subgroup, data for the specified year and the previous year have been combined to increase subgroup sample sizes and thus provide more stable estimates.

Note. From Monitoring the Future: National Survey Results on Drug Use, 1975–2002. Volume I: Secondary School Students by L. D. Johnston, P. M. O'Malley, & J. G. Bachman, 2003, Lansing, MI: University of Michigan (NID Publication No. 03-5375). Bethesda, MD: National Institute on Drug Abuse.

TABLE 5.7

Trends in 2-Week Prevalence of Five or More Drinks in a Row by Subgroups for 8th and 10th Graders[a]

8th Graders

	1991	1992	1993	1994	1995	1996	1997	1998	1999	2000	2001	2002	2001–2002 Change
Total (%)	12.9	13.4	13.5	14.5	14.5	15.6	14.5	13.7	15.2	14.1	13.2	12.4	-.8
White[b]	—	12.7	12.6	12.9	13.9	15.1	15.1	14.1	14.3	14.9	13.8	12.7	-1.1
Black	—	9.6	10.7	11.8	10.8	10.4	9.8	9.0	9.9	10.0	9.0	9.4	+.3
Hispanic	—	20.4	21.4	22.3	22.0	21.0	20.7	20.4	20.9	19.1	17.6	17.8	+.1
College plans													
None or < 4 years	24.4	26.4	29.3	29.3	29.2	29.9	30.3	30.5	33.9	29.3	29.6	28.1	-1.5
Complete 4 years	11.1	11.5	11.3	12.5	12.7	13.3	12.5	11.6	13.0	12.3	11.2	10.9	-.3

10th Graders

	1991	1992	1993	1994	1995	1996	1997	1998	1999	2000	2001	2002	2001–2002 Change
Total (%)	22.9	21.1	23.0	23.6	24.0	24.8	25.1	24.3	25.6	26.2	24.9	22.4	-2.4*
White	—	23.2	23.0	24.5	25.4	26.2	26.9	27.0	27.2	28.1	27.4	25.5	-1.9
Black	—	15.0	14.8	14.0	13.3	12.2	12.7	12.8	12.7	12.9	12.6	12.4	-.2
Hispanic	—	22.9	23.8	24.2	26.8	29.6	27.5	26.3	27.5	28.3	27.7	26.5	-1.2
College plans													
None or < 4 years	33.0	31.8	35.1	36.4	37.5	38.2	39.4	38.2	39.3	39.3	40.2	34.3	-5.9**
Complete 4 years	20.8	18.9	19.3	18.7	21.5	22.3	21.7	22.2	21.8	22.5	22.4	20.4	-2.0*

[a]Level of significance of difference between the two most recent classes: *p = .05, **p = .01, ***p = .001. — indicates data not available.
[b]To derive percentages for each racial subgroup, data for the specified year and the previous year have been combined to increase subgroup sample sizes and thus provide more stable estimates.

Note. From *Monitoring the Future: National Survey Results on Drug Use, 1975–2002. Volume I: Secondary School Students* by L. D. Johnston, P. M. O'Malley, & J. G. Bachman, 2003, Lansing, MI: University of Michigan (NID Publication No. 03-5375). Bethesda, MD: National Institute on Drug Abuse.

acceptable use of alcohol by adults, has limited comprehensive efforts to curb youth drinking.

With good reason adults are more worried about youth drinking and driving than drinking per se. The CDC estimates that the risk of being involved in a motor vehicle crash is greater for teenagers than for older people; indeed, car crashes are the number one cause of adolescent deaths.[45] And too many of these crashes involve alcohol. In 1998, 21% of the fatally injured drivers ages 15–20 years were legally drunk. (The risks of death for younger youths are just as high, with estimates of 21% of traffic fatalities among children ages 0–14 years involving a drunk driver.) Not only do youth drink and drive, but also about one third of high school students ride in cars with drivers who have been drinking alcohol.[46]

Highly visible organizations, such as Mothers Against Drunk Driving (MADD) and Students Against Drunk Driving (SADD), work to prevent drinking and driving–related accidents and fatalities, primarily through a scare approach that targets younger populations. One typical approach by SADD is to tour high school campuses with a display of a wrecked car from a fatal accident, sometimes accompanied by gruesome accident-scene photos or pictures of drunken youth covered in vomit. Research information from literature on antitobacco campaign effectiveness suggests that a consequence-based scare approach or romantic-rejection approach that makes drinkers look unappealing will have little impact on reducing teen drinking and driving.

Until recently, the media were not used as a medium for influencing youth's decisions not to drink and drive. In contrast to the widely visible antitobacco campaign, there have been no similar efforts to influence youth from drinking and driving. However, there is evidence this is slowly changing. During the summer of 2003, the National Highway Traffic Safety Administration, in association with law enforcement agencies around the country, applied a Congress-approved budget of $11 million toward advertisement campaigns designed to deter drinking and driving.[47] The 30-second ads that began appearing in June of 2003, include the tag line message "if you drink, you drive, you lose." Notably, this campaign is relatively new, is applied in only a small number of states, and only applied during a specific time period (e.g., Fourth of July). Therefore, it is impossible to tell what effect these ads are having on drinking and driving behavior. Still it is a promising step toward better recognition of a very challenging and dangerous problem.

Targeting Binge Drinking

There is wider recognition and concern for the rising numbers of young binge drinkers—especially on college campuses,[48] where alcohol plays a role in at least 1,400 deaths yearly.[49] In the past decade, there has been a push among campuses nationwide to adopt a social norms advertising campaign to reduce college drinking. The rationale is that if students believe other students drink only moderately (as opposed to heavily), then they will behave similarly. This approach seems logical, especially when there is evidence that students often have exaggerated notions of how much their peers drink. For example, in a study of 48,000 students on 100 campuses nationwide, researchers found that at campuses where most students claimed to drink only once a month, *90%* of students held the perception that their peers drank much more heavily (several drinks a day, several times a week).[50]

In this approach, campuses deluge their bulletin boards with messages informing students of how much their "average" peer drinks. For example, one might report that "2 of 3 students do not drink on big party nights" or that "55% of students consume fewer than five drinks when they drink." Given true "normative" data, youth might be likely to raise the question, "Have I had too much to drink" *sooner* than if they have exaggerated norms.

Notably, there is evidence that this tactic may be effective.[51] For example, at the University of North Carolina at Chapel Hill, random breathalyzer tests found that 66% of students had no alcohol in their blood when they returned to their dorm rooms.[52] At the University of Arizona, 65% of students report drinking only moderately, 79% had not used marijuana, and 92% reported that they had not used any other form of illegal drug in the past 30 days.[53]

It is worth noting that these studies are not without their methodological weaknesses. In contrast to the studies above, other researchers employing different methodological strategies report that social norming programs have no impact on drinking behavior on college campuses.[54] Another concern we have is what happens when the "norm" that is presented in such advertising campaigns represents a higher level of drinking for certain individuals. Does this message now give them "permission" to start drinking or to drink more? Clearly, more research needs to be done in this area.

Although these approaches can be successful on college campuses, it isn't clear whether a similar approach would work at the high school level, where few teens see binge drinking as risky behavior. One problematic aspect of this approach with high school students is the inevitable political maelstrom it would conjure. As noted in chapter 4, there are sharp debates over the context of sex education curricula in schools, partly because many believe that if sex were openly discussed, more teens would assume it was an accepted behavior. Similarly, the publication of drinking rates of underage drinkers would likely elicit the same kind of adult concern. If schools openly admit that a small percentage of teens drink, would that information encourage drinking? Or, in some cases, would it be encouraging if normative information is especially high?

DRUG USE

Most recent studies report that teen drug use is in decline.[55] Data from the 2002 MTF study show that youth drug use is on the decline. Specifically, illicit drug use is on the decline across all three grade levels (8th, 10th, and 12th) and for all three prevalence reporting periods (annual, lifetime, and 30 day).[56] According to one survey, there was a dramatic drop in drug use among the 12- to 17-year-old population from 1997 to 1999. There was a 21% drop in the proportion of 12- to 17-year-olds who reported they had used an illegal drug in the month before they were surveyed.[57] Marijuana use, specifically, dropped sharply, declining by 26% in the same age group. Unfortunately, in the age group of 18–25 years, the drug use problem has increased.[58] The use of illicit drugs in this age group rose 28% in the last 2 years. Despite these recent short-term trends, statistics suggest that, overall, the proportion of the 18- to 25-year-olds who reported using illicit drugs 20 years ago was much higher (38%) than the proportion of that same age group today (15%).

It is discouraging, however, that the trend of cocaine, inhalant, and hallucinogen use hasn't changed over the past few years.[59] Approximately 9.5% of students have used some form of cocaine (powder, crack, or freebase) during their lifetime, and 4% have used a form of cocaine at least one or more times during the past 30 days. Approximately 14.6% of students had sniffed glue, breathed in aerosol propellant from spray cans, or inhaled paints or spray to get high during their lifetime, and 4.2% had used inhalants at least one or more times during the past 30 days.[60]

Data from a recent national survey of adolescent drug behavior, the Youth Risk Behavior Survey (YRBS) sponsored by the CDC,[61] suggest that of a nationally representative sample of 9th–12th graders, 42.4% had used marijuana during their lifetime; 9.4% had used a form of cocaine; 14.7% had sniffed glue, breathed the contents of aerosol spray cans, or inhaled paints or sprays to get high; 3.1% had used heroin; 9.8% of students had used methamphetamines; 5% had used illegal steroids (without a doctor's prescription); and 2.3% had injected illegal drugs. Lifetime use of these substances varied greatly by gender for marijuana, heroin, and steroid use (boys used more often than girls). Ethnic and racial differences emerged as well for cocaine, inhalants, heroin, and methamphetamines (Hispanic and White students used more than Black students). Lastly, White students used steroids significantly more than Black students.

Perhaps most striking are data that show an increase in the percentage of small-town and rural American teens who use drugs. According to a report released in 2000, eighth graders in rural areas were more likely to have smoked marijuana; snorted cocaine; used inhalants, crack, amphetamines, and tranquilizers; smoked cigarettes; and used alcohol than eighth graders in the largest metropolitan areas.[62] Drug availability is rapidly increasing in these smaller rural areas; unfortunately, too few resources are being invested in fighting this growing problem. With few recreational opportunities for youth, inadequate numbers of health care providers, many uninsured residents, and insufficient tax revenues to support treatment facilities, small towns and rural areas are unable to prevent or combat youth drug use.

DARE

The Drug Abuse Resistance Education (DARE) program is probably the most visible antidrug program offered in schools. DARE's main message is that drugs are bad, will do one harm, and lead to major life problems. The program sends police officers into elementary classrooms to train children to simply say no if and when they are offered drugs. The model purposefully targets elementary students in an attempt to get to them while they are young.

Evaluations of DARE show the program to be ineffective. One reason is that the program is insensitive to developmental difference in attitudes toward and knowledge about drugs. The ill effects of drug use are not real to youth—especially when too much evidence seems to support the contrary: Many adults have tried drugs in their past and are leading healthy, responsible lives. As Richard Rothstein notes in a *New York Times* article, "Many successful adults use drugs casually. And experimentation by adolescents, most of whom still turn out O.K., continues."[63] The truth of this statement was visibly demonstrated during the 2000 elections, when questions surfaced regarding the drug history of candidates Gore and Bush. Gore admitted to smoking marijuana, and Bush admitted to cocaine use; he has also talked openly about his struggles with alcohol. And, in the presidential campaign, we learned that Bush covered up a previous citation for driving while under the influence of alcohol (DUI). How are modern youth supposed to believe a program such as the DARE program, which suggests that drug use will lead to destructive lifestyles when there is ample evidence—two presidential nominees—to the contrary?

The DARE model is currently being revamped. Its new curriculum targets adolescents (instead of elementary students) and embraces a more flexible cognitive-based approach (see Table 5.8). The problems with the just-say-no all-inclusive tag line is that it doesn't respect the varying contexts in which youth find themselves or that teens' perceptions of what one should say no to vary—just as they do for adults. Most important, youth need to know how to say no. While this new program addresses some of these flaws in the original DARE program, we have yet to see any data that it works or evidence that program implementation has radically changed.

TABLE 5.8
An Outline of the Updated DARE Program Curriculum Goals

The curriculum focuses on developing and extending students' capacities to:
1. Understand the nature of and risks associated with alcohol, drug, tobacco, and inhalant use.
2. Examine and understand their own beliefs related to alcohol, drug, tobacco, and inhalant use and consequences.
3. Communicate clearly and interact positively in social and interpersonal situations.
4. Develop and use assertiveness/refusal skills.
5. Recognize, defuse, and avoid potentially violent situations.
6. Make positive quality-of-life decisions.

Note. From *The New D.A.R.E. Program,* by D.A.R.E. America, 2002, Inglewood, CA: D.A.R.E. America. Copyright 2002 by D.A.R.E. America.

However, recent program modification that emphasize decision-making skills[64] is promising because it matches what is already known about the effectiveness of giving youth autonomy over their actions.

Considerably less advertising is aimed at convincing youth not to do drugs than at preventing teens from smoking. The antidrug ads that are developed may seem irrelevant to teens, or they may use ineffective scare or guilt tactics. For example, a White House media campaign tries to make the link between teen drug use and terrorism. In these ads, kids make claims like, "I helped murder families in Colombia" or "I helped kill a judge."[65] As we've noted throughout scare approaches are proven ineffective; but perhaps more importantly it is unconscionable to scare youth into believing they support terrorist activities by buying drugs from adults who manufacture them, and it is unconscionable to scare youth into believing they support international terrorism.

Promising Solutions

A review of the literature suggests that there is some consensus on what successful prevention/intervention TAD programs look like.[66] One common element across programs is strong adult guidance and mentoring. Youth, too, have voiced their desire for better quality connections with surrounding adults.[67] Especially in low-income, largely minority populations, programs that foster a sense of community and include adults who go out of their way to be there for youth are more successful at reducing risky behavior than those that do not.[68] When youth are given opportunities to participate in service learning (where autonomy and leadership skills are fostered) they are less likely to use drugs.[69]

Recently, the U.S. Supreme Court upheld the widespread use of random drug testing of public school students. The 5–4 decision concerned a program in Oklahoma schools to randomly test students who wanted to take part in extracurricular activities (such as athletics, drama, or music). However, the majority opinion was written in such a way as to suggest that any student could rightfully be tested for drugs. Even though the school over which this court decision was made did not have a major drug problem, one justice reasoned that "it would make little sense to require a school district to wait for a substantial portion of its students to begin using drugs before it was allowed to institute a drug testing program designed to deter drug use."[70] This flagrant antiyouth position, which implies that youth will inevitably use drugs, is a misguided attempt to control youth. Data are emerging that show drug testing is ineffective for deterring drug use.[71]

Different Reasons for TAD Use

A 2003 study released by the National Center on Addiction and Substance Abuse reports that female teens become habitual users of TAD more quickly than male teens.[72] Female teens get hooked faster than male teens using even lesser amounts of TAD. Motivations also differ according to gender. Female teens tend to use drugs to reduce stress and depression, whereas male teens do so to seek excitement and social status. Obviously, given these different reasons for using and physiological reactions to TAD it is likely that prevention programs and treatment programs need to be specialized for different youth. Further, it likely will keep youth from participating in programs that could have prevented drug use in the first place.

CONCLUSION

Society sends markedly mixed messages to youth about TAD use—adults seem to believe that TAD use among youth is already high, yet in many ways adults appear to condone TAD use. In actuality, the use of TAD by today's youth is less now than 20 years ago. Youth vary in the frequency and type of TAD they use. Teens who smoke tobacco once a month have different problems than those who smoke heavily on a daily basis. For some youths, the only drug-related vice is tobacco, whereas for others habitual heroin or inhalant use is a problem. There are age, gender, ethnic, and geographical (urban, rural) differences in TAD usage. Although interpretation of data on teen TAD use is complicated, it is clear that teens today use TAD less than those of their parents' cohort 20–25 years ago. However, early TAD use is a matter of concern.

    Treatment models that specifically target teens with TAD problems fail to understand one crucial fact: Teens' TAD habits and motivations to change vary enormously, depending on the individual young person.[73] Because youth culture is not monolithic, treatments that target teens' engagement in alcohol, tobacco, and drug use cannot be one-dimensional. A just-say-no campaign that focuses on a reductive idea—don't use any drug ever—means very little to young people who daily receive numerous media, cultural, and personal messages to the contrary. Youth have very different reasons for using drugs, alcohol, or tobacco, and their levels of use are equally various. Programs that aim to stop all students from engaging in illegal substance abuse will fail because unidimensional approaches ignore perplexing diversity of substance-abuse issues.

General Considerations

Because TAD behaviors are occurring earlier, it is important to begin educative programs earlier. The public must be actively taught to recognize the different forms of TAD. Approaches that teach strategies to say no or restrict use (e.g., carrying a half-full glass at a party) need to be researched and developed. Inspirational speakers who describe their journey of beating addiction and who encourage users to quit or dry out should be urged to talk bluntly about the difficult, embarrassing, and often arduous path to recovery. Students should be taught the percentage of TAD abusers who never recover. Too many young children do not know the dangers of inhalants, for example, and may experiment with them, unaware of possible consequences.

Prevention and intervention programs must be designed based on the developmental levels of the targeted youth. Young children may respond to adults who tell them to just say no; however, the game changes radically when one is trying to convey the same message to an adolescent. Although schools cannot become the only socializing agent for youth, it is appropriate for schools to include state-of-the-art information about the proven effects of alcohol, tobacco, and drug use. Literature presented to youth should acknowledge that society sends mixed messages about substance abuse. Teachers should encourage and challenge youth to think through issues and to make good decisions. Further, school prevention programs must recognize that some youth will become addicted abusers. Schools should be willing to provide referral services to students who need them.

The prevalence of tobacco products in many recent movies seems largely gratuitous and serves no purpose other than financial rewards of the movie industry in the form of payments from tobacco companies. When smoking rates are decreasing in the country, the dramatic increase in smoking in movies seems calculated and unnerving.[74] Iain Gately discusses this issue this way: "A Hollywood adviser had a simpler explanation—edginess: 'smoking has become part of the definition of edginess. And edginess is in.' "[75]

Although underage teens may be punished for smoking, there are no equivalent consequences for adults who provide cigarettes to teens. Closing

businesses for a week for repeated offenses or taking away licenses to sell tobacco products would send an unambiguous message that society does not
want youth to smoke. It is easy to punish and blame youth because they (unlike the adult sellers) are powerless.

Needed Research

Social norming approaches in colleges are useful in making youth aware
that their alcohol use is typical. Youth generally believe that their college
peers consume more alcohol than they actually do. Informing youth of the
truth makes them more responsible in their own use of alcohol. As noted,
there is some conflicting research on the effects of social norming approaches and further research is warranted. More studies of elementary
and middle school students would be useful to discover the degree to which
young students overestimate TAD use by their peers. If young students do
in fact overestimate peer TAD consumption, it might be effective in reducing TAD use to distribute social-comparison information to this age level as
well.

More research onto how parents do and can tell teens not to use drugs is
needed. Clearly, telling students to say no to drugs is unlikely to be effective. Parents (and other youth workers) need to explain why it is important
to say no and how teens can say no in ways that are socially appropriate to
them and their peers. If it is possible to identify more and less effective ad
approaches, shouldn't it also be possible to identify more and less successful rationales and strategies for telling youth not to do drugs?

Schools would seem to be an ideal place to discuss TAD and their negative effects. However, schools are already frequently criticized for devoting
too much time to non-subject-matter instruction, to the detriment of the
core curriculum. However, there are many who argue the opposite position: that students will progress more academically if some of their acute social needs are met.[76] More research is needed on citizens' and parents' expectations regarding TAD programs in the schools. Are parents as actively
supportive of TAD programs as they are of sex education programs?

Oddly, and distressingly, there seem to be fewer policymakers interested
in launching educative programs about drugs and alcohol. Why is this?
More basic research is needed on how policymakers see youth and their potential (cost vs. investment). As with public attitudes about teens' violent
and sexual behavior, it is clear that the public view of youth TAD use is exaggerated in negative ways. One myth noted was that teens' TAD use is increasingly common in rural areas (many citizens believe the TAD problem
is in the inner cities). Clearly, more research needs to be conducted with
rural teens to understand their conceptions and circumstances that are associated with their increased use of TAD. Are rural youths participating in

drugs more because of boredom, opportunity, community personalities, issues of individual identity, or enhanced peer pressure? At present, these questions cannot be adequately answered.

ENDNOTES

1. Gately, I. (2001). *La diva nicotina: The story of how tobacco seduced the world* (p. 348). New York: Simon & Schuster.

2. Zernike, K. (2001, February 4). Ritalin to the rescue: A children's story for our time. *New York Times,* p. 7.

3. Healton, C. G. (2000). *American Legacy Foundation statement.* Retrieved 2000, May 17, http://www.americanlegacy.org/

4. Lightfoot, C. (1997). *The culture of adolescent risk-taking.* New York: Guilford Press.

5. Siegel, J. T., & Burgoon, J. K. (2002). Expectancy theory approaches to prevention: Violating adolescent expectations to increase the effectiveness of public service announcements. In W. Crano & M. Burgoon (Eds.), *Mass media and drug prevention: Classic and contemporary theories and research* (pp. 163–186). Mahwah, NJ: Lawrence Erlbaum Associates.

6. A variety of developmental theories argue that a central need of young children is the acceptance/acknowledgment of caregivers. These include, but are not limited to, the following theories: cognitive (Piaget, J. [1929]. *The child's conception of the world.* New York: Harcourt, Brace.); social-emotional (Erikson, E. H. [1968]. *Identity: Youth and crisis.* New York: Norton.); moral (Kohlberg, L. [1969]. Stage and sequence: The cognitive-developmental approach to socialization. In D. Goslin (Ed.), *Handbook of socialization theory and research* (pp. 347–480). Chicago: Rand McNally; Gilligan, C. [1982]. *In a different voice: Psychological theory and women's development.* Cambridge, MA: Harvard University Press.); and attachment (Bowlby, J. [1969]. *Attachment and loss* (Vol. 1). New York: Basic Books.).

7. Wynder, E. L., & Graham, E. (1950). Tobacco smoking as a possible etiologic factor in bronchiogenic carcinoma: A study of 684 proven cases. *Journal of the American Medical Association, 143,* 329–336.

8. Massing, M. (1998, March 22). Strong stuff: Why beer won't go up in smoke. *New York Times Magazine,* p. 36.

9. This proposition has also been passed in Alaska, Arizona, Hawaii, Maine, Nevada, Oregon, and Washington State; however, government officials have threatened to penalize doctors who prescribe the illegal drug, and, therefore, few doctors have actually prescribed the drug to their patients. Recently, a judge in California ruled that the government cannot penalize doctors who do prescribe marijuana. Many are waiting for the government's response; see Kravets, D. (2000, October 30). U.S. can't punish doctors for pot advice, court says. *Arizona Republic,* pp. A1, A2.

10. Editorial. (2003, February 4). Misguided marijuana war. *New York Times,* p. A28.

11. This is slowly changing as the percentage of 8th and 10th graders who view inhalants as dangerous has increased over the 1990s; see Johnston, L. D., O'Malley, P. M., & Bachman, J. G. (2002). *Monitoring the future: National survey results on drug use, 1975–2001.* Lansing: University of Michigan, Institute for Social Research.

12. See Stolberg, S. G. (2002, September 19). Children's use of prescription drugs is surging, study shows. *New York Times,* p. A29.

13. For a recent review of the literature on attention deficit hyperactivity disorder, see Purdie, N., Hattie, J., & Carroll, A. (2002). A review of the research on interventions for attention

deficit hyperactivity disorder: What works best? *Review of Educational Research, 72*(1), 61–99.

14. Zernike, K. (2001, February 4). Ritalin to the rescue: A children's story for our time. *New York Times*, p. 7.

15. Although not a performance-enhancing drug, this drug is sometimes used by athletes to mask the evidence of other performance enhancing drugs and therefore is strictly considered a banned substance.

16. Verducci, T. (2002, June 3). Totally juiced. *Sports Illustrated, 96*(23), 34–48.

17. Pain in pro football. (2002, February 3). *New York Times*, p. 14; see also Sports section of *New York Times* (2002, January 31), section C, for example, Freeman, M. (2002, January 31). Painkillers a quiet fact of life in the NFL. *New York Times*, p. C17.

18. Wertheim, L. J. (2001, April 7). Jolt of reality. *Sports Illustrated, 98*(14), 69–78.

19. Johnston, L. D., O'Malley, P. M., & Bachman, J. G. (2001). *Monitoring the future: National results on adolescent drug use. Overview of key findings, 2000*. Lansing: University of Michigan, Institute for Social Research.

20. A copy of the Master Settlement Agreement can be obtained online, retrieved February 1, 2002, http://www.tobacco.neu.edu/msa/msa_analysis.pdf. Other information can also be obtained from the following Web sites, also retrieved February 1, 2002: http://www.naag.org/tobaccopublic/library.cfm and http://www.udayton.edu/~health/syllabi/tobacco/summary.htm

21. See, for example, Kelder, G., & Davidson, P. (Eds.). (1999, March 24). *The multistate Master Settlement Agreement and the future of state and local tobacco control: An analysis of selected topics and provisions of the multistate Master Settlement Agreement of November 23, 1998*. Retrieved February 20, 2002, from http://www.tobacco.neu.edu/msa/msa_analysis.pdf; Prepared by The Tobacco Control Resource Center at Northeastern University School of Law, Boston, MA. Also refer to Winter, G. (2002, February 14). Antismoking group sues to preserve an ad in campaign's tone. *New York Times*, p. A23.

22. Fischer, H. (2002, January 31). Hull would cut raises, use highway, tobacco funds to even budget. *Arizona Daily Star*, p. A6.

23. See King, C., & Siegel, M. (2001, August 16). The Master Settlement Agreement with the tobacco industry and cigarette advertising in magazines. *The New England Journal of Medicine, 345*(7), 504–511.

24. See Winter, G. (2002, June 7). Tobacco company reneged on youth ads, judge rules. *New York Times*, p. A8.

25. Johnston, L. D., O'Malley, P. M., & Bachman, J. G. (2001). *Monitoring the future: National results on adolescent drug use. Overview of key findings, 2000*. Lansing: University of Michigan, Institute for Social Research.

26. Johnston, L. D., O'Malley, P. M., & Bachman, J. G. (December 16, 2002). *Teen smoking declines sharply in 2002, more than offsetting large increases in the early 1990s*. Ann Arbor, MI: University of Michigan News and Information Services. Available online at www.monitoringthefuture.org; Accessed August 6, 2003.

27. See the most recent *Monitoring the Future* data available online at http://monitoringthfuture.org/ or notes published by NIDA, http://www.drugabuse.gov/NIDA_notes/NNVol17N6/tearoff.html

28. Federal Interagency Forum on Child and Family Statistics. (1999). *America's children: Key national indicators of well-being, 1999* (p. 37). Washington, DC: U.S. Government Printing Office.

29. Centers for Disease Control and Prevention. (1994). Surveillance for selected tobacco-use behaviors—United States, 1900–1994. *Morbidity and Mortality Weekly Report, 43* (SS-3); see

also Newton, C. (2001). *Generation risk: How to protect your teenager from smoking and other dangerous behavior.* New York: M. Evans.

30. Johnston, L. D., O'Malley, P. M., & Bachman, J. G. (December 16, 2002). *Teen smoking declines sharply in 2002, more than offsetting large increases in the early 1990s.* Ann Arbor, MI: University of Michigan News and Information Services. Available online at www.monitoringthefuture.org; Accessed August 6, 2003.

31. National Center on Addiction and Substance Abuse. (2003, August). National survey of American attitudes on substance abuse VIII: Teens and parents. New York: Copyright © by National Center on Addiction and Substance Abuse (CASA). Accessed September 3, 2003, from http://www.casacolumbia.org/usr_doc/2003_Teen_Survey.pdf

32. Taken from the History of Tobacco, Part III. Retrieved March 29, 1999, from http://www.historian.org/bysubject/tobacco3.htm

33. Research and Tobacco Development. (1977, March 21). Planning assumptions and forecast for the period 1978–1987 for R. J. Reynolds Tobacco Company. Reprinted online by thesmokinggun.com. For information about Camel's advertising strategies, go to http://www.thesmokinggun.com/tobacco/camelad1.html (retrieved July 1, 2002) or see http://tobaccofreekids.org/reports/smokescreen/marketingkids.shtml (retrieved July 1, 2002).

34. Ling, P. M., & Glantz, S. (2002). Using tobacco-industry marketing research to design more effective tobacco-control campaigns. *Journal of the American Medical Association, 287*(22), 2983–2989.

35. For example, smoking declines in Arizona and Florida are attributed in part to the aggressive ad campaigns designed to target youth; see Associated Press. (2000, March 2). Fla. kids' ads get credit for smoking drop. *Arizona Daily Star,* p. A6; Berry, W. (2001, May 25). CDC study confirms Arizona smoking fell 21%. *Arizona Daily Star,* pp. A1, A9; Sly, D. F., Hopkins, R., Trapido, E., & Ray, S. (2001). Influence of a counter advertising media campaign on initiation of smoking: The Florida "truth" campaign. *American Journal of Public Health, 91*(2), 233–238.

36. Bauer, U. E., Johnson, T. M., Hopkins, R. S., & Brooks, R. G. (2000). Changes in youth cigarette use and intentions following implementation of a tobacco control program: Findings from the Florida Youth Tobacco Survey, 1998–2000. *Journal of the American Medical Association, 284*(6), 723–728.

37. Bauer, U. E., Johnson, T. M., Hopkins, R. S., & Brooks, R. G. (2000). Changes in youth cigarette use and intentions following implementation of a tobacco control program: Findings from the Florida Youth Tobacco Survey, 1998–2000. *Journal of the American Medical Association, 284*(6), 723–728.

38. Burgoon, M., Alvaro, E., Broneck, K., Miller, C., Grandpre, J., Hall, R., & Frank, C. (2002). Using interactive media tools to test substance abuse prevention messages. In W. Crano & M. Burgoon (Eds.), *Mass media and drug prevention: Classic and contemporary theories and research.* Mahwah, NJ: Lawrence Erlbaum Associates.

39. Goldman, L. K., & Glantz, S. A. (1998). Evaluation of antismoking advertising campaigns. *Journal of the American Medical Association, 279*(10), 772–777.

40. Newman, A. (2001, February 4). Rotten teeth and dead babies. *New York Times,* p. 16.

41. Brehm, J. W. (1996). *A theory of psychological reactance.* New York: Academic Press; Alvaro, E. M., Grandpre, J. R., Burgoon, M., Miller, C. H., & Hall, J. R. (2000, June). *Adolescent reactance and anti-smoking campaigns II.* Paper presented at the Annual Conference of the International Communication Association, Acapulco, Mexico.

42. Lombardi, K. S. (2000, January 16). Underage drinkers getting younger and drinking more. *New York Times,* p. 1.

43. Lewin, T. (2002, February 27). Teenage drinking problem but not in way study found. *New York Times,* p. A19.

44. *No place to hide: Substance abuse in mid-size cities and rural America.* (2000, January). Washington, DC: United States Conference of Mayors, Drug Enforcement Administration, National Institute on Drug Abuse. Retrieved July 1, 2002, from http://www.casacolumbia.org/usr_doc/23734.PDF

45. The most recent statistics put out by the CDC estimate that the leading cause of death for individuals ages 10–24 years is accidents (unintentional). Information is found in CDC. (2002). Deaths: Leading causes for 2000. *National Vital Statistics Report, 50*(16). Retrieved November 20, 2002, from http://www.cdc.gov/nchs/data/nvsr/nvsr50/nvsr50_16.pdf

46. Retrieved March 26, 2002, from the CDC, http://www.cdc.gov/ncipc/factsheets/teenmvh.htm

47. Hakim, D. (2003, July 3). Advertising: Ads against drunken driving are aimed at a specific group and a specific weekend. *New York Times,* p. C5.

48. Zernike, K. (2000, October 3). Colleges shift emphasis on drinking. *New York Times,* p. A1.

49. Boylan, P. (2002, April 10). Study: Booze plays role in 1,400 college deaths yearly. *Arizona Daily Star,* p. A2.

50. Haines, M. P. (1996). *A social norms approach to preventing binge drinking at colleges and universities.* Washington, DC: U.S. Department of Education, Higher Education Center for Alcohol and Other Drug Prevention. Retrieved May 21, 2003, from http://www.edc.org/hec/pubs/socnorms.html

51. Johnston, L. D., O'Malley, P. M., & Bachman, J. G. (1992). *Drug use among American high school seniors, college students, and young adults, 1975–1991, volume 2.* Washington, DC: U.S. Government Printing Office.

52. As reported in Zernike, K. (2000, October 3). Colleges shift emphasis on drinking. *New York Times,* p. A1. The story is based on anecdotal information that supports the effectiveness of a social norms approach. Research on the effectiveness of social norming approaches is still underway, and no conclusive statements can be made regarding the effectiveness of the approach, although on some campuses, there is evidence of success. For example, see Haines, M. P. (1996). *A social norms approach to preventing binge drinking at colleges and universities.* Washington, DC: U.S. Department of Education, Higher Education Center for Alcohol and Other Drug Prevention. Retrieved May 21, 2003, from http://www.edc.org/hec/pubs/socnorms.html

53. Wager, T. (2001). UA receives grant to prevent binge drinking. *Arizona Daily Wildcat.* (Available online at http://wildcat.arizona.edu/papers/95/30/01_3_m.html)

54. Wechsler, H., et al. (2003, July). Perception and reality: A national evaluation of social norms marketing interventions to reduce college students' heavy alcohol use. *Journal of Studies on Alcohol, 64,* 484–494.

55. Wren, C. (1999, November 22). More teenagers disapprove of drug use, survey finds. *New York Times* p. A14; Stout, D. (2000, September 1). Use of illegal drugs is down among young, survey finds. *New York Times,* p. A18.

56. Johnston, L. D., O'Malley, P. M., & Bachman, J. G. (December 16, 2002). *Ecstasy use among American teens drops for the first time in recent years, and overall drug and alcohol use also decline in the year after 9/11.* Ann Arbor, MI: University of Michigan News and Information Services. (Available online at www.monitoringthefuture.org; Accessed August 6, 2003)

57. *No place to hide: Substance abuse in mid-size cities and rural America.* (2000, January). Washington, DC: United States Conference of Mayors, Drug Enforcement Administration, National Institute on Drug Abuse. Retrieved July 1, 2002, from http://www.casacolumbia.org/usr_doc/23734.PDF; see also Johnston, L. D., O'Malley, P. M., & Bachman, J. G. (1999). *National survey results on drug use from the Monitoring the Future study, 1975–1998: Volume I secondary school students.* Rockville, MD: U.S. Department of Health

and Human Services, Public Health Service, National Institutes of Health, National Institute on Drug Abuse.

58. *No place to hide: Substance abuse in mid-size cities and rural America.* (2000, January). Washington, DC: United States Conference of Mayors, Drug Enforcement Administration, National Institute on Drug Abuse. Retrieved July 1, 2002, from http://www.casacolumbia.org/usr_doc/23734.PDF

59. See remarks by Shalala, D. E. (2000, August 31). *Heading for home. National Household Survey press conference.* (Available online at http://www.hhs.gov/news/speeches/00831.html)

60. *No place to hide: Substance abuse in mid-size cities and rural America.* (2000, January). Washington, DC: United States Conference of Mayors, Drug Enforcement Administration, National Institute on Drug Abuse. Retrieved July 1, 2002, from http://www.casacolumbia.org/usr_doc/23734.PDF

61. Grunbaum, J., Kann, L., Kinchen, S., Williams, B., Ross, J. G., Lowry, R., & Kolbe, L. (2002). *Youth Risk Behavior Surveillance—United States, 2001, 51*(SS04). Washington, DC: Centers for Disease Control and Prevention.

62. *No place to hide: Substance abuse in mid-size cities and rural America.* (2000, January). Washington, DC: United States Conference of Mayors, Drug Enforcement Administration, National Institute on Drug Abuse. Retrieved July 1, 2002, from http://www.casacolumbia.org/usr_doc/23734.PDF; results are based on previously unpublished analysis of Monitoring the Future data.

63. Rothstein, R. (2000, September 27). Reality check is overdue in preventing drug abuse. *New York Times,* p. B12.

64. Lively, J. (2003, July 16). D.A.R.E. meeting focuses on new curriculum. *Messenger-Inquirer,* p. B1.

65. Bowman, D. H. (2002, February 13). Teen drug use and terror linked in television spots. *Education Week,* p. 3.

66. Eccles, J. S., & Templeton, J. (2002). Extracurricular and other after-school activities for youth. In W. G. Secada (Ed.), *Review of research in education* (Vol. 26, pp. 113–180). Washington, DC: American Educational Research Association.

67. Horatio Alger Association. (2001). *The state of our nation's youth, 2001–2002.* Alexandria, VA: Horatio Alger Association of Distinguished Americans. (Available online at http://www.horatioalger.com/); see also Loven, J. (2001, August). Teens want strong family ties, survey finds. *Arizona Daily Star,* p. A4.

68. See McLaughlin, M. W. (1993). Embedded identities: Enabling balance in urban contexts. In S. B. Heath & M. W. McLaughlin (Eds.), *Identity and inner-city youth: Beyond ethnicity and gender* (pp. 36–68). New York: Teachers College Press.

69. Youniss, J., McLellan, J. A., & Yates, M. (1999). Religion, community service, and identity in American youth. *Journal of Adolescence, 22,* 243–253.

70. Greenhouse, L. (2002, June 28). Justices allow schools wider use of random drug tests for pupils. *New York Times,* p. A1.

71. Original report documented in May 2003 issue of *Journal of School Health.* Results discussed by Yamaguchi, R., Johnston, L. D., & O'Malley, P. M. (2003, May 19). Student drug testing not effective in reducing drug use [online]. Accessed August 8, 2003 from http://monitoringthefuture.org/pressreleases/03testingpr.pdf

72. See a report on this by Associated Press. (2003, February 6). New addiction treatments, targeted to girls, are urged. *Arizona Daily Star,* p. A2; see the full report released in February, 2003, at http://www.casacolumbia.org/usr_doc/Formative_Years.pdf

73. Bauman, S., Merta, R., & Steiner, R. (2001). The development of an inventory to measure motivation to change in adolescent substance abusers. *Journal of Child and Adolescent Substance Abuse, 11*(2), 19–39.

74. See the full-page ad in the *New York Times* on Hollywood's use of smoking in movies: Hollywood movies push kids to smoke. What are the directors thinking? (2002, March 19). *New York Times*, p. A19; for more information, refer to http://www.smokefreemovies.ucsf.edu

75. Gately, I. (2001). *La diva nicotina: The story of how tobacco seduced the world* (p. 349). New York: Simon & Schuster.

76. See two special issues of the *Elementary School Journal* titled *Non-Subject-Matter Outcomes of Schooling, 99*(5) and *100*(5).

Healthy Living
and Decision Making

School tells parents: Kids are fat.
—*Washington Post* headline, March 2002

In 1999, 13% of children aged 6 to 11 years and 14% of adolescents aged 12 to 19 years in the United States were overweight. This percentage has nearly tripled for adolescents in the past 2 decades.
—Office of the Surgeon General[1]

It has been suggested that obesity-related costs 'may outstrip the costs of cigarette smoking, so I don't think we have a choice but to find ways to deal with it.'
—Dr. Marc Jacobson, Pediatrician, New York City[2]

The health of the next generation is at serious risk because teens don't receive enough guidance or support for healthy living. Adults are often too complacent about improving teens' health because they think young people are apathetic, and when adults do want good things for youth, some of their goals may undermine teens' healthy development. For example, there are health costs when success and achievement are overemphasized. Is there underemphasis on helping youth cope and make good decisions? Are rising obesity[3] and depression[4] rates related to exaggerated pressures to be successful in so many areas (school, work, community service, etc.) and inadequate adult guidance in dealing with these multiple pressures?

Youth's problems and shortcomings have always been overemphasized. Many programs aimed at helping youth target specific problem behaviors (interventions to stop smoking behavior, incarceration and rehabilitation for criminal behavior)—and some of these programs are good. But there

161

are too few coordinated and researched youth programs (in school or out of school) that view youth and their development as an integrated process.[5] Comprehensive programs have considerably stronger potential to reduce harmful habits and to lay a foundation for happy living than programs that view youth in terms of their separate identities (smokers, cheaters, failing students, overweight students, etc.).

We start the chapter by noting the many contradictory cultural messages about what it means to look, feel, and live soundly. If adults are confused about what constitutes health, how can they expect youth to know? Next, we identify two main areas of adolescent health that illustrate the complex nature and interrelatedness of the biological, social, and cognitive influences on youth health. The choice of these two topics (relationships with food and sleep) are used to illustrate the importance of adults sharing responsibility for youth health and being more sensitive to the challenging expectations imposed on youth who may be inadequately socialized to understand and cope with them.

In the last section, we discuss how schools, and to a lesser extent parents and community, can help address youth's health-related issues. In theory, students could obtain sufficient exercise and could gain health-enhancing guidance and information about good nutrition from school-based physical education and health programs.[6] However, schools generally are doing too little to educate students about nutrition and exercise—how to reduce the excessive fats in their food or how to be fit. This failure has far-reaching consequences: If society is unwilling to invest in youth's health, many young people will adopt poor health and nutrition habits that may impact them for a lifetime.

CONFUSING CONCEPTIONS OF HEALTH AND FITNESS

Unfortunately, opinions on what constitutes good health practices vary widely. For centuries—and especially over the last two decades—doctors and fitness enthusiasts have debated the positive and negative effects of various fitness strategies.[7] What follows is a brief synopsis of some recent trends in health and nutrition.

Some argue that health relies on the intensity of the workout, whereas others argue it is about duration. Some say weight lifting is essential; others advocate for cardiovascular regimens. An endless supply of fitness resources are now available, including videotapes for home use, personal trainers at local gyms, and a limitless supply of books about how to get in shape. Yet, these sources provide different and often contradictory advice about how to become fit. Despite the saliency of health issues and media attention, more Americans—both adults and children—are obese than ever before.[8] The historical belief that being overweight may help older adults offset the effects of aging is now being challenged.[9] Research is showing more conclusively that staying fit is crucial for Americans of all ages.

Fitness

The popularity of exercise boomed in the 1980s. Instead of the relatively unstructured, recreational activities of the past (sandlot games organized and supervised by youth), the fitness epidemic stressed high intensity, socially engaging group aerobics classes that combined contemporary music and dance moves to create structured workout routines. As evidence mounted that 30 min of aerobic exercise at least three times a week could lower the risk of heart disease and counteract depression, it became obvious that Americans could no longer ignore the benefits of a structured, well-designed fitness regimen.

Since at least the 1980s the adult health business has also exploded, selling diets, cookbooks, video workouts, exercise trends and equipment, and vitamins and herbal supplements. Fitness centers and community gyms are widely available, and many employers promote their employees' health and fitness, some by building fitness centers in their office buildings, so employees have immediate access—and fewer excuses for not working out. Others contract with personal trainers and aerobics instructors to offer fitness classes to employees.[10] And some businesses, such as Nike, make it a policy to allow employees to take time every day—even during the workday—to work out. Adults have many resources and opportunities for staying fit. Youth have not benefited substantially from this fitness explosion. Teens younger than 18 years of age are often banned from fitness centers because of potential liabilities associated with injuries to minors. But few worry about the consequences of keeping youth out of fitness centers—a decision that has even more potentially tragic consequences for future adults and health costs for society.

Strangely, although schools are a logical alternative venue to a paucity of community centers for educating youth and providing physical activity, school physical education (PE) programs have been markedly reduced. Budget cuts and increased emphasis on academics have led to severe reductions of PE in schools. Daily enrollment in PE classes between 1991 and 1995 dropped from 42% to 25% in high school.[11] And schools that once attempted to offer PE to all students now largely only serve the needs of students who choose to compete on school teams.

The Complexity of Nutrition

As with exercise, dietary issues are vehemently debated. Are organic fruits and vegetables better for us than non-organic ones? How much soy, carbohydrates, or protein should be in our diet? The *Journal of the American Medical Association* (*JAMA*) compared and contrasted the diets of various cultures, each of which assigns different degrees of importance to certain food items.[12] The U.S. Department of Agriculture (USDA) suggests that we have 2 to 3 servings of protein (meat, fish, poultry, dry beans, eggs, or nuts) a day, whereas the Asian diet calls for only weekly servings of protein. Similarly, vegetable oils are called for on a daily basis in the Asian diet, whereas the USDA recommends that fats and oils be used sparingly. We're advised to eat chicken instead of fatty beef, but, as is typically the case, adults often add rich sauces for taste. Youth notice these habits.

There are so many unhealthy, cheap ways to double or even triple our recommended daily intake. The fast food industry is a billion-dollar business. Adults accept and encourage fast food as an American staple. With restricted budgets and growing bodies, it is no surprise that many teens choose fast food. And fast food is becoming even more available to youth as fast food chains are increasingly present in schools and hospitals. A recent *JAMA* study reported that 38% of hospitals had regional or national fast food franchises on the grounds of their medical centers; four facilities had actually contracted with two chains simultaneously.[13] As will be discussed later, the saturation of fast food has inundated schools. Thus, institutions that are designed to cure and educate youth combine to symbolize that fast foods are okay.

ADOLESCENT HEALTH

Research about health and diet is complex and obviously contradictory at times.[14] Given the difficult issues of exercise and health for adults, it is easy to understand how complex and sometimes contradictory messages about health-related behaviors create considerable confusion for youth who are disadvantaged by less experience and restricted opportunity.

Youth Are Left Out

Increasingly, policymakers are eliminating physical education programs from school settings where all students could get appropriate information about health and adequate exercise.[15] Recently, President Bush advocated his fitness agenda at the White House, calling for America's increased attention to their daily levels of physical activity; however, his stance got very little press attention, and there is no indication that it has (or will) lead to greater social support or resources for youth health. In part, this lack of response to the president's call is a clue to his more salient legislation, No Child Left Behind, which we describe more fully in chapter 8. Unlike the president's fitness program, No Child Left Behind has sanctions (both rewards and punishments) for schools whose student achievement does not increase. Ironically, the president's call for higher achievement partially undermines his call for increasing the physical fitness of youth.

Not surprisingly, disadvantaged teens—like their parents—have fewer healthy opportunities than other youth. They tend to live in neighborhoods with poorly equipped gym or recreation facilities, or sometimes they live in neighborhoods with no facilities at all. These teens also attend schools with inadequate resources for quality PE curricula; they cannot even make up for the deficit in local parks because neighborhood parks too often have become centers for doing drugs, drinking alcohol, and engaging in criminal activity, not doing exercise.

Our culture fails to help youth adopt positive attitudes toward healthy behavior that carry over into adulthood. Most health concerns relating to adolescents are viewed as isolated problems that are presumably exclusive to the teen years. Obesity is an example. One solution to help overweight teens is to reduce their diet—take away all the fast food fare—or tell them to get off their "duff." Such shortsighted solutions don't work and are often seen by teens as patronizing or evening punishing attempts to control them.

RELATIONSHIPS WITH FOOD

We focus on the interrelated problems of dieting, body image, and overeating for two reasons. First, an astonishingly large number of teens are dissatisfied with the way they look. Second, youth abuse their relationships with food in numerous ways, undereating, overeating, starving themselves, or exercising excessively. We must understand the attitudes that precipitate these behaviors if we want to help youth more effectively.

Craving to Be Thin

Self-Loathing.   Teen boys and girls of all ethnicities are dissatisfied with their bodies, want to be thinner, or have distorted notions of their appearance. Estimates suggest that 30% to 50% of children and adolescents are worried about their weight. In one study of 9- to 11-year-olds, 33% of the girls and 17% of the boys worried about being fat.[16] In another study of 8- to 10-year-olds, 55% of girls and 26% of boys wanted to be thinner.[17] These concerns with body image start early. In another study, 21% of 5-year-old girls had weight concerns.[18]

The desire to be thinner increases with age. In a study of 9- to 11-year-olds, 30% of the 9-year-olds, 55% of the 10-year-olds, and 65% of the 11-year-olds worried about being too fat.[19] Both boys and girls worry about their looks; however their concerns differ, according to gender. Girls typically want to be thinner, and boys want to be muscular. Weight loss surgeries are increasing sharply for very young children and hospital costs for youth's obesity issues have increased substantially over the last 20 years.[20]

More children and youth are getting plastic surgery to alter their appearance. According to the American Society of Plastic Surgeons (which represents 97% of all board-certified physicians), there was an approximate 80% increase in cosmetic procedures for individuals under the age of 18 years since 1996 and a 138% since 1994. Specifically, there was a 370% increase in breast augmentation surgery and a 222% increase in liposuction for girls.[21] Research supports the obvious conclusion that dissatisfaction with body image is the major reason for these surgeries.[22]

Why are so many teens dissatisfied with how they look? One widely held view is that American culture's exaggeration of thinness as a beauty ideal causes young people to agonize when they don't match that ideal.[23] Jean Kilbourne argues persuasively that the prevalence of thin females in advertising is a significant, contributing factor to female anorexia. Although some males suffer from eating disorders, they represent such a small fraction of the affected population that most research on eating disorders focuses on women. Kilbourne argues that it is only logical that females are afflicted at higher rates than males because our culture values "thin women" and "strong men."[24] Women are represented in advertising images primarily as weak, submissive, and flawlessly beautiful. And, Kilbourne points out, many photographs are altered to create the impression that the models depicted have no blemishes or even pores. Such images seduce young women to value this norm.

Ethnic and cultural differences affect the definition of what constitutes a good body. In one study among Hispanic females of Latin American descent, adolescents who immigrated to the United States before age 17 years were more likely to idealize a thinner body type than those who immigrated after the age of 17 years.[25] Other research found that there are marked differences across Black girls and White girls in terms of body satisfaction. In general, Black girls are more likely to be satisfied with the way they look, a finding that has been attributed to their racial culture, in which larger women are accepted. More research on ethnic differences is needed to better understand how to help more youth to develop more appropriate views of their physical self.

Eating Disorders.   Extreme forms of eating disorders are relatively rare, and they afflict White adolescent females disproportionately. The highest incidence of anorexia occurs in the 10- to 19-year-old population, whereas bulimia exists primarily in the 19- to 23-year-old population.[26] The *Diagnostic and Statistical Manual of Mental Disorders* (*DSM–IV,* 4th ed.), published by the American Psychiatric Association, lists criteria for three major classifications of eating disorders, including anorexia nervosa, bulimia nervosa, and eating disorder not otherwise specified (EDNOS). Based on strict adherence to *DSM–IV* criteria, prevalence rates of the two most common and most severe disorders among adolescents are low, with estimates in the 0.5% to 1.0% range for anorexia nervosa and around 1.0% for bulimia.[27] However, in shocking contrast to relatively low rates of these extreme forms of eating disorders, some clinicians estimate that 50% or more of adolescents fit into a EDNOS diagnosis. Defined as the preoccupation with an imagined deficit in appearance that leads to distress in areas of social functioning, many teens suffer from EDNOS. There is an extremely wide range of eating disorder manifestations, affecting millions of youth, including, but not limited to, distorted body image, poor eating practices, and binging cycles.[28] Thus, although anorexia and bulimia are rare, the precursors to these severe eating dysfunctions are widely prevalent.

The high prevalence of depression and anxiety disorders among girls afflicted with anorexia or bulimia suggests that eating disorders are directly related to emotional problems. It isn't clear whether depression causes eating disorders or whether having an eating disorder causes depression; however, it seems obvious that intentional starvation and bingeing are self-destructive activities that preclude a healthy emotional state.

Sexually abused young girls are also more likely to develop eating disorders as adolescents. In one small study comparing abused adolescent girls with adolescent girls who were not abused, abused girls were more frequently reported to be dissatisfied with their weight and to purge and binge.[29] It isn't clear why abused girls tend to starve themselves. One reason could be because of an intense dissatisfaction with personal appearance that is somehow linked with earlier, sexual violations. Another could be due to intense negative emotions associated with the abuse that justifies self-destructive acts ("I'm no good, I'm worthless, I don't deserve to eat"). Also, parents with little education spend little time on proactive thinking and reacting strategies to counteract the pejorative effects of earlier abuse, and better-educated parents (perhaps in denial) continue to communicate "the thinner the better."

Young boys, striving to appear strong, often abuse weight control medications or steroids. They, too, have models who influence them: athletes who use supplements to beef up. High school athletes are pressured not only to bulk their bodies as quickly as possible but also in some cases to play when injured—a win-at-all-costs philosophy. The problem is so sufficiently widespread that it was discussed with alarm by members of the National Academy of Orthopedic Surgeons (NAOS) at their annual meeting in 2002. Coaches are known to not pull players soon enough and to rush them back into competition too quickly. This practice is widely condemned by the NAOS, the American Academy of Family Physicians, and the American College of Sports Medicine because of the increased risk for injury it poses to teens, who are 2 to 4 times more likely to sustain a second injury if they are playing with a concussion.[30]

Physical Activity

Although some young men and women are active in sports or personal fitness, it is clear that too many teens do not engage in sufficient physical activity. A 1996 surgeon general report notes four main trends in youth's lack of physical activity:[31]

1. Nearly half of American youths ages 12–21 years are not vigorously active on a regular basis.
2. About 14% of young people report no recent physical activity. Inactivity is more common among girls (14%) than boys (7%) and among Black girls (21%) than White girls (12%).
3. Participation in all types of physical activity declines strikingly as age or grade in school increases.
4. Only 19% of all high school students are physical active for 20 min or more, 5 days a week, in physical education classes.

This is unfortunate because ample evidence documented in the surgeon general's report shows that adolescents benefit from physical activity and that exercise need not be exceedingly difficult to be beneficial. The surgeon general report notes the following:

1. Moderate amounts of daily physical activity are recommended for people of all ages. This amount can be obtained in longer sessions of moderately intense activities, such as brisk walking for 30 min, or in shorter sessions of more intense activities, such as jogging or playing basketball for 15–20 min.
2. Greater amounts of physical activity are even more beneficial, up to a point. Excessive amounts of physical activity can lead to injuries, menstrual abnormalities, and bone weakening.
3. Exercise helps build and maintain healthy bones, muscles, and joints.
4. Exercise helps control weight, build lean muscle, and reduce fat.

TABLE 6.1
The Problem of Overweight Adolescents and Children

- In 1999, 13% of children ages 6 to 11 years and 14% of adolescents ages 12 to 19 years in the United States were overweight. This percentage has nearly tripled for adolescents in the past two decades.
- Risk factors for heart disease, such as high cholesterol and high blood pressure, occur with increased frequency in overweight children and adolescents compared with children with a healthy weight.
- Type 2 diabetes, previously considered an adult disease, has increased dramatically in children and adolescents. Overweight and obesity are closely linked to type 2 diabetes.
- Overweight adolescents have a 70% chance of becoming overweight or obese adults. This increases to 80% if one or more parent is overweight or obese. Overweight or obese adults are at risk for a number of health problems, including heart disease, type 2 diabetes, high blood pressure, and some forms of cancer.
- The most immediate consequence of overweight as perceived by the children themselves is social discrimination. This is associated with poor self-esteem and depression.

Note. From *The Surgeon General's Call to Action to Prevent and Decrease Overweight and Obesity*, by U.S. Department of Health and Human Services, 2001, Rockville, MD: Author.

Importantly, if adults continue to cut PE in schools, emphasizing academics over physical activity and withholding precious guidance and education about fitness, it shouldn't be surprising that many more teens will be out of shape. Youth's pervasive inactivity is one of the various factors that contribute to youth obesity.

Obesity

Although some teens are starving themselves, obesity is simultaneously surging throughout the adult and teen populations (see Table 6.1).[32] Rising rates of obesity are occurring at every age, ethnic, socioeconomic, and education level. In 1991, 29% of 18- to 29-year-olds were clinically obese; by 1998, this percentage had increased to 34%. Rising obesity rates are sufficiently alarming that the American Academy of Pediatrics was moved in the summer of 2003 to prepare a public document for the first time in its existence.[33] Specifically, they urge that all children be given a body mass index evaluation (height to weight ratio) each year as part of the annual physical exam. Early detection of problems hopefully can lead to quicker and more successful intervention. Although obesity is rising in every state,[34] it disproportionately affects ethnic minority children. Mexican American and Black children are twice as likely as non-Hispanic White children to be overweight.[35] The concern for teen obesity is serious because obesity is closely linked to severe health consequences, such as diabetes, gall bladder disease, high blood pressure, heart disease, and high cholesterol.[36]

Causes of Obesity.   Physiological characteristics, such as body type, me-tabolism, and genetic disposition to gain weight, vary widely in humans. Al-though the health benefits of maintaining a healthy weight are clear, it is equally clear that some people are genetically predisposed to become over-weight. For teens, the experience of genetically influenced obesity is trau-matizing because their peers often torment them mercilessly—and fail to recognize how hard they work to control their weight.[37]

A second challenge for adults and youth alike is that although there are many dieting choices aimed at weight loss, not every method is effective for every individual. In addition to the lack of universal effectiveness of numer-ous diets, information about weight loss strategies is often contradictory, con-fusing, or distorted. For example, one current popular diet, the Atkins diet, is supported by many members of the medical community, yet other physicians believe that recommending this diet to patients qualifies as malpractice.[38] Or consider the "magic" drug Phen Phen, once considered the fix for quick, easy weight loss—eventually the drug was recalled because of its dangerous link to heart failure. A similar phenomenon occurred with Ephedra.

Trauma of Obesity.   Overweight teens are often cut off from safe and use-ful information about how to reduce and control their weight. Often an obese youth experiences taunts and criticisms from her or his peers. In one study, 72% of college-age women recalled being teased as children, usually about the way their face looked or their body weight and shape.[39] In an-other study, girls (48%) were more likely to report appearance-related teas-ing than boys (29%), with the most common type including verbal refer-ences to poor physical appearance (39%) and being overweight (13%).[40] In the face of rejection or criticism by peers, teens may hide or deny their problems and be embarrassed to ask for help. PE programs aimed at large groups rather than individuals are unlikely to educate or encourage them to lose weight. Support systems are often ineffective; parents may not know how to help or may worsen the situation by buying the wrong kinds of food. And in many schools, lunches provide few healthy choices.

Nutritional Support.   Adults have considerably more latitude in food choices than do teens because they are able to buy and cook food for them-selves. Most adolescents have less autonomy in dieting because parents make food and cooking decisions. When parents have bad eating habits, these habits are directly passed on to their children. And when schools do not emphasize healthy eating and fitness to make up for (or supplement) what families do, schools effectively abandon students to future health risks.

As a case in point, because adults are often unavailable to give advice, many teens seek advice from others via the Internet. In July 2002, one girl—using Internet chat rooms designed to help anorexics—created the goal of reducing her daily caloric intake from 500 to 200.[41] Her goal received wide support from peers also suffering with anorexia. It's unfortunate that teens must rely on advice from a misinformed support group of other anorexic youths cheering them on. Anorexic young girls finding their primary support online instead of with parents or other adults is another egregious example of leaving youth to socialize each other.

"Do As I Say, Not As I Do" Gone Amuck

In the spring of 2002, some middle and elementary schools in Pennsylvania and Florida sent confidential letters home informing parents that their daughter or son was overweight or at risk for being overweight—an action that gained national media attention. Not surprisingly, media treatment of the story varied considerably. The *Washington Post*[42] described the schools' actions, framing them from mostly a positive slant (the school carefully wrote letters, and it was a good decision because obesity is a serious and growing problem). The *New York Times,* however, reported details of the story that had been left out of the *Post*'s version, and that possibly changed readers' perceptions of what happened. For example, in Florida, the children were asked to carry the letters home, a decision that resulted in contentious debates among school board members and parents about the possible impact on children's self-esteem.

The *Times* offered a more balanced perspective, reporting positive and negative responses from parents. Many parents were unhappy with the communication and felt judged. Others viewed it as an opportunity to change diets and exercise regimens at home. Although informing parents in writing of health concerns (a common practice with hearing and vision screenings) isn't a bad idea per se, one wonders if schools that, according to one parent, serve pepperoni stromboli and that require students to take PE only once a week are doing enough.[43] Schools unfortunately are more likely to blame youth and to criticize them and their parents rather than add health and fitness instruction.

We believe that schools should proactively involve parents in nutrition programs before they label parents as indifferent (or ignorant) and their children as fat. The Office of the Surgeon General created a list of dietary and exercise recommendations to help overweight teens and their parents make good health decisions (see Table 6.2).

Unfortunately, the lunches served in many school cafeterias at best have marginal nutritional value and are typically saturated with fat. In fact, some schools, especially those that are underfunded, engage in corporate relationships with fast food and soda companies as a way to make money. If youth can have McDonald's, Pizza Hut, or Burger King for lunch, it reinforces poor eating habits that last into adulthood.[44] And bad food is not the

TABLE 6.2
Surgeon General's Suggestions for
Overweight Adolescents and Children

Physical Activity Suggestions

- Be physically active. It is recommended that Americans accumulate at least 30 min (adults) or 60 min (children) of moderate physical activity most days of the week. Even greater amounts of physical activity may be necessary for the prevention of weight gain, for weight loss, or for sustaining weight loss.
- Plan family activities that provide everyone with exercise and enjoyment.
- Provide a safe environment for your children and their friends to play actively; encourage swimming, biking, skating, ball sports, and other fun activities.
- Reduce the amount of time you and your family spend in sedentary activities, such as watching TV or playing video games. Limit TV time to fewer than 2 hours a day.

Healthy Eating Suggestions

- Follow the Dietary Guidelines for healthy eating (www.health.gov/dietaryguidelines).
- Guide your family's choices rather than dictate foods.
- Encourage your child to eat when hungry and to eat slowly.
- Eat meals together as a family as often as possible.
- Cut down on the amount of fat and calories in your family's diet.
- Don't place your child on a restrictive diet.
- Avoid the use of food as a reward.
- Avoid withholding food as punishment.
- Children should be encouraged to drink water and to limit intake of beverages with added sugars, such as soft drinks, fruit juice drinks, and sports drinks.
- Plan for healthy snacks.
- Stock the refrigerator with fat-free or low-fat milk, fresh fruit, and vegetables instead of soft drinks or snacks that are high in fat, calories, or added sugars and low in essential nutrients.
- Aim to eat at least 5 servings of fruits and vegetables each day.
- Discourage eating meals or snacks while watching TV.
- Eating a healthy breakfast is a good way to start the day and may be important in achieving and maintaining a healthy weight.

Note. From *The Surgeon General's Call to Action to Prevent and Decrease Overweight and Obesity,* by U.S. Department of Health and Human Services, 2001, Rockville, MD: Author.

only culprit; more schools allow students to have sodas, which may double their daily caloric intake. This is an unconscionable practice because soda is a prime contributor to obesity, dental erosion, and diabetes.[45]

Some schools have serious budget problems and a decision to bring in fast food may be considered an adequate trade-off if the monies supply students with books—and if it means that students will eat. One aspect of the school's impact on nutrition (or malnutrition) that is rarely discussed is the number of students who choose not to eat any meal at school, either because they cannot afford it or because the food is simply unappetizing. In schools where most of the student population qualifies for the free lunch and free breakfast program, it is not uncommon for some students not to eat lunch at all because their choices are seen as unappetizing.

In some cases, the food choices may indeed be unappetizing. However, in other cases, it is because students have been set up to prefer foods high in fat or, like adults, to add salt, sugar, or special fattening sauces such as mayonnaise, to "spruce up" a food dish. As one journalist noted, "In a Kubrickian twist, the goo needed to enliven chicken often turned out to add more fat to the dish than if you had prepared a slobbering old prime rib in the first place."[46]

Young students are increasingly being exposed to targeted advertising from fast food venues that market directly to them. Of course advertisers have always targeted children to some extent, but what is troubling at present is the intensity of efforts. For example, fast food advertising budgets increased from $12.5 billion in 1998 to $15 billion in 2002,[47] and the scope of advertising efforts have also increased. Susan Linn, a psychologist who studies children's marketing at Harvard University has observed, "It used to just be Saturday-morning television. Now it's Nickelodeon, movies, video games, the Internet and even marketing in schools."[48] Schools must do more to help students to become more knowledgeable about nutrition and the dangers of heavy use of certain foods. But fundamentally, schools must find a way to pay for school supplies and activities without depending on revenue from candy and soft drink sales.

Richard Rothstein, formerly of the *New York Times*, commented on the value of adequate nutrition needed for students to perform in schools, yet many schools provide woefully inadequate meals.[49] He notes that when dietary deficiencies exist, learning suffers, and children from low socioeconomic backgrounds are more at risk for poor diets and unequal access to balanced nutritional meals at schools. Society needs to provide schools with sufficient resources to provide adequate nutrition for youth.

SLEEPY TEENS

Not only are many teens poorly nourished or overweight, but they also get too little sleep—a problem that has gone almost unnoticed until recently.[50] Carskadon, a prominent researcher on adolescent sleep patterns, has suggested that adolescents are uniquely vulnerable to risks of excessive sleepiness, including daytime sleepiness, emotional changes, underperformance, and alterations in attention: Often they are too tired to pay attention to teachers and classwork, especially in classes perceived as boring.[51] The busiest adolescents are most at risk for excessive sleepiness. Our society makes multiple demands on its teenagers, expecting them to be constantly engaged in activities. Carskadon argues that teens who display moderately risky behavior (trying marijuana or alcohol for the first time) are more likely to make poor decisions or fail to control their impulses if they are also excessively sleepy:

> The background state of excessive sleepiness that is present in many teenagers represents an incremental risk in this already high-risk group, because it reduces the margin for safe experimentation. Thus, for example, a fully alert teenager might be able to cope adequately with a beer or two, whereas an already sleepy youngster is likely to be severely impaired due to the interaction of sleepiness and alcohol.[52]

Three main findings from research on adolescent sleep suggest ways to improve youth health. First, and most obvious, teenagers need more sleep than they typically get. It was once believed that a growing adolescent required less sleep as they approached adulthood. More recent data suggest the opposite: Teenagers, as they move from prepubescence into puberty, require more sleep than they will when they become adults. Adults need an average of 7.5 hr of sleep a night, whereas adolescents require an average of 9.2 hr of sleep per night.[53] Second, adolescents not only require more sleep at night but also tend to be sleepier throughout the day, even after a substantial night's rest. Changes occurring during puberty predispose teens to be tired a lot of the time, and getting enough sleep doesn't always eliminate daytime fatigue.[54]

Third, physiological changes associated with puberty affect students' phase preference delays (a preference for morning vs. evening wakefulness: the tendency for one to be either a night owl or a morning person).[55] Parents may see their teenagers' night owl behavior as irresponsible when they have to get up early to get to school on time. However, for many adolescents, late-night hormonal activity and biorhythms keep them up at night.[56] Adolescents are programmed to still be asleep during their first and second periods of the day. Although an optimal day for a teen would start around 11 a.m. and end around midnight, teens' school, work, and social obligations run counter to biology, posing significant motivational challenges. Consider the perspectives of just two Arizona teens: "I have to wake up at 6:45 a.m., and I am falling asleep at the wheel, literally. When I get to class, it all goes in one ear and out the other. Concentration is really, really hard." Another teen states, "I'm there, but I'm not awake. It takes me until 10 to function properly."[57]

Later School Times: One Potential Solution to Sleepiness

Some school districts, in response to adolescents' need for more sleep, have changed their school start times to later in the morning. In fact, changing very early school starting times has become a popular strategy that responds to adolescent sleep concerns—though not without unintended outcomes and problems.[58]

Results From an Experimental District. Results from one study found significant differences between students attending school district A (which adopted a start time 1 hr later) and students from school districts B and C (both of which did not change their start times). Students in school district A reported getting 1 hr of sleep more than students from school districts B and C. Their increased sleep was associated with less daytime sleepiness, less erratic sleep behaviors, and less depression compared with students in the early-start schools. District A students also reported getting higher grades.[59] Although it cannot be conclusively argued that more sleep caused the outcomes, the possible benefits of later start times in middle and high schools merits further investigation.[60]

Variation of Effects. It is important to note that students in the experimental district were unevenly affected by a later start time. Some students who were late nighters still experienced daytime sleepiness, whereas students who were morning people were less sleepy independent of whether their school started late.[61]

Later school times also affect families unevenly.[62] Although later school times were intended to allow teens to get more sleep, in some families, teens got less sleep because of familial demands (e.g., they still had to get up to help get siblings ready for school or to help with breakfast). In other families, teens' schedules were now more in sync with those of other family members, and the extra time allowed for more quality interactions among all family members. Some parents reported that their teens' attitudes and motivation toward school improved, whereas others felt their teens often expressed more frustration and experienced deteriorating attitudes toward school.

Later starting times also affected families from varying socioeconomic backgrounds differently. Given the changing family demographics (see chap. 1), there are fewer adults home in the early morning hours or the after-school hours. In some multiple-sibling families, for example, it is crucial that older adolescents get home from school on time to take care of their younger siblings who arrive later. When schools start later, some families have to adjust to having young latchkey children. If elementary schools changed to later starting times, it is likely that many working parents would have to find child care for both before and after school.

Schools are not solely responsible for accommodating teen sleep needs. If parents are more sympathetic to a teen's sleep cycle, then adjustments can be made in the home to accommodate it. For example, instead of engaging in conflicts over bedtime, parents might allow their teen greater latitude in late-night activities, thus reducing negative interactions, which often deplete energy and create a combatant environment instead of a supportive one. The problems associated with sleep-deprived youth are sufficiently large that the National Institutes of Health issued warnings to parents in 2003 about teens' sleep needs.[63]

MAKING SCHOOLING MAKE A DIFFERENCE IN YOUTH FITNESS AND OVERALL HEALTH

Currently, U.S. children get 20–40% of their total physical activity at school, with many children active only during PE programs. Unfortunately, PE programs are rapidly being cut or minimized by schools in favor of increased academic work. For some youth, their daily activity level at school has been decreased by almost half or in some cases completely. School lunch programs provide one fourth to one third of total school-day calories for participating children.[64] Unfortunately, few efforts have been made to decrease the amount of fat in school breakfasts and lunches.[65] Importantly, schools fail youth when they don't provide sound nutritional and physical fitness options.

Physical Education

School PE programs have been devalued, downsized, and, in some cases, eliminated.[66] Although PE programs have declined for various reasons, recently the push to eliminate or curtail PE programs has been fueled by the desire to find more time to prepare for standardized tests. Many elementary schools have PE only one time a week for 30 min. Middle schools tend to have PE for about 30–40 min but only three times a week, and in high school PE requirements vary from 4 years of required PE to no PE requirement at all. Often high schoolers who play sports get excused from PE. Although playing in a sport is a healthy activity, it may not be enough to provide sufficient daily exercise, and it almost certainly will not provide education for lifelong health. This lack is especially serious in the area of nutrition.

It is especially unfortunate that PE programs are being widely cut when studies show that exercise has powerful academic and motivational benefits for youth.[67] Participation in PE classes is positively related to increases in general physical activity levels; teens who take PE are more likely to lead active lifestyles that include more recreational sports involvement and less sedentary television viewing than those who do not have PE. And youth who are physically active tend to do better in school,[68] are less likely to drop out,[69] are less depressed,[70] and have more self-esteem.[71]

That so many public schools are eliminating or reducing PE creates additional health disadvantages for teens who live in low-income households and have unequal access to health care and health resources. As a case in point, Latinos are the largest minority group of children in the United States, representing 16% of the population 18 years of age and younger. And a disproportionate number of them suffer from health-related problems. According to a report released in July of 2002, Hispanic youths experience higher rates of asthma (11%) and are more than 13 times as likely to be infected with tuberculosis. A higher proportion of them have cavities (20% vs. 18% in U.S. schoolchildren). They are more likely to consider suicide (20% vs. 15% of Blacks and 18% of Whites) and experience higher rates of obesity and diabetes than their non-Hispanic peers.[72] A primary reason for the dramatic disparity between Hispanic and non-Hispanic populations is that a disproportionately larger number of Hispanic families have no health insurance. As the Hispanic population continues to grow (between 1990 and 2000, the Hispanic population jumped 58%), it seems prudent that we invest in ways to improve these health conditions for Hispanic (and all minority) youths. Expanding public school PE programs could help many students to receive needed exercise and related health information.

It is clear that youth need more chances for physical activity, but they also need information about life adjustment that can be an important part of physical education programs. In chapter 1, we argued that the general view that youth will inevitably exhibit risky behavior is overstated. We want to emphasize that although many teens are doing well (achieving in school, enjoying life, and developing effective social relations with peers and adults), preadolescence brings increased stress for many youth (and youth vary in how they handle this stress). Stipek, de la Sota, and Weishaupt,[73] after reviewing a considerable body of research, concluded that there is great variation among individuals in the hormonal changes associated with puberty; biological changes may cause a range of problems for some youth, including more emotional volatility, depression and anger, increased sexual interest, greater concern with peer acceptance, and more risk-taking behavior. Hence, youth need and can benefit greatly from life skills courses that enhance their ability to cope with issues of identity and peer pressure. And if out-of-shape youngsters are to improve their health, they need to at least increase the tolerance if not the active support of their peers.

Quality of Physical Education

The quality of PE instruction helps determine the extent to which physical activity is incorporated into a youth's life.[74] However, there is little research that empirically investigates the quality of PE programs and their effects on student outcomes such as academic achievement. In planning PE curricula, teachers and administrators must remember that simply to have a PE program is not enough: Only quality PE programs will measurably improve students' health.

What constitutes high quality is an important issue, and at present members of the National Association for Sport and Physical Education (NASPE) are debating content and performance standards.[75] Three standards recently recommended for consideration are: achieve and maintain a health enhancing level of physical fitness, demonstrate responsible personal and social behavior in physical activity settings, and choose physical activity for health, enjoyment, challenge, self-expression, and social interaction. These three standards are more fully described in Appendix A.

Many other programs are currently in operation working toward meeting such standards. There is a Web site that discusses more than 100 different individual teachers who share award-winning best practice ideas in physical education.[76] These programs are a far cry from programs of the 1950s–1980s that in part led to the demise of PE programs in schools. Undoubtedly, part of the reason that many parents have remained silent as PE programs are cut is because their own PE experiences were not very satisfying.

Positive Effects of Exercise for Girls

Regrettably, females haven't always been allowed to participate in sports and physical activities. In the late 1800s–early 1900s, women were confined to beanbag tosses, dancing, and calisthenics because they were believed to be too fragile to participate in rigorous male sports. This philosophy changed gradually, until 1972 when Title IX legislation made it illegal to discriminate against girls' participation in sports (and required a redistribution of funds across all sports for both men and women). Since then the number of females participating in sports has increased dramatically. For example, from 1986–1987 the number rose from 284,015 young women participating in high school sports to 1,836,356.[77] Indeed, the impact of this legislation suggests that when socially supported more females are willing (and quite able) to participate in sports.

After 30 years of Title IX, however, there continues to be debate over the role and impact of women in sports, and, unfortunately, female athletes are still frequently devalued. In the spirit of supporting their athletes, many fans, parents, and even coaches stereotype their female athletes by gender, not athleticism. At the University of Arizona, the gymnastics coach described his star gymnast as exemplifying ". . . what you want out of a female collegiate gymnast—beauty, class, elegance, grace and humble."[78] In response, a local resident who abhorred this description wrote a letter to the editor, arguing the athlete deserved to be judged by her athletic ability and grace under pressure, not her grace as a lady. Professional female athletes

are often admired for their femininity or looks instead of their athletic contributions (e.g., professional basketball players who end up in hair or
beauty product commercials).

Increased female participation in athletics gave rise to a plethora of studies documenting the beneficial effects of girls' participation in sports and
exercise. In comparison to those who participate in some sort of sport or
exercise, girls who do not participate are at higher risk for depression,[79]
lowered self-esteem and distorted body image.[80] These girls are also more
likely to have lower academic achievement and are more at risk for dropping out of school. Exercise has powerful effects on girls.[81] But although exercise has unique benefits for females, PE programs that serve to provide
recreational and health opportunities for all students, regardless of race,
ethnicity, socioeconomic status, age, or gender, are desperately needed.

Benefits of Team Sports for Youth

A high percentage of adolescents participate in some organized sports activity. Approximately 70% of male students and 53% of female students
(more than 10 million youth) reported participating on one or more sports
teams in school or nonschool settings. However, students' sports participation varied according to race (White, 30.6%; Black, 27.2%; Hispanic,
20.7%), according to gender (boys, 33.8%; girls, 23.1%), and according to
age (age 16 years and younger, 31.6%; older than 16 years, 25.4%). These
discrepancies are a point of concern when there are such great physical
benefits to sports participation. A survey of more than 14,000 teenagers
found that adolescents who were involved in team sports were less likely to
use drugs, smoke, have sex, carry weapons, or have poor eating habits.[82]

Although we endorse team sports for adolescents, it is clear that in some
cases athletes are taken advantage of by coaches, fans, team sponsors, and
sometimes parents. For example, a Westchester High School basketball
team in Los Angeles was one of 15 high school teams to receive $15,000 in
gear—$1,300 for each player.[83] Corporate sponsors spent more than
$20,000 sending the Westchester Comets to tournaments in Houston and
elsewhere. The Comets went on to a 32–2 record and won the California Division Championship, even though 12 members of the team did not live in
the high school's attendance area.[84]

There are known instances where parents and coaches put excessive
amounts of pressure on the athletes, sometimes resulting in violence
among the parents (e.g., recall the widely publicized fatal fight between
hockey dads), and parents have become much more likely to sue their children's coaches. There is a fine line between high expectations of student
athletes that promote healthy sportsmanship and abusive expectations that

control, manipulate, and put too much pressure on young, developing minds and bodies.

Community Support

We believe that more physical activity needs to occur in schools. However, in some settings, political forces may not allow the expansion or reintroduction of physical activity in schools. Hence, citizens must be alert to other ways to help youth to become more physically active. For example, a rich collection of roughly 80 programs that have been nationally recognized as programs with potential for addressing successfully issues of poor nutrition, obesity, and inactive life styles can be found online.[85] These nationally recognized programs provide valuable information for individuals and organizations to enhance youth health. Table 6.3 identifies a few of these programs and their sponsors.

TABLE 6.3
Model Programs for Improving Youth Health

Program	Sponsor
A Garden in Every School	California Department of Education, Nutrition Services Division
Alabama Physical Activity Enhancement Project	Alabama Department of Education
A Taste of Family Fitness	Indiana Department of Education, Division of School and Community Nutrition Program
Body Weight and Body Image Lessons for Adolescents	Pennsylvania Department of Education via Voluntary school districts
California Adolescent Nutrition and Fitness Program	California Adolescent Nutrition and Fitness Program (CANFit)
Cleveland Universal Breakfast Program	Cleveland Municipal School District
Cooking with Kids Albuquerque	Albuquerque Public Schools Food and Nutrition Department
Exemplary Physical Education Curriculum	Michigan Governor's Council on Physical Fitness, Health and Sports
Success-Oriented P.E.	Seattle Public Schools
Nutrition Education in Philadelphia Public Schools	Food Services Division, School District of Philadelphia
Los Angeles Unified School District Nutrition Network	Los Angeles Unified School District
Healthy Choices	Massachusetts Department of Public Health

Note.   More information on these and other programs that are having positive effects on student health can be found online at http://www.edcenter.info/. We acknowledge Dave Griffey, a professor of physical education at the University of Arizona, who made us aware of this Web site.

TABLE 6.4
What Communities Can Do to Promote Youth Health

- Provide quality, preferably daily, K–12 physical education classes and hire physical education specialists to teach them.
- Create opportunities for physical activities that are enjoyable, that promote adolescents' and young adults' confidence in their ability to be physically active, and that involve friends, peers, and parents.
- Provide appropriate physically active role models for youth.
- Provide access to school buildings and community facilities that enable safe participation in physical activity.
- Provide a range of extracurricular programs in schools and community recreation centers to meet the needs and interests of specific adolescent and young adult populations, such as racial and ethnic minority groups, women, persons with disabilities, and low-income groups.
- Encourage health care providers to talk routinely to adolescents and young adults about the importance of incorporating physical activity into their lives.

Note. From *The Surgeon General's Call to Action to Prevent and Decrease Overweight and Obesity,* by U.S. Department of Health and Human Services, 2001, Rockville, MD: Author.

The surgeon general has also urged broader community support to promote youth health, as noted in Table 6.4. Elsewhere, educational researchers and policy leaders have summarized additional ways in which the community and the school can partner to develop after-school programs.[86]

CONCLUSION

We discussed the unique difficulties that teens face in leading healthy lives. On one level, there are biological factors that must be acknowledged. Some teens gain weight more easily than others; many succumb to excessive sleepiness brought on by physiological changes. On another level, teens are coping with emerging abstract cognitive abilities and evolving emotions. Exposure to contradictory messages (e.g., when one diet is valued over another) and to salient messages about ideal physical appearance may cause confusion or distress for young people who are susceptible to media power. Until self-identity constructs are integrated and more mature cognitive strategies are in place, adolescents will be especially vulnerable to suggestive messages and social pressures. Unless more adults play an active role in mediating external messages, youth will be left to socialize each other, a situation that will make them more vulnerable to inappropriate decisions.

The definition of good health, as well as the formula for achieving it, remains elusive. Even those in health-related fields (doctors, physical educators) disagree on what is best for the typical adult. What is best for the typical teen is even more elusive because of the variations in individual skills, understanding, opportunities, and motivation. Yet it is critical that teens be encouraged to adopt health habits, so they will carry healthy decision-making skills into adulthood.

Too many teens have unhealthy body images, and these concerns, which vary, may drive some to excessive and self-destructive behavior. Teens' poor nutrition is too often matched by inadequate sleep and exercise. Ironically, despite an increase in our knowledge about exercise and nutrition, our use of this knowledge and the promotion of physical activities has declined in public schools. Although participation rates in organized sports are up, many youths are not part of these groups. Hence, an opportunity for physical activity is denied to many school-age students.

General Considerations

Youth are criticized (often unjustly) because of excessive tobacco, alcohol, and drug (TAD) use, sexuality, and violence. Society generally attempts to convince youth to reduce, if not totally stop, these behaviors. In the area of youth health, society has a grand chance to tell youth do something—more physical activity, better weight management, and nutrition—yet not enough educators, parents, or citizens are doing their share to create programs where youth can participate in safe and exciting health programs. Needed also are broader vision of youth. Youth are not just smokers or drinkers or good athletes. It is important to plan programs that see and respond to youth as social beings with various strengths and weaknesses.

Adults complain that youth watch too much TV and consume too many violent movies. They fear that teens will act out the sex acts and engage in TAD violations that they see in the media. Youth are viewed by many adults as sedentary to the point of laziness and that, when they do act, it is too often in the form of crime, violence, or other forms of antisocial behavior. Youth are blamed for their sloth, obesity, and selfish behavior. Despite such attitudes, adult society leaves youth more unsupervised in the after-school hours than ever before. And it is widely known that youth are most likely to experiment widely with their sexuality and various risk-taking behaviors, including crime for some youth, in the hours following school dismissal. Further, this is the time when many crimes against youth by adults also take place. Thus, it seems unfortunate and lamentable that youth are blamed by adults, while simultaneously adults deny youth places to play, exercise, and engage in creative activities, allowing school yards and neighborhood parks to go unused. Youth notice these things.

Schools are in an optimal position to teach youth wellness lessons and proactive health habits that will endure into adulthood. Teens who participate in organized sports benefit physically and socially. Unfortunately, White students are more likely to participate in sports than Blacks and Hispanics, and, given that school-wide PE programs are being cut, more programs and funding need to be directed toward helping young minority students learn about and participate in vital and nonviolent physical activity. Providing adequate PE opportunities for all students is vital.

Teens' sleep needs must be addressed. Lack of sleep is an important health problem that often gets overlooked. While parents and educators argue for better academic achievement and higher standards, too few recognize that tired, overworked, and overextended teens will be hard-pressed to do well (although many do). Although we believe teens need to get more sleep, we are equally aware that the impact of shifting school start times is not always positive. Although increased sleep among adolescents is associated with increased academic achievement, less absenteeism, mood elevation, and behavioral improvement,[87] it is clear that later school start times are not easily implemented and do not universally benefit students and families. Some students might drop their participation in after-school activities because later school dismissal forces them to walk home after dark.

Needed Research

Confusing and conflicting health wisdom abounds. Adolescents should be surveyed to assess accurately their knowledge of health issues and to identify the kinds of programs needed to educate them effectively. It is unclear exactly what youth know about good nutrition and exercise habits, and it is even less clear how (or if) they act on that information. Business communities spend millions of dollars talking to teens to learn more about their consumer interests. Schools could profitably spend more time discussing what youth want to know about health.

It is critical to better understand how youth's attitudes toward and knowledge about health and nutrition vary based on cultural backgrounds. According to the CDC, the Hispanic/Latino population disproportionately suffers from conditions such as HIV/AIDS, obesity, asthma, suicide, and teen pregnancy. More research is needed to identify the unique risk factors associated with various subcultures.

The physical plants of schools should be open to more students after normal school hours. Surely, the insurance and supervision costs would be more than offset by students' opportunities to engage in fun but appropriate physical activity, to learn more about their nutritional needs, and to discuss academic issues and interests with adults. Research on such programs might find that positive experiences with schools in these settings may strengthen general attitudes about the value of education per se.

Further, it is vital that schools develop and evaluate programs that educate youth on tolerance. Too many youth suffer from social discrimination as a result of being overweight. Therefore, youth need quality intervention, not only to become fit but also to value the importance of not criticizing overweight peers. More research is needed, too, on how best to disseminate health information: what content should be taught at what grade level and how best to involve students in the learning of appropriate content skills and values.

Some might think that it is self-evident that schools spend time finding out what youth want to know about health; in fact, much instruction is wasted when topics are dealt with before youth are interested in them, and, of course, instruction is of limited value when it comes after teens have made health-related decisions. Similarly, golden rules logic—not making fun of overweight students—is easier said than achieved. Needed is careful research that develops strategies and tests them for helping youth to become more tolerant of one another.

Data suggest that boys and girls who are bulimic or anorexic suffer from highly distorted body images and depression and are likely to have been abused. These are important health issues and could be addressed by clearer and more focused health programs in schools that directly assess teens' perceptions of their bodies and other factors associated with eating disorders.

APPENDIX A[88]

Standard 1: Achieves and Maintains a Health-Enhancing Level of Physical Fitness

The intent of this standard is for students to have both the ability and willingness to accept responsibility for personal fitness leading to an active, healthy lifestyle. Students develop higher levels of basic fitness and physical competence as needed for many work situations and active leisure participation. Health-related fitness components include cardiorespiratory endurance, muscular strength, and endurance, flexibility, and body composition. Expectations for students' fitness levels are established on a personal basis, taking into account variation in entry levels, rather than setting a single standard for all children at a given grade level or comparing one student to another. Students progress in their ability to participate in moderate to vigorous physical activities that address each component of health-related fitness. Moreover, students become more skilled in their ability to plan, perform, and monitor physical activities appropriate for developing physical fitness. For elementary children, the emphasis is on an awareness of fitness components and having fun while participating in health-enhancing activities that promote physical fitness. Middle school students gradually acquire a greater understanding of the fitness components, how each is developed and maintained, and the importance of each in overall fitness. Secondary students are able to design and develop an appropriate personal fitness program that enables them to achieve desired levels of fitness.

Standard 2: Demonstrates Responsible Personal and Social Behavior in Physical Activity Settings

The intent of this standard is achievement of self-initiated behaviors that promote personal and group success in activity settings. These include safe practices, adherence to rules and procedures, etiquette, cooperation and teamwork, ethical behavior in sport, and positive social interaction. Key to this standard is developing respect for individual similarities and differences through positive interaction among participants in physical activity. Similarities and differences include characteristics of culture, ethnicity, motor performance, disabilities, physical characteristics (e.g., strength, size, shape, gender, race, and socioeconomic status. Achievement of this standard in the lower elementary grades begins with recognition of classroom rules and procedures and a focus on safety. In the upper elementary levels, children learn to work independently, with a partner, and in small groups. Throughout elementary school, students begin to recognize individual similarities and differences and participate cooperatively in physical activity. In the middle school, adolescents identify the purposes for rules and procedures and become involved in decision-making processes to establish the rules and procedures to guide specific activity situations. They participate cooperatively in physical activity with persons of diverse characteristics and backgrounds. High school students initiate responsible behavior, function independently and responsibly, and positively influence the behavior of others in physical activity settings. They are expected to be able to participate with all people, recognize the value of diversity in physical activity, and develop strategies for inclusion of others.

Standard 3: Chooses Physical Activity for Health, Enjoyment, Challenge, Self-Expression and Social Interaction

The intent of this standard is to develop an awareness of the intrinsic values and benefits of participation in physical activity that provides personal meaning. Physical activity provides opportunities for self-expression and social interaction and can be enjoyable, challenging, and fun. These benefits develop self-confidence and promote positive self-image, thereby enticing people to continue participation in activity throughout the life span. Elementary children derive pleasure from movement sensations and experience challenge and joy as they sense a growing competence in movement ability. At the middle school level, participation in physical activity provides important opportunities for challenge, social interaction, and group membership, as well as opportunities for continued personal growth in physical skills and their applied settings. Participation at the high school level continues to provide enjoyment and challenge as well as opportunities for self-expression and social interaction. As a result of these intrinsic benefits of participation, students will begin to actively pursue lifelong physical activities that meet their own needs.

ENDNOTES

1. Taken from Office of the Surgeon General. (2001). *The surgeon general's call to action to prevent and decrease overweight and obesity.* Rockville, MD: U.S. Department of Health and Human Services. Retrieved April 10, 2002, from http://www.surgeongeneral.gov/topics/obesity/calltoaction/CalltoAction.pdf

2. Quote taken from article by Tanner, L. (2003, August 4). Body-mass checks urged for all kids. *Arizona Daily Star,* p. A5.

3. Ogden, C. L., Flegal, K. M., Carroll, M. D., & Johnson, C. L. (2002). Prevalence and trends in overweight among U.S. children and adolescents, 1999–2000. *Journal of the American Medical Association, 288,* 1728–1732.

4. Birmaher, B., Ryan, N. D., Williamson, D. E., Brent, D. A., & Kaufman, J. (1996). Childhood and adolescent depression: A review of the past 10 years. Part II. *Journal of the American Academy of Child and Adolescent Psychiatry, 35,* 1575–1583.

5. See Weissberg, R. P., & Kumpfer, K. L. (Guest Eds.). (2003, June/July). Special Issue: Prevention that works for children and youth. *American Psychologist, 58*(6/7).

6. Robinson, T. N., & Killen, J. D. (2001). Obesity prevention for children and adolescents. In J. K. Thompson & L. Smolak (Eds.), *Body image, eating disorders, and obesity in youth: Assessment, prevention, and treatment* (pp. 261–292). Washington, DC: American Psychological Association.

7. For example, see Sallis, J. F., McKenzie, T. L., Kolody, B., Lewis, M., Marshall, S., & Rosengard, P. (1999). Effects of health-related physical education on academic achievement: Project SPARK. *Research Quarterly of Exercise and Sport, 70*(2), 127–134; U.S. Department of Health and Human Services. (2000, Fall). *Promoting better health for young people through physical activity and sports.* Washington, DC: Author. (Available online at http://www.cdc.gov/nccdphp/dash/healthtopics/physical_activity/promoting_health/pdfs/ppar.pdf)

8. Mokdad, A. H., et al. (2001). The continuing epidemics of obesity and diabetes in the United States. *Journal of the American Medical Association, 286*(10), 1195–1200.

9. In one of America's largest circulation magazines, *AARP,* it was reported (based on data from the CDC) that obesity is affecting older Americans with much greater frequency than ever before. See Stolberg, S. G. (2003, March/April). There's an obesity epidemic among 50+ Americans. *AARP: The Magazine, 1*(1A), 66–70. A 1998 *New England Journal of Medicine* article reviewed the health histories of 325,000 White adults and found that, although overweight people were overall more likely to die from all causes, the increased risk was only slight by the age of 65 years and nonexistent over the age of 75. See Stevens, J., et al. (1998). The effect of age on the association between body-mass index and mortality. *New England Journal of Medicine, 33*(1), 1–7.

10. Indeed, as a personal trainer in New York City, the first author worked for several businesses, attending offices to train individuals or groups of employees and saw firsthand the growing presence of fitness awareness within corporate institutions.

11. U.S. Department of Health and Human Services. (1996). *Physical activity and health: A report of the Surgeon General.* Washington, DC: Author.

12. Mitka, M. (2000). Where the elite meet to eat—A CME course? *Journal of American Medical Association, 284*(7), 817–818.

13. Cram, P., Nallanothu, B. K., Fendrick, A. M., Saint, S. (2002). Research letter: Fast food franchises in hospitals. *Journal of the American Medical Association, 287*(22), 2945–2946. It is important to note that these conclusions were based on a small sample of 16 hospitals chosen because they had been rated as honor roll hospitals by *US News & World Report.* Thus, more research needs to be done to accurately describe relationships between fast food corporations and hospitals.

14. U.S. Department of Health and Human Services. (1996). *Physical activity and health: A report of the surgeon general.* Atlanta, GA: Author.

15. U.S. Department of Health and Human Services. (1996). *Physical activity and health: A report of the surgeon general.* Atlanta, GA: Author.

16. Gustafson-Larson, A., & Terry, R. (1992). Weight-related behaviors and concerns of fourth-grade children. *Journal of the American Dietetic Association, 92,* 818–822.

17. Wood, C., Becker, J., & Thompson, J. K. (1996). Body image dissatisfaction in preadolescent children. *Journal of Applied Developmental Psychology, 17,* 85–100.

18. Smolak, L., & Levine, M. P. (2001). Body image in children. In J. K. Thompson & L. Smolak (Eds.), *Body image, eating disorders, and obesity in youth: Assessment, prevention, and treatment* (pp. 41–66). Washington, DC: American Psychological Association.

19. Mellin, L., Irwin, C., & Scully, S. (1992). Prevalence of disordered eating in girls: A survey of middle-class children. *Journal of the American Dietetic Association, 92,* 851–853.

20. See Kimm, S. Y. S., & Obarzanek, E. (2002). Childhood obesity: A new pandemic of the new millennium. *Pediatrics, 110,* 1003–1007.

21. Sarwar, D. B. (2001). Plastic surgery in children and adolescents. In J. K. Thompson & L. Smolak (Eds.), *Body image, eating disorders, and obesity in youth* (pp. 341–366). Washington, DC: American Psychological Association.

22. Sarwar, D. B., Wadden, T. A., Pertschuk, M. J., & Whitaker, L. A. (1998). The psychology of cosmetic surgery: A review and reconceptualization. *Clinical Psychology Review, 18,* 1–22.

23. Lewinsohn, P., Striegel-Moore, R. H., & Seeley, J. R. (2000). Epidemiology and natural course of eating disorders in young women from adolescence to young adulthood. *Journal of the American Academy of Child and Adolescent Psychiatry, 39,* 1284–1292.

24. Kilbourne, J. (2000). *Killing us softly 3.* Northhampton, MA: Media Education Foundation. (For further info, see http://jeankilbourne.com/video.html)

25. Lopez, E., Blix, G., & Blix, A. (1995). Body image of Latinas compared to body image of non-Latina White women. *Health Values: The Journal of Health Behavior, Education & Promotion, 19*(6), 3–10; as cited in Dounchis, J. Z., Hayden, H. A., & Wilfley, D. E. (2001). Obesity, body image, and eating disorders in ethnically diverse children and adolescents. In J. K. Thompson & L. Smolak (Eds.), *Body image, eating disorders, and obesity in youth* (pp. 67–98). Washington, DC: American Psychological Association.

26. Turnbull, S., Ward, A., Treasure, J., Jick, H., & Derby, L. (1996). The demand for eating disorder care: An epidemiological study using the General Practice Research Database. *British Journal of Psychiatry, 169,* 705–712.

27. Thompson, J. K., & Smolak, L. (2001). Body image, eating disorders, and obesity in youth: The future is now. In J. K. Thompson & L. Smolak (Eds.), *Body image, eating disorders, and*

obesity in youth: Assessment, prevention, and treatment (pp. 1–18). Washington, DC: American Psychological Association.

28. Thompson, J. K., & Smolak, L. (Eds.). (2001). *Body image, eating disorders, and obesity in youth: Assessment, prevention, and treatment.* Washington, DC: American Psychological Association.

29. Neumark-Sztainer, D., et al. (2000). Sexual abuse increases the risk of succumbing to eating disorders among teen-age survivors, both male and female. *International Journal of Eating Disorders, 28,* 249–258.

30. Associated Press. (2002, February 17). Athletes face inadequate medical care. *New York Times,* p. 14.

31. U.S. Department of Health and Human Services. (1996). *Physical activity and health: Adolescents and young adults.* Washington, DC: Author.

32. Mokdad, A. H., et al. (2001). The continuing epidemics of obesity and diabetes in the United States. *Journal of the American Medical Association, 286*(10), 1195–1200; see also Ogden, C. L., Flegal, K. M., Carroll, M. D., & Johnson, C. L. (2002). Prevalence and trends in overweight among U.S. children and adolescents, 1999–2000. *Journal of the American Medical Association, 288,* 1728–1732; Associated Press. (2000, December 15). We're getting fatter, government warns. *Arizona Daily Star,* p. A8.

33. American Academy of Pediatrics. (2003, August). Prevention of pediatric overweight and obesity. *Pediatrics, 112*(2), 424–430 [online], accessed August 9, 2003, from http://www.aap.org/policy/s100029.html

34. Mokdad, A. H., Serdula, M. K., Dietz, W. H., Bowman, B. A., Marks, J. S., & Koplan, J. P. (1999, October 27). The spread of the obesity epidemic in the United States, 1991–1998. *Journal of the American Medical Association, 282*(16), 1519–1522.

35. Editorial. (2002, November 29). America's epidemic of youth obesity. *New York Times,* p. A32; see also the Centers for Disease Control and Prevention, National Center for Health Statistics.

36. Must, A., Spadano, J., Coakley, E. H., Field, A. E., Colditz, G., & Dietz, W. H. (1999). The disease burden associated with overweight and obesity. *Journal of the American Medical Association, 282*(16), 1523–1529.

37. Shapiro, J. P., Baumeister, R. F., & Kessler, J. W. (1991). A three-component model of children's teasing: Aggression, humor, and ambiguity. *Journal of Social and Clinical Psychology, 10*(4), 459–472.

38. Kolata, G. (2000, October 18). No days off are allowed, experts on weight argue. *New York Times,* pp. A1, A18.

39. Cash, T. F. (1995). Developmental teasing about physical appearance: Retrospective descriptions and relationships with body image. *Journal of Social Behavior and Personality, 23,* 123–130.

40. Shapiro, J. P., Baumeister, R. F., & Kessler, J. W. (1991). A three-component model of children's teasing: Aggression, humor, and ambiguity. *Journal of Social and Clinical Psychology, 10,* 459–472.

41. Morris, B. R. (2002, June 23). A disturbing growth industry: Websites that espouse anorexia. *New York Times,* p. 8.

42. Loviglio, J. (2002, March 22). School tells parents: Kids are fat. *Washington Post.* Retrieved March 27, 2002, from http://www.washingtonpost.com/ac2/wp-dyn/A2326Mar22/

43. Morris, B. R. (2002, March 26). Letter on students' weight ruffles parents. *New York Times,* p. F7.

44. Schlosser, E. (2001). *Fast food nation: The dark side of the all-American meal.* Boston: Houghton Mifflin.

45. Ludwig, D. S., Peterson, K. E., & Gortmaker, S. L. (2001). Relation between consumption of sugar-sweetened drinks and childhood obesity: A prospective, observational analysis. *Lancet, 357,* 505–508; see also Fried, E. J., & Nestle, M. (2002, November 6). The growing political movement against soft drinks in schools. *Journal of the American Medical Association, 288,* 2181.

46. Reynolds, J. (2002, April 7). Belly up. *New York Times Magazine,* p. 71.

47. Barboza, D. (2003, August 3). If you pitch it, they will eat. *New York Times,* section 3, p. 1.

48. Quote taken from Barboza, D. (2003, August 3). If you pitch it, they will eat. *New York Times,* section 3, p. 1.

49. Rothstein, R. (2001, August 1). When there's simply not enough food for thought. *New York Times,* p. A15.

50. Richardson, L. (1995, December 27). To sleep, perchance to stay awake in class. *New York Times,* pp. A1, B16; Brooks, A. (1996, October 31). For teen-agers, too much to do, too little time for sleep. *New York Times;* Martin, D. (1999, August 1). Late to bed, early to rise makes a teen-ager tired. *New York Times,* Section 4A; Johnson, K. V. (1998, June 24). Schools slow to wake up to teens' need to sleep in. *USA Today,* p. 4D; Hellmich, N. (2000, March 28). A teen thing: Losing sleep. *USA Today,* pp. 1A, 9A; Holt, G. (1996, August 26). Schools start too early, experts say. *Seattle Post-Intelligencer,* pp. A1, A8; Skinner, M. S. (2000, June 23). Adults get wake-up call on teen sleep cycles. *Arizona Daily Star,* p. A1; Konski, T. (2000, June 30). Getting some shut-eye. *Arizona Daily Star,* p. B7.

51. Dahl, R. E. (1999, January). The consequences of insufficient sleep for adolescents: Links between sleep and emotional regulation. *Phi Delta Kappan, 80*(5), 354–359.

52. Carskadon, M. A. (1990). Adolescent sleepiness: Increased risk in a high-risk population. *Alcohol, Drugs, and Driving, 5/6,* 317–328.

53. Wolfson, A. R., & Carskadon, M. A. (1998). Sleep schedules and daytime functioning in adolescents. *Child Development, 69*(4), 875–887.

54. Carskadon, M. A., Wolfson, A. R., Acebo, C., Tzischinsky, O., & Seifer, R. (1998). Adolescent sleep patterns, circadian timing, and sleepiness at a transition to early school days. *Sleep, 21*(8), 871–875; Carskadon, M. A. (1990). Patterns of sleep and sleepiness in adolescents. *Pediatrician, 17,* 5–12; Carskadon, M. A., & Dement, W. C. (1987). Sleepiness in the normal adolescent. In C. Guilleminault (Ed.), *Sleep and its disorders in children* (pp. 53–65). New York: Raven Press.

55. Carskadon, M. A., Acebo, C., Richardson, G. S., Tate, B. A., & Seifer, R. (1997). Long nights protocol: Access to circadian parameters in adolescents. *Journal of Biological Rhythms, 12,* 278–289.

56. Carskadon, M. A., Vieira, C., & Acebo, C. (1993). Association between puberty and delayed phase preference. *Sleep, 16*(3), 258–262.

57. Skinner, M. S. (2000, June 23). Adults get wake-up call on teen sleep cycles. *Arizona Daily Star,* p. A1.

58. Wahlstrom, K. L. (1999, January). The prickly politics of school starting times. *Phi Delta Kappan, 80*(5), 345–347; Kubow, P. K., Wahlstrom, K. L., & Bemis, A. E. (1999, January). Starting time and school life: Reflections from educators and students. *Phi Delta Kappan, 80*(5), 366–371; Carskadon, M. A. (1999, January). When worlds collide: Adolescent need for sleep versus societal demands. *Phi Delta Kappan, 80*(5), 348–353.

59. Frederickson, J., & Wrobel, G. D. (1997). *School start time study: Technical report, Vol. II.* Minneapolis: Center for Applied Research and Educational Improvement, University of Minnesota.

60. Although students in school district A also received higher grades than students from districts B and C, this should be interpreted with caution. Although it is possible that later

school times and subsequently greater amounts of sleep are more conducive to better learning and higher academic achievement, these grade differences could be due to other factors, such as grade inflation or that students in school district A spend more time on homework than students from other districts. Higher achievement could also be attributed to a halo motivation effect where students are motivated to perform in schools they perceive are treating them as special and different.

61. Wahlstrom, K., Wrobel, G., & Kubow, P. (1998, November). *Minneapolis Public Schools start time study: Executive summary*. Minneapolis: Center for Applied Research and Educational Improvement, University of Minnesota.

62. Information in this section comes from Wrobel, G. D. (1999, January). The impact of school starting time on family life. *Phi Delta Kappan, 80*(5), 360–364.

63. McDonough, S. (2003, January 29). NIH urges parents to help kids value sleep. *Arizona Daily Star*, p. A3; see also National Institutes of Health's *Educating Youth About Sleep and Drowsy Driving*, National Center on Sleep Disorders Research, National Heart, Lung, and Blood Institute (Available online at http://www.nhlbi.nih.gov/health/prof/sleep/dwydrv_y.pdf); see also the site sponsored by the Sleep Disorders Clinic that targets the education of youth on sleep (http://www.nhlbi.nih.gov/health/public/sleep/starslp/index.htm)

64. Robinson, T. N., & Killen, J. D. (2001). Obesity prevention for children and adolescents. In J. K. Thompson & L. Smolak (Eds.), *Body image, eating disorders, and obesity in youth* (pp. 261–292). Washington, DC: American Psychological Association.

65. Robinson, T. N., & Killen, J. D. (2001). Obesity prevention for children and adolescents. In J. K. Thompson & L. Smolak (Eds.), *Body image, eating disorders, and obesity in youth* (pp. 261–292). Washington, DC: American Psychological Association.

66. Chase, R. (2000, June 7). Why kids are unfit. *Arizona Daily Star*, p. A2.

67. Kientzler, A. (1999). Fifth- and seventh-grade girls' decisions about participation in physical activity. *Elementary School Journal, 99*(5), 391–414.

68. Eccles, J. S., & Barber, B. L. (1999). Student council, volunteering, basketball, or marching band: What kind of extracurricular involvement matters? *Journal of Adolescent Research, 14*, 10–43.

69. Eccles, J. S., & Barber, B. L. (1999). Student council, volunteering, basketball, or marching band: What kind of extracurricular involvement matters? *Journal of Adolescent Research, 14*, 10–43.

70. Barber, B. L., Eccles, J. S., & Stone, M. R. (2001). Whatever happened to the jock, the brain, and the princess? Young adult pathways linked to adolescent activity involvement and social identity. *Journal of Adolescent Research, 16*, 429–455.

71. Whitehead, J. R., & Corbin, C. B. (1997). Self-esteem in children and youth: The role of sport and physical education. In K. R. Fox (Ed.), *The physical self: From motivation to well-being* (pp. 175–203). Champaign, IL: Human Kinetics.

72. See Flores, G., et al. (2002). The health of Latino children: Urgent priorities, unanswered questions, and a research agenda. *Journal of the American Medical Association, 288*(1), 82–93.

73. Stipek, D., de la Sota, A., & Weishaupt, L. (1999, May). Life lessons: An embedded classroom approach to preventing high-risk behaviors among preadolescents. *Elementary School Journal, 99*(5), 433–452.

74. For example, Pensgaard, A. M., & Roberts, G. C. (2000). The relationship between motivational climate, perceived ability and sources of distress among elite athletes. *Journal of Sports Sciences, 18*, 191–200.

75. NASPE standards can be found online at http://www.aahperd.org/naspe/pdf_files/input_standards.pdf

76. See http://www.pecentral.org/bp/TempBestPracticesDisplay.asp?room=All/; our thanks to Dave Griffey, a professor of physical education at the University of Arizona, who made us aware of this Web site.

77. The Center for Research on Girls and Women in Sport. (1997). *Physical activity and sport in the lives of girls: The President's Council on Physical Fitness and Sports Report* (p. 44). Minneapolis: University of Minnesota.

78. Editorial. (2002, April 15). Judge female gymnasts only on athletic abilities. *Arizona Daily Star*, p. B4; Harris, T. (2002, April 6). The perfect balance. *Arizona Daily Star*, pp. C1, C6.

79. Morgan, W. P. (1994). Physical activity, fitness and depression. In C. Bouchard, R. J. Shephard, & T. Stephens (Eds.), *Physical activity, fitness and health* (pp. 851–867). Champaign, IL: Human Kinetics.

80. Jaffee, L., & Manzer, R. (1992). Girls' perspectives: Physical activity and self-esteem. *Malpomene: A Journal for Women's Health Research, 11*(3), 14–23; Jaffee, L., & Ricker, S. (1993). Physical activity and self-esteem in girls: The teen years. *Melpomene: A Journal for Women's Health Research, 12*(3), 19–26; Jaffee, L., & Lutter, J. M. (1995). Adolescent girls: Factors influencing low and high body image. *Malpomene: A Journal for Women's Health Research, 14*(2), 14–22.

81. Kientzler, A. (1999). Fifth- and seventh-grade girls' decisions about participation in physical activity. *Elementary School Journal, 99*(5), 391–414.

82. Pate, R., Trost, S., Levin, S., & Dowda, M. (2000). Sports participation and health-related behaviors among U.S. youth. *Archives of Pediatrics and Adolescent Medicine, 154,* 904–911.

83. All-American [Editorial]. (2002, April 14). *Arizona Daily Star*, p. B8.

84. All-American [Editorial]. (2002, April 14). *Arizona Daily Star*, p. B8.

85. See http://www.edcenter.info/AFHK/whatsworking/viewall.php/

86. See Adair, J. K., Chung, A., & Stonehill, R. B. (2003). Ensuring quality and sustainability in after school programs: How partnerships play a key role. In M. M. Brabeck, M. E. Walsh, & R. E. Latta (Eds.), *Meeting at the hyphen: Schools-universities-communities-professions in collaboration for student achievement and well-being* (pp. 201–220). Chicago: National Society for the Study of Education.

87. Wahlstrom, K., Wrobel, G., & Kubow, P. (1998, November). *Minneapolis Public Schools start time study: Executive summary*. Minneapolis: Center for Applied Research and Educational Improvement, University of Minnesota.

88. More information about these standards and how they can be measured can be found on the American Alliance for Health, Physical Education, Recreation, and Dance (AAHPERD) Web site at http://www.aahperd.org/. These three standards are among six that are more fully described in a document found on the Web at: http://www.aahperd.org/naspe/pdf_files/input_standards.pdf. We thank Gay M. Timken, an Assistant Professor of Physical Education at the University of Arizona, for making us aware of this Web site.

Chapter 7

Working Teens

Teens are injured at the work place at nearly twice the rate of adults and it is estimated that at least one teen is hurt on the job every 40 seconds, while one dies every five days.

—U.S. Committee on Health and Safety Implications
of Child Labor, 1998[1]

I would never work at a McDonald's . . . and when I was looking for a job, my brother warned me not to take a job at a McDonald's or a Burger King. I guess he thought it would bring down his reputation to have a brother working at a place like that.

—16-year-old David Neuzil[2]

The question of whether young people should work while they are still in school is vigorously debated. Some adults question whether youth should work at all, whereas others believe the central issue is not whether youth should work but how much. Research on how working affects youth academically and socially provides no conclusive answers: Some youths benefit from holding a job; others do not. And some benefit from working more hours—keeping constantly busy—whereas for others working too much has deleterious social or academic effects. Ultimately, one constant seems to be that the quality of teens' working experiences largely determines whether working is beneficial or detrimental. Unfortunately, many adults believe for teenagers any job is good.

As with other aspects of teens' lives, beliefs about youth employment are stereotypical, failing to recognize the enormous range of positive contributions of working youth—which are undervalued and minimized—and the physical dangers of certain jobs. When beliefs about the "average" youth worker and job are stereotyped, it makes it harder for adults to give guidance to teens who are searching for ways to connect schooling to real-world goals. As we discuss later, data reveal that a majority of youth have misguided conceptions of what it takes to hold certain types of jobs.

It is surprising and disturbing that American teens are viewed as lazy[3] when so many of them work and go to school. Americans who exhort the need for our youth to be world class should take pleasure in knowing that America leads the world in the number of high school students who work while enrolled in school. Gerald Bracey compared 12th graders in various countries and found that 55% of American students work more than 3 hr a day, whereas considerably lower percentages of students from other countries work a comparable amount (Australia, 25%; Canada, 39%; Iceland, 26%; Netherlands, 26%; New Zealand, 27%; and Norway, 27%[4]). Too many Americans judge the capacities of American youth only in terms of how they compare academically to students in other industrialized nations; however, American youth are involved in many more activities than their international peers.[5]

This chapter begins by exploring the demographics of student workers. Who works? What kinds of jobs do they hold? What effect does working have on students' scholastic achievement and feelings about school? Next, we discuss the range of opinions youth hold about work experiences. Some youth workers can be more selective about jobs than ever before because of their advanced computer skills.[6] Still, youth choose all kinds of jobs to help them meet college or career goals. They are strongly motivated to succeed, but often they lack the self-awareness and knowledge to make decisions that lead to their future goals. Lastly, we discuss the reasons youth work, and the role of work in teens' lives. Many teens are socialized to believe that work is primarily a way to achieve material goods.

STUDENT WORKERS

In the early 1900s, all capable family members worked to support the family.[7] Youngsters' labor and income were critically needed in most families, and children commonly dropped out of school if there was a need at home. Young people who stayed in school typically came from more privileged backgrounds or families, where education was a high priority. At the beginning of the 20th century, work, for many teens, was a requirement for economic survival, and school, for many, was an unaffordable luxury.

By the 1950s, it was more common to see teens in schools and not in jobs.[8] Fewer teens worked because it was not an economic necessity—most families were doing well in the strong postwar economy of the 1950s.[9] However, this quickly changed as more parents began to worry that teens weren't busy enough—they had too many idle hours, and, therefore, students were encouraged to take part-time, after-school jobs. And, as we discuss later, teens were also lured to work by a consumer culture that created new product needs for youth.

The popularity of working and going to school—being a student worker—grew suddenly. In 1940 only 2.4% of American youth worked and went to school. The student-worker phenomenon quickly spread. Between 1947 and 1985 there was a 65% increase in student workers, and by the late 1990s, approximately 52% of all 16- to 19-year-olds worked and went to school.[10] The shift from the full-time student or worker to full-time student and part-time worker is remarkable.

Modern youth workers include male and female teens of all ages, from all ethnic and socioeconomic backgrounds. Still, it is more common for some types of students to work than it is for others. Older teens (17- and 18-year-olds) work more hours a week than younger teens (13- to 16-year-olds). More than half of all 10th graders have worked, and nearly all 11th and 12th graders have worked at some point during high school.[11] Roughly 40% to 60% of high school students are employed at any one time.[12] Eighty percent of high school seniors had a job at least once while in high school, with most working 15–20 hr a week.[13]

Gender Differences

Although about the same percentages of male and female youths work, their work experiences vary widely.[14] Gender-role stereotypes and societal expectations play a large role in determining the types of jobs that boys and girls get. Young men are expected to be stronger and more risk taking than are young women. Thus, boys are more likely to work in manual labor jobs than are girls. Conversely, girls are expected to be better with people and more nurturing and thus are more likely to work at jobs such as baby-sitting or retail sales. Because of these discrepancies in job types, boys' safety is more frequently compromised.[15] Young men are typically believed to be capable of handling dangerous equipment or materials; however, they may also be poorly supervised, and many more boys are injured on the job than girls. Girls, in contrast, have safer jobs, but those jobs pay less.

Gender wage discrimination begins early. As with adult workers, young men typically outearn young women. In one study, male students ages 16–19 years reported annual incomes of $4,624.62, whereas girls reported earning $3,325.64 annually. The effects of this disparity have been associated with gender-related income-entitlement beliefs.[16] When boys and girls are asked what they believe their income should be for specific jobs, boys typically report higher figures than do girls. Differences in wages are unfortunate, but worse these disparities in both entitlement beliefs and actual earnings foster a continuing belief among girls that they are entitled to less or that they must work harder for equal recognition. Although income inequities by gender are slowly decreasing, the discrepancies may still be sufficiently large to lead to lowered income-entitlement beliefs and a sense of marginalization from society among females.[17]

Ethnic and Socioeconomic Differences

Work experiences vary sharply according to socioeconomic and ethnic background. A larger proportion of White youths work than do Black youths,[18] and a larger proportion of youths from high-income families work than do youths from lower income families. In 1995, 18.8% of young Blacks had jobs, compared with 38.6% of young Whites.[19] A 1998 report estimated that by the age of 15 years, 22.2% of Whites, 23.1% of Hispanics, and 16.4% of Blacks held their first job. And by the age of 17 years, 82.8% of Whites, 79.1% of Hispanics, and 69.5% of Blacks had job experiences.[20] Similarly, in 1999, the U.S. Department of Labor estimated that 60% of working teens came from families whose income was more than $51,000, whereas 22% were from families making $27,300–$50,999, and 15% were from families making less than $27,300.[21] Thus, White, middle-class youths are more likely to hold jobs than their poorer, ethnic minority peers.

These job discrepancies reflect the paucity of job opportunities available to minority teens, who are likely to live in impoverished neighborhoods. For these teens, lack of access to jobs is a significant problem because employment often helps minority teens stay in school. Kaufman and Rosenbaum studied the effects of the Gautreaux program in Chicago, where most Black families were given vouchers to move from their racially discriminating, low-rent housing projects to other inner city private neighborhoods or to mostly White suburban neighborhoods.[22] Kaufman and Rosenbaum examined how living in different geographic locations affected students' grades, their chances of finishing high school, their likelihood of going to college, and their ability to get a job. They found that Black youths who moved to mostly White suburbs benefited more than those who moved to other inner city, mostly Black neighborhoods. And they also noted that Black youths who moved to suburban areas had richer and higher quality opportunities for both jobs and education than did teens who moved to other inner city neighborhoods.

Although employment rates and conditions[23] are worse for minority teens than for Whites, the past decade has seen some improvements for minority teens. A booming job market throughout the 1990s was credited with a rise in employment rates for young Black men. One 1999 report indicated a jump in the percentage of employed, less-educated Black men in poor ur-

ban areas (from 52% to 64%).[24] Indeed, the progression of the 1990s—
booming job markets, decreasing unemployment rates, and shifts in labor
areas—offered more opportunities to minority teens than ever before.[25]
Still, jobs for youth today are held by a disproportionately high percentage
of middle-class White teens, and the jobless rate of young Black men is twice
that of young White men.[26]

Modern Jobs

From 1996 to 1998 the primary jobs held by youths ages 14–17 years were
service occupations (food preparation and service) and sales occupations.[27]
As youth get older, more of them work in service-oriented jobs (33% of 14-
year-olds, 37% of 15-year-olds, and 37% of male 15- to 17-year-olds, and
41% of female 15- to 17-year-olds held service jobs). A minority of teens are
employed in other jobs, such as managerial, professional and technical,
farming and fishing, labor and construction.

For young workers (under the legal age of 14 years) there are many informal jobs, such as baby-sitting, mowing lawns, shoveling snow, walking
pets, and so on. When polls ask teens to make a distinction between formal
and informal jobs, 76% of adolescents report having worked at a formal job
by the age of 16 years, but 92% have started work even prior to this age, if
informal jobs are considered. The U.S. Department of Labor estimates that
50% of 12-year-olds worked in informal jobs (such as baby-sitting or yard
work) in 1995–1997 with an equal number of boys and girls working, and
Whites working more than Blacks or Hispanics (see Table 7.1). Interestingly, the cross-section of working 12-year-olds from a range of household
incomes was relatively equal. This sharply contrasts with statistics of older
youth workers, who primarily come from middle- and upper income homes
(see Table 7.2).

An extremely lucrative job for many teens today is computer work. During the technological boom of the 1990s many teens were needed to fill
computer-related positions. In the summer of 2000, there were national reports that traditional summer jobs (camp counselor, lifeguard) were not
filled because not enough teens applied for these positions. Many teens
were holding out for more lucrative and meaningful positions—such as in
the computer industry.[28] One effect of American teens' selectivity was that
summer employers were hiring international youths at higher rates than
ever before. According to the Council of International Education, a nonprofit organization that helps foreign students get jobs in the United States,
10% more foreign youths were brought into the country in the summer of
2000 than in the year 1999.[29]

In preparation for summer of 2002, and then again in the summer of
2003, New York City looked to foreigners to fill the 1,200 lifeguard open-

TABLE 7.1
Percent of Youths Engaged in Work Activities
While Age 12 Years in 1995–1997, by Type of Job,
Sex, Race, Hispanic Origin, and Household Income

Age in 1995–1997 and Characteristic[a]	% With a Work Activity	% Engaged in	
		Baby-sitting	Yard Work
Total, while age 12 years	49.6	55.6	39.7
Sex			
Male	48.3	26.3	65.8
Female	51.0	84.9	13.6
Race and Hispanic Origin			
White	56.5	54.06	40.1
Black	36.2	46.9	41.7
Hispanic origin	36.0	61.3	37.0
Household Income			
Less than $25,000	48.7	50.1	45.9
$25,000 to 44,999	52.2	51.2	41.5
$45,000 to 69,999	53.8	55.6	39.1
$70,000 and over	53.9	61.5	39.1

[a]The National Longitudinal Survey of Youth 1997 consists of young men and women who were ages 12 to 16 years on December 31, 1996. Race and Hispanic-origin groups are mutually exclusive. Totals include American Indians, Alaskan Natives, and Asians and Pacific Islanders not shown separately. "While age 12 years" refers to the entire year between the individuals' 12th and 13th birthdays. All rows exclude individuals who were not yet 13 years of age when interviewed.

Note. From *Report on the Youth Labor Force,* by A. M. Herman, 2000, Washington, DC: U.S. Secretary of Labor.

ings needed to supervise its 53 pools and 14 miles of beaches.[30] Notably, although some American youth have grown more selective in their summer employment, there is evidence that lifeguard positions in New York City were being given more often to international youths because they were better swimmers than their American peers. And, even though the job market is the worst it has been in years, and many employers are opting for older employees rather than hiring teenagers,[31] there is still evidence that American teens are more selective and that foreign workers were filling a substantial number of available jobs during the 2003 summer months.[32]

Getting Hurt on the Job

Prior to 1900, child labor was a widespread phenomenon, with children as young as 6 and 7 years of age expected to work up to 13 hours a day in factories for menial wages. In 1938, the Fair Standards Labor Act (FSLA), the first legislative initiative to protect youth, was passed, setting a minimum

TABLE 7.2
Employment Status of Persons 15 to 17 Years of Age by Family Income in
Previous Year, March 1980, 1990, and 1999

| | | Family Income in 1998 Dollars[a] | | | |
Indicator and Characteristic	Total in Families	Less Than $27,300	$27,300–$50,999	$51,000–$79,999	More Than $79,000
	Employment Population Ratio				
Total, 15–17 years, March 1999	23.9	15.0	22.1	29.5	29.5
Male	23.3	14.2	21.5	29.0	28.5
Female	24.6	15.9	22.6	30.0	30.5
Age 15 years	9.7	6.2	9.7	12.1	10.9
Age 16 years	24.8	16.0	21.8	32.3	29.7
Age 17 years	37.0	23.1	36.1	42.3	45.6
White, 15–17 years	26.9	17.3	25.4	32.1	30.4
Black, 15–17 years	11.9	9.9	8.5	16.9	21.4
Hispanic origin, 15–17 years	14.6	10.9	15.4	19.6	22.1
Total, 15–17 years					
March 1990	26.6	16.5	27.0	29.7	35.3
March 1980	28.4	17.6	26.8	34.5	36.9
	Unemployment Rate				
Total, 15–17 years, March 1999	18.7	30.6	22.8	13.9	12.0
Male	20.1	34.7	24.8	13.7	13.1
Female	17.1	26.3	20.7	14.2	10.9
Age 15 years	22.3	37.1	27.7	15.8	9.5
Age 16 years	20.8	29.9	31.0	11.1	15.1
Age 17 years	16.2	29.1	14.3	15.4	10.5
White, 15–17 years	16.4	26.8	18.9	12.9	12.5
Black, 15–17 years	38.5	45.0	51.9	26.3	11.1
Hispanic origin, 15–17 years	24.1	32.4	20.8	19.9	11.8
Total, 15–17 years					
March 1990	17.8	29.6	18.9	15.2	9.9
March 1980	19.3	30.1	20.5	16.3	13.1

[a]Income divisions were determined using quartiles in 1998. Divisions for earlier years were determined by deflating 1998 income categories by the CPI-U-RS.

Note. From *Report on the Youth Labor Force*, by A. M. Herman, 2000, Washington, DC: U.S. Secretary of Labor.

age of employment and guidelines for the safety of young laborers.[33] Today's federal government continues to search for ways to protect its youth workforce. In May 2002, the Youth Rules! initiative was established to strengthen federal and state regulation of today's youth workforce.[34] As yet there are no data to document the effects of this initiative for protecting and guiding youth.

Despite this legislation, too many teens are hurt or exploited on the job. Teens are injured on construction jobs at nearly twice the rate of adults, and those working in agriculture are at 4.4 times greater risk of dying than youths employed in any other job.[35] Approximately one teen is hurt on the job every 40 seconds, and one dies every 5 days.[36] The occupational deaths of workers under the age of 17 years from 1992 to 1998 varied between 62 and 70; 89% of deaths were boys, and 29% were under the age of 15. Youth are most at risk when they work in agriculture, retail trade, or construction.

A major risk factor for youth is poor adult supervision. In other cases, teens take on tasks that surpass their capabilities to impress the boss or because they are ordered to do so. In Apache Junction, Arizona, one 17-year-old boy died after an unsecured trench in which he was digging collapsed. In another example, a 15-year-old boy, who worked for a window-washing company, asked to be put on the roof to act as the safety harness for his partner washing windows below him—a dangerous job that is illegal for underage workers. The previous workers had unsecured the safety rig, and because the youth wasn't trained to secure the rig, he was pulled 10 stories to his death. These deaths illustrate the physical dangers youth face when asked to perform unsupervised jobs beyond their capabilities. They also illustrate the importance of quality supervision on the job site. Many teens go beyond regular job expectations because they assume adults know what is best. After all, they are raised to be compliant with adult authority.[37] As one construction employer noted following the death of the teen from a collapsed trench, "Kids just assume that the adults will tell them if there's any way they could get hurt—but the adults aren't looking out for them."[38] And in the current job market it may even be easier for employers to neglect their supervisory responsibility to youth, thinking teens are lucky just to have a job.

WORK AND SCHOOL

Does Work Increase Achievement?

All types of teens work in all kinds of jobs. Therefore, it is not surprising that research on how work impacts academic outcomes is mixed. Although some data suggest there is no relationship between number of hours worked and school achievement, a large body of evidence suggests that the more hours youth work, the more likely it is that their grades will drop.[39] Another researcher, however, suggests a more complex relationship between work and achievement. Gerald Bracey conducted a cross-national investigation of the relationship between weekly work hours and SAT performance.[40] He found a linear association between work and SAT scores in foreign countries but a curvilinear association for American students. Specifically, American students who worked up to 14 hr a week scored a 506 on the SAT (above the international average), whereas those who worked 24–35 hr per week scored a lower 474. Interestingly, those who worked more than 35 hr per week had an average SAT score of 484, which was the same score for those who didn't work at all.

Although on average evidence suggests that working a large number of weekly hours results in lowered achievement, it is oversimplifying to believe that this happens to all students. Indeed, many students who work 20 hr a week or less do not exhibit decreased academic performance; they continue to perform at acceptable levels.[41]

Work and Students' Connection to Their Schools

Researchers have also documented connections between working experiences and both positive (e.g., participation in extracurricular activities, positive attitudes toward school) and negative (absenteeism, truancy, dropping out) relationships to school. Proponents of youth employment argue that working enhances and reinforces prosocial skills, communicative skills, and a sense of responsibility that motivate students to become more involved in school. Some research found a positive link between working and student participation in extracurricular activities[42] and documented that increased work is associated with increased levels of self-esteem, motivation, responsibility, and communication skills—attributes associated with successful school experiences.[43]

Other research, however, found that working while in school has negative consequences, such as pulling youth away from school goals.[44] Working a greater number of hours is associated with high rates of absenteeism[45] and dropping out of school.[46] In an attempt to gain a more detailed understanding of why some students who work a lot drop out of school, researchers analyzed numbers of working hours and dropout rates in connection with the types of jobs youth hold. In a national study of more than 20,000 students, researchers found that the type of job one holds predicts the likelihood of dropping out.[47] Students who had jobs in the manufacturing and service sectors were most likely to drop out of school. Those with jobs in the retail sector had no greater risk of dropping out, and students doing agricultural work were more likely to remain in school.

One can only hypothesize why jobs in the manufacturing and service sectors are linked to higher dropout rates. Perhaps these jobs are more lucrative, and the financial benefits pull students from school. A more cynical hypothesis is that perhaps these jobs contribute to a belief that school experiences aren't relevant to the real world. That is, students drop out because school is seen as a waste of time—not related to real life.[48] However, other explanations are possible. For example, agricultural and retail sales jobs demand harder labor and better social skills, respectively. Perhaps the kinds of students who land these jobs have stronger abilities in these areas, which keeps them in school.

Controlling Youth Work

Despite the inconclusiveness of research on working and achievement, some states have passed legislation to control how much teens work. In Washington State, for example, workers under 18 years of age are restricted to 4 hours of work a day during the week and 8 hr a day on Friday through Sunday. They cannot work more than 6 days a week, and they cannot start before 7 a.m. or finish after 10 p.m. during the week or after midnight on weekends.[49] This policy, though useful for some students, may be counter-productive for others, who benefit greatly from the flexibility of being able to work longer hours while going to school.

Although the federal government outlined a set of provisions and safety regulations for protecting working youth, states vary widely in their own child labor law regulations. For example, the federal government stipulates that youth under the age of 16 years can work a maximum of 3 hr on any given school day and no more than 18 hr during an entire week. Although many states have similar working limits, they vary on how many hours youth may work daily and weekly. Delaware allows 4 hr of work a day; Maryland allows up to 23 hr per week.[50]

WHAT ADULTS MIGHT NOT KNOW
ABOUT STUDENT WORKERS

Teens Are Selective

Because more teens are earning large salaries for skilled positions, fast food service jobs are increasingly devalued. Whereas once it was good enough just to earn any income, many youth today are picky about how they earn it. Fewer suburban, upper middle-class teens are willing to work in a fast food setting. As some teens say, "It's not considered cool, working at a fast food place."[51] Another student views these "low-class" jobs with disdain because they are not investments in the future: "I won't do any of that. The pay's too low and there's no future."[52] Many students want jobs where they can use and build skills that are valuable for future jobs. Interestingly, although many adults believe that any kind of job is a positive experience for youth, some teens are extremely (and reasonably) selective about the jobs they want.

Working for College

Teens' work experience provides colleges with evidence of social maturity and responsibility. College applicants who have work experience are viewed as financially responsible, conscientious, and ambitious compared to their nonworking peers. Many teens work to bulk up their college application packets; others work to explore personal interests, and some work for both reasons.

Some students decide to take time out between high school and college to gain more work-related experiences and a broader perspective on possible career options. Students who take time off between high school and college do so to save money for college tuition, to take a break from school, to explore various career paths before committing to a 2- or 4-year institution.[53] Some adults argue that adolescents should have the option to enter the adult working world at an earlier age rather than waiting until after college.[54] However, statistics show that students who go to college straight from high school are more likely to finish college than students who delay. Better adult guidance is important for students planning to delay college to ensure their decision is in their best interests.

Traits for Finding and Securing Jobs

Although youth are often believed to be apathetic about their futures, most are, on the contrary, motivated; they have goals, future plans, and ambitions, and they exhibit many job-related abilities. Tragically, however, many teens get little guidance from parents or schools on how to prepare for their goals. In their book *The Ambitious Generation,* Barbara Schneider and David Stevenson[55] conclude that too many adolescents set unrealistic career goals, pursuing careers that have far fewer openings available than there are students who want to train for these careers. They report that 5 to 6 times more adolescents want to pursue medical and law-related careers than there are available openings. They also note that many students are motivated to pursue a career, but often these motivations aren't aligned with realistic achievement outcomes or knowledge of educational requirements. For example, they estimate that although 44% of students have aligned ambition (their skills, success expectations, and understanding of their future field is aligned with prospects for a career in that field), a majority, 56%, have misaligned ambitions. And 16% expect to need less education than is obtained by the average worker in their desired occupation.[56]

Although the researchers note that many students ultimately change their goals, the problem remains of youth failing to understand the appropriate educational route. The authors provide an example of a young student who wanted to be a filmmaker and who prepared for his dream by working at a local theater and studying film. Unfortunately, the university he chose to attend wouldn't allow him to study theater in the 1st year.[57] Given that so many teens don't know how to plan their career and educational futures, one goal of guiding youth in part-time jobs should be to help them develop goal-setting and volitional skills.[58]

Job Finding Skills

As most adults know, being out of work and having to find a job can be harrowing—especially if one needs that job to survive. The same is true for youth—both for those who have to get a job to help put food on the table and for those who look for work to buy the items they feel they have to have. Whether they want to work at a local McDonald's, intern at a local business, or baby-sit for a neighbor, teens must have skills to be successful. To be good employees, they must display assertiveness, self-motivation, responsibility, friendliness, and an ability to communicate. Working teens, on the whole, demonstrate all of these qualities. Yet the positive qualities of so many youth workers remain unrecognized and undervalued. Although some young people dislike their jobs—often understandably so, if supervisors are unfair or abusive—many of the millions of teens who work display a range of impressive skills and characteristics that can help them find and keep jobs.

Starting Young

A startling percentage of very young teens work. A 1997 survey found that 57% of 14-year-olds and 65% of 15-year-olds worked in some capacity, and 28% of all 14- to 16-year-olds worked both during the summer and during the school year.[59] Interestingly, when youth only worked during the summer, they worked approximately 54% of the available summer weeks. In contrast, when students worked both during the summer and during the school year, they worked 77% of the summer weeks.[60]

Those young workers also need a variety of skills to get jobs. For example, to become a trusted baby-sitter for neighborhood children, teens must be able to network and socialize appropriately and have a trustworthy reputation.

Work Ethic

The potential for huge financial payoffs is no longer limited to those who have worked their way up the corporate ladder. The Internet explosion of entrepreneurial opportunities allowed many young, creative, and energetic executives to become instant millionaires. It is difficult to know the potential impact instant success has on youth and their attitudes toward work, but it undoubtedly has had both positive and negative effects that require more study.

The example of instant millionairehood suggests to teens that rapid financial rewards are possible and that even disadvantaged life circumstances can be transcended. Although it is vital that youth, especially minority youths who disproportionately inhabit high-poverty, high-crime neighborhoods, have hope for the future, it is equally important that instant success not be glamorized. In April of 2002, it was announced that a 20-year-old first-time lottery player had one of three winning tickets to a $58 million jackpot. The press attention she received for her instant wealth glamorized a system in which the odds of winning are only 1 in 76 million.[61] Similarly, the instant success of computer guru Bill Gates, and many others, may mask the connection between ability, effort, persistence, and success.

Unfortunately, when the media glamorize instant wealth, young people may be negatively affected. First, the potential for huge financial payoffs has been presented as the primary (and only) important goal of work: Adults model a belief that money is the definition of personal happiness. This assumption devalues rewards of a successful, productive life. Secondly, instant gratification in the form of easy personal wealth is sometimes portrayed as the norm. The truth is that most workers must invest time, energy, and creativity before seeing significant financial payoffs. Lastly, major corporate businesses, who are now being brought to task for misreporting billions of dollars in profits, are modeling for youth that many adults covet financial gain over ethical principles. We should be more concerned about how these events affect youth.

Dispositions Are Shaped by Variety of Experiences

Youth's work commitments and the quality of their jobs vary dramatically. These variations in skills, safety, pay, and other dimensions are illustrated in Boxes 7.1–7.5.

The scenarios described in Boxes 7.1–7.5 highlight both positive and negative issues youth face. Julia works part-time with a flexible schedule and for a friendly manager. Julia's family is not financially reliant on her income, allowing Julia autonomy and freedom in her career pursuits and spending habits. As a valued employee, Julia has career opportunities and increasingly assumes more responsibility. Although her future goals are unrelated to her present job, her hard-work attitude keeps her motivated. A hard-work belief system is necessary to be successful in after-school jobs.

Miguel has been working (in both a paid and an unpaid capacity) in his father's business most of his adolescent life. Miguel has always felt it was his

---

BOX 7.1. Julia: Working for extras.

Julia, a sophomore in high school, is getting ready for her dinner shift at the local McDonald's. She works part-time (approximately 15 hr a week) for a manager who provides flexible work schedules to meet the needs of his high school employees. Julia enjoys going to work because she works with all of her friends, which keeps her current on the social events in her school. Additionally, because her parents are not reliant on her income, she uses her earnings to buy clothes, CDs, and concert tickets. Julia's career goals include becoming a doctor or a lawyer. Her grades in school are Bs and Cs, but she believes that grades don't matter much—only how hard you work.

BOX 7.2. Miguel: Aligned employment goals.

Miguel, a senior in high school, is currently in the 2nd hour of his shift at his father's bakery, where he works approximately 35 hr a week with his dad and brothers. He has been working there on an almost full-time basis since he was 12 years old, while also going to school full-time. Most of the money he earns goes toward family bills or college savings. He is in charge of the cake department and typically has to stay at work late into the evening to be sure everything is clean and to prepare for early morning pickups and deliveries. Miguel gets As and Bs in school and is hoping to go to college to become a business owner like his father. His major interests are computers, and he would like to one day be a CEO of an Internet start-up company.

BOX 7.3. Anthony: Negative working conditions.

Anthony, a junior in high school, is just getting ready for his all-night shift unloading shipments at a nearby national chain grocery store. He works three 12-hr shifts a week, moving large, heavy boxes. He tries not to miss many days of school, but he's often too exhausted or too physically sore to last the entire day. Anthony wants to quit, but his mother and younger brother rely on his income for rent and bills. He hopes one day to go to college to help secure a better job, but with failing grades in high school he doesn't think he can make it, and at this point he is thinking about dropping out.

BOX 7.4.   Natasha: Rich working opportunities.

Natasha, a junior in high school, has just returned home from her internship at Microsoft, where she works 10 hr a week (at her convenience) for minimum wage doing secretarial work. In addition to these 10 hr, Natasha meets with a mentor in the field of computers from whom she learns more about the business. Natasha's parents have already saved for her college tuition, so whatever money she makes goes directly toward recreational products and activities. Natasha gets straight As in school and wants to work in the computer industry as a network manager after college.

BOX 7.5.   Preteen workers.

Juanita, a seventh grader, is at home thinking about her upcoming baby-sitting job later that evening. Of all her baby-sitting jobs, she likes this one the most because the child she watches is 3-year-old, Benjamin, who is sweet and well behaved. Also, she can bring any one of her friends while she works, and she makes $5 an hour. Benjamin's family lives close to her on a nearby farm in a very large house. Juanita enjoys her baby-sitting jobs, and she likes spending the money she makes on things for herself and gifts for her family.

---

responsibility and obligation to help his father. Although he spends most of his time on cake-making activities, he has had exposure to financial and customer-service aspects of the business. Miguel's future career and academic goals are realistic, well thought out, and supported by his father—indeed, they are aligned with his future goal of owning his own business.[62]

Anthony works long hours in a job that frequently compromises his health and safety. He has many home responsibilities, and schooling is only a moderate priority. Anthony's boss is unforgiving and takes advantage of Anthony, who is his youngest employee. Anthony wants to move ahead and stay in school, but his neighborhood offers so few job opportunities that he feels lucky to have a job. Anthony's situation typifies those of many working teens employed in unfriendly environments that compromise the quality of their job experiences. Anthony also typifies young workers who, up against multiple obstacles, are at high risk of dropping out of high school.

Natasha is a conscientious and economically advantaged student who as a junior already works in a field aligned with her future interests. Like Julia, her earnings go toward recreation and personal purchases, but unlike Julia's job, Natasha's job simultaneously gives her valuable experience relevant to her future goals. As a bonus, Natasha receives academic credit for mentoring, and fieldwork gives her more flexibility in her school schedule.

Natasha's situation exemplifies a student with aligned ambitions and high-lights how schools and employers can work together for mutual benefit.

Juanita is motivated to help others and earn money. Her situation further extends the range of persons who make up the youth workforce and illustrates the kinds of jobs they hold. Juanita's working situation allows for a flexible schedule with great freedom to pick and choose her employer and work hours. She represents a part of the youth work force who work in informal jobs and whose skills and economic contributions go unnoticed.

SOCIALIZATION OF WORK

Youth employment is paradoxical and indicative of a culture in which adults have contradictory attitudes toward work:

> This is the paradox of youth employment: Such employment is valued by society despite extensive data suggesting that it can be associated with adverse and extreme consequences. To some extent, the paradox emerges from the mixed—and frequently contradictory—set of beliefs we hold about work and employment among adults, the view of work as both a source of human growth and fulfillment and a "curse" or burden imposed on humans as a punishment for original sin.[63]

Teens work for many reasons, but the most common reason is for money. In one study in which teens were asked the chief reasons why they were employed, 38% of working teens responded, "In order to earn money for things I really needed"; 36% replied, "I didn't really have to work, but I wanted to have money for the 'extras.' "[64]

Youth and Big Business

It is no surprise that youth work to purchase entertainment and material goods. Youth live in a culture saturated with highly advertised material goods. Big business spends millions of advertising dollars targeting youth. Nike ads illuminate the power of their shoe in promoting a Michael Jordan-esque athleticism. Clothing ads for popular name-brand clothing appeal to teens by using young, beautiful models. Big businesses even seek out youth to act as consultants to help with marketing strategies and product management.[65]

Appealing images lure large numbers of teens to participate in a culture designed by advertisers—participation that requires cash in hand. Although advertisers don't force or cause teens to work, the barrage of attractive advertising images is closely related to many teens' efforts to

obtain extra spending money to buy those "necessary" items made so desirable in the ads.

Teens' Spending

Marketers are well aware of teens' economic influence: Teens spend billions of dollars each year. Peter Zollo, author of *Wise Up to Teens: Insights into
Marketing and Advertising to Teenagers,* notes that the fast-growing youth market is a veritable gold mine. He estimated that there were 31 million individuals ages 12 to 19 years in 1999—7 million more than there were in 1991.
And experts project these numbers will grow to reach 34 million by the year
2010.[66] Teens' combined income (including both earnings from paid jobs
and money given to them by parents through allowances or on an as-
needed basis) grew considerably throughout the 1990s. In 1998, youth collectively received $121 billion, a figure up from $86 billion in 1993.[67] Similarly, it is estimated that teens spent about $140 billion during 1998, up
from an estimated $109 billion in 1995.[68]

Where does this income come from? Approximately 52% say they receive their income on an as-needed basis from parents; 48% report receiving money from odd jobs, 39% from gifts, 31% from part-time jobs, 30%
from allowances, 10% from full-time jobs, and 3% from their own businesses.[69] Older teens' (ages 18–19 years) weekly income is 4 times that of
younger teens (ages 12–15 years), and, on average, boys' weekly income
($84) is higher than girls' weekly income ($71). Boys spend more (average
of $59/week) of their own money than do girls ($53/week); however, girls
spend more family money, which decreases the male-female spending difference to $1.[70]

Marketing to Teens: The Good, the Bad, and the Ugly

The relationship of big-name retailers (The Gap, Coca-Cola, Old Navy,
Abercrombie and Fitch) and the youth culture is symbiotic. Youth depend
on the fashion market to inform them of the newest trends in fashions or
activities, and, conversely, they rely on youth to tell them which kinds of
products they want. This is not necessarily a bad relationship; however,
there are increasing numbers of instances where the boundaries of what
big businesses are willing to do for profit are blurred. Although not all companies purposefully take advantage of youth spending—indeed, many engage in community partnerships to benefit local youth[71]—there are some
businesses that exploit teens' spending power.

Many companies trade technological equipment to schools for information about students. In the fall of 1998, ZapMe! made deals with schools to
furnish them with a computer lab, providing up to 15 computers, free soft-

ware, and Internet access.[72] However, as part of this agreement, schools agreed to allow them access to student identification numbers for marketing and advertising purposes. Many citizens saw this as a gross violation of student rights. One letter sent to state governors by a youth advocacy group asserted the following:

> In essence, ZapMe! plants computers in the schools as advertising delivery, market research and surveillance machines. It turns the schools and the compulsory schooling laws into a means of gaining access to a captive audience of children in order to extract market research from them and to advertise to them. Parents entrust their children to the schools—especially public schools—for the purpose of learning and developing character, not to serve as guinea pigs for advertising and marketing firms.[73]

In addition to the ethical issues of marketing to children, schools have experienced technological difficulties with the equipment provided by ZapMe! In a survey of 900 schools conducted in January 2000, 46% said that their experience with ZapMe! was *somewhat worse* or *much worse* than they had expected when they signed up. Only a third believed it was *somewhat* or *much better*.[74]

Although the company changed its practices since these initial allegations and problems, ZapMe! corporate leaders argue that they were providing a valuable service for children, assisting financially struggling schools that otherwise couldn't afford computers and Internet access. Further, they argued that by offering a Web browser with filtering capacities, they kept children safe from undesirable Web sites, staving off parental and teacher worries about what children see while surfing the Internet.

Another company, N2H2 Inc., was tagged as a corporate predator by Commercial Alert, a Washington-based group founded by consumer advocate Ralph Nader. As with ZapMe!, N2H2 was using its Internet filtering services to collect marketing information from millions of unsuspecting children.[75] Ironically, although social scientists are held to rigid human-subjects guidelines for collecting information on children—information that could lead to better designed programs—Internet companies often have carte blanche access.

Big Business Meets Public Schooling

The marriage between big business or the media and schools is not a new phenomenon.[76] Joel Spring notes the following:

> In 1904, the advertising manager of the *Atlantic Monthly* wrote that the far-sighted advertising begins with the female child so that the brand name fol-

lows her "to school, thrusts its self upon her as she travels, and all uncon-
sciously engraves its self up her memory."[77]

Soft drink companies, such as Coca-Cola, have for a long time paid for
the privilege of being the sole soda provider in schools. Athletic companies,
such as Nike, have been offering seductive bonuses to prominent schools to
display their insignia. Although there are benefits to this kind of relationship, there is also much reason to believe that such practices can interfere
with and distract from the real purposes of schooling. Why would businesses vote to pay for increased taxes that provide more funds to support
schools if keeping schools lean increases the likelihood that schools will sell
advertising space cheaply to the business community?

In response to harsh criticism that it has been marketing products with
poor nutritional value for kids, Coca-Cola announced that it will reform
how it markets products in schools.[78] A Coca-Cola executive stated that
Coca-Cola will end its exclusive contracts with a limited number of schools,
include milk and juice in some of its machines, and let schools determine
where to place machines. Some critics argue that this is simply another marketing ploy by the company to keep its presence in schools; others argue
that the proposed changes will impact kids' health positively. Our own
stance is that any practice that offers incentives to schools to sell potentially
harmful products is problematic. It is especially troublesome for adults to
blame students for a problem created by adults (vending machines and
high-caloric foods are placed in schools but students are blamed for being
fat and they and their parents are left alone to "figure out" how to address
the problem).

The Darker Side of Adolescent Economics

Some teens turn to illegal methods to earn money.[79] In one study, investigators found that (based on a population of homeless adolescent runaways),
of those who chose to remain on the street and use no social services, 88%
of teens panhandled, 62% stole, 50% sold drugs, and 42% engaged in prostitution.[80] Teens who engage in illegal activity for money represent a tragic
faction of the youth subculture who often are forced into situations where
survival is the main goal. But some youths choose to engage in illegal activity for the main purpose of making quick and easy cash. Whether teens secure money by legal or illegal means, that so many youth actively participate
in the American economy is at least in part due to high-intensity marketing
aimed at youth, which creates an appetite for products, and hence, a need
for money.

CONCLUSION

Characteristics of teen workers and the types of jobs they hold have changed dramatically over the past century. American teen workers today typically hold jobs in the service and retail sectors, work part-time while attending school, come from middle-class backgrounds, and spend money on luxury items. Teens work for many reasons. Some teens use employment as an opportunity to buy discretionary luxury items, other teens contribute to the support of their family, and other teens save money for college. Obviously, there are many other reasons that teens work. Still, the one undeniable fact is that youth work. Despite their reputation as being lazy, youth work, and they are ambitious and goal driven.

Teens also have varied work experiences. Young men and women typically choose different kinds of jobs, and within those jobs there is wide differentiation of quality and experience. Boys work in jobs that require physical labor more frequently than do girls, which puts boys at a higher risk of injury. In contrast, girls suffer from a lowered sense of perceived income entitlement and therefore are at risk for an ongoing sense of marginalization by society. It is difficult to know exactly how this impacts future work-related attitudes and adjustments; however, it is arguable that both boys and girls carry with them attitudes about work learned when they held jobs as teenagers.

Whether teens should work, and for how long, is debatable. Some teens work without any negative consequences for their academic performance or social participation. Given that some teens choose to work and others have to work, we have seen that work, at least working a minimum number of hours, is not related in any causative way to lowered academic achievement. Some youth work, make academic progress, and participate in varied social activities. Others experience lowered achievement and disconnection from their schools.

General Considerations

It is time that ample employment opportunities be offered to students from every socioeconomic and ethnic background. Teens who live in economically depressed neighborhoods (primarily minority youths) simply don't have the same opportunities to work as those from more affluent areas. Therefore, it seems vital that legislators find ways to invest in job opportunities for more youth, especially for those in low-income neighborhoods.

Newspaper stories rarely discuss the exploitation of youth by their employers. A society that cares about its youth would demand assurance that youth are safe and treated fairly on the job and that they are learning positive values and work skills. Given that today's youth—and their future productivity—are critical to the maintenance of society, it would seem that society should be more concerned about what youth learn on the job. Yet Americans are largely indifferent to teens' work experiences.

Despite claims to the contrary, teens are motivated to be busy. They work, they study, and they are ambitious. It is unfortunate that there are not more adult counselors and mentors available to help youth cope with the many tasks they address and teach them how to use time wisely. The unique capabilities of young workers are typically overlooked.

The rationale behind capping or monitoring teens' work commitments, based on research, is seemingly logical—many teens' grades suffer with increased work. However, it would be misguided to institute hour limits as a blanket policy for several reasons. First, instituting a working cap during the school week assumes that all students are equally benefited or disadvantaged by the amount they work. This is illogical because students and their jobs vary widely. Some students thrive when they work 25 hr a week and participate in multiple extracurricular activities, whereas other students can work only a minimal amount if they also want to keep up with their schoolwork. A 25-hr-a-week job that requires students to employ complex thinking skills arguably affects students and their schooling differently than a 25-hr-a-week job that demands minimal thinking skills.

Second, caps assume that getting good grades is the only noble goal of schooling. For some, getting average grades is acceptable, especially if the student is supplementing their schooling with real-life working experiences. Lastly, for students who aren't as successful academically, work may be one of the few successful experiences they have. Therefore, to limit a students' time spent in their successful endeavors because they are struggling in school seems counterproductive.

Needed Research

Most research on teenage work has been supplied by surveys. Although surveys can provide useful information about associations between number of hours worked and school grades, they cannot explain the reasons for these associations, nor can they explain the many exceptions to the data (the class president who works 35 hr a week). More research on students' direct reports in interviews would be helpful in describing more fully the aspects of jobs that students find most and least satisfying. Further information on how teenagers cope with job problems (e.g., the boss who changes a work schedule with little notification time) and the success of such strategies would be useful for teens and their parents.

Research should also address the experiences of teen work across gender, socioeconomic status, and ethnicity. For example, how do female workers cope with the fact that they are paid less? Do they try to increase their pay or accept lower wages as a given? How do teenage girls conceptualize the importance of work and pay in contrast to boys? Is it less important? Why? It is possible that teen work may have subtle but important effects on students' socialization, especially as it relates to issues of developing appropriate attitudes toward work.

As noted earlier, the cross-section of working 12-year-olds was relatively equal, but older youth workers are more likely to come from White and more affluent households. Further, research needs to clarify if this is discrimination per se or whether other factors are involved. For example, this might have to do with transportation or job-application skills—neither of which is needed for casual jobs that 12-year-olds do. Or lack of employment for older minorities may be based at least in part by stereotypes that adults hold.

Given that teens' work experiences vary so widely, research could profitably explore the quality of their job experiences. An important first step in this endeavor is to define what *quality* means in a youth job. There are significant contributing factors, which include the nature of the employer–youth relationship, job fairness and flexibility, form and level of adult supervision, job safety, and how the job environment respects goals of schooling and teens' academic achievement. Given that youth derive their attitudes toward the broader world in part from work experiences, more attention needs to be paid to the quality of job conditions for youth.

The federal government attempted to invest monies into disadvantaged neighborhoods to encourage better partnerships between community businesses and youth who are their future employees. In the federal School-to-Work initiative,[81] monies were given to motivated individuals who wanted to sponsor working opportunities for kids who would academically and socially benefit from a connection to the working world. Unfortunately, this program did not invest enough funds for us to evaluate the progress or impact of such a program. Thus, valuable information has been lost about how certain subgroups of youth benefit from various kinds of working experiences. We believe it is crucial that more monies be invested in adequate research and evaluation of how employment affects teens' lives and their schooling. However, when times get tight, youth are among the first to suffer. In the spring of 2002, President Bush announced his intention to decrease federal monies allocated to Youth Opportunity grants (instituted by the Clinton administration and designed to impact youth in low-income neighborhoods) significantly.[82]

In the previous chapter, we noted that teens need more sleep than most adults realize. Yet adults want students to hold jobs, participate in school activities, and donate time to the community (and in the next chapter, we see that youth are to increase their work in school). Thus, the real question is not how much work teens can accommodate but how much available time they have for any activity other than school and work. No doubt the relationships between work and grades vary because youth do so many things other than schoolwork and jobs. More research needs to be done examining the total time expenditure of teens in a typical week. How can time for school, work, and play best be scheduled? Youth need the chance to learn these decision-making skills.

ENDNOTES

1. U.S. Committee on Health and Safety Implications of Child Labor. (1998). *Protecting youth at work: Health, safety, and development of working children and adolescents in the United States.* Washington, DC: National Academy Press.

2. From Johnson, D. (2001, January 8). For teenagers, fast food is a snack, not a job. *New York Times,* pp. A1, A13.

3. Farkas, S., & Johnson, J. (with Duffett, A., & Bers, A.). (1997). *Kids these days: What Americans really think about the next generation.* New York: Public Agenda; see also Duffett, A., Johnson, J., & Farkas, S. (1999). *Kids these days '99: What Americans really think about the next generation.* New York: Public Agenda.

4. Bracey, G. (1998, September). Tinkering with TIMSS. *Phi Delta Kappan, 80,* 32–38.

5. In another international comparison, labor participation rates for youth ages 16–19 years were as follows: United States, 53.5; Spain, 25.1; Mexico (ages 15–19 years), 45.0; Japan, 17.0; Greece (ages 15–19 years) 16.6; Argentina (ages 14–19 years), 34.4; and Germany (ages 15–19 years), 32.6; see Committee on the Health and Safety Implications of Child Labor. (1998). *Protecting youth at work: Health, safety, and development of working children and adolescents in the United States.* Washington, DC: National Academy Press.

6. Even now with the economy at a 9-year low there are still marketable opportunities for students with technology skills; see Leonhardt, D. (2003, June 6). Unemployment rate rises to 9-year high of 6.1%. *New York Times,* p. A1.

7. For a brief overview of young workers in America, see Herman, A. M. (2000, June). *Report on the youth labor force.* Washington, DC: U.S. Secretary of Labor. Retrieved July 2, 2002, from http://www.bls.gov/opub/rylf/pdf/rylf2000.pdf; or Hine, T. (1999). *The rise and fall of the American teenager.* New York: Avon Books.

8. Spring, J. (2003). *Educating the consumer-citizen: A history of the marriage of schools, advertising, and media.* Mahwah, NJ: Lawrence Erlbaum Associates.

9. Clearly, minority Americans did not benefit from the postwar economy to the extent that White middle-class families did. But most Americans were better off in the 1950s than in the 1940s. Hine, T. (1999). *The rise and fall of the American teenager.* New York: Avon Books.

10. Bureau of Labor Statistics. (2000). *The employment situation: January 2000.* Washington, DC: U.S. Department of Labor. (Available online at http://www.bls.org)

11. Manning, W. (1990). Parenting employed teenagers. *Youth and Society, 22,* 184–200.

12. Committee on the Health and Safety Implications of Child Labor. (1998). *Protecting youth at work: Health, safety, and development of working children and adolescents in the United States.* Washington, DC: National Academy Press.

13. Schneider, B., & Stevenson, D. (1999). *The ambitious generation: America's teenagers motivated but directionless.* New Haven, CT: Yale University Press.

14. Committee on the Health and Safety Implications of Child Labor. (1998). *Protecting youth at work: Health, safety, and development of working children and adolescents in the United States.* Washington, DC: National Academy Press; Barling, J., & Kelloway, E. K. (1999). *Young workers: Varieties of experience.* Washington, DC: American Psychological Association.

15. Barling, J., & Kelloway, E. K. (1999). *Young workers: Varieties of experience* (p. 71). Washington, DC: American Psychological Association.

16. Barling, J., & Kelloway, E. K. (1999). *Young workers: Varieties of experience.* Washington, DC: American Psychological Association.

17. Kelloway, E. K., & Harvey, S. (1999). Gender differences in employment and income experiences among young people. In J. Barling & E. K. Kelloway (Eds.), *Young workers: Varieties of experience.* Washington, DC: American Psychological Association.

18. Greenberger, E., & Steinberg, L. (1986). *When teenagers work: The psychological and social costs of adolescent employment* (p. 19). New York: Basic Books.

19. Committee on the Health and Safety Implications of Child Labor. (1998). *Protecting youth at work: Health, safety, and development of working children and adolescents in the United States* (p. 49). Washington, DC: National Academy Press.

20. Committee on the Health and Safety Implications of Child Labor. (1998). *Protecting youth at work: Health, safety, and development of working children and adolescents in the United States* (p. 49). Washington, DC: National Academy Press.

21. Herman, A. M. (2000). *Report on the youth labor force.* Washington, DC: U.S. Department of Labor. (Available online at http://www.bls.gov/opub/rylf/pdf/rylf2000.pdf)

22. Kaufman, J. E., & Rosenbaum, J. E. (1992). The education and employment of low-income Black youth in White suburbs. *Educational Evaluation and Policy Analysis, 14*(3), 229–240.

23. Committee on the Health and Safety Implications of Child Labor. (1998). *Protecting youth at work: Health, safety, and development of working children and adolescents in the United States* (p. 50). Washington, DC: National Academy Press.

24. Nasar, S., & Mitchell, K. (1999, May 23). Booming job market draws young Black men into fold. *New York Times,* pp. 1, 21.

25. Nasar, S., & Mitchell, K. (1999, May 23). Booming job market draws young Black men into fold. *New York Times,* pp. 1, 21.

26. Nasar, S., & Mitchell, K. (1999, May 23). Booming job market draws young Black men into fold. *New York Times,* pp. 1, 21; also see Herman, A. M. (2000). *Report on the youth labor force.* Washington, DC: U.S. Department of Labor. (Available online at http://www.bls.gov/opub/rylf/pdf/rylf2000.pdf)

27. Herman, A. M. (2000). *Report on the youth labor force.* Washington, DC: U.S. Secretary of Labor. (Available online at http://www.bls.gov/opub/rylf/pdf/rylf2000.pdf)

28. In one *New York Times* article, it was reported that one student charged $25–$30 per hour for computer consulting work.

29. Sharpe, R. (2000, July 24). Summer help wanted: Foreigners please apply. *Business Week,* p. 32.

30. Steward, B. (2002, April 15). *Baywatch:* The Bronx? *New York Times,* p. A23; see also Brick, M. (2003, May 21). *Baywatch* it isn't for lifeguard recruits. *New York Times,* p. A28.

31. Zernike, K. (2003, July 14). Teenagers facing hard competition for summer jobs. *New York Times.*

32. Greenhouse, I. (2003, July 20). Young foreign workers fill summer shortages. *New York Times,* p. 24.

33. Herman, A. M. (2000). *Report on the youth labor force.* Washington, DC: U.S. Secretary of Labor. (Available online at http://www.bls.gov/opub/rylf/pdf/rylf2000.pdf)

34. For more information, see the U.S. Department of Labor Web site (http://www.dol.gov/) or, more specifically, the Youth Rules! Web site (http://www.youthrules.dol.gov/).

35. Herman, A. M. (2000). *Report on the youth labor force.* Washington, DC: U.S. Secretary of Labor. (Available online at http://www.bls.gov/opub/rylf/pdf/rylf2000.pdf)

36. U.S. Committee on Health and Safety Implications of Child Labor. (1998). *Protecting youth at work: Health, safety, and development of working children and adolescents in the United States.* Washington, DC: National Academy Press.

37. For example, see Berliner, D. (1997). Educational psychology meets the Christian right: Differing views of children, schooling, teaching, and learning. *Teachers College Record, 98*(3), 381–416.

38. Kiger, P. (2000, April). Risky business: When teens do adult work. *Good Housekeeping,* pp. 114–117, 210.

39. Marsh, H. W. (1991). Employment during high school: Character building or subversion of academic goals. *Sociology of Education, 64,* 172–189; Warren, J. R., LePore, P. C., & Mare, R. D. (2000). Employment during high school: Consequences for students' grades in academic courses. *American Educational Research Journal, 37*(4), 943–969.

40. Bracey, G. (1998, September). Tinkering with TIMSS. *Phi Delta Kappan, 80,* 32–38.

41. Mihalic, S. F., & Elliott, D. (1997). Short- and long-term consequences of adolescent work. *Youth and Society, 28*(4), 464–498.

42. Mihalic, S. F., & Elliott, D. (1997). Short- and long-term consequences of adolescent work. *Youth and Society, 28*(4), 464–498.

43. Mihalic, S. F., & Elliott, D. (1997). Short- and long-term consequences of adolescent work. *Youth and Society, 28*(4), 464–498.

44. Barling, J., & Kelloway, E. K. (1999). *Young workers: Varieties of experience.* Washington, DC: American Psychological Association.

45. Schoenhals, M., Tienda, M., & Schneider, B. (1997). *The educational and personal consequences of adolescent employment.* Unpublished manuscript. (Available from authors at the Department of Sociology, University of Chicago)

46. See Lawton, S. B. (1994). *Part-time work and the high school student: Costs, benefits, and future. A review of the literature and research needs.* Ontario, Canada: Ontario Institution for Studies in Education, Toronto, Department of Educational Administration. (ERIC Document Reproduction Service No. ED420728)

47. McNeal, R. (1997, July). Are students being pulled out of high school? The effect of adolescent employment on dropping out. *Sociology of Education, 70,* 206–220. These researchers controlled various variables, such as ethnicity and socioeconomic status, as a way of minimizing selection effects.

48. Newmann, F. M. (1996). Introduction: The school restructuring study. In F. Newmann & Associates (Eds.), *Authentic achievement: Restructuring school for intellectual quality.* San Francisco: Jossey-Bass; Newmann, F. M., Wehlage, G. G., & Lamborn, S. D. (1992). The significance and sources of student engagement. In F. M. Newmann (Ed.), *Student engagement and achievement in American secondary schools.* New York: Teachers College Press; Good, T., & Brophy, J. (2003). *Looking in classrooms* (9th ed.). New York: Longman.

49. For information on laws regarding youth labor laws in the state of Washington, go to http://www.leg.wa.gov/wac/index.cfm?fuseaction=chapterdigest&chapter=296-125

50. For a summary of state-by-state child labor standards, go to http://www.dol.gov/esa/programs/whd/state/nonfarm.htm#footd

51. Johnson, D. (2001, January 8). For teenagers, fast food is a snack, not a job. *New York Times,* pp. A1, A13.

52. Higuera, J. J. (2000, May 30). Teen jobs go begging. *Arizona Daily Star,* pp. D1, D2.

53. Lee, L. (1998, August 2). What's the rush? Why college can wait. *Education Life: New York Times,* pp. 24–25, 42.

54. Botstein, L. (1999, May 17). Let teen-agers try adulthood. *The New York Times,* p. A25.

55. Schneider, B., & Stevenson, D. (1999). *The ambitious generation: America's teenagers motivated but directionless.* New Haven, CT: Yale University Press.

56. Percentages may not add up to 100% due to rounding.

57. For other case study examples, see Schneider, B., & Stevenson, D. (1999). *The ambitious generation: America's teenagers motivated but directionless.* New Haven, CT: Yale University Press.

58. In educational research, the concept of *volition* is defined as the skills necessary to carry out goals. For example a student may be motivated to participate in a classroom discussion; however, he or she may lack the skills or know-how to ask questions. Therefore, the student's lack of participation is not due to a lack of motivation but to a lack of skills that impeded the expression of the student's motivation. For example, see Corno, L. (1993). The best-laid plans: Modern conceptions of volition and educational research. *Educational Researcher, 22*(2), 14–22.

59. U.S. Department of Labor, Bureau of Labor Statistics. (1999). *Employment experience and other characteristics of youths: Results from a new longitudinal survey.* Washington, DC: Author. (ERIC Document Reproduction Service No. ED429229)

60. U.S. Department of Labor, Bureau of Labor Statistics. (1999). *Employment experience and other characteristics of youths: Results from a new longitudinal survey.* Washington, DC: Author. (ERIC Document Reproduction Service No. ED429229)

61. McNaughton, D. (2002, April 21). Lottery winner can't afford simplicity. *The Atlanta Journal and Constitution,* p. 5P; Jones, A. (2002, April 19). It's sun, sand for lottery winner as parents take the spotlight. *The Atlanta Journal and Constitution,* p. 7C.

62. Schneider, B., & Stevenson, D. (1999). *The ambitious generation: America's teenagers motivated but directionless.* New Haven, CT: Yale University Press.

63. Barling, J., & Kelloway, E. K. (1999). *Young workers: Varieties of experience.* Washington, DC: American Psychological Association.

64. Greenberger, E., & Steinberg, L. (1986). *When teenagers work: The psychological and social costs of adolescent employment* (p. 30). New York: Basic Books.

65. Margaret, I. (1996, August 8). Consultants with tender faces: Big companies ask children how to sell to children. *New York Times,* pp. C1, C4.

66. Zollo, P. (1999). *Wise up to teens: Insights into marketing and advertising to teenagers* (2nd ed., pp. 19–20). Ithaca, NY: New Strategist Publications.

67. Zollo, P. (1999). *Wise up to teens: Insights into marketing and advertising to teenagers* (2nd ed., p. 10). Ithaca, NY: New Strategist Publications.

68. Zollo, P. (1999). *Wise up to teens: Insights into marketing and advertising to teenagers* (2nd ed., p. 7). Ithaca, NY: New Strategist Publications.

69. Zollo, P. (1999). *Wise up to teens: Insights into marketing and advertising to teenagers* (2nd ed., p. 14). Ithaca, NY: New Strategist Publications. Percentages may not add up to 100% due to rounding.

70. Zollo, P. (1999). *Wise up to teens: Insights into marketing and advertising to teenagers* (2nd ed.). Ithaca, NY: New Strategist Publications.

71. Youth Rules! was started in May of 2002 by the U.S. Department of Labor to strengthen awareness of the federal and state rules about the youth workforce. The rules, among

other things, aim for a balance between work and school. The purpose is to create and endorse positive and safe experiences for youth that will help them prepare for careers in the future. The site is dedicated to giving quick access to the federal and state rules for youth employment and other pertinent information to help educate the public. In part, Youth Rules! will help spread awareness by creating and circulating information, a curricula for educators, using public service announcements, training people regarding the federal and state regulations, and using other types of publicity, such as stickers, posters, bookmarks, and checklists. U.S. Department of Labor. (2002). *About Youth Rules!* Washington, DC: Author. (Available online at http://www.youthrules.dol.gov/about.htm)

72. There are several Web sites dedicated to uncovering the marketing practices instituted by ZapMe! that are seen as unethical. For example, see http://zdnet.com.com/2100-11-517919.html?legacy=zdnn or http://www.commercialalert.org/zapme.html or http://www.internetstockreport.com/tracker/article/0,1785,1711_290501,00.html or the public document put out by ZapMe! and presented to the Federal Trade Commission (in June of 1999), defending its practices, http://www.ftc.gov/privacy/comments/zapme.htm (retrieved July 2, 2002).

73. Mendels, P. (2000, February 2). Criticism for company offering free computers to schools. *New York Times,* p. B10.

74. Zehr, M. A. (2000, March 15). Some schools feel burned by ZapMe! offer. *Education Week,* p. 5.

75. Trotter, A. (2001, February 7). Company criticized for collecting data on children. *Education Week, 20,* 3.

76. General Accounting Office. (2000). *Public education: Commercial activities in schools* (GAO/HEHS-00-156). Washington, DC: Author.

77. Spring, J. (2003). *Educating the consumer-citizen: A history of the marriage of schools, advertising, and media.* Mahwah, NJ: Lawrence Erlbaum Associates.

78. Zernike, K. (2001, March 14). Coke to dilute push in schools for its products. *New York Times,* p. A11.

79. Investigators who acquired these data sets remind us that statistics are obtained only from those teens who actually seek medical or social services, and therefore information gleaned from these reports is likely to underestimate the extent to which teens engage in illegal acts for money.

80. Stanford Center for the Study of Families, Children, and Youth. (1991). *The Stanford studies of homeless families, children, and youth.* Stanford, CA: Stanford University.

81. The School-to-Work Initiative was instituted in 1994. However, it ended in October, 2001. Relevant information associated with state-by-state School-to-Work programs can be found at www.doleta.gov or www.ed.gov/offices/OVAE (retrieved July 2, 2002).

82. Pear, R. (2002, January 31). Bush budget will seek cuts in programs for job training. *New York Times,* p. A1.

Chapter 8

Youth and Education

After decades of business-as-usual, school reform, too many of our nation's children still cannot read . . . After spending $125 billion . . . over 25 years, we have virtually nothing to show for it.

—R. Paige, Education Secretary[1]

The adolescent peer culture in contemporary America demeans academic success and scorns students who try to do well in school.

—L. Steinberg, 1996[2]

The young men and women of America's future elite work their laptops to the bone, rarely question authority, and happily accept their positions at the top of the heap as part of the natural order of life.

—D. Brooks, 2001[3]

There is a widespread myth that today's youth are less committed to education than their parents, grandparents, and their foreign peers. This myth has been prevalent since the 1983 national report *A Nation at Risk*. In this chapter, we systematically debunk the myth of teen as educational laggard. We show that today's students are as diligent as ever and that a higher percentage of youth, including those from low-income households, are enrolled in college than ever before.

Oddly, despite the documented high educational performance of youth, there is a demand for higher performance, a push that comes more from policymakers than from parents. Indeed, many parents don't mind their teens achieving at somewhat lower academic levels if it means that they can participate in other activities and be better rounded.[4] Still, many teens feel pressured to do more.

Policymakers and educational experts do not speak with a single voice. Generally, legislators want higher achievement, though some demand that youth be more community minded; others place more emphasis on individual academic accomplishments. Clearly, if youth are to commit to school and community, they must manage their time wisely. Yet it is equally clear that youth lack guidance about how to set appropriate goals and make good time-management decisions.[5] Especially problematic is that many policymakers, while demanding higher achievement from students, fail to acknowledge the inadequate resources that many schools receive.[6] This is tragic because growing evidence shows that school- and state-level resources are closely related to student achievement.[7]

In the case of at-risk schools whose students perform poorly, adults are willing to label youth, their teachers, and these schools as failures, even though many "failing" schools are denied fundamental resources. Unfortunately, criteria for determining schools' success or failure are inconsistently defined and carelessly applied. Recently, federal, state, and local school districts' lists of failing schools differed notably.[8] What do students think when policymakers carelessly describe them and their schools as failing? Some social scientists believe that schools described as failures are often the victims of indifferent policymakers who deny them needed resources or present them with unreasonable demands of graduation requirements. As but one example of the unrealistic demands being placed on students is the fact that the state of California has postponed its high school exit exam until 2006 because of its high failure rates.[9] Increasingly, the states are recognizing that they are using poor tests with unrealistic expectations for judging students.

Adults send contradictory messages to youth about the importance of education. Teens are told to excel, but in some high schools honor graduates are not even honored at graduations. Youth are told that early college admission is important and that they need to take national tests in their junior year, while at the same time they're encouraged to hold part-time jobs and to be active in school and community activities. Pressures for early college admission and higher levels of academic performance are creating trickle-down pressures for younger students to achieve academically.

It is time to break this cycle of multiple—and often conflicting—demands made on youth before more youth are fractured—forced to develop inadequate and contradictory images of themselves. School is important, but students are also social beings,[10] and their future contributions to society depend as much on their social growth as on their academic growth.

THE FAILURE OF AMERICAN EDUCATION

Since the Soviets' launching of *Sputnik* in 1957, and especially following the report, *A Nation at Risk* in 1983, American schools have been criticized as woefully inadequate. Neither teachers nor students work hard, critics have charged, and indifferent parents seldom visit their children's classrooms. Parents, students, and teachers were all blamed for school failures, and policymakers urged all participants to work harder in schools[11] and to spend more time on homework.

The launching of *Sputnik* sent shock waves through 1957 America, spawning national alarm that American education (especially in math and science) had allowed our nation to lag so far behind that our economy and very survival were at risk. American education was flawed, and radical, immediate reform was needed. It was argued that mathematics classes were too accessible, math was not taught in a formal, abstract fashion (e.g., set theory). The New Math curriculum proposed as a solution was soon rejected even as a partial solution. Subsequently, America won the space race in the 1970s and 1980s with scientists who graduated from the allegedly inferior high schools of the 1950s.[12]

In 1983, the federal government sponsored a national commission to explore the "horrible" state of American education, and the ensuing document, *A Nation at Risk*, loudly proclaimed the failure of our educational system:

> Our nation is at risk. Our once unchallenged preeminence in commerce, industry, science, technology and innovation is being overtaken by competitors throughout the world. . . . If an unfriendly foreign power had attempted to impose on America the mediocre educational performance that exists today, we might well have viewed it as an act of war. As it stands, we have allowed this to happen to ourselves. We have even squandered the gains in student achievement made in the wake of the *Sputnik* challenge.[13]

The prescription called for more education, including longer school days and years, and more homework. In many schools, these work-harder prescriptions were enacted.

Ironically, in the 1990s, American businesswomen and men (who had graduated from the alleged deficit high schools of the 1960s and 1970s) won the economic war. Despite the improving economy from 1983 to 1994, the shrill sequel to *A Nation at Risk*—*Prisoners of Time*—appeared in 1994. This document, like most sequels, had less impact than the original. Nonetheless, this report exerted considerable pressure for reform, and a new crisis and new Zeitgeist solutions were again issued. The *Prisoners of Time* document called for many reforms, but the central message was that high school students in America were receiving considerably less instruction in basic core areas than foreign students. The report noted that Americans spent only 1,460 hr on core subjects, whereas in Japan, France, and Germany 3,170 hr, 3,280 hr, and 3,528 hr, respectively, were spent on core subject-matter instruction. The commission asserted that these differences were alarming and warranted a national call for more time spent on basic subject matters.

A host of editorials followed, echoing the report's contention that in-creasing time on core subjects was a good idea. One editorial[14] included a quote from the report: "The traditional school day must now fit in a whole set of requirements for what has been called the new 'work of the schools'—education about personal safety, consumer affairs, AIDS, conser-vation in energy, family life, and driver's training."

Tom Good responded to the absurdity of eliminating important subject-matter areas simply because students in other countries did not spend time on them:

> If the curriculum includes some study in family life, it is because some politi-cal constituency and citizens thought this content would improve the curricu-lum. Perhaps educators and citizens were concerned because children were having children and children were killing children. They may have thought that information about family life and personal safety might allow sixth grad-ers to make it to high school so that they could receive extra instruction in his-tory. Were these citizens and policymakers wrong?[15]

Although it is encouraging that in the past decade, more social scientists are seeing the need for treating the social and emotional needs of students,[16] it is still the case that policymakers focus almost exclusively on student achieve-ment. This is especially ironic and tragic because parents want schools to do much more than focus purely on subject-matter learning.

Good News

In the 1990s, several social science scholars began to note that the data on average student performance did not match policymakers' assertions that average school performance was inadequate. David Berliner and Bruce Biddle, in their book *The Manufactured Crisis,* carefully documented that students in the 1990s were as good on average as students of yesterday, and that this was true of a wide range of school outcomes.[17] Berliner and Biddle and other educators and social scientists[18] convincingly argued that not only were students on average doing as well as those of earlier generations but also that many more students from low-income households were en-rolled in education at all levels.

Since the publication of *The Manufactured Crisis,* it has become almost routine for various educational groups to archive the good news of Ameri-can schools.[19] And, there is much good news to comment on:

1. Math and reading scores are increasing.[20]
2. Students are taking tougher courses.[21]
3. Students are taking more academic courses.[22]

4. More students are reading more as a part of schoolwork.[23]

5. SAT scores are increasing.[24]

6. ACT scores are increasing.[25]

7. The number of college degrees is increasing.[26]

8. More public schools than private schools offer advanced placement (AP) exams.[27]

9. More students are taking AP exams.[28]

10. More students are graduating from high schools.[29]

11. More high school graduates are completing college.[30]

These are notable gains. The 2000 National Assessment of Educational Progress (NAEP) test showed that 4th, 8th, and 12th graders' reading performances have increased steadily since 1992—reaching their highest level in 2000. Similarly, in the 1990s math scores increased for all age groups, and the proportion of students achieving the two highest levels in mathematics performance doubled for Grade 4, increased by 80% for Grade 8, and grew by 41% for Grade 12.

Many more students are taking SAT exams than in the past, and more high school graduates go to college. SAT scores continue to rise. Math SAT scores have risen 22 points since 1980, 13 points alone in 1990. Verbal gains have been less significant, but still SAT verbal scores have increased by 6 points since 1990. ACT test scores have also shown notable improvement, to the point that roughly half of high school seniors who take the ACT examination score at a level sufficient for admission to highly selective colleges.

NAEP Data

NAEP tests have been administered for more than 30 years, and they have become recognized as the gold standard for educational progress. Policymakers are asking increasingly for their use to validate state exams.[31] The evidence from NAEP testing is clear. As can be seen in Table 8.1, students have consistently held performance standards over time,[32] and current reading and mathematics scores are higher than 1970s scores in all six comparisons—and significantly so in five of the six comparisons.

The state-to-state variation in performance is remarkable. For example, science scores in Maine, North Dakota, Montana, and Wisconsin are exceedingly high in comparison to students' scores in Louisiana, Hawaii, Mississippi, and California. These data make it clear that discussions of average student performance are misleading. Still American youth—on average—are not performing worse than they did 30 years ago.

TABLE 8.1
NAEP Scores Over Time

Reading:
  9-year-olds: The average score in 1999 is higher than in 1971.
  13-year-olds: The average score in 1999 is higher than in 1971.
  17-year-olds: The average score in 1999 is higher than in 1971 but not significantly so.
Mathematics:
  9-year-olds: The average score in 1999 is higher than in 1973.
  13-year-olds: The average score in 1999 is higher than in 1973.
  17-year-olds: The average score in 1999 is higher than in 1973.

Note.   From *NAEP 1999 Trends in Academic Progress: Three Decades of Student Performance,* by
J. R. Campbell, C. M. Hombo, and J. Mazzeo, 2000, Washington, DC: U.S. Department of Education.

TIMSS: International Data

Another alleged Achilles heel of American education is our students'
poor performance in international comparisons (i.e., the Third International Mathematics and Science Study—TIMSS). President Clinton, in his
1999 State of the Union Address, asserted that, although American students were doing better (SAT scores and math scores on the NAEP were
increasing), there remained an acute educational problem: "While our
fourth graders outperform their peers in other countries in math and science, our eighth graders are around average, and our twelfth graders rank
near the bottom."[33]

There are various problems with the TIMSS data. First, American scores
at all grade levels show huge variation; wide variation in any set of scores
means that an average is not useful in assessing typical performance. The
range (from top to bottom) in school performance was higher in America
than in most countries. A second issue is the comparability of student populations. Gerald Bracey noted that our 12th-grade students are younger
than those in many countries, so in actuality American students were competing against 13th- and 14th-grade students.[34] Some countries only tested
high school students who were in concentrated math and science programs, and in some countries students had studied physics for 3 years
prior to taking the TIMSS. Bracey also pointed out that at least 23% of the
items on the advanced mathematics tests assumed that students had taken
a calculus course.[35]

The material covered in a curriculum correlates with students' performance on standardized tests.[36] If a teacher goes through the curriculum more
slowly than their colleagues, that teacher's students will be penalized on
tests that measure knowledge of more advanced topics. Consider that in Japan all eighth-grade students must take algebra, even those enrolled in vo-

cational tracks, but in the United States, some students take algebra, but many do not. Thus, it is not surprising that on average Japanese students score higher on the TIMSS mathematics test—which tests for knowledge of algebra—than do American students.

An analysis that focused on only American students who had taken algebra found, however, that these American students had scores higher than those of Japanese students.[37] Lower scores on TIMSS items often only reflect a curriculum issue. It makes no sense to test students on content that they have not been taught. Perhaps a more relevant question is whether algebra should be required at the sixth, seventh- or eighth-grade level.

American Students Perform at Different Levels on the TIMSS

A recent study based on 1999 TIMSS scores by the U.S. Department of Education and the International Association for the Evaluation of Educational Achievement compared the performance of eighth graders in selected American individual school districts (and states) with the performance of eighth graders in other countries. In this comparison, Singapore was ranked first in mathematics (604)[38] and Naperville School District No. 203 in Illinois was ranked first in science (584).[39] In contrast, an American school district ranked last in the comparisons in both mathematics and science (Miami-Dade County Public Schools, Florida). These data confirm what some educational researchers have known for years: America contains not only some of the best schools in the world but also some of the worst. As can be seen in Table 8.2, individual states (e.g., Michigan) outperformed many countries (including Australia, England, Belgium, and Canada). Interestingly, some of the highest-performing educational states in America were not included in the study.

Denial and Confusion

Despite the positive nature of data from educational testing in American schools, many still see the seeds of a crisis and find a need for radical reform:[40]

> Even though Connecticut performed slightly better than the U.S. average, Thomas Murphy, a spokesman for the State Education Department, said that the state found that its schools may be teaching some mathematics and science skills later than their international competitors. "We want to look at our sequencing and what was on the exam," he said, "and determine whether we're addressing those skills early enough."[41]

TABLE 8.2
Eighth-Grade TIMSS Comparisons

District/Country	Average Scale Score on TIMSS	
	Mathematics[a]	Science[b]
United States	502	515
By State		
Connecticut	512	529
Idaho	495	526
Illinois	509	521
Indiana	515	534
Maryland	495	506
Massachusetts	513	533
Michigan	517	544
Missouri	490	523
North Carolina	495	508
Oregon	514	536
Pennsylvania	507	529
South Carolina	502	511
Texas	516	509
By District[c]		
Naperville School District, Illinois	569	584
Miami Dade, Florida	421	426
International[d]		
International average (all countries)	487	488
Australia	525	540
Belgium	558	535
Canada	531	533
England	496	538
Hong Kong	582	530
Japan	579	550
Singapore	604	568

[a]Mathematics scores from *Mathematics Benchmarking Report: TIMSS 1999—Eighth Grade Achievement for U.S. States and Districts in an International Context,* by I. V. Mullis et al., Boston: Boston College, International Study Center. Copyright 2001 by IEA.

[b]Science scores from *Science Benchmarking Report: TIMSS 1999—Eighth Grade Achievement for U.S. States and Districts in an International Context,* by M. O. Martin et al., Boston: Boston College, International Study Center. Copyright 2001 by IEA.

[c]Not all districts are reported here. These are only the highest and lowest scoring districts.

[d]These represent only a sample of selected international test score results. See full report for comprehensive list of results.

At the time, Glenn W. "Max" McGee, the state superintendent of schools in Illinois, indicated that he anticipated copying Naperville's success by distributing videotapes of modeled teaching, classroom materials, and so forth and sharing those with a low-scoring district in Chicago.[42] (Perhaps instead of sending videotapes, McGee should consider enticing some of the Naperville teachers to teach in Chicago.)

Murphy and McGee's reactions appear spurious. Why should American schools teach certain mathematics and science skills earlier simply because it is done in Singapore or Sweden? After all, many American students eventually exceed the performance of students in other countries.[43] Research indicates that a curriculum that works in one context often does not work in other contexts or for other dependent measures.[44] Our point is not to debate Mr. Murphy or Mr. McGee; we stress, however, that education will not benefit from such simplistic plans.[45]

Need for a Different Curriculum: Higher Standards

As noted elsewhere,[46] there is an emerging argument that traditional achievement standards are no longer applicable to the current society, and the current push by policymakers and politicians is for schools to be held accountable to different and higher standards. However, high standards alone do not necessarily ensure better teaching or higher achievement. In fact, there is no consensus on what *higher* means or how it should be implemented. Higher can mean learning the same content earlier. However, sometimes it means making the same content harder. Too often, a higher standard means knowing more facts or concepts about the Civil War (or another subject), but not being more knowledgeable of integrated and defendable explanations of the causes of the War or its effects (short or long term) on the American economy. Higher standards, in some cases, simply means more information, not more knowledge.

Importantly, at the time policymakers started pushing for what they termed higher standards, extant data suggested that the test scores of students in states with higher standards were actually lower than those of students in states with presumably lower standards.[47] Policymakers are distinguished by asking for standards that are not only higher but are so artificially high that students fail; for example, in Virginia and Arizona, 90% of students failed exams that presumably represent policymakers' expectations for performance. As noted elsewhere,[48] increasing standards may be a laudable goal in some instances, but when only 10% of students pass a test, the effort is ridiculous and self-defeating. It is important to note that these are not isolated cases. Earlier we noted the outcry in California over high school graduation tests and recently, there has been an outcry over the Regents Physics test in New York, a test that college professors of physics have noted is unreasonable.[49]

It has been shown that even when high standards are imposed on school curricula, many students, especially minority students and those from low-income households, still do not receive the instruction that they need in these courses to succeed on tests. Although standards are mandated, it is clear, at least in some schools, that policies on tracking and other related issues prevent students from receiving the instruction they need.[50] Given the exaggerated negative views of youth, and testing-standards policies that will only demonstrate teens' failure, it seems important to explore the motivation for developing unrealistic tests. Are such practices designed to suggest that youth, especially minority youths, do not deserve resources in their schools?[51]

Why Change the Curriculum?

Ironically, leaders in other countries envy our public school system. During President Clinton's trip to China in 1998, he appeared on a radio show with Mr. Xu, the mayor of Shanghai, and learned that Mr. Xu wanted Chinese education to be more like American education. Mr. Xu noted:

> In Chinese education, we talk about the filling of information into the student, whereas in the United States they try to make the student more able. They try to teach you to have the ability to do things. So Chinese are very good at tests, but not necessarily when it comes to scientific research.[52]

It could be that Mr. Xu was just being a good host to President Clinton; however, there are official reports from other countries that also indicate an interest in improving students' ability to think creatively. For example, an official document from the Ministry of Education in Singapore argues the case this way:

> Our [Singapore] education system should not be judged solely by the number of A's our students get in major national examinations nor by the high standing of our students in international comparisons of science and mathematics achievement. Equally important is the quality of the people the education system produces—their integrity and character; their attitudes toward work, their ability to be team-players, and their sense of responsibility and commitment to society. In short, an education that encompasses a balanced development of the whole personality—moral, cognitive, physical, social, and aesthetic.[53]

Other countries have also deemphasized standardized testing and are interested in educating students to be more willing to take risks and creatively apply what they know.[54] Korea and Japan have been moving to make their educational systems more like American public education. In 1994, a Korean presidential commission recommended less emphasis on standardized testing and more on developing students' initiative and performance.[55] Still, our government and media continue to extol the virtues of foreign education. Consider, for example, the comments made by *New York Times* journalist Nicholas Kristof in November of 2002:

> Chinese students may not have a lot of fun, and may lag in subjects in which some American students excel, such as sex, drugs, and rock 'n' roll. But these kids know their calculus and are driven by a work ethic and thirst for education that make them indomitable.[56]

Competitiveness and Achievement

Some have urged American schools to become more competitive, and by this, they mean for students to score higher on narrow standardized achievement tests. However, the real success of American schools may be due to their encouragement of students to pursue diverse topics and activities in school that may lead to greater creativity in job performance after school. Gerald Bracey recently correlated the relationship between the Current Competitiveness Index (CCI) that is calculated by the World Economic Forum with test scores from the TIMSS. The 75 nations were ranked on the basis of their CCI, and 41 countries took part in TIMSS. For 38 countries there were data from both, and it was on this basis that Bracey concluded that the relationship between test scores in math and competitiveness is .23. As can be seen in Table 8.3, Finland, the United States, and the Netherlands top the global competitiveness score and Russia, Romania, and Bulgaria are at the bottom of this index.

Dangers of High-Stakes Testing

Audrey Amrein and David Berliner examined the effects of high-stakes testing (e.g., a required test for high school graduation) and found that states with high stakes attached to tests did not predict student performance on other measures.[57] They reasoned that a high-stakes test (that judges the quality of the teacher or school or students) may be misleading because of unintended consequences (the curriculum narrowly focuses on test content) or because of corruption (tests are invalidly administered or scored). Amrein and Berliner argued that higher scores on a single high-stakes test may not be predictive of general learning. To test this hypothesis, they compared those 18 states adopting a high-stakes test before and after its adop-

TABLE 8.3
Ranks of 38 Nations on Global Competitiveness
and TIMSS Mathematics Scores

Country	Rank	Math Score
Finland	1	21*
United States	2	29
Netherlands	3	10
Germany	4	24
Switzerland	5	9
Sweden	6	23
England	7	26
Denmark	8	28
Australia	9	17
Singapore	10	1
Canada	11	19
France	12	14
Austria	13	13
Belgium	14	6
Japan	15	4
Iceland	16	31
Israel	17	22
Hong Kong	18	5
Norway	19	27
New Zealand	20	25
Chinese Taipei	21	2**
Ireland	22	18
Spain	23	31
Italy	24	34*
South Africa	25	38
Hungary	26	15
Korea	27	3
Portugal	28	32
Slovenia	29	11
Czech Rep.	29 (35)+	8
Thailand	30 (38)+	20
Slovak Rep.	31 (39)+	9
Latvia	32	30
Greece	33 (43)+	33
Lithuania	34 (49)+	35
Colombia	35 (56)+	35
Russia	36 (58)+	16
Romania	37 (61)+	37
Bulgaria	38 (65)+	12

*These nations did not participate in the original TIMSS. Ranks are computed from scores on TIMSS-R, which used the same tests.

**Taiwan did not participate in the original TIMSS, so TIMSS-R scores were used to compute ranks. In addition, the nation is listed as Chinese Taipei because of the People's Republic of China insistence on this designation.

+ Ranks in parentheses are the ranks for those countries when compared to the full slate of 75 countries ranked by the World Economic Forum.

Note. From "Test Scores, Creativity, and Global Competitiveness," by G. W. Bracey, 2002, *Phi Delta Kappan, 83*(10), pp. 738–739. Copyright 2002 by Phi Delta Kappan International. Reprinted with permission.

tion and in comparison to a national trend line. In particular, they compared student performance on the ACT, SAT, NAEP, and advanced placement (AP) tests. They found across these various analyses that student learning remains at roughly the same level or a slightly lower level than it was before high-stakes testing was implemented. They lamented that so much money (more than $100 million) and person hours have been expended in the preparation, scoring, and analyses of tests that have not enhanced student performance and, in some cases, appear to have lowered student performance. Preparation for these tests not only takes time away from other student activities (playing chess, writing for pleasure) but also may lower performance on other educational tests.

Others have investigated the relationship of high-stakes testing and student achievement and reported different results, in part due to different methodological approaches. For example, in comparison to the Ambrein and Berliner study that compared states using high-stakes tests with the national average, Margaret Raymond and Eric Hanushek[58] compared high-stakes tests with those states having no accountability program. They found that high-stakes test states did increase the typical performance of a student moving from fourth grade to eighth grade by 1.6%, which was twice the rate of states with no accountability programs.[59] Further, in another study, Carnoy and Loeb created a composite index to measure the strength of accountability in each state. In comparing states with stronger accountability and states with lesser accountability, they found that states with stronger accountability had significantly higher NAEP math test scores. They also reported that accountability was related to decreases in the Black–White achievement gap.[60]

These data will continue to be debated and analyzed by other social scientists,[61] but at best, if it is true that the massive and costly high-stakes testing has increased students' average percentile progress by less than one percentile point over 4 years, then even if these results were sustained, it seems hardly worth it. The possible trade-offs of increased student anxiety, dropouts, and loss of activities hardly seem worth the cost.

As an extension of this debate, the most recent 2003 SAT scores have just become available for analysis (as we finalize the book in September 2003). These data show that students' performance on this exam is at its highest level in 36 years. Has the increase in state standards and testing played a major role in students' increasing SAT performance? Bob Schaeffer, director of the National Center for Fair and Open Testing (FairTest), noted that high-standards/high-stakes states like Texas and Florida registered but modest gains in contrast to lower accountability states like Vermont which showed more robust gains. As Schaeffer notes, this data "undermines the claim that high-stakes tests improve overall education quality."[62]

UNDERESTIMATING YOUTH'S EDUCATIONAL PERFORMANCE

Why, given strong evidence to the contrary, was there a strident media argument in the early 1990s that our schools were woefully inadequate?[63] Youth and their teachers were characterized as indifferent, inadequate, and unwilling to work hard. This description is grossly inaccurate. During the 1990s, the press consistently criticized schools and youth for their inadequate educational performance. Why did the media choose to perpetuate the myth that our schools were failing?

We do not believe that the media systematically decided to exaggerate teens' deficiencies or to pillar them as part of some conspiracy. However, the pressures that have induced the media to exaggerate teen sexuality, violence, and so on are the same forces that worked to distort the reporting of their good educational progress. In part, the media always emphasize negative news, and the educational reporting on youth is consistent with this general pattern. Further, media coverage of education highlights the episodic aspects without any, or very little, in-depth analysis. It is easy to exaggerate teens' irresponsibility, such as high dropout rates in some cities, when the conditions of students' lives are not reported. Perhaps the press suffers from a too low opinion about youth that leads many reporters not to look at context or disconfirming evidence.

Media's View of Youth

It is discouraging to see the misleading headlines that frequently are used to describe educational performance. Consider the following headline: "Although SAT scores fell, number of A's increased."[64] This representation has major problems. The headline is largely pejorative, but the content of the article revealed that math SAT scores increased and reading SAT scores stayed about the same, and, although the article discussed grade inflation at length, it failed to report that students made notable progress on AP tests. High school students' scores went up in math (a subject that is taught in high school) and stayed the same in reading (a subject not taught in most high schools[65]).

On July 11, 2003, Tamar Lewin used this headline, "New report on students' skills reinforces good news and bad."[66] The report focuses on students' writing progress as measured by the National Assessment of Educational Progress' 2002 writing assessment. The report noted that average fourth-grade scores increased by four points and a three-point gain occurred at the eighth-grade level. And roughly, 85% of fourth- and eighth-graders were sufficient in basic writing ability. These gains were significantly reliable. In contrast, Lewin noted, "And the average 12th-grade score fell two points—too small a decline to be statistically significant, but certainly no cause for celebration, particularly considered to next to the 12th-graders' declining reading scores." Although this headline is not blatantly wrong, it is misleading and on balance negative about students' school performance.

Significant findings of improvement in writing at the fourth- and eighth-grade levels for students of all ethnic backgrounds and for low-income students as well is equated (in the headline) with nonsignificant changes at the twelfth-grade level. This is especially misleading since reading and writing are not taught in most twelfth-grade classrooms.

The media's distortion of performance in American schools is so negatively slanted that many have argued that it affects citizens' beliefs about the general quality of schooling. The *Phi Delta Kappan* regularly reports citizens' high marks of local schools but low scores of national schools. The authors of a Phi Delta Kappa/Gallup Poll concluded that, "The low grades given the *nation's* public schools are primarily media induced. Whereas people learn first hand about their *children's* schools, they learn about the nation's schools primarily from the media" [italics included in original quote].[67] These misperceptions about poor schools undoubtedly make many Americans reluctant to invest more money in public schools.

Leading the Media

The media are not the only segment of American culture that distorts the truth about schools in this country. Social scientists' heavy reliance on reporting data in terms of averages, at times and perhaps inadvertently, lead to misunderstandings about American education. For example, a book authored by Laurence Steinberg (with Bradford Brown and Sanford Dornbusch) received extensive publicity, including a story in *Newsweek*. It exemplifies our argument about the dangers of episodic reporting. Steinberg wrote the following:

> More than one-third of the students we surveyed showed signs of being emotionally disengaged from school, as indexed by measures of mind-wandering, lack of interest, or inattentiveness. Half of the students we surveyed say their classes are boring. A third say they have lost interest in school, that they are not learning very much, and that they get through the school day by fooling around with their classmates. And remember, ours was a sample of "average" students in "average" American schools—not a sample of "high-risk" youngsters in "high-risk" school settings.[68]

Steinberg made various claims, including the statistics that two thirds of students surveyed said they had cheated on a school exam and that almost 9

out of 10 students had copied someone else's homework. Further, he indicated that fewer than 1 in 5 students said their friends thought it was important to get good grades in school and that roughly 20% of all students said
they do not try as hard in school because they are fearful of peer rejection.
Steinberg concluded, "The adolescent peer culture in contemporary America demeans academic success and scorns students who try to do well in
school."[69]

To explore the variability of teens' perceptions on some of the topics
that Steinberg studied, we conducted our own study, involving more than
700 students in two schools. Details of the study can be found elsewhere;[70]
however, we want to make a few points about the misconceptions associated
with the reporting of averages. Figures 8.1, 8.2, 8.3, and 8.4 provide data
that we obtained in the junior high and high school with regard to students' perceptions of peer pressure. These perceptions were quantified
both in terms of gender and students' grade point averages.

As shown in Fig. 8.1, male and female students in the junior high did not
feel pressure from peers to perform at lower levels. The data are similar in

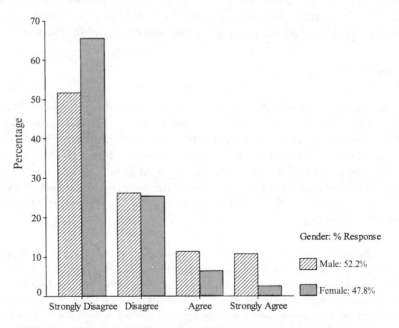

FIG. 8.1.   Response distribution of peer pressure by gender in a junior high
school: If I get good grades, my friends make fun of me. From "Underestimating Youth's Commitment to Schools and Society: Toward a More Differentiated View," by T. L. Good, S. L. Nichols, and D. L. Sabers, 1999, *Social Psychology of Education, 3,* 1–39. Copyright 1999 by Kluwer Academic/Plenum
Publishers. Reprinted with permission. Based on a sample of 358 junior high
students, ages 12 to 15 years.

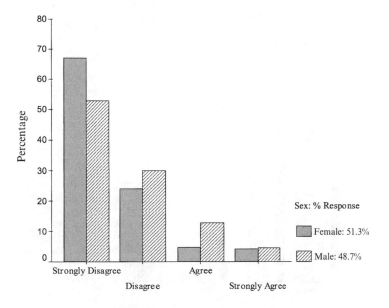

FIG. 8.2. Response distribution of peer pressure by gender in a high school: If I get good grades, my friends make fun of me. From "Underestimating Youth's Commitment to Schools and Society: Toward a More Differentiated View," by T. L. Good, S. L. Nichols, and D. L. Sabers, 1999, *Social Psychology of Education, 3,* 1–39. Copyright 1999 by Kluwer Academic/Plenum Publishers. Reprinted with permission. Based on a sample of 347 high students in Grades 9 through 12.

the high school, as shown in Fig. 8.2. In Figs. 8.3 and 8.4 these data are reported by students' achievement levels. Clearly, female and male students and students who are doing well report different perceptions of the peer culture than those who are not. But despite this variation, it is apparent that the notion of a pernicious, intractable peer culture, as implied by Steinberg, is simply untenable. What is most misleading in reports like Steinberg's, which suggest that 20–25% of students perform poorly because of peer pressure, is that the statistics imply that other students are indifferent or unaffected by the peer culture. However, the data presented in all the figures show that students generally perceive that their peers support their achievement. Overwhelmingly, students strongly disagree with the assertion that peers negatively influence their performance. And our study showed that by many other measures, students' attitudes and beliefs were varied but were generally pro school.

There is no monolithic youth culture that actively works to disrupt academic performance in schools or to pressure students to perform poorly. However, there is research to show that in some schools peer cultures can be detrimental.[71] But a broad review of the literature shows that although in

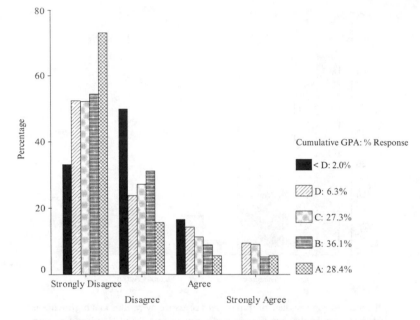

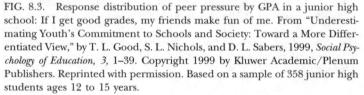

FIG. 8.3.   Response distribution of peer pressure by GPA in a junior high school: If I get good grades, my friends make fun of me. From "Underestimating Youth's Commitment to Schools and Society: Toward a More Differentiated View," by T. L. Good, S. L. Nichols, and D. L. Sabers, 1999, *Social Psychology of Education, 3,* 1–39. Copyright 1999 by Kluwer Academic/Plenum Publishers. Reprinted with permission. Based on a sample of 358 junior high students ages 12 to 15 years.

some schools a peer culture makes it more difficult for academic goals to be highly valued, in other schools the peer culture actively supports achievement.[72] Rather than lament that peer cultures fail to support achievement, we need to understand why the peer culture supports scholarship heavily in some schools but less so in other schools. Unfortunately, despite the growing evidence that peer groups have negative and positive effects on students' achievement, the media continue the myth that peer groups are universally hostile to students who achieve.

Peer Groups Are Permeable

Barbara Schneider and David Stevenson, in their book *The Ambitious Generation,* illustrated that American teens are not a monolithic group controlled by peers. On the contrary, they found that peer arrangements are very fluid.[73] When asked to describe their closest friends, the change in peer affiliations from 10th to 12th grade was dramatic. "Almost three-quarters of

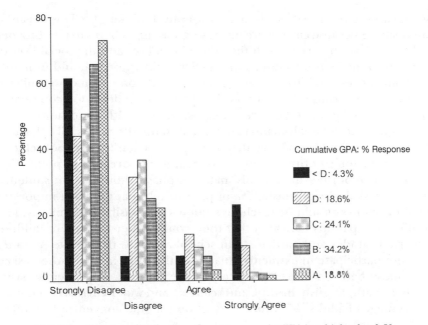

FIG. 8.4.   Response distribution of peer pressure by GPA in a high school: If I get good grades, my friends make fun of me. From "Underestimating Youth's Commitment to Schools and Society: Toward a More Differentiated View," by T. L. Good, S. L. Nichols, and D. L. Sabers, 1999, *Social Psychology of Education, 3*, 1–39. Copyright 1999 by Kluwer Academic/Plenum Publishers. Reprinted with permission. Based on a sample of 347 high students in Grades 9 through 12.

the closest friends named during the senior year had not been mentioned during the sophomore year."[74] Peer group memberships were fluid, and students moved across groups because of their changing interests or conflicts. Thus, individual autonomy appeared to have more impact than group influence. Students could choose different groups and were not "owned" by a particular peer configuration. These findings stand in sharp contrast to the common view that the teen peer group is invariantly antischool, antisuccess, and antiachievement.

DIVERSE ATTITUDES ABOUT THE PURPOSE OF SCHOOLS

Citizens, parents, and policymakers disagree about what schools should be held accountable for teaching. Some citizens feel strongly that schools should teach primarily subject-matter knowledge (math, science, English); others believe equally strongly that schools should teach various non-subject-matter topics (social skills, morality, critical thinking).[75] This debate is intensifying because citizens are increasingly asking schools to play broader roles than ever before in both the educational lives and the social lives of students. Indeed, some citizens who believe that schools should primarily be academic institutions even argue for the inclusion of some non-subject-matter goals because there is no other place for students to acquire adequate knowledge in certain areas (e.g., sex and health education).

Despite the federally-mandated higher standards across all 50 states, there is considerable evidence that many parents don't see school achievement as the top priority. In 1999, in one large and prestigious poll,[76] 43% of parents reported that schools' main emphasis should be on students' academic skills. In contrast, 47% of parents felt that the most important goal of schools should be teaching students responsibility. Similarly, in a 1996 poll,[77] parents indicated that they would rather have their children receive C grades and participate in school activities than make A grades but not participate in extracurricular activities. And in 2002, when asked to choose between narrow curricula (focusing only on academic basics such as math, English, history, and science) and wider curricula, a higher percentage of adults (57%) believed schools should concentrate on offering more variety.[78]

Students encounter dramatically mixed messages daily about the importance of achievement. (Should I be an honor student? Can I participate in band if it means I might get an occasional B?) For example, state-mandated exams stress academic achievement, but that influence is mediated when colleges want well-rounded students. Messages about achievement are further mediated by high school students' employers, who do not ask for information about academic performance. If some teens are confused as to what constitutes appropriate achievement in schooling, it is easy to understand why.

SOME REAL PROBLEMS IN EDUCATION:
SOCIAL CAPITAL AND FISCAL RESOURCES

It is ironic that policymakers want to have a say in areas such as curriculum planning and evaluation, where they have little competence, while ignoring their fundamental role of obtaining and allocating needed educational funds equitably. In the 1990s, while some researchers were disputing the myth of failing schools, others were pointing to the inadequate resources available to some schools. For example, Tom Good and colleagues noted in two special issues of the *Educational Researcher*[79] (the flagship journal of the American Educational Research Association) that policymakers were misguided in their definitions of educational problems, and their focus on student achievement did not address other more molar problems of schooling.

There is a crisis in some of our schools, especially urban and rural ones. These schools typically serve a high percentage of students from low-income homes and have fewer resources (books, labs, computers), less-qualified teachers, and inappropriately low expectations. Rhona Weinstein, in her book *The Power of Expectations in Schooling*,[80] illustrated the comprehensive set of expectation factors—home, school, and community—that serve to erode the aspirations and performance of students when adults perceive them to have little talent.

Although teachers' expectations can be communicated in diverse ways and although some students are more sensitive to performance cues than others, some of the more common ways in which low expectations are communicated are presented in Tables 8.4 and 8.5. Many students are set up for failure when they enter school. Students from poorer households often have fewer skills for reading the social environment (e.g., knowing when to ask and when not to ask for help);[81] hence, their intellectual curiosity is more prone to be seen as misbehavior by the teachers.[82] These dynamics are often further exaggerated for low-income students who come from different ethnic groups than their teachers. Teachers' low performance expectations for Black children have frequently been cited as one of the reasons Black students do not achieve as well as White students.[83] Students who grow up in low-income households are especially likely to be affected by stereotyped beliefs about low ability levels from low-income students if they perceive intelligence to be predetermined as compared to perceiving it as relatively malleable.[84] Too many students from low-income households do not attend schools that expect and support academic achievement.

Much research demonstrates that children's development is substantially impacted by social capital. Social capital has been defined in various ways,[85] but the essential idea is that some communities (both rich and poor) are marked by shared trust, communication, friendship, community organization, and a willingness to supervise youth. It has been argued that "Social capital keeps bad things from happening to good kids."[86] Poverty is the single most powerful variable that contributes to numerous undesirable social conditions (e.g., teenage pregnancies, dropping out of school). Less well understood is that social capital is the next most powerful predictor of several indices of well-being next to economic capital. High-poverty areas marked by low social capital are markedly inferior to those impoverished areas with high social capital. Robert Putnam correlated social capital with measures of child well-being developed by the Annie E. Casey Foundation and found that when states high in social capital (Iowa, Minnesota, Nebraska, North Carolina, Vermont) were compared to states low in social capital (Mississippi, Louisiana, Alabama, South Carolina, Georgia, Tennes-

TABLE 8.4
How Teachers Interact With Students Believed
to Be Less Capable Than Their Peers

1. Waiting less time for lows to answer a question (before giving the answer or calling on someone else)
2. Giving lows answers or calling on someone else rather than trying to improve their responses by giving clues or repeating or rephrasing questions
3. Inappropriate reinforcement: rewarding inappropriate behavior or incorrect answers by lows
4. Criticizing lows more often for failure
5. Praising lows less often for success
6. Failing to give feedback to the public responses of lows
7. Generally paying less attention to lows or interacting with them less frequently
8. Calling on lows less often to respond to questions or asking them only easier, non-analytic questions
9. Seating lows farther away from the teacher
10. Demanding less from lows (e.g., teach less, gratuitous praise, excessive offers of help)
11. Interacting with lows more privately than publicly and monitoring and structuring their activities more closely
12. Differential administration or grading of tests or assignments, in which highs but not lows are given the benefit of the doubt in borderline case
13. Less friendly interactions with lows, including less smiling and fewer other nonverbal indicators of support
14. Briefer and less-informative feedback to questions of lows
15. Less eye contact and other nonverbal communication of attention and responsiveness (forward lean, positive head nodding) in interaction with lows
16. Less use of effective but time-consuming instructional methods with lows when time is limited
17. Less acceptance of use of lows' ideas
18. Exposing lows to an impoverished curriculum (overly limited and repetitive content, emphasis on factual recitation rather than on lesson-extending discussion, emphasis on drill and practice tasks rather than application and higher-level thinking tasks)

Note. From Thomas L. Good & Jere E. Brophy. Looking in Classrooms, 9e, 2003. Published by Allyn and Bacon, Boston, MA. Copyright © 2003 by Pearson Education. Reprinted by permission of the publisher.

see, New Mexico, and Arizona), the former ranked consistently higher in various measures of child well-being.[87] Specifically, high-social-capital states had lower percentages of low birth weight babies, infant mortality, child and teen deaths, teenage births, juvenile violent crime, and teen truancy.

Economic Capital

There are at least two American school systems—one serving the affluent, the other educating the poor. The enormous difference between schools and between states in educational performance is evident. We started this

TABLE 8.5
General Dimensions of Teachers' Communication
of Differential Expectations and Selected Examples

Task Environment	Students Believed to Be More Capable Have:	Students Believed to Be Less Capable Have:
Curriculum, procedures task definition, pacing qualities of environment	More opportunity to perform publicly on meaningful tasks	Less opportunity to perform publicly, especially on meaningful tasks (supplying alternate endings to a story vs. learning to pronounce a word correctly)
	More opportunity to think	Less opportunity to think (since much work is aimed at practice)
Grouping practices	More assignments that deal with comprehension understanding (in higher-ability groups)	Less choice on curriculum assignments—more work on drill-like assignments
Locus of responsibility for learning	More autonomy (more choice in assignments, fewer interruptions)	Less autonomy (frequent teacher monitoring of work, frequent interruptions)
Feedback and evaluation practices	More opportunity for self-evaluation	Less opportunity for self-evaluation
Motivational Strategies	More honest/contingent feedback	Less honest/more gratuitous less contingent feedback
Quality of teacher relationships	More respect for the learner as an individual with unique interests and needs	Less respect for the learner as an individual with unique interests and needs

Note. From Good, T., & Weinstein, R. Classroom expectations: One framework for exploring classrooms, in K. Kepler-Zumwalt (Ed.). *Theory into practice.* Copyright © 1986 Association for Supervision and Curriculum Development (www.ascd.org). Reprinted with permission from ASCD.

chapter with a quote from Education Secretary Rod Paige, who lamented the high cost of education in light of the inadequate results. Solid research data suggest, however, that students in states that spend more on education have higher scores on all types of evaluative tests than those in states that spend less.[88] It is obvious that some schools need more resources. Arianna Huffington, writing in May of 2001, asserted, "By now there should be nobody who doesn't agree that how much money we spend per pupil makes a difference."[89] Unfortunately, many policymakers refuse to acknowledge the clear link between educational performance and resources.

Bruce Biddle examined the relationship between students' 1996 NAEP performance, state spending for education, and child poverty rates.[90] States that spent more money on education had higher NAEP scores (the correlation was +.43) and there was an exceedingly high and negative correlation

TABLE 8.6
Correlations of Adjusted State Per Pupil Spending
With Percentage of Students Scoring at the Proficient
or Below-Basic Levels on Various NAEP Tests in 1996 and 1998[a]

Level	Subject	Correlation With Per Pupil Spending	
		1996	1998
Proficient	Fourth-grade reading	+.478*	+.562*
	Fourth-grade math	+.548*	
	Eighth-grade reading		+.536
	Eighth-grade math	+.533*	
	Eighth-grade science	+.477*	
Below basic	Fourth-grade reading	−.460*	+.540*
	Fourth-grade math	−.495*	
	Eighth-grade reading		+.434*
	Eighth-grade math	−.478*	
	Eighth-grade science	−.426*	

*significant at the p = .01 level.
[a]All grade levels and subjects are not measured each year. All data available for 1996 and 1998 are presented here.
   Note.   From "State-to-State Data Comparison: All Students Achieving at High Levels," 1999, *Education Week.*

(−.70) between state child poverty rates and state NAEP performance (high poverty rates were associated with low NAEP scores). Elsewhere, Thomas Good and Jennifer Braden calculated students' 1996 NAEP scores in reading, science, and mathematics and found a sizable correlation between the adjusted average state spending for education and students' NAEP achievement scores.[91] As shown in Table 8.6, test scores of students who were performing at a proficient level were linked to higher state spending, and below-basic scores were linked to lower state spending.

Crowded and Inadequate Schools.   A June 2000 report by the U.S. Office of Education showed that there is no general crisis in the physical facilities of American schools. However, some schools have acute problems. Twenty-five percent of schools are overcrowded; schools with a large minority student body are most likely to be seriously overcrowded. Roughly 10% of schools have 25% more students than the legal building capacity allows. Further, 20–25% of schools reported less than adequate conditions for life safety features, roofs, electric power, plumbing, heating, and ventilation. In terms of six environmental conditions—heating, lighting, building security, ventilation, air quality, and noise control—43% of schools reported at least one unsatisfactory environmental factor and two thirds of those schools reported more than one deficiency. Schools with the highest levels of poverty were more likely to have unfavorable environmental conditions.[92] In one study, 70% of teachers reported that crowded and inadequate buildings interfered with instructional activities and increased their stress and absenteeism. Students are active observers, and it is likely that their teachers' stress was felt by them in ways that might undermine their own confidence.[93] Clearly, although there is no widespread crisis in school buildings, there is a crisis of physical resources in many schools serving the poor.

Crowded conditions and inflexible and inadequate physical plants in poor school districts complicate and sometimes increase other schools' reform efforts. In 1996, the California legislature committed more than $1 billion a year to reduce class size from the state average of 30 students in K–3 classrooms to a maximum of 20 students. Obviously this was easier to accomplish in schools that averaged 24 students in those grades and that had extra space than in schools that were overcrowded and had an average of 34 students per class. Not surprisingly, most schools that were overcrowded, with limited space, were those serving low-income students. These schools had to hire more teachers to reduce the class size to 20, and to do this they often had to hire unqualified teachers. In addition, because they had no space, they had to capture space in their buildings by taking it away from other legitimate programs. On balance this reform lost resources for low-income schools and their students.[94]

Inadequate Libraries in Low-Income Schools. Reading materials are often markedly different in schools serving affluent students and in schools serving poor students.[95] In one study of first-grade classrooms, libraries in poor schools were found to be 40% smaller than those in more affluent schools. There were also important differences in how reading was taught. Students in the enriched environment saw that reading had many purposes and could be found in many forms.

A Qualitative Gap in Technology.[96] Students' computer access has increased in some low-income schools. For example, the difference in access to computers in high-income schools (1 computer for every 4.7 students) and in low-income schools (5.3 students per computer) is small. However, the technology gap between high-income and low-income schools is huge when measured in terms of computer quality, teacher knowledge of computers, classroom Internet access, speed of connections, and so forth. In schools where less than 11% of students qualify for free lunch, 74% of classrooms have Internet connections. In stark contrast, in schools where 71% (or more) of students qualify for free lunch, only 39% of classrooms have Internet connections. Access to technology varies from state to state. Table 8.7 indicates that, generally, in states with fewer minority students and children living in poverty, students have better access to computers.

TABLE 8.7
Computer Opportunities Across 50 States

State	% Children in Poverty	% Minority Students	Students Per Instructional Computer
Alabama	24.1	38.9	5.0
Alaska	10.1	37.8	3.7
Arizona	26.1	46.0	4.8
Arkansas	16.3	27.8	5.1
California	23.3	63.0	7.2
Colorado	13.4	30.5	4.6
Connecticut	11.7	29.5	5.4
Delaware	16.1	38.4	4.4
District of Columbia	45.3	95.9	5.8
Florida	21.9	45.7	4.2
Georgia	23.3	44.5	4.7
Hawaii	15.1	79.5	5.8
Idaho	20.1	13.3	3.8
Illinois	13.5	39.3	4.9
Indiana	12.0	15.7	3.7
Iowa	15.4	9.2	3.8
Kansas	12.9	20.3	3.3
Kentucky	18.6	11.9	4.2
Louisiana	29.2	50.8	6.8
Maine	14.0	3.2	4.6
Maryland	6.9	45.7	5.6
Massachusetts	13.8	23.4	5.2
Michigan	15.4	25.6	5.1
Minnesota	15.4	16.0	4.2
Mississippi	21.6	52.5	6.4
Missouri	15.6	20.3	4.5
Montana	22.0	13.5	3.1
Nebraska	16.2	14.0	3.7
Nevada	13.7	41.1	6.1
New Hampshire	14.3	4.1	6.1
New Jersey	12.0	39.2	4.6
New Mexico	26.0	63.8	4.9
New York	24.2	44.8	5.3
North Carolina	21.3	38.2	5.2
North Dakota	20.6	10.6	3.6
Ohio	17.9	18.9	4.4
Oklahoma	19.3	33.8	4.6
Oregon	19.3	33.8	4.6
Pennsylvania	18.0	21.2	4.6
Rhode Island	19.4	24.5	6.5
South Carolina	18.1	44.8	5.0
South Dakota	11.7	13.0	3.2
Tennessee	18.1	27.1	5.4

(Continued)

TABLE 8.7
(Continued)

State	% Children in Poverty	% Minority Students	Students Per Instructional Computer
Texas	21.8	56.9	4.3
Utah	13.8	13.1	5.5
Vermont	13.5	3.2	4.9
Virginia	9.0	35.7	4.7
Washington	11.1	24.7	4.7
West Virginia	27.5	5.2	3.9
Wisconsin	13.5	18.6	3.7
Wyoming	14.6	11.6	3.0

Note. From *Education Week: Technology Counts*, *20*(35), pp. 70–104. Copyright 2001 by Education Week. Reprinted with permission.

Dropouts

Children who come from poor homes often attend schools that do not expect them to perform well and that have inadequately prepared teachers who treat students in ways that are likely to reinforce their own low expectations for the students. These students often attend schools where the physical plant is ugly, sometimes dangerous. Further, the schools they attend are typically starved for resources, including labs, books, and computers. It is no surprise that many of these students drop out. A report by the U.S. Department of Education showed that minority youths drop out more often than their White counterparts. The dropout rate for White boys is 9%; White girls, 8.2%; Black boys, 11.1%; Black girls, 12.9%; Hispanic boys, 30%; and Hispanic girls, 30%. Since 1991, dropout rates have varied, 11–13% for low-income students, 4–6% for middle-income students, and 1–3% for high-income students.[97]

These figures on dropouts are discouraging but are likely to seriously underestimate the problem. For example, it has become clear in the Houston school system (which had been widely recognized as making good achievement gains) that many poor performing students were pushed out by school administrators and these pushed-out students were not counted as dropouts. Diana Jean Schemo notes that in a recent state audit in Texas, of 16 middle and high schools, it was ". . . found that more than half of the 5,500 students who left their school in the 2000–2001 school years should have been declared as dropouts but were not."[98] And tragically, it is becoming clear that Houston is not alone in pushing students out and failing to claim them in official dropout accounts.

PREPARING FOR AND GETTING INTO COLLEGE

In Table 8.8, we present a few findings from a 2002 report summarizing college admission trends.[99] The report emphasized that "selectivity at four-year institutions has increased. More is being required of students, who are meeting the challenge in increasingly large numbers."[100]

In 2001, the report of the National Commission on the High School Senior Year contended that increased educational attainment is a critical goal:

TABLE 8.8
Highlights in College Admission

Enrollment
- Between 1979 and 1999, the annual number of high school graduates in the United States decreased by over a quarter million students, but total undergraduate enrollment in higher education increased substantially.
- Between 1985 and 1999, the average number of applications per enrolled first-time, first-year student increased dramatically, and thus yield rates—the proportion of accepted applicants who enroll at any given institution—decreased dramatically.

Recruitment
- Public institutions have increased their efforts to recruit out-of-district/out-of-state and international students.
- Institutions in all sectors are making greater use of marketing or public relations consultants than in previous years.
- Four-year institutions continue to raise their academic qualifications for new students. Nearly 60 percent had increased their academic qualifications for the entering class of 1999 compared to 1998.

Admissions, Policies, Practices, and Standards
- The percentage of institutions reporting that they required admissions test scores remained essentially constant at over 90 percent of institutions reporting over the period of 1979 to 2000.
- High school GPA or rank was consistently the most important factor in admissions decisions between 1979 and 2000, and admissions test scores were consistently second in importance.
- Admissions officers at four-year private institutions perceived that standards were higher in 2000 than five years previously (i.e., 1995), and overall acceptance rates decreased. Four-year public institutions indicated that standards had not changed in the last five years, and overall acceptance rates did not change.

Equity
- Between 1985 and 1999, the average number of applications per enrolled first-time, first-year student in four-year public and private institutions increased for all racial/ethnic groups, with the greatest increases occurring for Asian and Hispanic students.
- Between 1985 and 1999, increasing application rates were accompanied by lower acceptance rates for all groups except white students and students of unknown racial/ethnic identity.

Note. From *Summary Report, Trends in College Admission 2000: A Report of a Survey of Undergraduate Admissions, Policies, Practices, and Procedures,* by H. Breland, J. Maxey, R. Gernand, T. Cumming, and C. Trapani, 2002, Tallahassee, FL: Association for Institutional Research.

In the agricultural age, post secondary education was a pipe dream for most Americans. In the industrial age it was the birthright of only a few. By the space age, it became common for many. Today, it is just common sense for all.[101]

The report argued that it is irresponsible to view 12 years of education as acceptable and that at least 15 years of education are necessary. The report called for a sharper definition of the purposes of the senior year and recommended the following:

Instead of functioning as a rest stop between the demands of elementary and secondary education and whatever follows, the final year should serve as a consummation of what already has been accomplished and a launching pad for what lies ahead.[102]

The commission wants to turn the senior year into a more intensive learning experience by encouraging students to explore life options and gain new knowledge and skills. "Ideally every senior should complete a capstone project, perform an internship, complete a research project, participate in community service, or take college-level courses."[103] Many policymakers, in contrast, want to concentrate students' attentions not on thinking and creating but on a narrow but difficult high-stakes graduation test.

The report makes it clear that in contrast to earlier times (except the period immediately following World War II and the influx of GIs to the college campus), today's student body is more heterogeneous than ever before. The changing demographics and their effects on college students are presented in Table 8.9.

Early Admission

The pressures of getting into college—especially top colleges—have increased to the point that many parents lobby to get their child into the right preschool. And many middle school students are being prepared for the college work they will face in the ninth grade. Elementary school students' recess periods have been eliminated, so they can have more time for academics.[104]

In part, this new pressure has been created by colleges' use of early admission procedures. Early admission requires that applications be submitted in the fall of the senior year, which means that students' 9th-, 10th-, and 11th-grade records will be the only grades that the college considers. Pressure on students starts earlier because decisions are made earlier. Some younger students even participate in SAT course preparations and take, and retake, ACT and SAT exams in hopes of getting a high score.

TABLE 8.9
The New Shape of Postsecondary Education

• Fewer than one-fifth of today's college students meet the stereotype of an 18–22-year-old living on campus and attending college full time.
• Women, working adults, part-timers, and students drove the enrollment bulge of the 1980s and 1990s over the age of 25.
• Today's new breed of student is interested in four dimensions of postsecondary education: convenience, service, quality, and low cost.
• The students want a stripped-down version of higher education, minus the wealth of electives and student activities.
• There are some 3,600 institutions of higher education in the United States, enrolling about 15 million students.
• About one-third of those institutions are community colleges enrolling about one-half of all students and experiencing double the growth of four-year institutions.
• One of the fastest growing degree-granting institutions in the United States in the last 20 years is University of Phoenix, a for-profit institution offering a limited number of majors, few electives, and instruction by part-time faculty during the evenings and weekends.
• More than 1,000 "corporate universities" already exist, providing instruction and training for their own workers in everything from food preparation to high-end electronics assembly.

Note.   From *Raising Our Sights: No High School Senior Left Behind,* by the National Commission on the High School Senior Year, 2001, Princeton, NJ: Woodrow Wilson National Fellowship Foundation. Copyright 2001 by Woodrow Wilson National Fellowship Foundation. Reprinted with permission.

Given that college admission decisions have been high pressure since the 1960s, what propels an interest in adding to pressures already inherent in the system? This seems especially ironic because college admission decisions are not extremely competitive except for the top 100 colleges or so. Most of the 3,000 colleges take most students who apply. What accounts for the pressure for early-decision admission? James Fallows argues that early-decision admission practices occur because prestigious universities want to increase their status.[105]

College Prestige

College prestige is based on selectivity. If a university accepts only one student per three applicants, it is more selective than the university that accepts two students per three applications. Selectivity, in effect, measures how many students a college rejects. However, students also reject schools. A student may be accepted by the University of Illinois, Yale, and Harvard but decide to attend Stanford. The most prestigious schools are defined as those that reject large numbers of students and where students are likely to come if offered the chance. Early admission allows colleges to improve both their yield—the number of students that a school must accept to fill its freshman class—and selectivity. If a school takes one third or one fourth of its students in early admissions in the fall, it will need fewer students (i.e., accept fewer students for admission) to fill its quota during the regular admission period in the spring semester. Fallows contends that early-decision practices of elite colleges is a racket:

> Early-decision programs—whereby a student applies early to a single school, receives an early answer, and promises to attend if accepted—have added an insane intensity to middle-class obsessions about college. They also distort the admissions process, rewarding the richest students from the most exclusive high schools and penalizing nearly everyone else. But the incentives for many colleges and students are as irresistible as they are perverse.[106]

Early admission decisions have no costs to colleges, and they can enhance their selectivity and yield. For most students, there is nothing to gain except more and earlier pressure. Importantly some students are advantaged by the early admission process because it provides them with an easier admission opportunity. Christopher Avery and colleagues examined 500,000 applications from 14 selective colleges and concluded that an early application provided an advantage comparable to scoring 100 points higher on the SAT.[107] Fallows notes:

> For instance, a student with a combined SAT score of 1400 to 1490 (out of 1600) who applied early was as likely to be accepted as a regular-admission student scoring 1500–1600. An early student scoring 1200 to 1290 was *more* likely to be accepted than a regular student scoring 1300–1390.[108]

Rising College Costs

At present college tuitions are increasing and many Americans are finding their budgets strained. However, despite reasons for increasing aid to college students, recent federal actions have led researchers to estimate that $270 million for students' financial aid will be lost because of changes in eligibility for the highly popular Pell Grant program. This is because of a new formula that is being used to gauge whether students will qualify for financial support. Greg Winter reports that hundreds of thousands of students will end up with smaller Pell awards and estimates that about another 84,000 students will no longer qualify for funding. Winter also reports that the $270 million lost is just the first step ". . . since it does not consider the further cuts in student awards that will probably occur once the new formula is applied to billions of dollars in state awards and university grants."[109]

It seems both ironic and tragic that at a time when the federal government and many individual states are encouraging more from students at all
grade levels (and as noted, sometimes these demands are excessive to the
point of being ludicrous), the federal government is cutting aid to potential
college students. On the one hand, policymakers are asking students to
make greater commitments to education and to realize that their future job
depends on achieving a college education while at the same time reducing
financial support available for students to attend college.

CONCLUSION

American youth and their schools have been widely criticized by the press
and policymakers because of their alleged low performance on achievement tests and because of their low educational commitment. But average
performance in American schools contradicts these dismal assessments. It
is as high as it has ever been, and more Americans from low-income families
are graduating from high school and college. Because of the active work of
some social scientists, many members of the community, including the media, have shifted their arguments and now admit (sometimes grudgingly)
that performance on average is reasonably good in American schools.

However, many policymakers react to this good news by arguing that it is
not enough and that higher standards are needed if we are to be a viable
economy in the 21st century. These arguments for higher standards are
specious, and too often the mandate for higher standards only results in
shifting more advanced curricula to lower grades: moving college calculus
into the high school and moving algebra from the middle school into elementary schools without sufficient research on the short- and long-term
consequences of more content sooner.

Unfortunately, there are many problems in American education, including unequal access to high-quality teachers, to technology, and to adequate
physical plants. Students from high-income families almost invariably attend highly equipped schools. Students who come from low-income families often are taught in poor schools with few resources. Policymakers who
know little about education are most willing to make curriculum and testing decisions, but too many legislators are unwilling to address their legislative responsibility for equity in excellence and education.

The control of American education has been a hot political topic from
the start. Arguments for higher achievement standards are primarily articu-
lated by the business community, with backing from legislators. In sharp
contrast, parents and many citizens express alarm at growing academic
pressures, in part because they interfere with traditional experiences for
youth in this country. Teenagers are expected not only to be serious stu-

dents but also to grow socially and to engage in extracurricular activities, to date, and to assume various responsibilities in the community so that their intellectual development is matched by their social development.

Although many factors lead to increased pressure on American youth, one clear source comes from the college admission process. Ironically, only 100 or so colleges in the country are truly competitive; however, those colleges drive the system. The most recent manifestation of this pressure has been early admission, the impact of which trickles down from the high school to create pressure in middle schools and elementary schools. These pressures are counterproductive and dangerous.

The student voice in educational decision making has been understudied and underused. However, it is clear that American youth feel tremendous pressure to achieve. When teenagers are asked, they say their chief concerns and worries are not violence or drugs but rather getting good grades in school and being admitted into a good college.[110] Given that many teens are ambitious and want to attend college, we need to provide them with more useful information in high school that will help them align educational and career goals. As we pointed out earlier, many teens receive insufficient guidance in this area.

General Considerations

American citizens want more out of their K–12 schools than subject-matter instruction, and it is increasingly clear that the high-standard movement is not fueled by the wishes of citizens but by professional groups and business interests. Citizens want American children and teenagers to be well rounded and to experience various extracurricular activities, as well as part-time jobs, volunteer work, dating, music, and so on. It is time to stop demanding that American youth do everything well. Some educators have reasoned that the range of activities in which students engage contributes to the future creativity of our citizens past high school and college.[111] If schools are to continue to nurture social growth, creativity, and communicative skills in addition to subject-matter knowledge, citizens must be more active in the educational debate. The current excessive drive for more, sooner, is not logical, and there is no empirical research to support its desirability.

Critics of public schools often use 1970 as a benchmark of educational success. However, various researchers have illustrated that this claim is false: Average student performance is as high today as in the 1970s. However, support for students has deteriorated. Today, a higher percentage of students live in poverty than the students of 1970. The gap between schools serving high- and low-income students has widened. Students who come from affluent homes in contrast to less affluent ones enjoy better physical plants, better curriculum resources, and better teachers in their schools. And more students, both poor and affluent, are returning to unsupervised homes and lives when the school day ends. These general considerations lead us to the unhappy conclusion that societal attitudes are more to push and to blame youth than to support them in constructive ways.

Needed Research

What do students make of adults' educational policies? What do they think of policymakers who criticize them for their low performance in comparison to students elsewhere who are older and who have had advanced coursework in math and science? What do students who attend physically unattractive—and sometimes dangerous—buildings think about their value to society? It would seem that children must at some level learn that they mean little to society when they are forced to attend schools under these circumstances. It's like "putting our beautiful children in a garbage can."[112]

What do students think when they are asked to meet unreachable goals and their failures are published in the newspaper? What do students in Virginia think when they read in the newspaper that 93% of their schools are failing? What do students think when they learn that in various states students and schools have been given failing grades because tests were inadequately scored? What do students think when they are told they need to improve their science learning only to find that their textbooks are replete with serious errors? How do youth react to President Bush's statement at the Yale Commencement, "to the C students, I say you, too, can be President of the United States."[113] What do students think when a mandated test is not taken by educational leaders who demand it?[114]

Although some of the questions raised here are polemical, they are raised in a serious context. Social scientists must collect data from youth about how they interpret adults' messages to them about their educational performance and motivation. There is anecdotal evidence that some youth are aware of these contradictions,[115] but it is unclear how this affects their behaviors and attitudes toward education over time. We need to understand better how youth mediate these contradictory messages about their education. And more research is needed on other youth attitudes toward education, including the day-to-day instruction and content they receive.

ENDNOTES

1. Educational failure (Editorial). (2001, April 16). *Arizona Daily Star*, p. B6.
2. Steinberg, L. (1996). *Beyond the classroom: Why school reform has failed and what parents need to do about it* (p. 71). New York: Simon & Schuster.

3. Brooks, D. (2001, April). The organization kid. *The Atlantic Monthly, 287*(4), 40.

4. Rose, L., Gallup, A., & Elam, S. (1997). The 29th annual Phi Delta Kappa/Gallup Poll of public's attitudes toward the public schools. *Phi Delta Kappan, 79*(1), 47; Elam, S. M., Rose, L. C., & Gallup, A. M. (1996). The 28th annual Phi Delta Kappa/Gallup Poll of the public's attitudes toward the public schools. *Phi Delta Kappan, 77*(1), 41–59; Rose, L. C., & Gallup, A. M. (2002). The 34th annual Phi Delta Kappa/Gallup Poll of the public's attitudes toward the public schools. *Phi Delta Kappan, 84*(1), 41–56.

5. Schneider, B., & Stevenson, D. (1999). *The ambitious generation: America's teenagers motivated but directionless.* New Haven, CT: Yale University Press.

6. National Research Council. (2001). *Making money matter: Financing America's schools.* Washington, DC: National Academy Press.

7. Biddle, B. (1997). Foolishness, dangerous nonsense, and real correlates of state differences in achievement. *Phi Delta Kappan, 79*(1), 8–13.

8. Schemo, D. J. (2002, November 27). New federal rule tightens demands on failing schools. *New York Times,* pp. A1, 16.

9. Winter, G. (2003, July 10). California will wait until 2006 to require high school graduates to pass exit exams. *New York Times,* p. A16.

10. McCaslin, M., & Good, T. L. (1996). The informal curriculum. In D. Berliner & R. Calfee (Eds.), *The handbook of educational psychology* (pp. 622–670). New York: Macmillan.

11. National Commission on Excellence in Education. (1983). *A nation at risk: The imperative for educational reform.* Washington, DC: U.S. Department of Education.

12. Conant, J. (1959). *The American high school today.* New York: McGraw-Hill. In this book, Conant details the "weaknesses" of the American high school.

13. National Commission on Excellence in Education. (1983). *A nation at risk: The imperative for educational reform.* Washington, DC: U.S. Department of Education.

14. Wasted days (Editorial). (1994, May 7). *Arizona Daily Star,* p. A18.

15. Good, T. (1996). Teaching effects and teacher evaluation. In J. Sikula, T. Buttery, & E. Guyton (Eds.), *Handbook of research on teacher education* (2nd ed., pp. 617–666). New York: Simon & Schuster.

16. For example, the American Psychological Association put forth a special issue of the *American Psychologist,* the flagship journal of the organization, which focused purely on prevention efforts that work for children and youth. Articles focus on comprehensive approaches to health risk prevention. See Weissberg, R. P., & Kumpfer, K. L. (Guest Eds.). (2003, June/July). Special Issue: Prevention that works for children and youth. *American Psychologist, 58*(6/7).

17. Berliner, D., & Biddle, B. (1995). *The manufactured crisis: Myths, fraud, and the attack on America's public schools.* Reading, MA: Addison-Wesley Publishing.

18. Bracey, G. (1997). *The truth about America's schools: The Bracey Reports, 1991–1997.* Bloomington, IN: Phi Delta Kappa Educational Foundation; Henig, J. R. (1994). *Rethinking school choice.* Princeton, NJ: Princeton University Press; Rothstein, R. (1997). *What do we know about declining (or rising) student achievement?* Arlington, VA: Educational Research Service.

19. For example, as of this writing, both the National School Boards Association and the National Education Association (NEA) provide data about the good performance of American schools. The 11 points presented in this chapter are based on data provided in the NEA Web site, http://www.nea.org/publiced/goodnews/

20. National Center for Education Statistics. (2001). *NCES, The nation's report card: 4th grade reading 2000* (NCES 2001-499). Washington, DC: U.S. Department of Education, Office of Educational Research and Improvement. Retrieved July 9, 2002, from http://nces.ed. gov/nationsreportcard/pdf/main2000/2001499.pdf; National Center for Education

Statistics. (1999, March). *NCES, the 1998 reading report card for the nation and the states, March 1999* (NCES 2000-500). Washington, DC: U.S. Department of Education, Office of Educational Research and Improvement. (Available online at http://nces.ed.gov/ nationsreportcard/pdf/main1998/1999500.pdf)

21. National Center for Education Statistics. (2001). *NCES, the 1998 high school transcript study tabulations: Comparative data on credits earned and demographics for 1998, 1994, 1990, 1987, and 1982 high school graduates* (NCES 2001-498). Washington, DC: U.S. Department of Education, Office of Educational Research and Improvement. Retrieved July 9, 2002, from http://nces.ed.gov/pubs2001/2001498.pdf

22. National Center for Education Statistics. (2000). *The condition of education, 2000* (NCES 2000-062). Washington, DC: U.S. Department of Education, Office of Educational Research and Improvement. Retrieved July 9, 2002, from http://nces.ed.gov/pubs2000/ 2000062.pdf

23. National Center for Education Statistics. (2000). *NCES, NAEP 1999, trends in academic progress: Three decades of student performance* (NCES 2000-469). Washington, DC: U.S. Department of Education, Office of Educational Research and Improvement.

24. College Entrance Examination Board. (2001). *2001 college bound seniors: A profile of SAT program test takers.* New York: The College Board. Retrieved July 9, 2002, from http:// www.collegeboard.com/sat/cbsenior/yr2001/pdf/NATL.pdf

25. National Press Release. (2001). *ACT, Inc. "ACT national press release for 2001 ACT scores."* Iowa City, IA: American College Testing Program. Retrieved July 9, 2002, from http:// www.act.org/news/releases/2001/08-15-01.html

26. National Center for Education Statistics. (2000). *The condition of education, 2000* (NCES 2000-062). Washington, DC: U.S. Department of Education, Office of Educational Research and Improvement. Retrieved July 9, 2002, from http://nces.ed.gov/pubs2000/ 2000062.pdf

27. Taken from College Board, AP Web site. See http://apcentral.collegeboard.com/article/ 0,1281,150-156-0-2059,00.html for a breakdown of state-by-state information, and for a national overview of public versus private school test-taking rates, see the summary tables provided at http://apcentral.collegeboard.com/repository/01_national_8128.pdf

28. See the summary tables of AP test scores provided at http://apcentral.collegeboard.com/ repository/01_national_8128.pdf; also see National Center for Education Statistics. (1999). *The condition of education, 1999* (NCES 1999-022). Washington, DC: U.S. Department of Education, Office of Educational Research and Improvement. Retrieved July 9, 2002, from http://nces.ed.gov/pubs99/condition99/pdf/1999022.pdf

29. Snyder, T., & Hoffman, C. (2001). *Digest of education statistics, 2000* (NCES 2001-034). Washington, DC: U.S. Department of Education, Office of Educational Research and Improvement.

30. Snyder, T., & Hoffman, C. (2001). *Digest of education statistics, 2000* (NCES 2001-034). Washington, DC: U.S. Department of Education, Office of Educational Research and Improvement.

31. Diverse participants in the educational debate with diverse philosophies have agreed that something like the National Assessment of Educational Progress (NAEP) is needed if states are to be compared with one another; How to close the achievement gap (Editorial). (2001, June 2). *New York Times,* p. A22; Olson, L. (2001, March 14). Experts preach caution on use of "precious" NAEP. *Education Week,* pp. 1, 34–35.

32. Campbell, J. R., Hombo, C. M., & Mazzeo, J. (2000). *NAEP 1999 trends in academic progress: Three decades of student performance* (NCES 2000-469). Washington, DC: U.S. Department of Education, Office of Educational Research and Improvement, National Center for Education Statistics.

33. President's State of the Union Address. (1999, January 21). *New York Times,* p. A21.

34. Bracey, G. (1998). Tinkering with TIMSS. *Phi Delta Kappa, 80,* 32–38.

35. Bracey, G. (1998). Tinkering with TIMSS. *Phi Delta Kappa, 80,* 32–38.

36. Good, T., Grouws, D., & Beckerman, T. (1978). Curriculum pacing: Some empirical data in mathematics. *Journal of Curriculum Studies, 12,* 75–81.

37. Data presented by Ian Westbury on data from the second international study. This was presented in Berliner, D., & Biddle, B. (1995). *The manufactured crisis: Myths, fraud, and the attack on America's public schools.* New York: Addison-Wesley.

38. Mullis, I. V., et al. (2001, April). *Mathematics benchmarking report: TIMSS 1999-eighth grade, Achievement for US states and districts in an international context.* Boston: Boston College, International Study Center. (Available online at http://isc.bc.edu/timss1999b/mathbench_report/t99b_math_report.html)

39. Martin, M. O., et al. (2001, April). *Science benchmarking report: TIMSS 1999-eighth grade, Achievement for US states and districts in an international context.* Boston: Boston College, International Study Center. (Available online at http://isc.bc.edu/timss1999b/sciencebench_report/t99b_sciencebench_report.html)

40. Various reactions to this report were presented in *Education Week.*

41. Hoff, D. J. (2001, April 11). A world-class education eludes many in the U.S. *Education Week, 20*(30), 15.

42. Hoff, D. J. (2001, April 11). A world-class education eludes many in the U.S. *Education Week, 20*(30), 16.

43. For example, David Berliner and Bruce Biddle contend that American students are more creative than students elsewhere because they delay specialization until the college years. See Berliner, D., & Biddle, B. (1995). *The manufactured crisis: Myths, fraud, and the attack on America's public schools.* New York: Addison-Wesley.

44. Good, T., & Grouws, D. (1979). The Missouri mathematics effectiveness project: An experimental study of fourth-grade classrooms. *Journal of Educational Psychology, 71,* 355–362.

45. Elsewhere, Good and Braden (2000) illustrated the various simplistic plans that have been generated over time for "solving" educational problems. Good, T., & Braden, J. (2000). *The great school debate: Choice, vouchers, and charter schools.* Mahwah, NJ: Lawrence Erlbaum Associates.

46. Good, T., & Nichols, S. (2001). School effects: Subject-matter and non-subject-matter outcomes of schooling. In N. Smelser & P. Baltes (Eds.), *The international encyclopedia of the social and behavioral sciences* (Vol. 20, pp. 13583–13589). Oxford: Pergamon.

47. Camilli, G., & Firestone, W. (1999). Values and state ratings: An examination of the state-by-state indicators in *Quality Counts. Educational Measurement: Issues and Practice, 35,* 17–25.

48. Good, T., & Braden, J. (2000). *The great school debate: Choice, vouchers, and charter schools.* Mahwah, NJ: Lawrence Erlbaum Associates.

49. Dillon, S. (2003, July 18). Outcry over Regents physics test, but Albany won't budge. *New York Times,* p. A15.

50. Alexander, N. (2002). Race, poverty, and the student curriculum: Implications for standards policy. *American Educational Research Journal, 39*(3), 675–693.

51. Good, T., & Nichols, S. (2001). School effects: Subject-matter and non-subject-matter outcomes of schooling. In N. Smelser & P. Baltes (Eds.), *The international encyclopedia of the social and behavioral sciences* (Vol. 20, p. 13587). Oxford: Pergamon.

52. Faison, S. (1998, July 1). Clinton enjoys radio stint: No violence, drugs or sex. *New York Times,* p. A10.

53. Ministry of Education. (1998). *Learning to think thinking to learn: Towards thinking schools, learning nation.* Singapore: Author.

54. Rothstein, R. (2001, May 16). Weighing students' skills and attitudes. *New York Times,* p. B8.

55. Rothstein, R. (2001, May 16). Weighing students' skills and attitudes. *New York Times,* p. B8.

56. Kristof, N. D. (2002, November 22). China's super kids. *New York Times,* p. A27.

57. Amrein, A. L., & Berliner, D. (2002). High-stakes testing, uncertainty, and student learning. *Educational Policy Analysis Archives, 10*(18). Retrieved July 10, 2002, from http://epaa.asu.edu/epaa/v10n18

58. The study was brought to our attention in an *Education Week* article: Viadero, D. (2003, April 16). Study finds higher gains in states with high-stakes tests. *Education Week, 22*(31), 10. Also, for the original study, Raymond, M., & Hanushek, E. (2003, March). Shopping for evidence against school accountability. *Education Next.* (Available online at http://www.educationnext.org/unabridged/20033/hanushek.pdf)

59. Importantly, the methods employed in this study have been disputed. In a review of their study, Ambrein and Berliner argue that Raymond and Hanushek's strategy for comparing states with and without high-stakes legislation was flawed because states "move in and out of the high-stakes testing scene within each intra-test period." The first author received a version of Ambrein and Berliner's critique before it went to press.

60. The authors would like to thank David Berliner for sharing the study by Martin Carnoy and Susanna Loeb with us. Carnoy, M., & Loeb, S. (2002, March). *Does external accountability affect student outcomes? A cross-state analysis.* Stanford University School of Education.

61. Indeed, others have begun to conduct analyses to further examine arguments Amrein and Berliner initially made. For example, see Rosenshine, G. (2003, July 18). High-stakes testing: Another analysis. *Educational Policy Analysis Archives, 11*(23). Retrieved August 8, 2003, from http://epaa.asu.edu/epaa/v11n23/

62. SAT math scores are highest in 36 years. *Arizona Daily Star,* pp. A1, A7.

63. Good, T., Nichols, S., & Sabers, D. (1999). Underestimating youth's commitment to schools and society: Toward a more differentiated view. *Social Psychology of Education, 3,* 1–39; Gough, P. (1994). Shame on the press. *Phi Delta Kappan, 75,* 355; Berliner, D., & Biddle, B. (1998). The lamentable alliance between the media and school critics. In G. Maeroff (Ed.), *Imaging education: The media and schools in America.* New York: Teachers College Press; Maeroff, G. (Ed.). (1998). *Imaging education: The media and schools in America.* New York: Teachers College Press.

64. Schackner, B. (1997, September 1). Although SAT scores fall, number of A's increased. *Arizona Daily Star,* pp. A1, A9.

65. Good, T., Nichols, S., & Sabers, D. (1999). Underestimating youth's commitment to schools and society: Toward a more differentiated view. *Social Psychology of Education, 3,* 1–39.

66. Lewin, T. (2003, July 11). New report on students' skills reinforces good news and bad. *New York Times,* p. A9.

67. Rose, L., Gallup, A., & Elam, S. (1997). The 29th annual Phi Delta Kappa/Gallup Poll of public's attitudes toward the public schools. *Phi Delta Kappan, 79*(1), 47.

68. Steinberg, L. (with Brown, B. B., & Dornbusch, S. M.). (1996). *Beyond the classroom: Why school reform has failed and what parents need to do about it* (p. 19). New York: Simon & Schuster.

69. Steinberg, L. (with Brown, B. B., & Dornbusch, S. M.). (1996). *Beyond the classroom: Why school reform has failed and what parents need to do about it* (p. 71). New York: Simon & Schuster.

70. Good, T., Nichols, S., & Sabers, D. (1999). Underestimating youth's commitment to schools and society: Toward a more differentiated view. *Social Psychology of Education, 3,* 1–39.

71. Farmer, T., Leung, M., Pearl, R., Rodkin, P., Cadwallader, T., & Van Acker, R. (2002). Deviant or diverse peer groups? The peer affiliations of aggressive elementary students. *Journal of Educational Psychology, 94*(3), 611–620. John Ogbu (2003) has argued that Black youth may be especially sensitive to pejorative peer pressure in some schools; see Ogbu, J. U. (2003). *Black American students in an affluent suburb: A study of academic disengagement.* Mahwah, NJ: Lawrence Erlbaum Associates.

72. Bank, B. (1997). Peer cultures and their challenge for teaching. In B. J. Biddle, T. L. Good, & I. F. Goodson (Eds.), *The international handbook of teachers and teaching* (Vol. 2, pp. 879–973). Dordrecht, The Netherlands: Kluwer.

73. Schneider, B., & Stevenson, D. (1999). *The ambitious generation: America's teenagers motivated but directionless.* New Haven, CT: Yale University Press.

74. Schneider, B., & Stevenson, D. (1999). *The ambitious generation: America's teenagers motivated but directionless* (p. 198). New Haven, CT: Yale University Press.

75. Rose, L., Gallup, A., & Elam, S. (1997). The 29th annual Phi Delta Kappa/Gallup Poll of the public's attitudes toward the public schools. *Phi Delta Kappan, 79*(1), 41–56.

76. Rose, L. C., & Gallup, A. M. (1999). The 31st annual Phi Delta Kappa/Gallup Poll of the public's attitudes toward the public schools. *Phi Delta Kappan, 81*(1), 4–56.

77. Elam, S. M., Rose, L. C., & Gallup, A. M. (1996). The 28th annual Phi Delta Kappa/Gallup Poll of the public's attitudes toward the public schools. *Phi Delta Kappan, 77*(1), 41–59.

78. Rose, L., & Gallup, A. M. (2002). The 34th annual Phi Delta Kappa/Gallup Poll of the public's attitudes toward the public schools. *Phi Delta Kappan, 84*(1), 41–56.

79. Good, T. (1996). Educational researchers comment on the educational summit and other policy proclamations from 1983–1997. *Educational Researcher, 25,* 4–6.

80. Weinstein, R. (2002). *The power of expectations in schooling.* Cambridge, MA: Harvard University Press.

81. Becker, B., & Luthar, S. (2002). Social-emotional factors affecting achievement outcomes among disadvantaged students: Closing the achievement gap. *Educational Psychologist, 37*(4), 197–214.

82. Good, T., & Nichols, S. (2001). Expectancy effects in the classroom: A special focus on improving the reading performance of minority students in first grade classrooms. *Educational Psychologist, 36*(2), 113–126.

83. Darling-Hammond, L. (2000). New standards in old inequities: School reform and the education of African-American students. *Journal of Negro Education, 69,* 263–287; see also Jencks, C., & Phillips, M. (Eds.). (1998). *The Black–White test score gap.* Washington, DC: Brookings Institute.

84. Aronson, J., Fried, C., & Good, C. (2002). Reducing the effects of stereotype threat on African-American college students by shaping theories of intelligence. *Journal of Experimental and Social Psychology, 38*(2), 113–125; Régmer, I., Huguet, P., & Marcmonteil, J. (2002). Effects of socioeconomic status (SES) information on cognitive ability inferences: When low-SES students make use of a self-threatening stereotype. *Social Psychology of Education, 5,* 253–269.

85. Putnam, R. D. (2000). *Bowling alone: The collapse and revival of American community.* New York: Simon & Schuster.

86. Putnam, R. D. (2000). *Bowling alone: The collapse and revival of American community* (p. 296). New York: Simon & Schuster.

87. Annie E. Casey Foundation. (2000). *Kids count data book: State profiles of child well-being.*

88. Biddle, B. (1997). Foolishness, dangerous nonsense, and real correlates of state differences in achievement. *Phi Delta Kappan, 79*(1), 8–13.

89. Huffington, A. (2001, May 8). If schools are broke, don't fix them. *Arizona Daily Star.*

90. Biddle, B. (1997). Foolishness, dangerous nonsense, and real correlates of state differences in achievement. *Phi Delta Kappan, 79*(1), 8–13.

91. Good, T., & Braden, J. (2000). *The great school debate: Choice, vouchers, and charter schools.* Mahwah, NJ: Lawrence Erlbaum Associates.

92. Lewis, L., Snow, K., Farris, E., Smerdon, B., Cronen, S., & Kaplan, J. (2000). *Condition of America's public school facilities: 1999* (NCES 2000-032). Washington, DC: U.S. Department of Education, National Center for Education Statistics.

93. There are considerable data to illustrate that even young students are well aware of classroom behaviors. For example, see Weinstein, R., & Middlestadt, S. (1975). Student perceptions of teacher interactions with male high and low achievers. *Journal of Educational Psychology, 71*(4), 421–431; Cooper, H., & Good, T. (1983). *Pygmalion grows up: Studies in the expectation communication process.* New York: Longman.

94. Stecher, B., Bohrnstedt, G., Kirst, M., McRobbie, J., & Williams, T. (2001, May). Class size reduction in California. *Phi Delta Kappan, 82*(9), 670–674.

95. Duke, N. (2000). For the rich it's richer: Print experiences and environments offered to children in very low- and very high-socioeconomic status first-grade classrooms. *American Educational Research Journal, 37*(2), 441–478.

96. From Trotter, A. (2001, May 10). Closing the digital divide. *Education Week, XX*(35), 37–44.

97. National Center for Education Statistics. (2002). *The condition of education 2002: Status dropout rates, by race/ethnicity.* Washington, DC: U.S. Department of Education, Office of Educational Research and Improvement.

98. Schemo, D. J. (2003, July 11). Questions on data cloud luster of Houston schools. *New York Times,* p. A1.

99. Breland, H., Maxey, J., Gernand, R., Cumming, T., & Trapani, C. (2002). *Trends in college admission 2000: A report of a survey of undergraduate admissions policies, practices, and procedures.* Tallahassee, FL: Association for Institutional Research. (Available online at http://airweb.org/trendsreport.pdf)

100. Breland, H., Maxey, J., Gernand, R., Cumming, T., & Trapani, C. (2002). *Trends in college admission 2000: A report of a survey of undergraduate admissions policies, practices, and procedures* (p. vii). Tallahassee, FL: Association for Institutional Research. (Available online at http://airweb.org/trendsreport.pdf)

101. National Commission on the High School Senior Year. (2001). *Raising our sights: No high school senior left behind* (prologue). Princeton, NJ: Woodrow Wilson National Fellowship Foundation.

102. National Commission on the High School Senior Year. (2001). *Raising our sights: No high school senior left behind* (p. 11). Princeton, NJ: Woodrow Wilson National Fellowship Foundation.

103. National Commission on the High School Senior Year. (2001). *Raising our sights: No high school senior left behind* (p. 22). Princeton, NJ: Woodrow Wilson National Fellowship Foundation.

104. Blatchford, P. (1998). *Social life in schools: Pupils' experience of breaktime and recess from 7–16 years.* Bristol, PA: Falmer Press; Ohanian, S. (2002). *What happened to recess and why are our children struggling in kindergarten?* New York: McGraw-Hill.

105. Fallows, J. (2001, September). The early-decision racket. *The Atlantic Monthly, 288*(2), 37–52.

106. Fallows, J. (2001, September). The early-decision racket. *The Atlantic Monthly, 288*(2), 37.

107. Avery, C., Fairbanks, A., & Zeckhauser, R. (2001, August). *What worms for the early bird: Early admissions at elite colleges.* Cambridge, MA: Harvard's Kennedy School of Government.

108. Fallows, J. (2001, September). The early-decision racket. *The Atlantic Monthly, 288*(2), 37–52.

109. Winter, G. (2003, July 18). Formula will reduce educational grants, report says. *New York Times,* p. A13.

110. Shell Oil Company. (1999, Summer). *The Shell Poll: Teens under pressure, coping well, 1*(4). (Available online at http://www.shell.com/)

111. Berliner, D., & Biddle, B. (1995). *The manufactured crisis: Myths, fraud, and the attack on America's public schools.* New York: Addison-Wesley.

112. See the documentary titled *Children in America's Schools with Bill Moyers.* A coproduction of the Sant/Hayden Co., South Carolina ETC, Nebraska ETV; this film was based on the book by Jonathan Kozol: Kozol, J. (1991). *Savage inequalities: Children in America's schools.* New York: Crown.

113. Bruni, F. (2001, May 22). Bush warmly embraces Yale, but his reception is mixed. *Arizona Daily Star,* p. A1.

114. Jaime Molera, the former state superintendent for education in Arizona, refused to take the AIMS test. His predecessor, Lisa Graham Keegan, did actually take the 3-hr test and passed it (by narrow margin). Molera refuses to take AIMS test. (2001, June 1). *Arizona Daily Star,* p. A1.

115. In the spring of 2003 in Tucson, Arizona, high schoolers held a town hall meeting where they raised concerns over the validity of the statewide test (Arizona Instrument to Measure Standards—AIMS). At this meeting, students were acknowledging how the test was affecting the quality of teaching they were receiving.

Chapter 9

Enhancing the Future of Youth

For the first time in the history of our country, the educational skills of one generation will not surpass, will not equal, will not even approach, those of their parents.

—National Commission on Excellence in Education, 1983[1]

Study of 50 states and the District of Columbia finds dearth of well-qualified teachers for the students who need them most.

—*Education Week*, 2003[2]

For Americans, the probability of living a long life has never been so high. Today's youth will live longer and healthier lives than those of past generations.[3] Over decades, infant mortality rates and the proportion of high-risk, low birth weight births have declined steadily, while the percentage of American children who receive potentially lifesaving immunizations in early childhood has increased. For teenagers, life has improved steadily. The number of teenage pregnancies and abortions has declined steadily.[4] Data show that youth achievement is steadily increasing, despite the youth population that is tested being increasingly diverse.[5]

In spite of such promising conditions overall, teen suicide rates are alarmingly high,[6] yet the topic of teen suicide gets less media attention than teenage violence, which is prevalent in the media. This lack of attention to the real problems teens face (poverty, hopelessness, unending expectations, despair)[7] is typical of a society in which teens are increasingly asked to do more but are given less guidance and support. Childhood and adolescent obesity rates are alarmingly high—and more youth are having surgery to "correct" obesity or low self-esteem.[8] Sexually transmitted disease (STD) and youth victimization rates continue to be high and disproportionately affect poor, minority youth (see chap. 3 and 4).[9] Also, we know that White boys are most likely to commit suicide, and White girls are most likely to run away from home, and youth from all social classes and ethnicities are not given the resources and adult guidance they need (or want). There is a large and growing gap between the haves and the have nots, especially in terms of educational opportunities.[10] Many youth live in poverty[11]—and alarmingly, policymakers show callous disregard for their problems.[12] Many youth from all social classes and ethnic groups do not receive the economic or social support they deserve, and in fact, in many areas support is actually decreasing.

The title of the widely cited 1983 report *A Nation at Risk* proved to be an accurate description of the state of our society, although not in the way the report specified.[13] As depicted in the first epigraph, this report erroneously[14] suggested that our students' poor academic performance placed the country at serious risk. Given this belief about the need for increasing educational performance, the second epigraph suggests that although society is willing to blame youth, it is unwilling to provide adequate educational resources for students (this is especially the case for those who come from low-income families).

Our nation is not at risk because youth are underperforming but because adults are. To the extent that our society is at risk is not because of defective teens but rather because of a society that is careless in its education, guidance, general support, and even its knowledge of youth. Too many teens live in inadequate, even appalling circumstances. Yet we consistently put the burden on them to rise above such conditions and be successful. Given the extent of the problems that characterize many teens' lives—absent parents, poverty, and dangerous environments—it is ludicrous to blame youth for not living up to what are often unattainable expectations for many. Our analysis leads us to the firm conclusion that the basic problem is not defective kids but a society that is careless in its guidance and support of youth.[15] This careless indifference creates various threats to youth. Ten of these dangers are presented in Table 9.1.

A pro-youth stance would be more likely if citizens realized how much of an asset young people are and how well they are performing. In Table 9.2, we identify 10 of the many aspects of youth to celebrate. Data supporting these claims have been presented in previous chapters. Youth are doing better than expected in many areas and are highly motivated to achieve, have connections with one another and surrounding adults, and look to the future. Unfortunately, these aspects are ignored or discounted by many adults; this is a difficult perceptual problem to overcome because a considerable body of research shows that bad news is vastly more likely to create enduring impressions than is good news.[16]

TABLE 9.1
Ten Critical Threats to America's Children

1. Plague of poverty	Roughly 1 in 5 children live in poverty and more than 3 million experienced hunger in 1998. Children who are deprived of nutrition during brain's critical formative years score lower on academic tests.
2. Abuse and neglect at home	Child abuse and neglect rose to 41 percent between 1988 and 1997. Children who are abused typically experience problems later in life including juvenile crime, poor academic performance and drug and alcohol abuse.
3. Violent crime	Juvenile crime rates are on the decline. However, between 1979 and 1996 more than 75,000 American children and teens were killed and another 3,775,000 wounded by firearms.
4. Dangerous escapes	Alcohol and drug use, although declining, are still at a high level. Every year, 3 million American teens are infected with AIDS, HIV and other sexually transmitted diseases.
5. Children having children	There is a steady decline in teenage pregnancy. However, we still have the highest teen pregnancy and birth rates among western industrialized nations.
6. Inadequate child care	Affordable quality child care is beyond the reach of many low income families. Some studies have shown that many of the child care facilities in the United States are poor to mediocre quality and many are staffed by inadequately trained workers.
7. Lack of health care	In 1998, an estimated 11.1 million children younger than 18 had no health insurance. Quality health care and mental health services can address an array of problems that if left untreated, often explode into severe family or community problems.
8. Absent parents	Parents must take more responsibility for their children's actions. Parents must have a better grasp of their children's activities, their friends, and the conflicting messages they receive about violence, drugs and sex from television, movies and music.
9. New pressures in the classroom	America's elementary and secondary schools face a variety of complex challenges in educating children including overcrowded classrooms, high dropout rates, and threats and fears of violence.
10. Dangers in the environment	Every year, about 8,000 children in the US develop some form of cancer, most often leukemia or brain cancer. Government scientists suspect environmental hazards to be the cause. And, more than 900,000 children have elevated levels of lead in their bloodstream, putting them at risk for a variety of health and behavioral problems.

Note. From *Ten Critical Threats to America's Children: Warning Signs for the Next Millennium,* by the National League of Cities, National School Boards Association, Joe DiMaggio Children's Hospital, and Youth Crime Watch of America, 1999, Washington, DC: Author.

TABLE 9.2
What We Should Know About Youth

1. Youth have good moral values.[17]
2. Many teens are energetic and determined to make a difference.[18]
3. Many teens help out or are willing to help out adults in their community.[19]
4. Many teens are achieving at very high educational levels, and for some this is in spite of incredibly busy and hectic schedules.[20]
5. Youth watch less TV than do adults.[21]
6. Many teens make positive choices every day, and for some they do so in spite of peer pressures to conform.[22]
7. Youth drug use is declining.[23]
8. Youth alcohol use is declining.[24]
9. Youth tobacco use is declining.[25]
10. Teen pregnancy and birth rates are declining.[26]

There are many ways to enhance the quality of teens' lives (see Table 9.3). Some of these are readily achievable (spend more time with youth), whereas others require economic investments and strategic planning to be achieved. Yet policymakers have ignored many easily accomplished solutions (provide tax breaks for low-income families) and denied needed resources (cutting Head Start, reducing money to after-school programs) that address the more complex problems.

In this chapter, we outline a strategy for helping youth. It is not possible to propose solutions that apply to all youth because youth vary widely in resources, talents, and ambitions. For example, all teens need a productive and safe environment in the after-school hours. But some teens need instituted opportunities for productive accomplishments, whereas other teens have so many after-school opportunities that adults need to help them to use their time more selectively. Therefore, we cannot pretend to present magic formulas to help all youth. However, we present a powerful

TABLE 9.3
What We Should Be Doing for Youth

1. Youth need (and want) more contact with adults.[27]
2. Youth need more guidance in defining work and career goals.[28]
3. Youth mental health needs must be better addressed (e.g., depression, suicide).[29]
4. Adult violence against youth must be reduced.[30]
5. Youth and their parents need/want more education on sex.[31]
6. Teens' pressures to get good grades and get into the "right" college must be better recognized and reduced when possible.[32]
7. Youth must be provided with better and more enriching after-school activities.[33]
8. Youth need more sleep and time for reflection.[34]
9. Youth need better education on nutrition and exercise to reduce the epidemic of obesity and ensure lifelong health.[35]
10. Teens' accomplishments merit more accurate media coverage.[36]

way for looking at the effects of devaluing youth and propose a strategy for changing societal expectations and behaviors toward youth.

CHANGING EXPECTATIONS ABOUT YOUTH

Adults Devalue Youth

Youth are often undervalued and sometimes horrifically devalued. And, to add fuel to the fire, many adults carelessly disregard youth and deny them needed guidance. This indifferent attitude may affect youth overtly or in subtle ways that are difficult to pinpoint. For example, teens' reactions to such critical attitudes could range from indifference to disappointment to radical rebellion, thus creating or maintaining a cycle of negativity, as shown in Fig. 9.1. In this model, adults' negative expectations for youth (defined as holding inaccurate and overly negative beliefs about youth) influence their actions toward youth (e.g., distrust youth, cause them to consume media with bias against youth, vote for legislators who treat youth harshly). Generally, this lack of good information about youth results in attempts to control or punish youth rather than support them. In this current climate, teens' bad behavior, which is widely reported on, confirms adults' expectations. Reciprocally, for some teens, an overly controlling and critical adult culture simply justifies their rebellion.

As a case in point, the belief that youth are dangerous and need to be controlled leads to spending money on school guards, metal detectors, and random body searches. These attempts to make school "safer" may in fact make youth more suspicious of peers and feel less secure.[37] Such actions (locker searches) may make youth more suspicious of adults and less willing to share information with them. Policies such as zero tolerance and three-strikes-you're-out may convince youth that adults are more interested in punishing them than helping them. Most important, spending money on control tactics reduces resources for investments into positive, proactive approaches, such as life skills training or after-school programs.

And this is not just a hypothetical argument. Interviews with teens illustrate their frustration and humiliation associated with the invasion of privacy in a zero-tolerance environment. As one 16-year-old put it when asked about the random body searches in her school, "It violates us. Some days you'll come to school and they'll just be like 'take your purse off, your jacket, your backpack.' " In another school, one student commented on the searches as "embarrassing. They're treating us like we're criminals. It's turning school into prison."[38] Tragically, these are not isolated incidences. High school newspapers across the country have published story after story uncovering the "nightmare" experiences of students who attend zero-tolerance

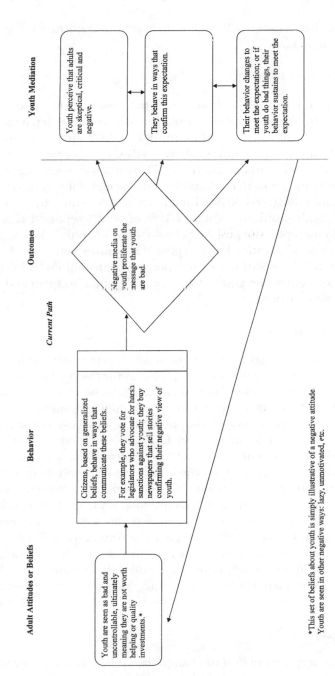

Adult Attitudes or Beliefs

Youth are seen as bad and uncontrollable, ultimately meaning they are not worth helping or quality investments.*

Behavior

Citizens, based on generalized beliefs, behave in ways that communicate these beliefs.

For example, they vote for legislators who advocate for harsh sanctions against youth; they buy newspapers that sell stories confirming their negative view of youth.

Current Path

Outcomes

Negative media on youth proliferate the message that youth are bad.

Youth Mediation

Youth perceive that adults are skeptical, critical and negative.

They behave in ways that confirm this expectation.

Their behavior changes to meet the expectation; or if youth do bad things, their behavior sustains to meet the expectation.

*This set of beliefs about youth is simply illustrative of a negative attitude.
Youth are seen in other negative ways: lazy, unmotivated, etc.

FIG. 9.1. An expectation model for improving the lives of youth.

schools, and there is even a Web site dedicated to reporting these "Zero Tolerance Nightmares."[39]

Adults Don't Listen to Youth

Data show that even parents—those closest to teens—may not listen closely enough to youth, as evidenced by sharp discrepancies between parents' and teens' perceptions of teens' contributions.[40] In a 2002 survey sponsored by the Search Institute, adults and youth were asked to describe their perceptions of how they relate to one another.[41] There was widespread agreement between adults and teens that adults don't do enough for youth. However, youth and adults disagreed on one fundamental issue—the extent to which adults view youth positively. Whereas 42% of adults reported that most adults they know report the positive behavior of youth, only 3% of youth believed that most adults they know report the positive behavior of youth. Very few youth believe adults see their positive contributions. Adults must do a better job convincing youth that they are listening to them and noticing their positive actions.

Changing Expectations

To effect positive changes for youth, we must change how we think about them (which in time may influence what we do for them). Figure 9.2 presents a change model. If adults' beliefs and attitudes became more positive, the cycle of negativity directed toward youth would lessen and, in time, change. Ultimately, youth would respond to these proactive measures and, feeling validated, try to live up to them. Certainly, this model doesn't apply evenly across the spectrum of all youth or adults. There are some adults who passionately advocate for the protection of youth,[42] and there are many youths who are doing well in spite of the cycle of negative expectations that currently exists. There are some teens, too, who, even if conditions changed radically, might still behave in undesirable ways because these opportunities came too late. Still, changing the normative societal view of youth, from seeing them as lazy and dangerous to seeing them as an important investment in the future, would markedly enhance the quality of life for many teens. In turn, youth who are integrated into society and better educated will pay great dividends to the society that nurtured them.

Course of Action

Our model conceptualizes how to change shared beliefs about youth; however, it is difficult to translate beliefs into action when problems are complex or broadly defined. We believe that if three core concepts are applied across populations and problem areas, it would increase the effectiveness of

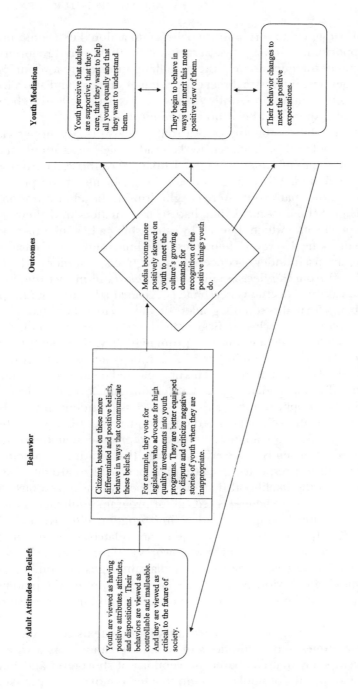

Adult Attitudes or Beliefs

Youth are viewed as having positive attributes, attitudes, and dispositions. Their behaviors are viewed as controllable and malleable. And they are viewed as critical to the future of society.

Behavior

Citizens, based on these more differentiated and positive beliefs, behave in ways that communicate these beliefs.

For example, they vote for legislators who advocate for high quality investments into youth programs. They are better equipped to dispute and criticize negative stories of youth when they are inappropriate.

Outcomes

Media become more positively skewed on youth to meet the culture's growing demands for recognition of the positive things youth do.

Youth Mediation

Youth perceive that adults are supportive, that they care, that they want to help all youth equally and that they want to understand them.

They begin to behave in ways that merit this more positive view of them.

Their behavior changes to meet the positive expectations.

FIG. 9.2. An expectation model for improving the lives of youth.

any program designed to turn positive beliefs into action. First, youth must be given opportunities to be active participants in their own development and in proposals intended to help them. Talking sincerely to a young person conveys genuine interest, a direct expression of support, and also allows him or her to have input on sensitive issues. This is likely to lead to better solutions than if there had been no communication.

For example, the community of Scarsdale, New York, an upper class mostly White neighborhood, has received considerable media attention for widespread problems of underage binge drinking.[43] As the 2003 prom season approached, and still reeling from all the problems of the previous year's prom season (many youth were caught drunk), the administration of Scarsdale High School decided they had to take matters into their own hands to protect youth which they did by establishing a few rules meant to thwart teen drinking. However, their rules of no limos and restricted access to the prom raised a thunder of concern from high school students who felt disenfranchised from the decision-making process (and in fact they were not consulted as these decisions were made). As one high school senior put it, "We are being treated as seventh graders on the way to a bar mitzvah."

In another community close to Scarsdale, the administration took a different approach to protecting youth on prom night, giving students the responsibility of "collectively coming up with a strategy that would insure everyone arrived sober and left sober." This approached seemed successful, at least in terms of giving students a sense of responsibility over their own actions, providing an opportunity, as the senior class president noted, "For [students] to take the reins [giving them] adult responsibility."[44] When adults show youth they care about their ideas and provide them opportunities to voice them, it sends a powerful message that youth are valued. In turn, when youth feel respected because their perspectives are taken seriously, it increases the likelihood that they will behave more responsibly.

A second condition we believe is critical for program implementation is research to continually improve and refine program effectiveness. Research can identify which program elements are related to youth success and which are not, as well as defining what works and for whom. For example, in chapter 5 we discussed the role of media campaigns in promoting or deterring smoking behavior. We noted research that showed the power of different types of antitobacco messages on youth's attitudes toward smoking. Controlled studies investigating the persuasive powers of varied media messages about smoking behavior across different contexts could discover the unique attitudes and motivations of teens who smoke. As a case in point, a recent study that compared perceptions of short-term and long-term harm and benefits of smoking found that teen smokers, nonsmokers, and those nonsmokers who were at greatest risk for future smoking held significantly different views of the short-term benefits and perceived safety of casual smoking[45]—a view that could seriously influence whether at-risk nonsmokers will smoke or whether current smokers will stop.

Ironically, the only segment of society that actively researches youth motivations is big business; by paying attention to youth they can market their products more successfully.[46] However, research can be used in other ways to empower youth. For example, research programs might identify strategies that would lead to productive and low-cost activities that help youth. Throughout this book we recommended specific types of research that would help to clarify the attitudes and behaviors of youth.

How can societal belief systems that are so entrenched throughout society (law enforcement, media, policymakers, citizens) be altered? Even if citizens listen more carefully to youth and make more proactive use of research, it is still difficult to know how and where to begin because major problems faced by young people and their parents are complex and overwhelming: teen pregnancy, youth violence, binge drinking. Often, students, parents, or schools are left alone to deal with overwhelming problems. To handle problems more realistically, it is necessary to understand that they are not just personal, parental, or school related. Rather, these are shared societal issues, and recognition of this fact is the third core concept that must be in place for successful change.

A SMALL-WINS APPROACH

Our thinking about the interface of family, school, student, and society was greatly influenced by McCaslin and DiMarino-Linnen.[47] Their historical review of the field of psychology and the beliefs of experts in that discipline about applying psychological principles to address social problems persuaded us that at times the field swings (and in other behavioral sciences as well) from overly pessimistic to widely enthusiastic perceptions of its value. If expectations are too high or too low, efforts to effect change will fail. And as these failures become more frequent and more visible, the problem becomes more intractable. McCaslin and DiMarino-Linnen identified Weick's work as a way to think about the value of small steps for addressing large-scale social problems.

Weick[48] defined a *small win* as the acceptance of small successes in pursuit of larger, more complicated ones. He noted that large-scale social problems (e.g., pollution, poverty) are so complex that they seem intractable, involving seemingly infinite variables and potential solutions. As a result, problem solvers seek solutions that are so ambitious as to be impossible to enact. Weick suggested that effective problem solving in these situations must begin by dissecting the larger, more diffuse problem into smaller, more definable and manageable units.

Unfortunately, small-wins approaches are not mounted in youth policy interventions. In contrast, social interventions for youth tend to be monolithic, one-size-fits-all approaches to reform. This is especially the case in education, where policymakers shift from one panacea to another in an elusive search for universal solutions to problems that vary from context to context.[49] The current federal law—No Child Left Behind—offers bold sanctions (positive and negative) for schools to improve student achievement; however, the goals are so broad to be unobtainable. For example, schools are expected to have all children performing at grade level in the space of a few years or face punitive sanctions, such as being taken over or closed down. To complicate things further, in the short run, if schools fail to meet "adequate progress," they receive public labels, such as "failing" or "underperforming." Further, when schools are successful in the short run, their hard work, and that of students and teachers, often go unrecognized. Why is this?

One reason is that the goals outlined in the No Child Left Behind legislation are too high and fail to recognize context. For example in some schools, the average sixth grader may be reading at the second-grade level. Hypothetically, if a school that obtains a year's growth such that at the end of the year, their sixth-grade students on average now read at third-grade level, there should be public recognition, personal pleasure, and renewed effort to continue to improve. However, what occurs is that, in many instances, these schools are still seen as failing, and in some cases resources are denied. In time, such perceptions may lead to the conclusion that these schools are failing because of poor effort rather than the recognition of extant potential and how to mobilize it.

However, despite this historical tendency to use global and underresearched strategies for educational change, this history can be changed. We present three examples of small wins that have had successful effects on intended outcomes. These illustrate the core of small-wins philosophy and its power for affecting change.

Small-Wins Examples

The approach of Alcoholics Anonymous for helping alcoholics typifies a small-wins approach. Alcoholics are advised not to try to beat their addiction outright but to take it 1 day at a time. Reducing the overwhelming problem of general addiction to a day-by-day struggle (or in some cases hour by hour) reduces the anxiety, stress, and fear of failure associated with the larger, more difficult-to-solve problem of addiction. This approach to addiction is very powerful for many.

Weick discussed the smaller win of the feminist movement in desexing the English language as more successful than the larger win of the Equal

Rights Amendment. He notes that this consciousness-raising act had enormous impact on the broader social society by getting individuals to be more cognizant of the words they chose and to resist traditional gendered language. We believe a small win of changing the language used to discuss youth can, over time, have positive effects.

Rothstein reports that in one California school district the superintendent noticed that attendance and test score data were positively related—schools with low attendance also had poor test scores. He also noticed that low attendance was associated with health care availability and cost. Families in his district, primarily poorer Mexican Americans (some who spoke almost no English), often avoided health care because of high costs, lack of insurance, and lack of Spanish-speaking, friendly staff. He created a mobile health care unit that was accessible and friendly to this specific population. The result was that children stayed in school more and were sick less often, and, as a result, test scores rose.[50] Efforts to improve attendance have resulted in performance gains in other school districts as well. The key to improving attendance, however, is not mandating strict truancy regulations but making school a place where students feel safe and want to be.[51]

Applying Small Wins to Youth

Small-wins thinking can be applied to many youth issues. We review some major topics presented in the book and propose illustrative small-wins strategies for effecting positive changes for youth. Across each area, we confine our small-wins proposal to school contexts. We do this in part because one must clearly define the context to which a small win is applied for maximum effectiveness. Also, we locate our review of small wins in schools because schools have great potential for affecting large numbers of youth.

Violence. Youth violence is not as widespread as citizens believe. The misconception that it is out of control exists in part because the media exaggerate and oversimplify when reporting youth violence (see chap. 3). Erroneous but entrenched beliefs in the violent nature of teens have helped to legitimize harsh sanctions against youth violence. In Table 9.4 we outline an example of how to apply a small-wins approach to our expectation model (see Fig. 9.2) to change how youth violence is viewed. Eliminating youth violence outright is, of course, next to impossible because the problem has myriad causes, and the multiplicity of causes makes it impossible to pinpoint one cure-all solution. Rather, there are many ways to define a small win that changes violence patterns—one that works in one setting may not be effective in another. Even experts disagree about the extent to which violent behavior is predictable and about which prevention strategies are most effective.[52]

TABLE 9.4
Small Wins—An Application of the
Expectation Model Depicted in Fig. 9.1

Normative Societal Expectations:
Attitude: Youth are prone to violence because it is in their nature.
Behavior: Set up reactive, punitive policies to combat violence.
Outcomes: No significant changes in violence because youth are not given other options
Small Wins Course of Change:
1. Redefine the problem in terms of resources and opportunities: Fact: Youth violence is more likely to occur during the after-school hours of 3 and 7 p.m.
2. Many teens, especially low-income teens, do not have fun, rewarding activities in which to participate during these hours, increasing the likelihood of them getting into trouble.
3. Start small: pick one small, specific geographic area such as a suburb of a city, or the neighborhood that surrounds an urban elementary school.
4. Invest as much as possible into creating teen centers and include youth in the decision-making process to ensure contextual relevance.
5. Evaluate program effectiveness and identify successful program elements through research.
6. Publish in the press research results highlighting the successes of the program.
7. Youth violence decreases because of the program. Simultaneously, adults begin to view youth as less violent than previously believed because of the widespread recognition youth are changing.
See the Small Win:
More youth are engaged in productive activities in one small context than before. A well-run teen center is established in one area of the country, and youth have more things to do there.
Celebrate the Small Win:
Publicize teens' positive actions—celebrate the positive things youth are doing in front page news.
See Normative Expectations Change:
Because adults are exposed to wider visibility of youth's positive actions in the media, they begin to recognize that violence is partly due to environment, and blame is redirected away from youth and toward resource inequities.

   In 2001, the surgeon general's office (led by David Satcher, surgeon general at the time) reviewed research investigating the effectiveness of various violence prevention and intervention programs.[53] He reported that a range of programs can be effective in certain contexts. For example, the more effective programs with middle- and high-school-age students are skills based. Here the small success of educating students in life skills can lead to a broader success of reducing violence. The middle school years are a critical time to intervene; much research suggests that teens' self-confidence dips as they move from the more family-like environment of elementary school to what is frequently a benign-neglect (unless students get into trouble) bureaucracy of middle schools.[54] In elementary schools, effective violence prevention involves a focus on behavior management and sense of safety.

The surgeon general's report discusses the essential components of model programs at the middle- and elementary-school levels. Among the more effective components of programs that reduce youth violence are life skills training, behavior monitoring and modification, and pro-youth program development. Life skills training specifically shows high promise for reducing risky behaviors associated with violence. For example, the Life Skills Training (LST)[55] program targets students in middle or junior high school and includes three main curriculum components: self-management skills, social skills, and information and skills related specifically to drug use. Program effects include lowered risk of inhalant, narcotic, and hallucinogen use. The Midwestern Prevention Project (MPP)[56] also targets middle school students with the goal of reducing gateway (initial) drug use risks associated with the transition from early adolescence to middle through late adolescence. Program effects include reduced daily smoking and reduced marijuana and hard-drug use through the age of 23 years. Although these programs target drug use per se, the high correlation of drug use and violence[57] suggests that they might deter violent behavior as well.

The Seattle Social Development Project (SSDP) targets children in the early elementary school grades (when generally students' self-concepts are high) and focuses on goals that establish better connections among children, their families, and schools. Importantly, this program found empirical support across the widest range of independent researchers, in comparison to other programs that were evaluated, such as the LST and MPP.[58] Project evaluations show that students involved in them displayed a reduction in aggression and antisocial and self-destructive behavior. Follow-up evaluations show that at age 18 years, students who had participated in the program were likely to feel more connected to school than students who did not participate.

These specific programs are empirically validated examples of how to redefine violence in ways that help youth who lack skills or resources, instead of blaming them. They also show how different approaches are necessary in different contexts. In elementary school, students respond better to behavior management techniques that make them feel safe. In contrast, middle school students require life skills training. Unfortunately, the range of effective approaches is rarely discussed in the public forum. Violence continues to be seen as abhorrent teen behavior—and largely unpreventable—rather than as a correctable problem.

Sexuality. Adults must put their discomfort aside if teens' sexual health is to improve. Data show that youth want sex information, and parents want schools to address it (see chap. 4). However, sex education is so heavily politicized as a moral issue that money and resources are directed away from programs and curricula that could improve the sexual health of many teens. This reluctance to confront sex education issues in the schools is problematic because it contradicts the way sex is portrayed throughout the media. The media's role in promulgating society's values about youth sex is so insidious and contradictory that it makes a difficult job (providing youth with skills to make sound decisions) even more challenging. In entertainment, sex and sexuality are defined by the physical beauty of youth. To be young is to be sexy. Journalism media use real-life stories to portray youth as sex craved, irresponsible beings who leave babies in trash cans. Certainly, some teens make tragic decisions; however, it is counterproductive to blame them totally when they live in a sexually charged media environment and go to school with abstinence-only educational programs. Youth are bound to stray—sometimes way off—when they are denied critical information, skills, and guidance.[59]

One small-wins strategy is to give youth a better-developed future orientation. Many youth don't see beyond the present, and some avoid looking into the future because their surrounding environment is bleak. As a result, youth turn to each other for comfort and engage in risky behavior without foreseeing dire consequences because of unfounded fear or futility (the only thing I can do is have a baby). Research has shown that for some a focus on life/educational options can result in better decisions and fewer pregnancies.[60] Once youth are able to foresee their future as positive and productive, many won't want to jeopardize it. More research is needed to see how best to develop and maintain a future-oriented perspective.

Although there is relatively wide consensus that violence is bad, there is enormous variability in beliefs about what is appropriate sexual behavior. Table 9.5 provides some suggestions about potentially successful approaches to sex education in our schools. At the heart of these suggestions is the assumption that teachers, parents, and schools should talk openly and freely and that teachers and parents should attempt to agree on the sex-education content covered in schools. Parent, teacher, and student conversations about these issues can be a highly successful small-wins approach.

Health. In chapter 6 we noted the alarming movement to eliminate physical education (PE) programs from schools so that students can spend more time on academics. A recent survey reported that more than 75% of parents did not want PE classes at their children's school reduced in favor of other classes.[61] Too often these parental preferences are ignored by policymakers, who want schools to focus narrowly on subject-matter content goals. Additionally, in chapter 6 we discussed a wide range of health concerns, such as problems of over- and undereating and sleep deprivation.

Schools have great potential for meeting the health needs of their students, but proposed solutions are difficult to implement because schools vary in resources and problems. A small win in the area of youth health is

TABLE 9.5
Recommendations for School-Wide Sex Education Policies

Educate Boys and Girls Separately.

Initially, it is important that boys and girls be given safe, same-sex environments in which to explore sex issues—especially ones relevant to each gender. For example, although both sexes need to address safe sex practices to prevent unwanted pregnancies and STDs, there are gender-specific issues, such as rape for girls and, for boys, how to behave appropriately (e.g., not pressure girls). Further, given that girls are physically developing earlier, it seems important to provide them a safe environment in which to learn how to handle premature hormonal changes. Although general sex education can occur in mixed gender classes, it seems that at least some time should be allowed in single-gender settings.

Abolish Abstinence-Only Models.

This approach doesn't work. If community members insist on a message of abstinence, then schools, in respect to their wishes, could adopt abstinence-based models that teach abstinence as the ideal but also incorporate critical information on safe sex practices. However, the information on sex and sexuality must be more explicit and include controversial topics (e.g., morning after pill, STD transmission, how to talk to a partner about condom use) as well as core issues of sex education (pregnancy). Too many youth are ill informed on sex-related topics and, therefore, at high risk for STDs including HIV and unwanted pregnancies.

Sex Education Curricula Should Incorporate Issues of Diversity.

Discussions that suggest that certain lifestyles are immoral or wrong alienate many youth already at risk for poor developmental outcomes.

Sex Education Curricula Should Be Mandatory.

Students from at least the 7th grade on should be exposed to consistent sex education lessons that keep pace with teens' ongoing development through 12th grade.

Include Issues of Harassment.

There are too many instances of verbal and sexual harassment in schools. Thus, it is vital that any sexual education materials emphasize tolerance and respect.

Commit Adequate Time in Classes.

Many of today's health education programs involve too little time in the classroom. Given that students develop radically over the course of their K–12 schooling, it is vital that enough time be allotted to sex educational curricula.

Incorporate Government-Sponsored Research Programs.

Consistent with the surgeon general's recommendations, we believe that more research must be conducted on sexual education programs throughout the country. It is vital that we have a way to judge the effectiveness of various intervention approaches in affecting teens' decisions about sex.

Include the Concept of Healthy Body Image.

If students learn how to be healthy, there is a better chance they will feel better about their own bodies and avoid self-destructive behaviors, such as promiscuity or eating disorders.

Stock Libraries With Sex-Related Information.

Libraries should include a broader range of materials relevant to all aspects of youth sexuality. Resources that are rich with information about the nuances of sexual and romantic relationships (when/how to say no; what is it like to be in love) are as important as books that detail the physiology of sex.

better defined by addressing one health issue at a time. For example, local communities could begin by focusing squarely on the problem of soda intake of youth. One way to enhance the nutritional value of students' intake at schools could be to remove soda from school grounds.[62] It is promising that some states are proposing to eliminate soda from school grounds.[63] However, this policy action may well have unintended consequences if students are not provided with nutritious alternatives. If soda is removed, many students will still find ways to get their caffeine/sugar fix (as adults do). Thus, it is not sufficient to just remove soda; it is also critical to provide healthy options, such as smoothies, which are a rich source of vitamins, minerals, and proteins, or enhanced drinking water. A small win of eliminating soda and replacing it with another product could affect larger successes, such as good nutrition and more energy for academic work.

Economic repercussions have deterred school action, especially in low-income schools, where profits from soda machines are needed to buy basic necessities, such as books and supplies. Astonishingly, even in light of all the information we have about the relationship of soda intake and obesity (and its relationship with other health problems such as diabetes), there are still schools that seek out financially lucrative deals with soda companies to provide revenue for school-related needs. In August 2003, one school district in Flint, Michigan, was hoping to make a deal with a soft drink company that would provide, according to the district's chief financial officer, "some funding that we can use to do some nice things for the kids." In this case, the funds would be put toward a playground. The message to students that they should buy health debilitating soda to fund a place where they can get some physical activity is alarmingly contradictory and troubling.[64]

Another small-win focus could be on the inactivity of students at school. Given that lack of activity contributes to poor adolescent health and obesity, it is important for schools to try harder to increase students' activity levels. When youth don't exercise, especially at school, where they spend large amounts of time, it reinforces a sedentary lifestyle and increases the risk of obesity.

Parents could also initiate small wins in local schools. Parents who want to change their school lunch offerings could at first be deterred by obstacles such as changing federal laws about what constitutes a nutritious lunch or state funding. However, a group of citizens recently enacted a small-wins strategy that had the unintended consequence of making an impact at the national level. Citizens of Opelika, Alabama, brainstormed how they could influence local schools to provide healthier lunches to their students. Their efforts were nontrivial given the enormous cost typically associated with such a proposal. However, their successful solution was to draw on the local farming industry to provide students with more fruits and vegetables at lunchtime.

These citizens did not worry about all schools, the enormous costs associated with such large-scale change, or various regulations associated with healthy eating options. Their goals were to define the problem and solve it in terms of what is good nutrition at their local school. These efforts have been sufficiently clear and persuasive that a bill based largely on their plan has been introduced in Congress to change federal law. Importantly, if the citizens' goal had been to change federal law, they likely would have quickly failed. But their effort to reform one school seems to have paid significantly large dividends.[65]

Importantly, there is growing evidence that simple environmental conditions play a role in diet control. The fast food industry has long known that size, portion, and packaging all affect what we consume and indeed, when adolescents are served portions that are too large, they will consume it—not because they are hungry, but simply because it is there.[66] A 2003 study recently documented another way that environmental conditions can shape what we eat. In this study, researchers manipulated the prices and labels of high and low fat snack foods in vending machines across 12 high schools. Their findings indicated sales spiked significantly when low fat foods were reduced in price—even if it was just five cents—from the cost of the high fat alternatives. In contrast, labels which informed potential buyers of fat content had no effect on their choices.[67] This is a good example of a research-based small win that has great potential for effecting change and one that could easily be implemented. It is time that we address these conditions to help improve health as fervently as fast food advertisers do to sell their product.

In Table 9.6 we present 10 suggestions the U.S. surgeon general recommended in 2000.[68] In Table 9.7 we provide our own suggestions for increasing adolescent activity in schools. Students should be provided with more information about health; good health education should be better incorporated throughout their day and modeled throughout the curricula. Despite the boom in recent years of research and informative knowledge about nutrition and exercise, this knowledge has largely disappeared from the public school curriculum.[69] The school curriculum should require daily physical activity[70] and integrate appropriate health information throughout the daily routine. This is a small-win strategy that schools and parents can successfully enact.

Employment. In chapter 7 we noted that most high school students work while attending school, providing clear evidence that many youth work and most want to. However, the range of their work experience is enormous—some are employed in jobs that enhance their school experiences; others are involved in manual-labor-type jobs with little or no link to the educative process. Some jobs provide safe, well-supervised environments with appropriate adult modeling, whereas other work is extremely unsafe and poorly

TABLE 9.6
Strategies for Promoting Participation in Physical
Activity and Sports Among Young People

---

1. Include education for parents and guardians as part of youth physical activity promotion initiatives.
2. Help all children, from prekindergarten through Grade 12, to receive quality, daily physical education. Help all schools to have certified physical education specialists, appropriate class sizes, and the facilities, equipment, and supplies needed to deliver quality, daily physical education.
3. Publicize and disseminate tools to help schools improve their physical education and other physical activity programs.
4. Enable state education and health departments to work together to help schools implement quality, daily physical education and other physical activity programs.
   - With a full-time state coordinator for school physical activity programs
   - As part of a coordinated school health program
   - With support from relevant governmental and nongovernmental organizations
5. Enable more after-school care programs to provide regular opportunities for active, physical play.
6. Help provide access to community sports and recreation programs for all young people.
7. Provide coaches and recreation program staff with the training they need to offer developmentally appropriate, safe, and enjoyable physical activity experiences for young people.
8. Enable communities to develop and promote the use of safe, well-maintained, and close-to-home sidewalks, crosswalks, bicycle paths, trails, parks, recreation facilities, and community designs featuring mixed-use development and a connected grid of streets.
9. Implement an ongoing media campaign to promote physical education as an important component of quality education and long-term health.
10. Monitor youth physical activity, physical fitness, and school and community physical activity programs in the nation and each state.

Note. From *Promoting Better Health for Young People Through Physical Activity and Sports,* by the U.S. Department of Health and Human Services, 2000, Silver Spring, MD: Author.

supervised, with adult supervisors who model inappropriate, unethical behavior (e.g., taking advantage of young, inexperienced workers). How long teens should work is necessarily an individual decision. In aggregate, data suggest that the more time spent on the job, the more deleterious the effects on social and academic development. However, for some teens (even those who work many hours), work is linked to positive outcomes, such as growth of self-esteem and stronger connections to schools.

Data show that many teens have misaligned ambitions[71] and are unable to connect what they learn in school to future jobs. It is critical that schools and local businesses work together to provide students with more realistic future goals and to be sure that jobs are safe and well supervised. There are many ways communities could achieve this goal. One small-wins approach is for high schools to develop a student worker bill of rights. This document would express many important values for students (and their employers).

TABLE 9.7
School Policy Suggestions for Healthier Teens

1. Improve teacher education on health and physical awareness.
2. Provide a resource room for teachers and students that will have available resources rich with information about the benefits of exercise and proper nutrition.
3. Have schools sponsor health clubs that involve students who educate their peers on appropriate health-related concerns. They could inform the school body through a variety of strategies, including a student newspaper, a news leaflet, and video/audio announcements.
4. Incorporate physical activity into instructional lessons.
5. Provide students with brief rest periods and allow students to stretch throughout the day or to meditate.
6. Provide ample amounts of water to prevent student dehydration.
7. Improve nutrition throughout the schools.
8. Explore options for replacing traditional PE programs with wellness programs where youth health is redefined as physical, psychological, emotional, and spiritual integration.[72]

For example, an official position taken by the school to protect students in their work environment clearly communicates the value schools place on the safety and welfare of their students. Similarly, a document that outlines how the school will foster students' work schedules and experiences (e.g., integrate work-related experiences into the curricula, help students with time management) shows students that the school cares about them beyond the boundaries of the physical environment.

Another small win would be to increase the quality and number of business–school partnerships. In the fall of 2002, Caroline Kennedy was hired as a chief fundraiser for New York City public schools,[73] and in the spring of 2003 she announced that her first goal would be to raise $75 million for a new training academy for principals.[74] Her appointment was made with the assumption that her extensive contacts and public profile would bring much-needed attention and economic assistance to public schools. This is a promising step toward recognizing the importance of business and foundation support for public schools and one that helps model the belief that schools are a good investment.

These partnerships could help youth see the function of their education in preparing them for future careers (see chap. 7). Further, community business leaders who take an active interest in youth enhance themselves as well as youth. After all, local adolescents are likely future employees, and, therefore, businesses should view them as a valuable resource. Even if teens pursue employment opportunities elsewhere, it is important that local businesses help to instill in teens the work ethic and job skills required for them to be successful contributors to society at large. When youth positively contribute to society, everyone benefits.

Since 2000 and the slide of the American economy, job support for youth seeking new skills and job training has radically diminished. As the economy improves, funds to support youth employment and training must be restored, especially in the inner cities, where dropout rates have become very high.

Education.   America is ambivalent about its students. Youth are encouraged to be active members of the school community (band, basketball team, choir, etc.), be members of the social community (provide community service), and be economic workers as well as scholars in school. Yet despite the empirical documentation that youth today are more ambitious than the youth of the 20th century, many Americans report feeling skepticism and disillusionment with teens' motivations and intentions. The current media frenzy publicizing failing students and failing schools leads many adults to conclude that youth lack motivation and do not care about academics. We demonstrated that these beliefs are false—more students are achieving than ever before, more are taking and doing well on standardized tests, such as AP tests and the SAT.

Rothstein suggested a strategy for improving educational performance of students that we would call a small win.[75] In his March 7, 2001, *New York Times* column, Rothstein noted that too much emphasis is placed on student achievement based on test scores. Billions of dollars are spent on creating and scoring these tests to make statements such as "schools are failing" or "students aren't making adequate progress in math." The results appear to show that not only are students underachieving, but also they are unmotivated. Such views result in a punitive educational environment (e.g., students must pass a test to get diploma). Rothstein argues that trying to fix a smaller problem that is more readily identifiable (increasing student attendance through better health care) is more likely to affect the broader, more diffuse, and harder-to-define goal of increased achievement.

He points out that a political plan to invest $25–35 billion (or about $500 per student) to raise poor children's achievement scores is misplaced because the strategy of spending more money on testing students is overambitious, ill defined, and ultimately will be ineffective. Spending billions on student testing is often counterproductive because of the many competing reasons for why students' test scores raise, fall, or stay the same.[76] He argues that a more successful approach might be to focus on a definable problem, such as improving the dental health of poor children. Many impoverished children suffer from dental ailments that impede academic progress in schools. If the government invested only $2 billion (a much smaller amount than the hypothesized $25 billion) in dental care for these students, the benefits would improve not only students' health but also their ability to concentrate in schools and, in time, their achievement. Once in better health, youth might benefit from additional funds used for educational reform.

As noted in chapter 8, federal legislation and in many cases, state laws, are increasing expectations for student performance. And, as we have noted, these expectations are often inappropriately high, measured by tests with serious flaws, and given to students who do not have qualified teachers or attend schools that are increasing in size. Most tragically, it is clear that the resources which are mandated by the No Child Left Behind law to be provided from outside service providers to help youth who attend failing schools have not been forthcoming. For example, in New York City, about 250,000 children were entitled to free tutoring. Unfortunately, as Jane Gross of the *New York Times* notes, "... only 30,333 children requested tutoring, 12.5 percent of the 243,249 eligible. Of those, all but 2,640 were tutored by the very school system that had already failed them."[77] Citizens in New York City could help youth by making sure that youth and their parents know about resources to which they are entitled and to help to expand these resources—perhaps by volunteering to tutor children after school. Similarly, the media could do its part by more proactively helping communities be more alert to the needs of local schools. Instead of participating in a reactive blame game, why not advertise the problems as opportunities for community members to get involved?

As we noted the physical conditions of schooling (buildings, libraries, technology) and the quality of teachers need to be enhanced. Federal, state, and local governments must become better at addressing issues of unequal resources, and parents and local communities must press for small-wins solutions in their local schools. One current small-win area would be to work to establish criteria of successful schools to include increasing performance as well as absolute criteria for calling schools successful.

Enhance Student Opportunities and Voice in Schools

Although there may be good reasons for keeping students out of some social policy discussions, we believe that every effort should be made to increase students' voice in educational policy. Increasingly, students' rights in school settings are being stripped away. Some districts have instituted mandatory drug testing for students who want to participate in after-school activities;[78] others have even imposed random nicotine testing on students.[79] And students sometimes react to these intrusions as attacks on their character. In one southwestern district, officials brought drug-sniffing dogs onto high school and middle school campuses. Although school officials indicated that there were growing drug problems on campus that needed to be dealt with, many students reacted negatively. One student responded, "Being told that we can't be trusted and that we are nothing more than pill-popping, joint-smoking, coke-snorting criminals . . . does not enhance our self image and it definitely doesn't make us feel that we are respected and worthy."[80]

One example of expanding student voice in decision making could be through town halls and city councils. Legislators, educational officials, prominent business leaders, and media workers often convene to discuss youth issues (most frequently educational ones) and to make recommendations. However, these meetings are seldom attended by students, and seldom do students, if they do attend, play active roles. An exception was an educational town hall meeting held in Tucson, Arizona, in the fall of 2001. This meeting had three panels, including an educators' panel (which included a principal, a superintendent, a college professor, the head of a teachers' union, and so forth). The second panel was made up of parents, and the third was composed of students. The session, chaired by Tom Oliphant, columnist for the *Boston Globe,* allowed equal time for all panels to discuss related topics. A live audience as well as TV and radio audiences were also given the opportunity to learn from these three different perspectives. The five students, chosen from five different schools across the city, presented unique as well as common perspectives. Students learned from one another as problems in some schools had already been addressed in other schools (e.g., dealing with racial tensions). A small-wins strategy need not involve the entire community, although it is a plus when that does occur. Still, a town hall in a single school could have powerful effects in integrating and strengthening adult-student understanding and good will.

Changing the Media

Throughout the book, we commented on the role of media in defining youth culture and adults' attitudes toward youth. It is only reasonable, then, to argue for a small-wins approach to begin changing the way the media describe youth. The media have an incredibly vast presence in American culture; however, it is difficult to address issues of media influence. Do media sources print what their readers want or do they influence what people know and believe? Certainly, readers can select from and consume a range of media, including varying political beliefs (compare, e.g., *Atlantic Monthly, New Republic, Time, Newsweek*). (Teens, too, can choose their media: *Seventeen* or *Newsweek.*) However, adult media tend to present a monolithic, negative view of youth. There are few, if any, pro-youth adult commercial magazines, and most are not even neutral—they are hard on youth. There are, from time to time, special issues that identify problems for teens created by society or that celebrate them in certain ways. However, overall, the media are not bullish on youth.

In their 2003 book *The Press Effect,* Jamieson and Waldman provide an interesting analysis of reporting in the area of politics. However, their analysis of problems and their call for journalists to act as custodians of facts and to correct misconceptions and confusion applies to youth reporting as well. They suggest that one aspect of improving objectivity is for reporters to become more aware "of the lenses through which the reporters themselves see events and the frames that structure the stories they tell about them."[81] Helping media to achieve and maintain an open perspective on youth is critical because much of life—and in this regard, student accomplishments—are gray—not black or white. Hence, small accomplishments of youth are likely to be minimized or ignored if reporters hold a negative lens toward them.

We need to ask media to be more balanced in their reporting of youth. One small win might be for newspapers to print fewer negative stories about youth and to more prominently display positive ones. For example, newspapers could agree to include a daily or weekly youth section that would specifically address youth issues (e.g., pressures of high-stakes testing, inadequate opportunity for exercise, too little information on sexuality). As with business sections of most papers that follow economic trends, youth sections would provide a more objective look into the lives of youth and debunk the more typical depictions of youth through regular, in-depth descriptions of their achievements, responsible behaviors, dispositions, and so forth.

In addition, the accolades adults give youth must be seen as credible. For example, each year at graduation time the *Arizona Daily Star,* like most newspapers around the country, profiles a population of graduating high school seniors to highlight their academic and social successes. They also include stories about teens who have overcome tremendous obstacles to finish high school. Newspapers should provide more frequent positive reports like these on youth throughout the year. To praise youth only at graduation time may not be seen as genuine. Students are well aware of this lack of attention to their good educational performance. For example, students at the high school exposed to the drug sniffing dogs wrote editorials to the newspaper complaining that the misbehavior of some students was emphasized, while the good behavior of many students went unrecognized.

The media will not change without considerable pressure. Citizens must make it known that they want the full story about youth—their success and struggles as well as their failures. Individual citizens can create small wins each day by writing letters to the editor and by holding the media accountable for fair, unbiased reporting and for showcasing the positive and responsible things youth do, not just the negative ones.

Enhance the Role and Value of Research

As part of our small-wins framework, we have presented research questions at the end of chapters 1–8. These are but a few of the questions that merit inquiry. If we are to move beyond stereotypic views of youth, it is important to study their needs, actions, and aspirations. The view of lazy, indifferent, and dangerous youth do not hold up under close examination. Recent research has shown that youth are much more ambitious and motivated than they are commonly described by citizens and its media.[82] And, there is clear evidence that many of our youth are under tremendous pressure to excel in high school and in college.[83] Through research and active communication of it, social scientists can help the media to move beyond the stereotypic views of youth.

It is most satisfying that others too have been concerned to argue for a more positive attitude toward youth and a more proactive attempt to influence their development in positive ways.[84] We hope that additional research on youth will increase and that knowledge gleaned from it can be used to support, nourish, and guide youth.

CONCLUSION

Youth have not failed society, despite various reports that claim they are undereducated and uncaring. But arguably society has failed them. Society is careless in its socialization of youth; too often they are left to socialize themselves. We recognize the importance of teens discovering or exploring identities by separating from their parents and other adults and by spending more time with their peers. However, youth need increased attention, guidance, and help from adults as distinct from control and punishment.

Adults must realize that adolescence is primarily about the search for individual identity. They should take this search seriously. Youth want to be recognized as unique individuals. At the same time, they want to be viewed like everyone else. This poses a challenge for adults who have difficulty interacting with youth, who may appear to possess two personalities—one expressing individuality and one craving invisibility.

As teens move into adulthood, they must make tough decisions. They must select beliefs and values that make sense to them and that connect them to society.[85] Some of the things that teens reject as childish or as "not them" anymore may threaten adults who do not see these changes as progress. Yet for teens to mature, they must break from blind obedience to behavioral codes and move toward reasoned acceptance if they are to become both prosocial and self-reliant. What constitutes adult status is becoming even more complex in America as marriage, full-time jobs and other adult trappings are being delayed.[86]

In most civilizations there are creeds, religious beliefs, and philosophic ties that obligate the elders to teach and to provide for the young. In actuality, this process is a two-way street. The young need guidance, protection, and opportunity. In turn, adults need an opportunity to pay back and to provide for others. Psychologist Eric Erikson has called the major identity issue for older individuals "generativity."[87] Erickson believes that the search for identity is never fully complete until one achieves generativity—a feeling that one is comfortable with his or her life decisions and is helping others to move forward. Unfortunately, some adults don't integrate their lives and thus stagnate in their remaining years.

We argued in this chapter that society has become indifferent toward youth for various reasons, including seeing them as more violent and less motivated than they actually are. However, these beliefs once developed are difficult to change. In an effort to increase generativity toward our youth, we have provided a few strategies. These include listening to youth and making them an active participant in programs that are being designed for them. Youth problems are varied and complex. Solutions aren't always obvious, and we need more research to better understand how more effectively to encourage youth not to do drugs and how to design after-school programs that build real skills and help adolescents to have wholesome fun. Finally, collectively we must design a systematic series of small-wins strategies that improve the quality of opportunity for youth and their growth. These small wins need to be documented with research and widely disseminated.

The events of September 11, 2001, have had a tremendous impact on our nation. In the short term, the reality that life can end so suddenly caused many citizens to reflect on their own personal priorities. However, there also seemed to be a change (even if for a brief period of time) in the way we viewed each other. As a nation, there was a sense of common purpose and compassion for those who were at the wrong place at the wrong time. The same kind of compassion and concern must be directed toward youth. Changes in teens' living conditions are more likely if Americans believe young people to be worthy recipients of adults' help and guidance. Perhaps drawing on the emotions of September 11th to make a case for why youth deserve and require more adult advocates is bold. But we feel it to be a valid comparison. We do not allow or force our youth to be suicidal bombers, but we do allow thousands of them to be lost every year to preventable tragedies such as violence, depression and suicide, after-school crime, and drug or alcohol addiction. If we paid more attention to our youth and invested in ways to help them, perhaps more youth could be saved, and more youth would enjoy a better quality of life. Our youth—and our society—deserve nothing less.

ENDNOTES

1. National Commission on Excellence in Education. (1983). A nation at risk: The imperative for educational reform. *Elementary School Journal, 84*(2), 113–130.

2. Study of 50 states and the District of Columbia finds dearth of well-qualified teachers for the students who need them most. (2003, January 7). *Education Week.* Story is based on data drawn from the report *Quality Counts 2003: If I Can't Learn From You* (available online at http://www.edweek.org/sreports/qc03/templates/article.cfm?slug=17exec.h22) and a report available from Ed Week online at http://www.edweek.org/products/special-reports/

3. For century-long comparisons on the changes in life quality for adults and children, see Nichols, S., & Good, T. (2000). Education and society, 1900–2000: Selected snapshots of then and now. In T. Good (Ed.), *American education: Yesterday, today, and tomorrow. Ninety-ninth yearbook of the National Society for the Study of Education* (pp. 1–52). Chicago: University of Chicago Press.

4. Teenage birth rates have declined significantly from 1991–2000. See Ventura, S. J., Mathews, T. J., & Hamilton, B. E. (2002, May 30). Teenage births in the United States: State trends, 1991–2000, an update. *National Vital Statistics Reports, 50*(9). (Available online at http://www.cdc.gov/nchs/data/nvsr/nvsr50/nvsr50_09.pdf) The CDC also reports a decline in teen pregnancy rates; see CDC. (2000, July 14). National and state-specific pregnancy rates among adolescents—United States, 1995–1997. *Morbidity and Mortality Weekly Report, 49*(27). (Available online at http://www.cdc.gov/mmwr/PDF/wk/mm4927.pdf)

5. Berliner, D., & Biddle, B. (1995). *The manufactured crisis: Myth, fraud and the attack on America's public schools.* New York: Addison-Wesley.

6. Snyder, H. N., & Sickmund, M. (1999). *Juvenile offenders and victims: 1999 national report.* Washington, DC: Office of Juvenile Justice and Delinquency Prevention.

7. See chapter 3. Also, see work by Michael Males, who has written extensively about how the media exaggerates youth violence. For example, Males, M. (1994, March/April). *Bashing youth: Media myths about teenagers.* Retrieved August 14, 2002, from http://www.fair.org/extra/9043/bashing-youth.html

8. Reuters. (2002, October 9). Obesity in U.S. has surged, survey says. *New York Times.* Retrieved October 9, 2002, from http://www.nytimes.com/2002/10/09/health/; see also the National Center for Health Statistics Report, retrieved October 15, 2002, from http://www.cdc.gov/nchs/products/pubs/pubd/hestats/overwght99.htm; see also Associated Press. (2002, November 4). More youths having surgery for obesity. *Kansas City Star,* p. A7.

9. Some reports estimate that teens are victimized at twice the rate of others. See Miller, L. (2002, July 17). Teens victimized at twice the rate of others. *Arizona Daily Star,* p. A3.

10. Throughout 2001, the disparity in health insurance coverage between the rich and the poor grew. See Pear, R. (2002, September 30). After decline, the number of uninsured rose in 2001. *New York Times,* p. A21; see also Berliner, D., & Biddle, B. (1995). *The manufactured crisis: Myths, fraud, and the attack on America's public schools.* New York: Addison-Wesley; McCaslin, M., & Good, T. L. (1996). The informal curriculum. In B. Berliner & R. Calfee (Eds.), *The handbook of educational psychology* (pp. 622–670). New York: Macmillan.

11. U.S. Census Bureau. (2002, September 24). *Press briefing on 2001 income and poverty estimates.* Washington, DC: Author. (Available online at http://www.census.gov/hhes/income/income01/prs02asc.html); see also U.S. Census Bureau. (2002, September 26). *Poverty rate rises, household income declines, census bureau reports.* Washington, DC: Author. (Available online at http://www.census.gov/Press-Release/www/2002/cb02-124.html)

12. At the time of writing this book, congress had approved a tax law that omitted a $400 tax credit for millions of families with incomes between $10,500 and $26,625, although there

are continued debates about the legislation. See Herbert, B. (2003, June 2). The reverse Robin Hood. *New York Times*; see also Associated Press. (2003, June 6). House Republicans face pressure to pass child-credit. *New York Times*.

13. National Commission on Excellence in Education. (1983). A nation at risk: The imperative for educational reform. *Elementary School Journal, 84*(2), 113–130.

14. Subsequent analyses illustrated that this report was substantially in error. Berliner, D., & Biddle, B. (1995). *The manufactured crisis: Myth, fraud and the attack on America's public schools.* New York: Addison-Wesley; see also Bracey, G. W. (2000, October). The 10th Bracey report on the condition of public education. *Phi Delta Kappan, 82*(2), 133–144.

15. Some have argued that social change (e.g., growing divorce rates, increasing numbers of single-parent households, economic fluctuations) creates a social environment that affects the transition to adolescence. In the current climate, not enough is being done to help youth cope with such dramatic changes. For further discussion on the notion of how social changes affects adolescence, see Crockett, L. J., & Silbereisen, R. K. (Eds.). (2000). *Negotiating adolescence in times of social change.* New York: Cambridge University Press.

16. Some social scientists have argued that it takes seven pieces of good news to overcome one piece of bad news. Baumeister, R. F., Bratslavsky, E., Finkenauer, C., & Vohs, K. D. (2001). Bad is stronger than good. *Review of General Psychology, 5*(4), 323–370.

17. Horatio Alger Association. (2001). The state of our nation's youth, 2001–2002. Alexandria, VA: Horatio Alger Association of Distinguished Americans. (Available online at http://www.horatioalger.com); see also Loven, J. (2001, August). Teens want strong family ties, survey finds. *Arizona Daily Star,* p. A4.

18. Schneider, B., & Stevenson, D. (1999). *The ambitious generation: America's teenagers motivated but directionless.* New Haven, CT: Yale University Press.

19. Youniss, J., & Yates, M. (1997). *Community service and social responsibility in youth.* University of Chicago Press; Farkas, S., & Johnson, J. (1997). *Kids these days: What Americans really think about the next generation.* New York: Public Agenda, Horatio Alger Association. (2001). The state of our nation's youth, 2001–2002. Alexandria, VA: Horatio Alger Association of Distinguished Americans. (Available online at http://www.horatioalger.com)

20. See chapter 8. Also see Berliner, D., & Biddle, B. (1995). *The manufactured crisis: Myths, fraud, and the attack on America's public schools.* New York: Addison-Wesley; Campbell, J. R., Hombo, C. M., & Mazzeo, J. (2000). *NAEP 1999 trends in academic progress: Three decades of student performance* (NCES 2000-469). Washington, DC: U.S. Department of Education, Office of Educational Research and Improvement.

21. Roberts, D. F., Foehr, U. G., Rideout, V. J., & Brodie, M. (1999, November). *Kids and media @ the new millennium: A comprehensive national analysis of children's media use* (p. 1). Menlo Park, CA: Kaiser Family Foundation.

22. Individually, we all know youth who succeed and strive to meet laudable goals in spite of many pressures. See Shell Oil Company. (1999). *The Shell Poll: Teens under pressure, coping well, 1*(4). (Available online at http://www.shell.com). And many youth resist peer pressure to conform or do well in school in spite of peer pressure. Importantly, there is evidence that many teens do not feel peer pressure to do poorly in school. See Good, T., Nichols, S., & Sabers, D. (1999). Underestimating youth's commitment to schools and society: Toward a more differentiated view. *Social Psychology of Education, 3*, 1–39.

23. See chapter 5; Monitoring the Future Web site, http://monitoringthefuture.org/, or notes published by NIDA, http://www.drugabuse.gov/NIDA_notes/NNVol17N6/tearoff.html

24. See chapter 5; Monitoring the Future Web site, http://monitoringthefuture.org/, or notes published by NIDA, http://www.drugabuse.gov/NIDA_notes/NNVol17N6/tearoff.html

25. See chapter 5; Monitoring the Future Web site, http://monitoringthefuture.org/, or notes published by NIDA, http://www.drugabuse.gov/NIDA_notes/NNVol17N6/tearoff.html

26. Ventura, S. J., Mathews, T. J., & Hamilton, B. E. (2002). Teenage births in the United States: State trends, 1991–2000, an update. *National Vital Statistics Reports, 50*(9). Washington, DC: U.S. Centers for Disease Control and Prevention, Department of Health and Human Services. (Available online at http://www.cdc.gov/nchs/data/nvsr/nvsr50/nvsr50_09.pdf). The CDC also reports a decline in teen pregnancy rates. See CDC. (2000). National and state-specific pregnancy rates among adolescents—United States, 1995–1997. *Morbidity and Mortality Weekly Report, 49*(27). (Available online at http://www.cdc.gov/mmwr/PDF/wk/mm4927.pdf)

27. Shell Oil Company. (1999). *The Shell Poll: Teens under pressure, coping well, 1*(4). (Available online at http://www.shell.com/)

28. Schneider, B., & Stevenson, D. (1999). *The ambitious generation: America's teenagers motivated but directionless.* New Haven, CT: Yale University Press; Sum, A., Khatiwada, I., & Trub'skyy, M. (2002). *Left behind in the labor market: Labor market problems of the nation's out-of-school, young adult populations.* Chicago: Center for Labor Market Studies, Northeastern University. (Available online at http://www.nupr.neu.edu/2-03/left_behind.PDF)

29. Koplewicz, H. S. (2002). *More than moody: Recognizing and treating adolescent depression.* New York: Putnam.

30. Wilson, J. W. (2000). *Characteristics of crimes against juveniles.* Washington, DC: U.S. Department of Justice, Office of Juvenile Justice and Delinquency Prevention.

31. Hoff, T., & Greene, L. (2000, September). *Sex education in America: A view from inside the nation's classrooms.* Menlo Park, CA: Kaiser Family Foundation. (Available online at http://www.kff.org/)

32. National Commission on the High School Senior Year. (2001). *Raising our sights: No high school senior left behind.* Princeton, NJ: Woodrow Wilson National Fellowship Foundation. Note that youth are given mixed messages about their high school years and that conceptions about what the senior year in high school is supposed to be are especially confusing, and this confusion leads to more pressure for youth to do it all.

33. Carnegie Council on Adolescent Development. (1992). *A matter of time: Risk and opportunity in the nonschool hours* (Report of the Task Force on Youth Development and Community Programs). New York: Carnegie Corporation of New York.

34. Carskadon, M. A., Vieira, C., & Acebo, C. (1993). Association between puberty and delayed phase preference. *Sleep, 16*(3), 258–262; M. A. Carskadon (1990). Patterns of sleep and sleepiness in adolescents. *Pediatrician, 17,* 5–12; Carskadon, M. A., & Dement, W. C. (1987). Sleepiness in the normal adolescent. In C. Guilleminault (Ed.), *Sleep and its disorders in children* (pp. 53–65). New York: Raven Press.

35. Kimm, S. Y. S., & Obarzanek, E. (2002). Childhood obesity: A new pandemic of the new millennium. *Pediatrics, 110,* 1003–1007; U.S. Department of Health and Human Services. (1996). *Physical activity and health: Adolescents and young adults. A report of the surgeon general.* Washington, DC: Author. Retrieved May 19, 2003, from http://www.cdc.gov/nccdphp/sgr/summary.htm; Office of the Surgeon General. (2001). The surgeon general's call to action to prevent and decrease overweight and obesity. Rockville, MD: U.S. Department of Health and Human Services. Retrieved April 10, 2002, from http://www.surgeongeneral.gov/topics/obesity/calltoaction/CalltoAction.pdf; Mokdad, A. H., et al. (2001, September 12). The continuing epidemics of obesity and diabetes in the United States. *Journal of the American Medical Association, 286*(10), 1195–1200; see also Ogden, C. L., Flegal, K. M., Carroll, M. D., & Johnson, C. L. (2002). Prevalence and trends in overweight among U.S. children and adolescents, 1999–2000. *Journal of the American Medical Association, 288,* 1728–1732.

36. Males has noted, for example, the tendency of media to exaggerate youth violence. Males, M. A. (2000). *Kids and guns: How politicians, experts, and the press fabricate fear of youth*. Philadelphia: Common Courage Press. (Available online at http://www.commoncouragepress. com/); Jamieson and Waldman also remind us that the press tends to emphasize the negative in general. We feel that youth's educational accomplishments are notably ignored. Jamieson, K. H., & Waldman, P. (2003). *The press effect: Politicians, journalists, and the stories that shape the political world*. Oxford: Oxford University Press.

37. We are thankful to Amanda Rabidue for this observation (based on personal communication).

38. Quotes taken from an online story published by AlterNet, an online magazine. (http:// www.alternet.org/index.html) AlterNet's online magazine was launched in 1998 and asserts to provide a mix of news, opinion and investigative journalism on subjects ranging from the environment, the drug war, technology and cultural trends to policy debate, sexual politics and health issues. The story on Zero Tolerance was accessed August 9, 2003, from http://www.alternet.org/story.html?StoryID=16305

39. Many high school newspapers can be accessed online. For information on how to view these newspapers, see http://www.highschooljournalism.org/students/Schoolinf_Index. cfm (Accessed August 9, 2003). Also, for a list of "zero tolerance nightmares" that are posted online, see: http://www.ztnightmares.com/index.htm (Accessed August 9, 2003).

40. See Farkas, S., & Johnson, J. (1997). *Kids these days: What Americans really think about the next generation*. New York: Public Agenda.

41. The Search Institute. (2002). *Grading grown-ups 2002: How do American kids and adults relate?* Minneapolis, MN. (Available online at http://www.search-institute.org/norms/ gg2002.pdf)

42. We recognize that there are many nonprofit organizations created solely to advocate for the rights and safety of children. However, part of the problem is that these agencies are oftentimes poorly funded and hardly visible, and the effectiveness of their programs is underresearched.

43. Gross, J. (2002, October 8). A binge by teenagers leads a village to painful self-reflection. *New York Times*, p. B1.

44. Gross, J. (2003, June 6). In a fight against prom night drinking, a prohibition on limousines. *New York Times*.

45. Siegel, J. T., Alvaro, E. M., & Burgoon, M. (in press). Perceptions of the at-risk nonsmoker: Are potential intervention topics being overlooked? *Journal of Adolescent Health*.

46. Zollo, P. (1999). *Wise up to teens: Insights into marketing and advertising to teenagers* (2nd ed.). Ithaca, NY: New Strategist Publications.

47. McCaslin, M., & DiMarino-Linnen, E. (2000). Motivation and learning in school: Societal contexts, psychological constructs, and educational practices. In T. Good (Guest Ed.), *American education: Yesterday, today, and tomorrow. Ninety-ninth yearbook of the National Society for the Study of Education* (Part II, pp. 84–151). Chicago: Chicago University Press.

48. Weick, K. E. (1984). Small wins: Redefining the scale of social problems. *American Psychologist, 39*(1), 40–49.

49. Good, T., & Braden, J. (2000). *The great school debate: Choice, vouchers and charters*. Mahwah, NJ: Lawrence Erlbaum Associates.

50. Rothstein, R. (2002, September 11). Lessons: A mobile clinic delivers good health and grades. *New York Times*, p. B8.

51. For example, there is emerging literature to show that when students feel they are a part of the system, or feel like they belong, they are less likely to be absent than students who do not feel like they belong. Nichols, S. (2003). *The role of belongingness in middle school stu-*

dents' motivational adaptation to a new school: Do fresh starts make a difference? Unpublished doctoral dissertation, University of Arizona, Tucson.

52. Mulvey, E. P., & Cauffman, E. (2001). The inherent limits of predicting school violence. *American Psychologist, 56,* 797–802; Reinke, W. M., & Herman, K. C. (2002, October). A research agenda for school violence prevention. *American Psychologist, 57*(10), 796–797.

53. U.S. Department of Health and Human Services. (2000). *Youth violence: A report of the surgeon general.* Rockville: MD: Author.

54. Eccles, J. S., & Midgley, C. (1990). Changes in academic motivations and self-perceptions during early adolescence. In R. Montemayor, G. R. Adams, & T. P. Gullotta (Eds.), *Advances in adolescent development: From childhood to adolescence* (Vol. 2, pp. 134–155). Newbury Park, CA: Sage.

55. This program has less empirical support than others; however, based on the surgeon general's review of the literature, it has still yielded some empirical support. Importantly, more research is necessary to fully understand the potential impact of the program. For more information, see Botvin, G. J., Mihalic, S. F., & Grotpeter, J. K. (1998). Life skills training. In D. S. Elliot (Series Ed.), *Blueprints for violence prevention.* Boulder, CO: Center for the Study and Prevention of Violence, Institute of Behavioral Science, University of Colorado at Boulder.

56. For more detailed information on program evaluation, see Pentz, M. A., Mihalic, S. F., & Grotpeter, J. K. (1998). The Midwestern Prevention Project. In D. S. Elliott (Series Ed.), *Blueprints for violence prevention.* Boulder, CO: Center for the Study and Prevention of Violence, Institute of Behavioral Science, University of Colorado at Boulder.

57. U.S. Department of Health and Human Services. (2000). *Youth violence: A report of the surgeon general.* Rockville, MD: Author.

58. Hawkins, J. D., Catalano, R. F., Morrison, D., O'Donnell, J., Abbott, R., & Day, L. E. (1992). The Seattle Social Development Project: Effects of the first four years on protective factors and problem behaviors. In J. McCord & R. E. Tremblay (Eds.), *Preventing antisocial behavior: Interventions from birth through adolescence.* New York: Guilford Press; Mendel, R. A. (2000). *Less hype, more help: Reducing juvenile crime, what works—And what doesn't.* Washington, DC: American Youth Policy Forum.

59. A 2003 study found that the strategy of making condoms available in schools may improve HIV prevention practices among youth. See Blake, S. M., et al. (2003, June). Condom availability programs in Massachusetts high schools: Relationships with condom use and sexual behavior. *American Journal of Public Health, 93*(6), 955–962.

60. See U.S. Department of Health and Human Services. (2001). *The surgeon general's call to action to promote sexual health and responsible behavior.* Washington, DC: Author. Retrieved January 16, 2002, from http://www.surgeongeneral.gov/library/sexualhealth/; see also Hawkins, J. D., et al. (1999). Preventing adolescent health-risk behaviors by strengthening protection during childhood. *Archives of Pediatric and Adolescent Medicine, 153,* 226–234.

61. Kids' obesity a worry for parents. (2000, September 13). *Arizona Daily Star.*

62. For example, see U.S. Department of Health and Human Services. (2001). *The surgeon general's call to action to prevent and decrease overweight and obesity, 2001.* Rockville, MD: Author. Retrieved October 15, 2002, from http://www.surgeongeneral.gov/topics/obesity/calltoaction/CalltoAction.pdf

63. Bowman, D. H. (2001, October 3). States consider forbidding snack, soda sales. *Education Week,* p. 10.

64. Bach, M. (2003, August 21). Flint schools seek soft-drink cash. *The Flint Journal.*

65. Becker, E., & Burros, M. (2003, January 13). Eat your vegetables? Only at a few schools. *New York Times,* pp. A1, A12.

66. Barboza, D. (2003, August 3). If you pitch it, they will eat: Barrage of food ads takes aim at children. *New York Times,* pp. A1, A11.

67. This study was discussed in the *New York Times.* Goode, E. (2003, July 22). The gorge-yourself environment. *New York Times,* pp. D1, D7.

68. U.S. Department of Health and Human Services. (1996). *Physical activity and health: A report of the surgeon general.* Atlanta, GA: Author.

69. Gordon-Larsen, P., McMurray, R. G., & Popkin, B. M. (2000). Determinants of adolescent physical activity and inactivity patterns. *Pediatrics, 105*(6), 1–8.

70. Recently, a 1,000-page report sponsored by the Institute of Medicine (the medical division of the National Academies) urged that individuals exercise at least 1 hr a day. For the full report, see Institute of Medicine of the National Academies. (2002). *Dietary reference intakes for energy, carbohydrates, fiber, fat, protein and amino acids (macronutrients).* Washington, DC: National Academies Press. Retrieved October 15, 2002, from http://books.nap.edu/books/0309085373/html/R1.html#pagetop). For news release, see Brody, J. (2002, September 6). U.S. panel urges hour of exercise each day. *New York Times,* pp. A1, A16.

    Currently, the Center for Physical Activity and Weight Management at the University of Kansas has been funded to conduct research in schools on the effects of incorporating daily physical activity into instruction. See Brooks, J. R. (2002, July 14). Fighting obesity in the classroom: Study promotes lessons based on physical activity. *Arizona Daily Star,* p. A12.

71. Schneider, B., & Stevenson, D. (1999). *The ambitious generation: America's teenagers motivated but directionless.* New Haven, CT: Yale University Press.

72. We would like to thank Alesha Kientzler for bringing the idea of physical wellness to our attention.

73. Goodnough, A. (2002, October 2). Caroline Kennedy takes part as fundraiser for schools. *New York Times,* p. A1.

74. Goodnough, A., & Herszenhorn, D. M. (2003, June 4). Kennedy finding her footing as schools' rainmaker. *New York Times.*

75. Rothstein, R. (2001, March 7). Lessons: Reducing poverty could increase school achievement. *New York Times,* p. B9.

76. For a comprehensive literature review on effects of teachers on academic achievement, see Brophy, J., & Good, T. (1986). Teacher behavior and student achievement. In M. Wittrock (Ed.), *Handbook of research on teaching* (3rd ed., pp. 328–375). Washington, DC: American Educational Research Association.

77. Gross, J. (2003, August 29). Free tutoring reaches only fraction of students. *New York Times,* pp. A1, A19.

78. See also Greenhouse, L. (2002, June 28). Justices allow schools wider use of random drug tests for pupils. *New York Times,* p. A1.

79. Associated Press. (2002, October 8). Some U.S. schools test student urine to catch smokers. *Arizona Daily Star,* p. A3.

80. Sterba, J. (2002, November 28). Drug-dog sniffs miff students. *Arizona Daily Star,* pp. B1, B5.

81. Jamieson, K. H., & Waldman, P. (2003). *The press effect: Politicians, journalists, and the stories that shape the political world* (p. 197). Oxford, UK: Oxford University Press.

82. Schneider, B., & Stevenson, D. (1999). *The ambitious generation: America's teenagers motivated but directionless.* New Haven, CT: Yale University Press.

83. Humes, E. (2003). *School of dreams: Making the grade at a top American high school.* New York: Harcourt.

84. In 1998, a group of psychologists and researchers compiled all the evidence available at the time on the effects of positive youth development programs. This document can be

found online. See Catalano, R. F., Berglund, M. L., Ryan, J. A. M., Lonczak, H. S., & Hawkins, J. D. (1998, November 13). *Positive youth development in the United States: Research findings on evaluations of positive youth development programs.* Washington, DC: U.S. Department of Health and Human Services. Accessed September 4, 2003, from http://aspe. hhs.gov/hsp/PositiveYouthDev99/index.htm

85. McAdams, D. (1993). *The stories we live by: Personal myths and the making of the self.* New York: Guilford Press.

86. Based on a study conducted by the University of Chicago's National Opinion Research Center. See Web site for more information on report: http://www.norc.uchicago.edu/; Irving, M. (2003, May 9). College "kids" is no misnomer: Adulthood starts at 26, poll finds. *Arizona Daily Star,* p. A5.

87. Erikson, E. (1968). *Identity, youth and crisis.* New York: W. W. Norton.

Author Index

Note: **Boldface** page numbers contain full bibliographic descriptions of works cited. The number in parentheses is the multiple frequency of the author's name on the preceding page number.

Subject Index

Note 1: *Italic page numbers* and letters *f* and *t* following them indicate *figures* or *tables* on those pages. Behind leading page numbers, the **boldface** letter **n** precedes a numbered end note, e.g., locator 28**n**52 directs readers to page 28 and Note 52 on that page, whereas **nn** means multiple notes.

Note 2: Within the United States, specific states mentioned have separate main entries.

A

Abortions by youth, 96, 100, 101–102, 106, 111
Abortions in the U.S., *108f*
Abstinence, 122
    in sex education, 106, 107, 109, 116**n**12, 119**n**62, *275t*
Academic performance, 15, 189–190**n**60
    improvement policy on, *58f,* 227–228
    influences on, xiii, 51**n**4, *74t,* 154, 163, 165
    pressures on, 220, 234–237, *234f, 235f, 236f, 237f*
    state spending correlated with, 241–242, 254**n**31
    underestimation of, 232–237
    work force and youth, 199–201, 212
    See also Tests and scores
Acquired Immunodeficiency Disease Syndrome (AIDS) in youth, 102–104
ACT scores, 223, 231, 232

Adolescence
    definition of, xi–xii
    experiences during, 1–2, 3–5, 9–10, 25**n**10
    identity development during, 91, 114**n**4, 284–285
    myth of, 1–29
    puberty in, 91, 287**n**15
Adolescents. *See* Youth
Adult attitudes toward youth, 3–24, *12f, 13f*
    critical, ix–xi, 21, 26**n**24, *265f*
    erroneous, 260–261, *263t*
    indifferent, 72, 161, 163, 264–266, 285
    research needed on, 284
    sexuality and, 91–92, 95–96, 102
    stereotypical, 193, 201, 284
Adults
    absence of, and effect on youth, xi, 37, *38f,* 47, 96
    antitobacco campaigns and, 137–138, *139t–140t*
    as controlling, 142, 151–152, 162, 165, 264